AN EXEGETICAL SUMMARY OF
REVELATION 12–22

AN EXEGETICAL SUMMARY OF REVELATION 12–22

Second Edition

Ronald L. Trail

SIL International

Second Edition
© 2006, 2008 by SIL International

Library of Congress Catalog Card Number: 2008923522
ISBN: 978-155671-196-1

Printed in the United States of America

All Rights Reserved
No part of this publication may be reproduced, stored in a retrieval system, or transmitted in any form or by any means without the express permission of SIL International. However, brief excerpts, generally understood to be within the limits of fair use, may be quoted without written permission.

Copies of this and other publications
of SIL International may be obtained from

International Academic Bookstore
SIL International
7500 West Camp Wisdom Road
Dallas, TX 75236-5699, USA

Voice: 972-708-7404
Fax: 972-708-7363
academic_books@sil.org
www.ethnologue.com

PREFACE

Exegesis is concerned with the interpretation of a text. Exegesis of the New Testament involves determining the meaning of the Greek text. Translators must be especially careful and thorough in their exegesis of the New Testament in order to accurately communicate its message in the vocabulary, grammar, and literary devices of another language. Questions occurring to translators as they study the Greek text are answered by summarizing how scholars have interpreted the text. This is information that should be considered by translators as they make their own exegetical decisions regarding the message they will communicate in their translations.

The Semi-Literal Translation

As a basis for discussion, a semi-literal translation of the Greek text is given so that the reasons for different interpretations can best be seen. When one Greek word is translated into English by several words, these words are joined by hyphens. There are a few times when clarity requires that a string of words joined by hyphens have a separate word, such as 'not' (μή), inserted in their midst. In this case, the separate word is surrounded by spaces between the hyphens. When alternate translations of a Greek word are given, these are separated by slashes.

The Text

Variations in the Greek text are noted under the heading TEXT. The base text for the summary is the text of the fourth revised edition of *The Greek New Testament,* published by the United Bible Societies, which has the same text as the twenty-sixth edition of the *Novum Testamentum Graece* (Nestle-Aland). Dr. J. Harold Greenlee researched the variants and has written the notes for this part of the summary. The versions that follow different variations are listed without evaluating their choices.

The Lexicon

The meaning of a key word in context is the first question to be answered. Words marked with a raised letter in the semi-literal translation are treated separately under the heading LEXICON. First, the lexicon form of the Greek word is given. Within the parentheses following the Greek word is the location number where, in the author's judgment, this word is defined in the *Greek-English Lexicon of the New Testament Based on Semantic Domains* (Louw and Nida 1988). When a semantic domain includes a translation of the particular verse being treated, **LN** in bold type indicates that specific translation. If the specific reference for the verse is listed in *A Greek-English Lexicon of the New Testament and Other Early Christian Literature* (Bauer, Arndt, Gingrich, and Danker 1979), the outline location and page number is given. Then English equivalents of the Greek word are given to show how it is translated by commentators who offer their own translations of the whole text and, after a semicolon, all the versions in the list of abbreviations for translations. When reference is made to "all versions," it refers to only the versions in the list of translations. Sometimes further comments are made about the meaning of the word or the significance of a verb's tense, voice, or mood.

The Questions

Under the heading QUESTION, a question is asked that comes from examining the Greek text under consideration. Typical questions concern the identity of an implied actor or object of an event word, the antecedent of a pronominal reference, the connection indicated by a relational word, the meaning of a genitive construction, the meaning of figurative language, the function of a rhetorical question, the identification of an ambiguity, and the presence of implied information that is needed to understand the passage correctly. Background information is also considered for a proper understanding of a passage. Although not all implied information and background information is made explicit in a translation, it is important to consider it so that the translation will not be stated in such a way that prevents a reader from arriving at the proper interpretation. The question is answered with a summary of what commentators have said. If there are contrasting differences of opinion, the different interpretations are numbered and the commentaries that support each are listed. Differences that are not treated by many of the commentaries often are not numbered, but are introduced with a contrastive 'Or' at the beginning of the sentence. No attempt has been made to select which interpretation is best.

In listing support for various statements of interpretation, the author is often faced with the difficult task of matching the different terminologies used in commentaries with the terminology he has adopted. Sometimes he can only infer the position of a commentary from incidental remarks. This book, then, includes the author's interpretation of the views taken in the various commentaries. General statements are followed by specific statements, which indicate the author's understanding of the pertinent relationships, actors, events, and objects implied by that interpretation.

The Use of This Book

This book does not replace the commentaries that it summarizes. Commentaries contain much more information about the meaning of words and passages. They often contain arguments for the interpretations that are taken and they may have important discussions about the discourse features of the text. In addition, they have information about the historical, geographical, and cultural setting. Translators will want to refer to at least four commentaries as they exegete a passage. However, since no one commentary contains all the answers translators need, this book will be a valuable supplement. It makes more sources of exegetical help available than most translators have access to. Even if they had all the books available, few would have the time to search through all of them for the answers.

When many commentaries are studied, it soon becomes apparent that they frequently disagree in their interpretations. That is the reason why so many answers in this book are divided into two or more interpretations. The reader's initial reaction may be that all of these different interpretations complicate exegesis rather than help it. However, before translating a passage, a translator needs to know exactly where there is a problem of interpretation and what the exegetical options are.

ABBREVIATIONS

COMMENTARIES AND REFERENCE BOOKS

Alf   Alford, Henry. *Alford's Greek Testament, an Exegetical and Critical Commentary.* Vol. 4. 1875. Grand Rapids: Baker, 1980.

BAGD   Bauer, Walter. *A Greek-English Lexicon of the New Testament and Other Early Christian Literature.* Translated and adapted from the 5th ed., 1958 by William F. Arndt and F. Wilbur Gingrich. 2nd English ed. revised and augmented by F. Wilbur Gingrich and Frederick W. Danker. Chicago: University of Chicago Press, 1979.

Be   Beckwith, Isbon T. *The Apocalypse of John.* New York: MacMillan, 1919; reprinted, Eugene: Wipf and Stock Publishers, 2001.

BNTC   Caird, G. B. *A Commentary on the Revelation of St. John the Divine.* Black's New Testament Commentaries, edited by Henry Chadwick. London: Adam & Charles Black, 1966.

EC   Thomas, Robert L. *Revelation 8–22 An Exegetical Commentary.* Chicago: Moody Press, 1995.

Hu   Hughes, Philip Edgcumbe. *The Book of the Revelation.* Grand Rapids: Eerdmans, 1990.

ICC   Charles, R. H. *A Critical and Exegetical Commentary on The Revelation of St. John.* The International Critical Commentary. Edinburgh: T. & T. Clark, 1920.

Ld   Ladd, George Eldon. *A Commentary of the Revelation of John.* Grand Rapids: Eerdmans, 1972.

LN   Louw, Johannes P., and Eugene A. Nida. *Greek-English Lexicon of the New Testament Based on Semantic Domains.* New York: United Bible Societies, 1988.

Lns   Lenski, R. C. H. *The Interpretation of St. John's Revelation.* Minneapolis: Augsburg, 1963.

NIC   Mounce, Robert H. *The Book of Revelation.* Revised ed. The New International Commentary on the New Testament, edited by F. F. Bruce and Gordon D. Fee. Grand Rapids: Eerdmans, 1977.

NIGTC   Beale, G. K. *The Book of Revelation, A Commentary on the Greek Text.* The New International Greek Testament Commentary. Grand Rapids: Eerdmans, 1999.

NTC   Bruce, F. F. *The Revelation to John.* A New Testament Commentary, edited by G. C. D. Howley. Grand Rapids: Zondervan, 1969.

Sw   Swete, Henry Barclay. *Commentary on Revelation.* Grand Rapids: Kregel Publications, 1977.

TH   Bratcher, Robert G. and Howard A. Hatton. *A Handbook on The Revelation to John.* New York: The United Bible Societies, 1993.

TNTC	Morris, Leon. *The Book of Revelation, an Introduction and Commentary*. Tyndale New Testament Commentaries. Revised Edition. Grand Rapids: Eerdmans, 1987.
Wal	Walvoord, John F. *The Revelation of Jesus Christ*. Chicago: Moody, 1966.
WBC	Aune, David E. *Revelation*. Word Biblical Commentary, Vols. 52a and 52b, edited by Ralph p. Martin. Nashville: Thomas Nelson, 1997 and 1998.

GREEK TEXT AND TRANSLATIONS

GNT	The Greek New Testament. Edited by B. Aland, K. Aland, J. Karavidopoulos, C. Martini, and B. Metzger. 4th ed. London, New York: United Bible Societies, 1993.
CEV	The Holy Bible, Contemporary English Version. New York: American Bible Society, 1995.
KJV	The Holy Bible. Authorized (or King James) Version. 1611.
NCV	New Century Version. Word Publishing, 1987.
NAB	The New American Bible. New York: Catholic Book Publishing Co, 1970.
NET	The Net Bible. New English Translation, New Testament. Version 9.206. WWW.NETBIBLE.COM: Biblical Studies Press, 1999.
NIV	The Holy Bible, New International Version. Grand Rapids: Zondervan, 1984.
NLT	The Holy Bible, New Living Translation. Wheaton, Ill.: Tyndale House Publishers, 1996.
NRSV	The Holy Bible: New Revised Standard Version. New York: Oxford University Press, 1989.
REB	The Revised English Bible. Oxford: Oxford University Press and Cambridge University Press, 1989.
TEV	Good News Bible, Today's English Version. 2nd ed. New York: American Bible Society, 1992.
TNT	The Translator's New Testament. London: British and Foreign Bible Society, 1973.

GRAMMATICAL TERMS

act.	active
fut.	future
impera	imperative
indic.	indicative
infin.	infinitive
mid.	middle
opt	optative
pass.	passive
perf.	perfect
pres.	present
subj.	subjunctive

MISCELLANEOUS

LXX	Septuagint
TR	Textus Receptus
OT	Old Testament
NT	New Testament

EXEGESIS OF REVELATION 12–21

DISCOURSE UNIT: 12:1–22:5 [NTC]. The topic is a tableaux of conflict and triumph.

DISCOURSE UNIT: 12:1–18:24 [EC]. The topic is the pouring out of the seven bowls.

DISCOURSE UNIT: 12:1–15:4 [NIGTC]. The topic is deeper conflict.

DISCOURSE UNIT: 12:1–14:20 [BNTC, EC, Ld, TH, TNTC; REB]. The topic is the great ordeal [BNTC], interlude [Ld], the dragon and the lamb [TH], seven significant signs [TNTC], seven visions [REB], the background of the bowls [EC].

DISCOURSE UNIT: 12:1–14:5 [NIC]. The topic is the conflict between the church and the powers of evil.

DISCOURSE UNIT: 12:1–15:4 [NIGTC]. The topic is deeper conflict.

DISCOURSE UNIT: 12:1–18 [EC, GNT, Sw, TH; CEV, NCV, TEV]. The topic is the woman and the dragon [GNT, TH; CEV, NCV, TEV], the woman the child and the dragon [EC, Sw].

DISCOURSE UNIT: 12:1–17 [Alf, Be, Hu, Ld, Lns, NIGTC, NTC, Wal; KJV, NAB, NLT]. The topic is the woman and the dragon [Alf, Lns; KJV, NAB, NLT], the woman, the child and the dragon [Hu, Ld, NTC], the conflict in heaven and earth [Wal], Satan's hostility to the Messiah [Be].

DISCOURSE UNIT: 12:1–13:1a [NIV]. The topic is the woman and the dragon.

DISCOURSE UNIT: 12:1–6 [Be, BNTC, Hu, NIC, NIGTC, NTC, TNTC; CEV, NET, NRSV]. The topic is the birth of the Messiah [BNTC], the birth of the child [Hu, NTC], the woman, the child and the dragon [NIC; NET], the woman and the dragon [CEV, NRSV], the woman clothed with the sun [TNTC], attempt to destroy the Messiah [Be].

12:1 And (a) great[a] sign[b] was-seen in heaven[c], (a) woman clothed[d] (with) the sun, and the moon under her feet and (a) crown of-twelve stars on her head,

LEXICON—a. μέγας (LN 78.2, 87.22): 'great' [BNTC, EC, LN (78.2, 87.22), Lns, WBC; KJV, NAB, NCV, NET, NLT, NRSV, REB, TNT], 'great and wondrous' [NIV], 'great and mysterious' [TEV], 'important' [LN (87.22)], not explicit [CEV]. Here μέγας has two senses, 'important in meaning' and 'huge in appearance' [Alf, EC]. Μέγας does not refer to its size but rather to its effect on the one who saw it [TH]. See this word also at 6:17.

b. σημεῖον (LN 33.477) (BAGD 2.c. p. 748): 'sign' [EC, LN, Lns, WBC; NAB, NET, NIV, REB, TNT], 'portent' [BAGD, BNTC; NRSV], 'something important' [CEV], 'wonder' [Be; KJV, NCV], 'a significant event' [NLT], 'sight' [TEV]. Here it is used of a frightening, never-before-seen appearance [BAGD]. A σημεῖον is an object or event that has spiritual significance [TH].

c. οὐρανός (LN 1.5, 1.11) (BAGD 1.b. p. 594): 'heaven' [BAGD, EC, LN (1.11), Lns, WBC; KJV, NCV, NET, NIV, NLT, NRSV, REB], 'sky' [BAGD, Be, BNTC, LN (1.5); CEV, NAB, TEV, TNT]. Here it refers to the firmament or sky over the earth [BAGD, ICC, Ld, LN, NIC, Sw, TH, TNTC]. That it refers to 'sky' is supported by verse 4 where the dragon sweeps the stars to earth [Ld, NIC]. See this word also at 3:12.

d. perf. pass. participle of περιβάλλω (LN 49.3, 49.5) (BAGD 1.b.α. p. 646): 'to be clothed' [EC, LN (49.3, 49.5), WBC; KJV, NAB, NCV, NET, NIV, NLT, NRSV, TNT], 'to be robed' [BNTC; REB], 'to have put on' [BAGD], 'to be adorned' [LN (49.5)], 'to have thrown around' [Lns]. This passive verb is also translated actively: 'to wear' [BAGD]; and as a noun: '(whose) clothes' [CEV], '(whose) dress' [TEV].

QUESTION—What is the significance of the woman being clothed with the sun with the moon under her feet and a crown of stars on her head?

It indicates that she was honorable and majestic [Ld, Lns]. It shows her divine dignity [Be]. These serve to show her purity and that she came from Heaven and was protected by God [NIGTC]. The moon under her feet indicates her dominion while the crown indicates her royalty [Hu, NIC]. The crown indicates the believers' part in the royalty of Christ [NIGTC]. Being clothed with the sun symbolizes her beauty [Hu] and may picture her as being enveloped with brilliance [Ld].

QUESTION—Who does the woman represent?

1. She represents the church or the Messianic community [Alf, BNTC, Hu]. That she represents the Messianic community is supported by the phrase 'the rest of her children' which refers to the members of the church (see 12:17) [BNTC]. The shift from Mary to the church is to be expected [Hu].

2. She represents the nation of Israel [EC, Sw, Wal]. She is the godly remnant of Israel through whom the Messiah came [Sw, Wal]. There are many references in the OT that symbolize Israel as a travailing woman. The fact that she was clothed with the sun with the moon under her feet and crowned with 12 stars may refer to Genesis 37:9–10 where Joseph dreamed of his father Jacob as the sun, his mother Rachel as the moon and his 11 brothers as the stars. These features show that the woman symbolized Israel [EC].

3. She represents both the true Israel (the church) and faithful Israel of the OT [Be, ICC, Ld, NIC, NIGTC, NTC, TNTC]. She represents not only the true Israel, the Christian community, but also the true Israel of the OT as well [ICC]. She represents the ideal people of God in both the Old and New Testaments [Be, Ld]. Because she is both the church, as seen in verse

12:17, and the mother of the Messiah, it is best to see her as representing the people of God in general [Ld]. The early church thought of itself as a continuation of faithful Israel [NIC]. At first she is Israel who gives birth to the Messiah, later she is the church who is persecuted [TNTC].

QUESTION—How are the nouns related in the genitive construction στέφανος ἀστέρων δώδεκα 'crown of twelve stars'?

The crown was *made of* twelve stars [CEV] or had 12 stars in it [TH].

QUESTION—To what do the birth pangs refer?

The birth pangs refer to those of Mary when Christ was born.

12:2 and having[a] in womb[b] (a child), and she-cries-out suffering-birth-pangs[c] and being-pained[d] to-give-birth.[e]

LEXICON—a. pres. act. participle of ἔχω (LN 23.50) (BAGD I.2.j. p. 333): 'to have' [LN (57.1)]. The phrase ἐν γαστρὶ ἔχουσα 'in womb having' is translated: 'to be pregnant' [BAGD, LN, Lns, WBC; NCV, NET, NIV, NLT, NRSV, TNT], 'to be about to give birth' [CEV], 'to be about to bear a child' [REB], 'to be with child' [EC, WBC; KJV, NAB], 'to be soon to give birth' [BNTC; TEV].

b. γαστήρ (LN 8.68) (BAGD 2. p. 152): 'womb' [BAGD, LN], not explicit [BNTC, EC, Lns, WBC; all versions].

c. pres. act. participle of ὠδίνω (LN **23.54**) (BAGD p. 895): 'to suffer birth-pangs' [BAGD], 'to have birth pains, to suffer pain in connection with giving birth' [LN], 'to bear amid throes' [BAGD], 'to travail in birth' [KJV], 'to be in travail' [EC, Lns]. This verb is also translated as a noun: 'labor pains' [NET]; and as a phrase: 'in pain' [NIV], 'in the pain of labor' [NLT], 'in birthpangs' [NRSV], 'in labor' [WBC]. The phrase κράζει ὠδίνουσα 'she cries out suffering birth pangs' is translated: 'she cried out in her birth pangs' [**LN**]. The phrase ὠδίνουσα καὶ βασανιζομένη 'suffering birth pangs and being in pain' is translated: '(because of) the great pain' [CEV], 'with pain' [NCV], 'in the anguish/agony of her labor' [BNTC; REB], 'pain and suffering (of childbirth)' [TEV, TNT], 'in pain as she labored' [NAB].

d. pres. pass. participle of βασανίζω (LN 38.13) (BAGD 2.a. p. 134): 'to be pained' [BAGD; KJV], 'to be tormented' [BAGD, EC, LN], 'to be in torment' [Lns], 'to be tortured' [BAGD, LN], 'to struggle' [NET]. Βασανίζω refers here to birth-pangs [BAGD]. This verb is also translated as a noun: 'agony (of giving birth)' [NRSV]; and as a phrase: 'in the throes' [WBC].

e. aorist act. infin. of τίκτω (LN 23.52) (BAGD 1. p. 816): 'to give birth' [BAGD, EC, LN, Lns; NAB, NCV, NET, NIV, NRSV], 'to bear' [BAGD, LN], not explicit [CEV]. This verb is also translated as a noun: '(her) delivery' [NLT], 'childbirth' [WBC; TEV, TNT]. This active verb is also translated passively: 'to be delivered' [BNTC; KJV, REB].

QUESTION—What is the significance of the repeated reference to suffering in the phrase ὠδίνουσα καὶ βασανιζομένη 'suffering birth pangs and being in pain'?

The second part is synonymous with the first and explains it [Be]: suffering birth pangs, *that is*, being in pain. It emphasizes the intense suffering of the woman [TH].

QUESTION—To whom will the woman give birth?
1. She will give birth to the Messiah [BNTC, EC, ICC, Lns, NIC, NIGTC, NTC, Sw, TNTC]. Israel will give birth to the Messiah [TNTC].
2. She will give birth to Christ and his church [NIGTC]. The child born is not only Christ but the community of believers making the church [NIGTC].
3. She will not give birth to Christ [Ld, Wal]. The figure merely points to the sufferings of Israel [Wal]. This is an OT symbol and since it takes place in heaven, it does not refer to the historical birth of Jesus to Mary. Rather the events accompanying the following birth symbolize the hostility of Satan to God's anointed One [Ld].

12:3 **And another sign was-seen in heaven, and behold[a] (a) great[b] red[c] dragon[d] having seven heads and ten horns and seven crowns[e] on its heads,**

LEXICON—a. ἰδού (LN 91:13) (BAGD 1.a. p. 370): 'behold' [BAGD, EC, WBC; KJV], 'look' [BAGD, LN], 'lo' [Lns], 'suddenly' [NLT], 'there was' [TEV], 'it was' [NAB, TNT], not explicit [BNTC; CEV, NCV, NET, NIV, NRSV, REB]. Ἰδού is used because this symbol is astonishing and repulsive [Lns]. See this word also at 1:7.

b. μέγας (LN 79.123) (BAGD 1.a. p. 497): 'great' [BNTC, EC, LN, Lns, WBC; KJV, NRSV, REB, TNT], 'huge' [TH; CEV, NAB, NET, TEV], 'enormous' [TNTC; NIV], 'large' [BAGD, LN, TH; NLT], 'giant' [NCV]. Μέγας here indicates enormous size and strength [Lns]. See this word also at 6:4.

c. πυρρός (LN **79.31**) (BAGD p. 731): 'red' [BNTC, EC, **LN**, WBC; all versions except NAB, REB], 'fiery red' [LN, Lns; REB], 'flaming red' [NAB], 'red as fire' [BAGD]. See this word also at 6:4.

d. δράκων (LN **4.54**) (BAGD p. 206): 'dragon' [BAGD, BNTC, EC, **LN**, Lns, WBC; all versions]. A δράκων is a legendary animal. It is typically regarded as being a kind of monstrous winged serpent or lizard. Here it is a used to refer to the Devil [LN]. A dragon is an enormous serpent-like monster [Be]. No such creature actually exists and the reference to a dragon is made only to symbolize the ferocious, cruel, and enormous power of the devil [Lns].

e. διάδημα (LN **6.196**) (BAGD p. 182): 'crown' [BAGD; CEV, KJV, NCV, NIV, NLT, TEV, TNT], 'diadem' [BAGD, BNTC, EC, **LN**, Lns, WBC; NAB, NRSV, REB], 'diadem crown' [LN; NET]. A διάδημα was a symbol of the highest ruling power in a particular area [LN].

QUESTION—Whom does this dragon symbolize?
> It symbolizes the devil or Satan (see 11:9 and 20:2) [Alf, Be, BNTC, EC, Hu, Ld, Lns, NIC, NIGTC, NTC, TH, TNTC]. A dragon in the OT frequently symbolized an evil being [TNTC] or the enemy of Israel [EC, NIC, NIGTC], or Satan [WBC]. It symbolizes the revived Roman Empire and satanic strength [Wal].

QUESTION—What is indicated by the color red?
> It indicates the murderous work of the dragon [Be, EC, Hu, NIC, Sw, Wal], its oppressive character [NIGTC] or its fearsome character [Hu]. From 6:4, we find that the color red symbolizes hell and blood (6:4) [Lns]. Or, the red color may have not any particular significance [Ld].

QUESTION—What is indicated by the seven heads, seven crowns, and ten horns?
> The symbolism of these features are not to be pictured, such as having four horns on one head and one on each of the other six, or having two horns on four of the heads and one horn of the remaining two heads [Ld]. The description is plainly symbolical and it is impossible to draw such a picture of the dragon [Lns]. The seven heads and seven crowns may indicate the universality of the dragon's earthly kingdom [Alf] or his great power [Be, Ld]. The seven heads may indicate the great vitality of the dragon [TNTC] or the completeness of his power [NIC, Sw]. The seven heads with ten crowns indicates the totality of his oppressive power and its worldwide rule [NIGTC]. The crowns indicate royalty [Hu, Lns, NIGTC], or sovereignty [Sw], or authority [NIC, NIGTC, TH]. Seven crowns indicate authority over many nations [WBC] or sovereign worldwide authority [NIGTC]. Seven symbolizes divinity and indicates that unbelieving mankind crowns the dragon as their god [Hu]. The ten horns symbolize the great strength of the dragon [Hu, Ld, Lns, TNTC]. The ten horns indicate ten kingdoms of the revived Roman Empire. Of these ten, three were subdued by the little horn of Dan 7:8. This little horn is the world ruler during the great tribulation [Wal]. The seven heads are seven successive world empires, the diadems show that the empires are currently ruling (as John writes) and the ten horns (those of the final 3 empires) indicate the supremacy of the 10 kingdoms during the final three and a half years before the Second Coming [EC].

QUESTION—What OT Scripture points to a similar figure as this dragon?
> The fourth beast described in Daniel 7:7, 20 and 24 is a similar figure [Alf, BNTC, ICC, Ld, NIC, NTC, TH, Wal, WBC].

12:4 **And its tail sweeps-away**[a] **the third (part) of-the stars of heaven**[b] **and threw them to the earth.**

LEXICON—a. pres. act. indic. of σύρω (LN **15.212**) (BAGD p. 794): 'to sweep away' [BAGD, BNTC; NET, TNT], 'to sweep down' [WBC; NRSV, REB], 'to sweep out of' [NCV, NIV], 'to sweep from' [NAB], 'to drag' [EC, LN, Lns], 'to drag out' [**LN**; TEV], 'to drag down' [NLT], 'to drag from' [CEV], 'to draw' [LN; KJV], 'to pull' [LN].

b. οὐρανός (BAGD 1.c. p. 594): 'sky' [BNTC, Sw; CEV, NAB, NCV, NIV, REB, TEV, TNT], 'heaven' [BAGD, EC, WBC; KJV, NET, NRSV], not explicit [Lns; NLT]. Οὐρανός here refers to the starry heaven [BAGD]. See this word also at 12:1.

QUESTION—What do the stars symbolize?

1. They symbolize angels who fell with Satan in past history [EC, Hu, ICC, Lns, NTC]. This is supported by the fact that in 9:1 a star is seen as an angel and 12:8–9 speak of Satan and his angels [EC]. As this refers to the fall of Satan from Heaven with his angels, 12:7ff. refer to the event when Satan attacks Heaven in pursuit of the child [EC, ICC]. These are the fallen angels of Jude 6 [Lns].
2. They symbolize ungodly powers being represented by angels [BNTC, TH].
3. They symbolize angels and Israelite saints [NIGTC]. Two passages in Daniel associate God's people with stars (8:24 and 12:3) and one, 8:10, associates angels with stars. Further, Rev. 1:16, 20ff. show stars representing angels who represent the churches on earth. The focus here is on the persecution of God's people before the birth of the Messiah [EC].
4. They represent the dragon's enemies whom he subdues [Wal].
5. It may show that the dragon's activities in other spheres have repercussions on earth [TNTC].
6. The act of sweeping away the stars in the sky merely emphasizes the huge size of the dragon [Ld, NIC], and its awesome power [NIC].

QUESTION—What is the significance of the fraction, one-third?

It signifies a significant amount [Hu, NIC, TNTC], a significant minority [TNTC]. It signifies his great authority [EC].

QUESTION—What OT Scripture points to a similar figure?

Daniel 8:10 and 24 depict the Little Horn as throwing stars to the ground and trampling on them [Alf, BNTC, EC, ICC, Ld, Lns, NIC, NIGTC, NTC, Sw, TH, TNTC, WBC]. Daniel 7:7 tells about a beast with ten horns that was similarly frightening and strong [Hu].

And the dragon was-standing before the woman who is-about[a] to-give-birth, so-that when she-gives-birth-to her child it-may-devour[b] (it).

LEXICON—a. pres. act. participle of μέλλω (LN 67.62): 'to be about to' [BNTC, EC, LN, Lns, WBC; NAB, NET, NIV, NLT, NRSV, REB, TNT], 'to be ready to' [KJV, NCV], not explicit [CEV, TEV]. See this word also at 1:19 and 3:2.

b. aorist act. subj. of κατεσθίω (LN 23.4) (BAGD 1. p. 422): 'to devour' [BAGD, BNTC, EC, Lns; all versions except CEV, TEV], 'to eat' [CEV, NCV, TEV], 'to eat up' [BAGD, LN], 'to swallow' [WBC]. See this word also at 10:9 and 11:5.

QUESTION—Who is the child?

The child is Christ [Alf, BNTC, EC, Hu, Ld, Lns, NIC, NIGTC, NTC, TNTC, Wal].

QUESTION—What events show the dragon's attempt to devour the child?
Evidences of the dragon's attempts are: Herod's attempt to kill Jesus [BNTC, EC, Hu, Lns, NIGTC], the temptation in the wilderness and the crucifixion [BNTC, EC, Lns, NIGTC].

12:5 And she-gave-birth-to (a) son, (a) male[a] (child), who is-destined[b] to-shepherd[c] all the nations[d] with (an) iron rod.
LEXICON—a. ἄρσην (LN 79.102) (BAGD p. 110): 'male' [BAGD, LN], 'man' [LN]. The phrase υἱὸν ἄρσεν 'a son, a male' [EC, Lns] is also translated: 'a son, a male child' [WBC; NET, NIV, NRSV], 'a man child' [KJV], 'a male child' [BNTC; REB], 'a male child, a son' [TNT], 'a son, a boy' [NAB], 'a son' [CEV, NAB, TEV], 'a boy' [NLT].
  b. pres. act. indic. of μέλλω (LN 67.62, 71.36) (BAGD 1.c.δ. p. 501): 'to be destined' [BAGD, BNTC; NAB, REB], 'will certainly' [BAGD], 'must' [BAGD, LN (71.36)], 'to be to' [KJV, NLT, NRSV, TNT], 'would' [CEV], 'will' [Be, WBC; NCV, NIV, TEV], 'has to' [LN (71.36)], 'to be about to' [EC, LN (67.62), Lns], 'to be going to' [NET].
  c. pres. act. infin. of ποιμαίνω (BAGD 2.a.γ. p. 683): 'to rule' [LN; all versions except NAB], 'to govern' [LN], 'to shepherd' [Lns; NAB], 'to smash' [BNTC], 'to destroy' [EC], 'to drive' [WBC]. 'To shepherd with an iron rod' indicates ruling with complete authority, brutally defeating all enemies [TH]. It implies ruling with destructive results [BAGD]. See this word also at 2:27.
  d. ἔθνος (LN 11.55): 'nation' [LN]. The phrase τὰ ἔθνη 'the nations' [BNTC, EC, WBC; all versions] is also translated 'the Gentiles' [Be, EC, WBC], 'the heathen' [Lns]. See this phrase also at 2:26 and 11:2
QUESTION—What is the purpose of adding the word 'male' to 'son'?
The word 'male' emphasizes the masculine gender of the child [Lns, NIC, Sw, TNTC, Wal].
QUESTION—Who is the son the woman gave birth to?
The son is Jesus Christ [Alf, Be, EC, Hu, Ld, Lns, NIC, NTC, Sw, TH, Wal]. The fact that the child was caught up to God and his throne support the interpretation that this child was Christ [Wal]. Although this is a reference to Jesus, the birth does not refer to his birth at Bethlehem. The main point of the symbolism here is rather to show the hostility of Satan to God's chosen [Ld].
QUESTION—To what Psalm does this statement allude?
It alludes to Psalm 2:9 [Alf, EC, Hu, Ld, Lns, NIC, NIGTC, NTC, Sw, TH, TNTC, Wal].

And her child was-snatched-away[a] to God and to his throne.
LEXICON—a. aorist pass. indic. of ἁρπάζω (LN 18.4) (BAGD 2.b. p. 109): 'to be snatched away' [BNTC, LN, Lns; CEV, NLT, NRSV, TEV], 'to be snatched up' [NIV, REB, TNT], 'to be caught up' [WBC; KJV, NAB], 'to be caught away' [EC], 'to be snatched' [BAGD], 'to be taken away'

[BAGD, LN], 'to be taken up' [NCV, NET], 'to be seized' [LN]. The snatching away implies no resistance offered [BAGD].

QUESTION—To what does the verb ἡρπάσθη 'was snatched away' refer?

It refers to the Ascension of Christ [Alf, EC, Hu, Lns, NIC, NIGTC, Sw, TH, TNTC, Wal, WBC]. Although the Ascension of Christ is included here, the verb ἡρπάσθη probably alludes to Christ's resurrection [NIGTC]. The whole scene of the birth and being snatched away occurred in heaven, so it does not refer to the Ascension, but symbolically proclaims Christ's victory over the efforts of Satan to destroy him [Ld].

QUESTION—Who is the implied actor of the passive verb 'was snatched away'?

The actor is either God or an angel [TH].

12:6 And the woman fled[a] into the wilderness,[b] where she-has (a) place prepared[c] by[d] God there,

TEXT—Some manuscripts do not include ἐκεῖ 'there'. GNT does not mention this alternative. Ἐκεῖ 'there' is not included by KJV.

LEXICON—a. aorist act. indic. of φεύγω (LN 15.61) (BAGD 1. p. 855): 'to flee' [BAGD, EC, LN, Lns, WBC; all versions except CEV], 'to run' [CEV], 'to run away' [LN; NCV], 'to escape' [BNTC]. See this word also at 9:6.
- b. ἔρημος (LN 1.86) (BAGD 2. p. 309): 'wilderness' [BAGD, EC, LN, Lns, WBC; KJV, NET, NLT, NRSV, REB, TNT], 'desert' [BAGD, BNTC, LN; CEV, NAB, NCV, NIV, TEV], 'lonely place' [LN], 'grassland' [BAGD]. An ἔρημος is a mainly uninhabited area, usually with sparse vegetation [LN].
- c. perf. pass. participle of ἑτοιμάζω (BAGD 3. p. 316): 'to be prepared' [BAGD, EC, LN, WBC; all versions], 'to be made ready' [LN], 'to be put in readiness' [BAGD], 'to be kept in readiness' [BAGD]. See this word also at 8:6.
- d. ἀπό with genitive object (LN 90.7) (BAGD V.6. p. 88): 'by' [BNTC, EC, LN, NIC, WBC; NAB, NET, NIV, NRSV, REB], 'of' [Lns; KJV], 'from' [LN]. The phrase ἀπὸ τοῦ θεοῦ 'by God' is translated: 'by God's command' (not by God himself) [Alf, BAGD, EC]. This passive voice is also translated as active with God as the actor: 'God prepared' [CEV, NCV, NLT, TEV, TNT]. See this word also at 9:18.

QUESTION—What is the relationship of this verse to the account beginning in 12:13 where a woman also escapes to the wilderness?

The accounts are the same [ICC, Sw]. This one is less detailed than the one beginning in 12:13 [Alf, EC, Lns]. Although this event is the same as that in 12:13, it occurs as 12:13 shows, chronologically after the events described in 12:7–12, not before [Alf, EC, ICC].

QUESTION—To what does this escape into the wilderness allude?

1. It alludes to the flight of the church from the Roman army in A.D. 66 to Pella, east of the Jordan [NIC, NTC, Sw]. It may partly indicate the

escape to Pella but the purpose of the vision is to assure the church that God will protect her and enable her to endure in the face of martyrdom [NIC].
2. It alludes to the to the final three and a half years of the 70th week of Daniel [EC, Wal]. This must refer to the protection of a part of the nation of Israel during the great tribulation before Christ's return [Wal]. It refers to Israel as a whole and since it refers to the time of the Antichrist's rule, it cannot refer to the whole time from the Ascension to the Second Coming [EC].
3. It alludes to a period of time during which the true church is protected from the dragon [ICC, Ld, Lns, NIGTC]. This symbolic period of three and a half years refers to the final part of Satan's attempt to thwart God's purposes [Ld]. This period begins right after the Ascension of Christ and is that time when God protects the church and enables it to witness to the world (see 13:5) [NIGTC]. It refers to the time until Christ's coming and the wilderness indicates that the church is to be away from earthly grandeur as it exists in lowliness and much want [Lns].
4. It alludes to a virtual, not an actual place [BNTC, WBC]. This is a period when the true invisible church is being protected from any ultimate harm while the visible church is enduring persecution (11:2) [BNTC]. The three and a half years refers to a period of time that God limits [WBC].

so-that there they-may-take-care-of[a] her (a) thousand two-hundred sixty days.
LEXICON—a. pres. act. subj. of τρέφω (LN 23.6, 35.45) (BAGD 1. p. 825): 'to take care of' [LN (35.45); TNT], 'to give care to' [NLT], 'to nourish' [BAGD, EC, Lns], 'to feed' [BAGD; KJV], 'to provide food for' [BAGD, LN (23.6)], 'to support' [BAGD], 'to give food to eat' [LN (23.6)]. Τρέφω carries the implication that the food is adequate and is supplied over a considerable period of time [LN (23.6)]. This word is also translated passively: 'to be taken care of' [WBC; CEV, NAB, NCV, NET, NIV, TEV, TNT], 'to be nourished' [NRSV], 'to be looked after' [REB], 'to be sustained' [BNTC].
QUESTION—With what other event does this period correspond?
It corresponds to the same period when the two witnesses are prophesying in Jerusalem (see 11:2) [EC, Sw]. It corresponds to a period of persecution (see 11:2 and 13:5) [NIC].
QUESTION—Who are the 'they' who take care of the woman?
God provides for the woman's care, but his agents are not important enough to be specified [TNTC]. It is not stated who 'they' are, but perhaps it refers to the prophet and apostles who will nourish the church with their written words [Lns]. Many translations avoid the problem by translating in the passive, 'so that she may be taken care of' [BNTC, WBC; CEV, NAB, NCV, NET, NIV, NRSV, REB, TEV, TNT].

DISCOURSE UNIT: 12:7–18 [CEV, NET]. The topic is war in heaven [NET], Michael fights the dragon [CEV].

DISCOURSE UNIT: 12:7–12 [Be, BNTC, EC, Hu, NIC, NIGTC, NTC, TNTC, Wal, WBC; NRSV]. The topic is war in heaven [BNTC, NIC], Satan's expulsion from the heavens [Be], war in heaven, the dragon cast out [Hu], the expulsion of the dragon from heaven [EC], Satan cast out [TNTC, Wal], the defeat of the dragon [NTC; NRSV].

12:7 And there-was^a war^b in heaven,^{c} Michael and his angels waged-war^d with the dragon. And the dragon and its angels waged-war,
LEXICON—a. aorist mid. (deponent = act.) indic. of γίνομαι (LN 91.5): 'to be' [WBC; KJV, NCV, NIV, NLT, TNT], 'to break out' [BNTC; CEV, NAB, NET, NRSV, REB, TEV], 'to occur' [EC, Lns], 'there was' [LN].
  b. πόλεμος (LN 55.5) (BAGD 1.b. p. 685): 'war' [BNTC, EC, LN; all versions], 'battle' [BAGD, Lns, WBC]. See this word also at 9:7.
  c. οὐρανός (BAGD 1.d. p. 594): 'heaven' [BAGD; all versions]. Οὐρανός here refers to Heaven, not the sky [EC, NIC, TH]. Or οὐρανός here refers to the atmosphere, the place where the clouds hover [BAGD]. See this word also at 3:12.
  d. genitive articular infinitive of πολεμέω (LN **55.5**): 'to wage war' [BNTC, LN], 'to fight' [WBC; all versions except NAB], 'to battle' [Lns; NAB], 'to make war' [EC]. See this word also at 2:16.
QUESTION—When does this war occur?
  1. It will occur at the end of time [EC, ICC, NIC, Wal]. It occurs just before the last half of the Great Tribulation in the middle of Daniel's 70th week [EC]. Its occurrence marks the beginning of the Great Tribulation as predicted by Daniel 12:1 [Wal].
  2. It occurred some time in the past [Hu, Lns, NIGTC, NTC, Sw]. This verse depicts the effect of the exaltation of Christ and his victory over Satanic forces [Hu, Lns]. It depicts the counterpart in Heaven to what happened in 12:1–6 concerning the victory of Christ in his death and resurrection. That is, Michael's defeat of the devil in Heaven reflect Christ's resurrection and subsequent rule on earth. This marks the beginning of the last-day earthly-heavenly struggle between good and evil predicted by Daniel [NIGTC]. Jesus saw Satan fall from heaven (see Luke 10:18). That fall is pictured here [NTC].
  3. It should not be placed in the sequence of time [Ld]. The verse only assures those who experience evil on earth that evil is in fact a defeated force [Ld].
QUESTION—Who is Michael?
  He is an archangel (see Jude 9) [Alf, EC, Hu, Lns, Sw, TH, TNTC]. He is Israel's guardian angel (see Daniel 10:12, 21; 12:1) [Alf, Be, EC, ICC, Ld, Sw, TH]. He is the commander of the heavenly army [Be, Lns, TNTC].

QUESTION—How are the nouns related in the genitive construction οἱ ἄγγελοι αὐτοῦ 'his angels'?
They are the angels who are under Michael's command [TH, TNTC].
QUESTION—What was the cause of this battle?
It may have been an effort on Satan's part to overthrow the woman's son [EC, Sw] and regain his position in God's presence [EC, NIC, Sw].

12:8 and/but it-was- not -strong[a] (enough) nor was-found[b] place for-them (any) longer[c] in heaven.
TEXT—Instead of ἴσχυσεν 'it was strong', some manuscripts have ἴσχυσαν 'they were strong'. GNT does not mention this alternative. The reading 'they were strong' is taken by BNTC; KJV, NAB, and NRSV.
LEXICON—a. aorist act. indic. of ἰσχύω (LN **74.9, fn. 1**) (BAGD 3. 383): 'to be strong enough' [Lns; NCV, NIV], 'to be strong enough to win' [TNT], 'to be able to prevail' [**LN**, WBC], 'to be strong enough to prevail' [Be; NET], 'to prevail' [BAGD, EC; KJV], 'to have the strength to, to be very capable of' [LN], 'to win out' [BAGD]. It may be better to translate this: 'he was defeated' [**LN**; TEV], 'they were defeated' [NRSV], 'they were overpowered' [BNTC; NAB], 'he lost the battle' [CEV, NLT], 'he was too weak' [REB].
  b. aorist pass. indic. of εὑρίσκω (LN 27.27) (BAGD 1.b. p. 325): 'to be found' [BNTC, EC, LN, Lns; KJV], 'to be discovered' [LN]. This entire clause is translated: 'there was no longer any place for them in heaven' [BAGD, WBC; NET, NRSV], '(they) were forced out of their places in heaven' [CEV, NLT], 'they lost their place in heaven' [NAB, NCV, NIV, REB], '(they) were not allowed to stay in heaven' [TEV], 'there was no room left for them in heaven' [TNT]. See this word also at 2:2 and 9:6.
  c. ἔτι (BAGD 1.b.β. p. 315): 'longer' [BAGD, EC, WBC; NET, NRSV, TEV], 'more' [Lns; KJV], not explicit [BNTC; CEV, NAB, NCV, NIV, NLT, REB], 'in the end' [TNT]. See this word also at 3:12.
QUESTION—What relationship is indicated by καί 'and/but' that begins this verse?
  1. It indicates a conjoining relationship [Lns; KJV, NLT]: *and* it was not strong enough.
  2. It indicates an adversative relationship [BNTC, EC, WBC; all versions except KJV, NLT]: *but* it was not strong enough.

12:9 And the great dragon was-thrown-down,[a] the ancient[b] serpent,[c] the-one called (the) Devil[d] and Satan,[e] the-one deceiving[f] the whole inhabited-earth,[g] he-was-thrown-down to the earth, and his angels were-thrown with him.
LEXICON—a. aorist pass. indic. of βάλλω (LN 15.215) (BAGD 1.b. p. 131): 'to be thrown down' [CEV, NCV, NET, NLT, NRSV, REB, TEV, TNT], 'to be overthrown' [BNTC], 'to be thrown' [BAGD, LN, Lns], 'to be cast out' [KJV], 'to be cast down' [EC, WBC], 'to be hurled down' [NIV], 'to be driven out' [NAB]. See this word also at 2:10.

b. ἀρχαῖος (LN **67.98**) (BAGD 1. p. 111): 'ancient' [BAGD, **LN**, Lns, WBC; NAB, NET, NIV, NLT, NRSV, REB, TEV], 'old' [BNTC, EC; CEV, KJV, NCV], 'primeval' [TNT].
c. ὄφις (LN 4.52) (BAGD 3. p. 600): 'serpent' [BAGD, BNTC, EC, Lns, WBC; all versions except CEV], 'snake' [BAGD, LN; CEV, NCV], 'reptile' [LN]. Here ὄφις is used symbolically of the Devil [BAGD]. In Revelation this word is only used to indicate the Devil [TH]. See this word also at 9:19.
d. διάβολος (LN **12.34, fn. 4**): 'Devil' [BNTC, EC, **LN**, WBC; KJV, NLT, NRSV, REB, TEV, TNT], 'devil' [Lns; CEV, NAB, NCV, NET, NIV]. See this word also at 2:10.
e. Σατανᾶς (LN 93.330) (BAGD p. 744): 'Satan' [BAGD, BNTC, EC, LN, Lns, WBC; all versions]. Σατανᾶς means 'adversary' or 'opponent' [TH]. See this word also at 2:9.
f. pres. pass. participle of πλανάω (LN 31.8) (BAGD 1.b. p. 665): 'to deceive' [BAGD, EC, LN, Lns; KJV, NET, NLT, TEV], 'to mislead' [BAGD, LN], 'to fool' [CEV], 'to lead astray' [WBC; NIV, REB, TNT], 'to trick' [NCV]. This verb is also translated as a noun: 'deceiver' [BNTC; NRSV], 'seducer' [NAB]. See this word also at 2:20.
g. οἰκουμένη (LN 1.39) (BAGD 1.a. p. 561): 'inhabited earth' [BAGD, Lns], 'world' [BAGD, BNTC, LN, WBC; all versions except CEV], 'earth' [EC, LN]. The phrase τὴν οἰκουμένην ὅλην 'the whole inhabited earth' is translated: 'all humankind' [BAGD], 'everyone on earth' [CEV]. See this word also at 3:10.

QUESTION—To whom does the phrase ὁ ὄφις ὁ ἀρχαῖος 'the ancient serpent' refer?

It refers to the Devil, who in the form of a serpent, tempted Eve in the Garden of Eden (see Genesis 3:1-15) [Alf, EC, ICC, Lns, NIC, NIGTC, NTC, Sw, TH, TNTC].

QUESTION—Who is the implied actor of ἐβλήθη 'he was thrown down'?

Michael and his angels are the implied actors [Lns, TH]. God is the implied actor in the ultimate sense [WBC].

QUESTION—What is the function of the three-fold repetition of 'to be thrown down': (1) he was thrown down; (2) he was thrown down; (3) they were thrown down?

The repetition emphasizes the action [Lns]. It emphasizes the dishonorable manner in which he was expelled from heaven [EC]. The locations are symbolic; it means that Satan was removed from his place of power [Ld].

QUESTION—What is the function of the five-fold identity of the dragon: (1) the great dragon, (2) the ancient serpent, (3) the Devil, (4) Satan, (5) the one who deceives the whole earth?

It functions to make crystal clear who is being spoken about [EC].

12:10 And I-heard (a) loud voice in heaven saying, "Now has-come[a] the salvation[b] and the power[c] and the kingdom[d] of-our God and the authority[e] of-his Christ,[f]

LEXICON—a. aorist mid. (deponent = act.) indic. of γίνομαι (LN 13.80): 'to come' [EC; CEV, KJV, NAB, NCV, NET, NIV, NRSV, TEV], 'to come to exist' [LN], 'to come to be' [Lns], 'to occur' [WBC], 'to happen' [NLT], 'to be (the time for)' [BNTC; REB], not explicit [TNT]. 'Has come' has the meaning here of 'has come into existence' [TH].
- b. σωτηρία (LN 21.18): 'salvation' [EC, Lns; KJV, NAB, NCV, NET, NIV, NLT, NRSV, TEV], 'deliverance' [LN], 'victory' [WBC; REB], 'hour of victory' [BNTC]. This noun is also translated as a verb: 'to deliver' [TNT]. The phrase ἡ σωτηρία καὶ ἡ δύναμις 'the salvation and the power' is translated: 'saving power' [CEV]. It may be necessary to translate this noun as a verb: '(God) will save (his people)' [TH]. Σωτηρία means deliverance from danger and restoration to a former state of safety and well being [LN]. See this word also at 7:10.
- c. δύναμις (LN 76.1): 'power' [BNTC, EC, LN, Lns, WBC; NAB, NCV, NET, NIV, NLT, NRSV, TEV, TNT], 'time of his power' [REB], 'strength' [KJV]. The phrase ἐγένετο...ἡ δύναμις καὶ ἡ βασιλεία 'has come...the power and the kingdom' is translated '(God) has shown...his power as King' [TEV]. See this word also at 1:16.
- d. βασιλεία (LN 37.64): 'kingdom' [BNTC, EC, Lns, WBC; all versions except REB, TNT], 'sovereignty' [BNTC; REB, TNT], 'kingship' [WBC], 'rule, reign' [LN]. It may be necessary to translate this noun as a verb: '(God) will rule as king' [TH]. See this word also at 1:6.
- e. ἐξουσία (LN 37.35): 'authority' [EC, Lns, WBC; CEV, NAB, NCV, NET, NIV, NLT, NRSV, TEV, TNT], 'authority to rule' [LN], 'rightful rule' [REB], 'rightful reign' [BNTC], 'power' [KJV]. See this word also at 2:26 and 9:3.
- f. Χριστός (LN 53.82) (BAGD 1. p. 887): 'Christ' [BAGD, BNTC, EC, LN, Lns; KJV, NCV, NET, NIV, NLT, REB], 'Messiah' [BAGD, LN, WBC; NRSV, TEV, TNT], 'Anointed One' [NAB], 'own Chosen One' [CEV]. See this word also at 11:15.

QUESTION—Who is likely to be the one speaking?
1. It may be the voice of one of the martyrs under the altar (see 6:10) [EC, ICC, Ld, WBC]. The martyrs also use a loud voice to call out for their vindication [EC]. The voice is a man, not an angel because he calls believers 'our brothers' [ICC].
2. It may be the voice of an angel (see 19:10 and 22:9) [Be, NIC, TH, TNTC].
3. It may be the voice of one of the 24 elders (see 4:11; 7:12; 11:17) [Alf, NIC, Sw].
4. It may be the voice of the many saints in heaven [NIGTC].
5. It may be the voice of the tribulation saints [Wal].

QUESTION—In what sense have salvation and power and kingdom already come?

They have come in anticipation as a future event which is conceived of as already having happened [Be, EC, Ld, Wal, WBC]. The 'kingdom' here is used to indicate the millennial reign of Christ on earth [Wal]. Or, this event happened in the past and it depicts Christ's victory on the Cross of which Michael's victory in heaven was the counterpart [EC].

QUESTION—How are the nouns related in the genitive construction ἡ βασιλεία τοῦ θεοῦ ἡμῶν 'the kingdom of our God'?

The kingdom belongs to our God [Alf, EC]. The phrase means that our God rules or will rule as king [TH].

QUESTION—The phrase τοῦ θεοῦ ἡμῶν 'of our God' governs how many of the previous three nouns?

It governs all three nouns [Be, NIC]: the salvation *of our God*, the power *of our God*, and the kingdom *of our God*.

QUESTION—Is the possessive pronoun 'our' in the phrase 'our God' inclusive or exclusive?

It is inclusive [TH]: the God of you and us.

because the accuser^a of-our brothers^b has-been-thrown-down, the-one accusing^c them before our God day and night.

LEXICON—a. κατήγωρ (LN **33.429**) (BAGD p. 423): 'accuser' [BAGD, BNTC, EC, **LN**, Lns, WBC; KJV, NAB, NCV, NET, NIV, NRSV, REB, TNT], 'Satan' [CEV], 'Accuser' [NLT], 'one…who accused' [TEV].

b. ἀδελφός (LN 11.23) (BAGD 2. p. 16): 'brother' [BNTC, EC, LN, Lns; KJV, NAB, NET, NIV, REB, TNT], 'fellow believer' [LN]. The plural form 'brothers' is translated 'brothers and sisters' [WBC; NCV, NLT], 'comrades' [NRSV], 'our people' [CEV], 'believers' [TEV]. See this word also at 1:9.

c. pres. act. participle of κατηγορέω (LN 33.427) (BAGD 1.b. p. 423): 'to accuse' [BAGD, BNTC, EC, LN, Lns, WBC; all versions], 'to bring charges (against)' [BAGD, LN].

QUESTION—What relationship is indicated by ὅτι 'because'?

It indicates that the following clause is the grounds for the previous claim [EC, Lns, NIC, TNTC]: God's salvation, power, and kingdom have come *because* the accuser of our brothers has been thrown down.

QUESTION—What is indicated by the phrase ἡμέρας καὶ νυκτός 'day and night'?

It means 'continuously' or 'unceasingly' [EC, Hu, ICC, Sw, TH]. It compares with the same expression in 4:8 concerning the praises of the four living beings—the accuser accuses the brothers as continuously as the four living beings continuously praise God [EC].

QUESTION—To whom does the term τῶν ἀδελφῶν ἡμῶν 'our brothers' refer?

It refers to believers who are still living on earth and are being accused by Satan [Be, ICC].

12:11 And they conquered him by/because-of^a the blood of-the Lamb and by/because-of the word of-their testimony

LEXICON—a. διά with accusative object (BAGD B.II.4.a. p. 181): 'by' [BAGD, BNTC; all versions except CEV, NLT], 'through' [Hu, WBC], 'because of' [EC, Lns; CEV, NLT], 'by virtue of' [Alf]. See this word also at 1:9 and 2:3.

QUESTION—What is the function using the pronoun αὐτοί 'they' in addition to its inclusion in the verb morphology?

It functions to emphasize the pronoun [EC, Lns, NIC, TNTC]: *they themselves* conquered him.

QUESTION—What relationship is indicated by διά 'by/because of'?

1. It indicates the means of their victory [BAGD, Be, BNTC, Hu, Ld, NTC, TH, TNTC, Wal, WBC; all versions except CEV, NLT]: they conquered him *by* the blood of the Lamb. It is by means of the blood of the Lamb that they conquered Satan; the effect of what the Lamb did also works for them [TNTC].
2. It indicates the reason for their victory [Alf, EC, ICC, Lns, NIC, NIGTC, Sw; CEV, NLT]: They conquered him *because of* the blood of the Lamb. It was *because* Christ's blood was shed that they have victory over Satan [Alf, EC].

QUESTION—How are the nouns related in the genitive construction τὸν λόγον τῆς μαρτυρίας αὐτῶν 'the word of their testimony'?

1. The *word* is in apposition to *their testimony* [Be, EC, ICC, Ld, NIC, NIGTC, Sw, TH, Wal, WBC]: the word, *that is*, their testimony. It is the testimony that they gave [NIC]. They gave a personal testimony about Jesus [ICC, Ld, NIGTC, Sw, Wal]. They testified about the fact that the blood of Christ could save men from death [Ld].
2. They *testified* about the *word*, where word is the Word of God [Be, EC, TH]. The word is the gospel that they announced [TH].
3. The *word* is the Word of God and *their testimony* is the testimony of Jesus Christ (see 1:2 and 1:9) It indicates the contents of the book of Revelation [Lns].

QUESTION—To what does the word αἷμα 'blood' refer?

It refers to the sacrificial death of the Lamb [Hu, TH]. The Lamb is Christ and the blood is his blood that was shed on the cross [Ld].

and they-loved not their life to-the-point-of^a death.^b

LEXICON—a. ἄχρι (LN 84.19) (BAGD 1.c. p. 129): 'to the point of' [WBC], 'even to the point of' [NET], 'up to' [LN, Lns], 'even in the face of' [NRSV], 'faced with' [REB], 'unto' [BAGD, EC; KJV], 'so much that

(they were) afraid of' [NCV], not explicit [BNTC; CEV, NAB, NIV, NLT, TEV, TNT]. See this word also at 2:10.
  b. θάνατος (BAGD 1.a. p. 350): 'death' [BAGD, BNTC, EC, Lns, WBC; KJV, NAB, NCV, NET, NIV, NRSV, REB]. The phrase ἄχρι θανάτου 'up to death' refers to a devotion that does not shrink even from the sacrifice of one's life [BAGD]. This whole clause is translated: 'they were willing to give up their lives (and die)' [CEV, TEV], 'they were not afraid to die' [NLT], 'they set no value on their lives and were willing to die' [TNT], 'love for life did not deter them from death' [NAB]. See this word also at 1:18.

12:12 Therefore^a rejoice^b (O) heavens and the-ones living^c in them.
TEXT—Some manuscripts do not include the definite article οἱ 'the' before οὐρανοί 'heavens'. GNT does not deal with this alternative but includes it in brackets in the text, indicating doubt about including it.
LEXICON—a. διὰ τοῦτο: This phrase is translated 'therefore' [WBC; KJV, NET, NIV, REB], 'because of this' [EC, Lns], 'for this' [BNTC; TNT], 'then' [NRSV], 'so' [NAB, NCV], 'and so' [TEV], not explicit [CEV, NLT]. See this phrase at 7:15.
  b. pres. pass. impera. of εὐφραίνω (LN 25.122): 'to rejoice' [BNTC, LN, WBC; all versions except TEV], 'to be glad' [TEV], 'to make merry' [EC, Lns]. See this word also at 11:10.
  c. pres. act. participle of σκηνόω (LN 85.75) (BAGD p. 755): 'to live' [BAGD; CEV, NCV, NLT, TEV, TNT], 'to dwell' [BAGD, BNTC, EC, LN, WBC; KJV, NAB, NIV, NRSV, REB], 'to reside' [NET], 'to tent' [Lns]. See this word also at 7:15.
QUESTION—What relationship is indicated by the phrase διὰ τοῦτο 'therefore'?
  It indicates that this command to rejoice is given in response to the fact that the dragon of verse 10 had been thrown down [Alf, EC, NIGTC]: the accuser of our brothers has been thrown down *therefore* rejoice O heavens...! The coming of God's salvation, power, and kingdom also form part of this reason [NIGTC].
QUESTION—Who are the ones living in heaven?
  The ones living in heaven are the angels [Be, EC, Ld, NIC, TH]. Or, they are all those in heaven: the saints and other heavenly beings [NIGTC]. Or, this is directed to those who have been saved: the saints, apostles, and prophets mentioned in 18:20, although angels will join in the celebration [Lns].

Woe^a (to) the earth and the sea, because the Devil has-come-down to you having great wrath,^{b} knowing that he-has little^c time. ^{d}
TEXT—Following οὐαί 'woe', some manuscripts include τοῖς κατοικοῦσιν 'to the ones inhabiting'. GNT does not mention with this alternative. The reading 'to the ones inhabiting' is taken by KJV.
LEXICON—a. οὐαί (LN 22.9) (BAGD 1.c. p. 591): 'woe' [BAGD, BNTC, EC, LN, WBC; KJV, NAB, NET, NIV, NRSV, REB], 'how terrible for'

[TEV], 'it will be terrible for' [NCV], 'alas!' [BAGD; TNT], 'pity' [CEV], 'terror will come on' [NLT]. See this word also at 8:13.
  b. θυμός (LN 88.178) (BAGD 2. p. 365): 'wrath' [BAGD, LN; KJV, NRSV], 'fury' [BNTC, LN, Lns; NAB, NIV, REB, TNT], 'anger' [BAGD, EC, LN; NCV, NET, NLT], 'rage' [BAGD, LN; TEV]. This noun is also translated: 'to be angry' [WBC; CEV]. Θυμός indicates a more emotional reaction than a rational one [EC, Wal]. It indicates intense anger and implies passionate outbursts [LN].
  c. ὀλίγος (LN **59.13**) (BAGD 2.c. p. 563): 'little' [EC, LN; NLT], 'only a little' [**LN**, Lns; NET, TEV], 'short' [BAGD, BNTC, WBC; CEV, KJV, NAB, NIV, NRSV, REB, TNT], 'not much' [NCV].
  d. καιρός (LN **67.78**) (BAGD 2.a. p. 395): 'time' [BNTC, EC, **LN**, WBC; all versions], 'period of time' [LN], 'season' [Lns], 'right time' [BAGD]. See this word also at 1:3 and 11:18.
QUESTION—What relationship is indicated by the conjunction ὅτι 'because'?
  It indicates that the clause that follows is the grounds for the warning to earth and sea [EC, NIGTC, WBC]: Woe to the earth and sea *because* the Devil has come down to you having great wrath.
QUESTION—What relationship is indicated by the participle εἰδώς 'knowing'?
  It indicates a causal relationship telling why the Devil's anger is great [Alf, EC, WBC; KJV, NAB, NCV, NET, NIV, NRSV, TEV]: the Devil has come down to you having great wrath *because* he knows that he has little time.
QUESTION—What is meant by the phrase τὴν γῆν καὶ τὴν θάλασσαν 'the earth and the sea'?
  'Earth and sea' indicate the whole planet earth [EC, TH]. It refers to the people who live on the earth and the sea [Be, EC, Ld, Lns, NIGTC, TH, TNTC, Wal]. 'Earth' is used to indicate the people of the earth, but the function of 'sea' is uncertain [WBC]. The phrase includes those who live on the land and those who sail on the sea [Ld].
QUESTION—Against whom will the anger of the Devil be directed?
  1. It will be directed against the body of believers as 12:11, 13–17 show [Alf, BNTC, EC, Ld, Lns, NIC, NIGTC, TNTC, Wal, WBC]. They are the persecuted righteous people on earth who are the target of Satan's wrath [NIGTC, TNTC].
  2. It will be directed against the ungodly dwellers of earth whose only home is the earth and the sea, the people whom Satan will stir into fury against the church on earth [Lns].
QUESTION—What specific time is indicated here by 'little time'?
  It is the three and a half years of the reign of the beast of the sea (13:5) and it is the same as the time indicated in 12:6 and 14 [EC, NIGTC]. It also corresponds to the three and a half years spoken of in 11:2–3 and in Daniel 7–12 that depicts the end time persecution of the church [NIGTC]. It refers to the great tribulation which is followed by the binding of Satan for 1000 years [Wal]. It is the time between Satan's fall and the final judgment [NIC].

QUESTION—What indicates that this time is short?
Satan is soon to be bound for 1000 years before Christ comes. It is this that limits his time [Alf, EC, Wal]. The time remaining before Christ comes again makes the time short [TNTC]. The end of the age and establishing of God's Kingdom is near [NIGTC]. The final judgment is close [Lns]. The time is limited to the 1260 days referred to in 12:6 [Hu]. This short time refers to the three and on-half year reign of the beast from the sea (see 13:5) [EC].

DISCOURSE UNIT: 12:13-18 [EC]. The topic is the dragon's pursuit of the woman.

DISCOURSE UNIT: 12:13-17 [Be, BNTC, Hu, NIC, NIGTC, NTC, TNTC, WBC; NRSV]. The topic is the river of lies [BNTC], war on earth [NIC; NRSV], assault on the woman and her children [Be, Hu, NTC, TNTC, WBC].

12:13 **And when the dragon saw that it-was-thrown to the earth, it-pursued**[a] **the woman who gave-birth-to the male (child).**
LEXICON—a. aorist act. indic. of διώκω (LN **15.158**, 39.45) (BAGD 2. p. 201): 'to pursue' [EC, **LN** (15.158), Lns, WBC; NAB, NET, NIV, NLT, NRSV, TEV, TNT], 'to go in pursuit of' [BNTC; REB], 'to run after, to chase after' [LN (15.158)], 'to persecute' [BAGD, LN (39.45); KJV], 'to make trouble for' [CEV], 'to hunt for' [NCV], 'to harass' [LN (39.45)]. The aorist tense has an inchoative sense here: 'to begin to pursue' [TEV]; or it means: 'to try to make trouble for' [CEV]. Implied in the meaning is that this is a hostile kind of pursuit [EC, NIGTC, Sw, TH].
QUESTION—What is the sense of εἶδεν 'it saw'?
It means that it *perceived* or *realized* that it was thrown to the earth [BNTC, TH, WBC; CEV, NET, NLT, TEV]. This gives Satan's reaction to his defeat in heaven [TNTC].
QUESTION—On what verse does this account build?
This verse begins to fill in the details of the flight of the woman who fled into the wilderness. [Alf, BNTC, Ld, Lns, NIC, Sw].
QUESTION—What is the significance of this pursuit?
It marks the beginning of the great tribulation spoken of by Jesus in Matthew 24:15–22 [Wal]. It indicates the persecution of believers [Hu, NIGTC]. The woman had fled to the wilderness and now Satan pursues her into that wilderness [Ld].

12:14 **But/and there-were-given to-the woman the two wings of-the great**[a] **eagle,**[b]
TEXT—Some manuscripts do not include αἱ 'the' before δύο 'two'. GNT does not deal with this alternative. 'The' is not included by KJV.
LEXICON—a. μέγας (LN): 'great' [BNTC, EC, LN, Lns; KJV, NCV, NIV, NLT, NRSV, TNT], 'large' [LN, TH, WBC; TEV], 'huge' [CEV], 'giant' [NET], 'gigantic' [NAB], 'mighty' [REB]. See this word also at 6:4 and 12:3.

b. ἀετός (LN **4.42**) (BAGD p. 19): 'eagle' [BAGD, BNTC, **LN**, Lns, WBC; all versions], 'vulture' [LN]. See this word also at 4:7 and 8:13.

QUESTION—What relationship is indicated by καί 'but/and'?

1. It indicates an adversative relationship [BNTC, EC; CEV, NCV, NET, NLT, NRSV, REB]: It pursued the woman...*but* she was given two wings.
2. It indicates a conjoining relationship [Lns; KJV, TNT]: It pursued the woman...*and* she was given two wings.
3. It indicates a consecutive relationship [WBC]: It pursued the woman... *then* she was given two wings.

QUESTION—Who is the implied actor of ἐδόθησαν 'were given'?

The implied actor is God [Alf, Be, EC, TH], or an angel [TH].

QUESTION—What do the eagle and its wings symbolize?

The wings of an eagle symbolize: great strength and rapid flight [EC], easy and speedy flight [BAGD, TNTC], God's protection [NIGTC]. They allude to the figure of an eagle in Exodus 19:4 and Deuteronomy 32:11 where God tells Israel that he brought them out of Egypt on eagle's wings [EC, Lns, NIC, NIGTC, NTC, Sw, TNTC, Wal, WBC]. The eagle symbolizes God's deliverance and enablement [NIC]. It may allude to the fourth living creature that looked like a flying eagle (see 4:7) [Hu].

so-that she-might-fly into the wilderness to her place, where she-is-taken-care-of[a] there (for a) time and times and half (a) time from (the) presence[b] of-the serpent.

LEXICON—a. pres. pass. indic. of τρέφω (LN **35.45**): 'to be taken care of' [**LN**, WBC; CEV, NAB, NCV, NET, NIV, TEV], 'to be looked after' [REB], 'to be cared for' [NLT], 'to be nourished' [EC, Lns; KJV, NRSV], 'to be sustained' [BNTC; TNT] 'to be provided food, to be given food to eat.' [LN]. This nourishing is important because during this three and a half years no one will be able to buy or sell without the mark of the beast (see 13:17) [EC]. See this word also at 12:6.

b. πρόσωπον (LN 8.18, 85.26) (BAGD 1.c.α. p. 721): 'presence' [BAGD, EC, LN (85.26), WBC; NET], 'face' [LN (8.18), Lns; KJV]. The phrase 'from the presence of the serpent' is translated 'from the serpent' [BNTC; all versions except KJV, NET]. See this word also at 4:7.

QUESTION—What is symbolized by τὴν ἔρημον 'the wilderness'?

It symbolizes a place of safety or refuge [EC, Ld, NIC, WBC]. It is a place of refuge for true Israel during the last half of the 70th week [EC]. It symbolizes the fallen world [Hu]. The woman had already fled to the wilderness where she could become lost without food, but now she goes to a place prepared for her to be safely nourished in that wilderness [Lns].

QUESTION—Who is the implied actor of τρέφεται 'she is taken care of'?

God is the one who provides for her [Hu, TNTC] while the actual agent is left indefinite [TNTC].

QUESTION—What is indicated by καιρὸν καὶ καιροὺς καὶ ἥμισυ καιροῦ 'time and times and half a time'?

It is the same period of time referred to in Daniel 7:25 and 12:7 [Wal], and corresponds to the 1260 days of verses 11:3 and 12:6 [Alf, EC, Ld, Lns, NTC, TH, WBC], and the 42 months of verses 11:2 and 13:5 [Alf, EC, Hu, Ld, Lns, TH, WBC]. It is the three and a half years during which the serpent rules over the world [ICC]. It is three and a half years of severe persecution and martyrdom [Ld]. It indicates the time of the great tribulation [Wal]. It is the time from the enthronement of Christ until the judgment when God protects his people [Lns]. It indicates a limited time of intense suffering [TH]. The period indicates the entire existence of the church [Hu, NIGTC].

QUESTION—What is τοῦ ὄφεως 'the serpent'?

It is the same as the dragon of the preceding verses [EC, TH, TNTC, Wal].

12:15 **And the serpent spewed**[a] **out-of its mouth after the woman water as (a) river,**

LEXICON—a. aorist act. indic. of βάλλω (LN 47.2) (BAGD 1.b. p. 130): 'to spew' [BNTC, WBC; CEV, NAB, NIV, REB], 'to spout' [NET], 'to pour' [BAGD, LN; NCV, NRSV, TEV], 'to cast' [EC; KJV], 'to send' [TNT], 'to throw' [Lns]. This active verb is also translated by a passive: '(flood of water that) flowed' [NLT]. See this word also at 2:10.

QUESTION—If the 'river of water' is taken figuratively, what does it symbolize?

The river of water symbolizes: persecution [Hu, NIGTC, Sw], overwhelming evil [NIC, TNTC], destruction [WBC], deceit [BNTC], delusion [Lns]. In the OT, flooding water indicates overpowering evil (see Psalm 18:4 and Isaiah 43:2) [NIC].

so-that it-might-cause-to-be[a] **her carried-away-by-a-river.**[b]

LEXICON—a. aorist act. subj. of ποιέω (BAGD I.1.b.ι. p. 682): 'to cause to be' [LN, Lns; KJV], 'to make' [BAGD, EC], 'to make to be' [LN], not explicit [BNTC, WBC; all versions except KJV]. See this word also at 1:6 and 3:9.

b. ποταμοφόρητος (LN **15.205**) (BAGD p. 694): 'carried away by a river' [Lns], 'swept away by a river' [BAGD], 'swallowed up by the river' [EC], 'overwhelmed by a stream' [BAGD], 'carried away by a flood of water' [LN], 'carried off by a flood' [LN; KJV]. This entire clause is translated: 'that he might sweep her away (with the stream)' [BAGD, WBC; CEV, NET, NRSV, REB, TEV, TNT], 'to overtake the woman and sweep her away with the torrent' [NIV], 'to try to drown the woman with a flood of water' [NLT], 'to search out the woman and sweep her away' [NAB], 'so the flood would carry her away' [NCV], 'to engulf her in its flood' [BNTC]. The meaning of this clause is: 'that he might drown her' [BAGD].

QUESTION—What is the purpose of the 'river of water'?

The purpose of the flood is: to destroy God's people [Hu, Ld, NIGTC, Sw], to destroy the nation of Israel [Wal].

12:16 **And the earth helped**[a] **the woman and opened its mouth and swallowed the river that the dragon spewed out-of its mouth.**

LEXICON—a. aorist act. indic. of βοηθέω (LN 35.1) (BAGD 2. p. 144): 'to help' [BAGD, EC, LN, Lns, WBC; CEV, KJV, NCV, NIV, NLT, TEV], 'to come to the help of' [NRSV, TNT], 'to come to the rescue of' [BNTC; NAB, NET, REB], 'to come to the aid of' [BAGD].

QUESTION—What is the overall teaching of this verse?

It teaches that God uses whatever means he chooses to protect the church from attacks of Satan [Hu, Sw, TNTC, Wal].

QUESTION—What is indicated by ἡ γῆ τὸ στόμα αὐτῆς 'the mouth of the earth'?

It indicates an opening or fissure in the surface of the earth [BAGD, TH].

12:17 **And the dragon became-angry at the woman and went-away to-make war with the rest**[a] **of-her seed**[b]

LEXICON—a. λοιπός (LN 63.21) (BAGD 2.b.α. p. 480): 'rest' [BAGD, BNTC, EC, LN, WBC; all versions except KJV, NCV], 'remnant' [KJV], 'other' [BAGD; NCV], 'remaining ones' [LN, Lns]. See this word also at 2:24.

b. σπέρμα (LN 10.29) (BAGD 2.b. p. 762): 'seed' [EC, Lns; KJV], 'children' [BAGD, BNTC, WBC; CEV, NCV, NET, NLT, NRSV, TNT], 'offspring' [LN; NAB, NIV, REB], 'descendants' [LN; TEV], 'posterity' [LN].

QUESTION—Who are τῶν λοιπῶν τοῦ σπέρματος αὐτῆς 'the rest of her seed'?

1. These are Christians, the body of Christ on earth [BAGD, Be, ICC, Ld, Lns, NIC, NIGTC, NTC, Sw, TH, TNTC, Wal, WBC]. They are the woman's other children in contrast to the male child of verses 3 and 5 [Be, NIC, NIGTC, Sw, TH]. The facts that they observe God's commands and testify about Jesus indicate that they are Christians [NTC]. They may be particularly Gentile Christians [Hu, WBC]. They are Jewish believers in contrast to Israel as a whole (the woman). This includes the 144,000 spoken of in chapter 7 [Wal].

2. They are the 144,000 sons of Israel spoken of in chapter 7 who were sealed on their foreheads [EC].

QUESTION—What Scripture does this verse allude to?

It alludes to Genesis 3:15 in which God promises to put enmity between the serpent and the woman and between the serpent's seed and woman's seed [Be, BNTC, EC, NIC, Sw, WBC].

the-ones keeping the commands[a] **of-God and having**[b] **the testimony**[c] **of-Jesus.**

TEXT—Following Ἰησοῦ 'Jesus', some manuscripts possibly include Χριστοῦ 'Christ', GNT does not mention this alternative. The reading 'Christ' is taken by TR and KJV.

LEXICON—a. ἐντολή (LN 33.330) (BAGD 2.b. p. 269): 'commandment' [BAGD, BNTC, EC, LN, Lns, WBC; all versions except CEV, NCV], 'command' [BAGD; NCV], 'order' [BAGD, LN]. The phrase 'the ones keeping the commands of God' is translated 'the people who obey God' [CEV].

b. pres. act. participle of ἔχω (BAGD I.1.c.β. p. 332): 'to have' [EC, LN, Lns; KJV, NCV], 'to possess' [TNT], 'to hold to' [NET, NIV], 'to hold' [BNTC; NRSV], 'to hold fast' [Be], 'to maintain' [WBC; REB], 'to keep, to preserve' [BAGD], 'to give' [NAB]. The phrase ἐχόντων τὴν μαρτυρίαν Ἰησοῦ 'having the testimony of Jesus' is translated: 'are faithful to what Jesus did and taught' [CEV], 'are faithful to the truth revealed by Jesus' [TEV], 'confess that they belong to Jesus' [NLT], 'give witness to Jesus' [NAB]. See this word also at 2:6 and 12:2.

c. μαρτυρία (LN 33.262, 33.264) (BAGD 2.d.γ. p. 493): 'testimony' [BAGD, BNTC, EC, LN (33.264), Lns; KJV, NIV, NRSV], 'witness' [LN (33.262, 33.264); REB], 'message' [NCV]. The phrase τὴν μαρτυρίαν Ἰησοῦ 'the testimony of Jesus' is translated 'testimony about Jesus' [NET], 'what Jesus did and taught' [CEV], 'their witness to Jesus' [WBC], 'testimony given by Jesus' [TNT], 'the truth revealed by Jesus' [TEV]. This noun is also translated as a verb: 'to give witness to Jesus' [NAB], 'confess that they belong to Jesus' [NLT]. See this word also at 1:2.

QUESTION—How are the nouns related in the genitive construction τὰς ἐντολὰς τοῦ θεοῦ 'the commands of God'?

God gave the commands [EC].

QUESTION—What is indicated by ἐχόντων τὴν μαρτυρίαν Ἰησοῦ 'having the testimony of Jesus?

1. It indicates that they believed in the testimony that Jesus gave [Be, BNTC, EC, ICC, Lns, NIC, NIGTC, TH, TNTC; CEV, NCV, NET, TEV, TNT]. They made Jesus' life and teaching their guiding principle and bore witness to it by martyrdom [BNTC]. 'To have' here indicates 'to hold fast to' the truth that Jesus taught [Be]. This refers to the complete gospel, all that Jesus spoke while on earth [Lns].
2. It means that they testified about Jesus to others [Alf, Hu, NTC, Sw WBC; NAB, NET, NLT, REB].
3. It can be either 1 or 2 [Ld, NIGTC]. The basic meaning is the same whether it is taken to mean the testimony that Jesus bore and to which they held fast, or the testimony which they bore to Jesus [Ld]. The phrase is intended to be ambiguous and can be taken so as to include Jesus'

testimony to God given to the church and also the church's testimony to Jesus as it reproduces Jesus' testimony [NIGTC].

DISCOURSE UNIT: 12:18–13:18 [Be, NIGTC, WBC]. The topic is the warning to believers about false worship [NIGTC], the two beasts [Be, NTC, WBC].

DISCOURSE UNIT: 12:18–13:10 [Alf; NLT, NRSV]. The topic is the beast out of the sea [Alf; NLT], the first beast [NRSV].

12:18 And it-stood on the sand[a] of-the sea.
TEXT—Instead of ἐστάθη 'it stood', some manuscripts have ἐστάθην 'I stood'. GNT selects the reading 'it stood' with a B decision, indicating that the text is almost certain. The reading 'I stood' is taken by KJV.
LEXICON—a. ἄμμος (LN 1.64) (BAGD p. 46): 'sand' [BAGD, EC, Lns, WBC; KJV, NET, NRSV], 'shore' [**LN**; NAB, NIV, NLT], 'beach' [LN; CEV]. The phrase τὴν ἄμμον τῆς θαλάσσης 'the sand of the sea' is translated: 'seashore' [BAGD, BNTC; NCV, REB, TEV, TNT],
QUESTION—Is this a separate verse or is it part of 12:17 or 13:1?
1. It belongs with verse 17 [BNTC, Hu; NAB]: The dragon became angry and went away to make war…and it stood on the sand of the sea.
2. It is a separate verse 18 [BNTC, EC, WBC; CEV, NCV, NET, NLT, NRSV, REB, TEV, TNT].
3. It belongs with verse 13:1 [Lns, TNTC, Wal; KJV, NIV, REB]. It stood on the sand of the sea and I saw a beast.
QUESTION—What is the function of this verse?
This verse combined with the word εἶδον 'I saw' of 13:1, introduces a new vision [NIGTC].

DISCOURSE UNIT: 13:1–18 [GNT, Hu, Ld, NTC, TH, Wal; CEV, KJV, NCV, NET, TEV]. The topic is the two beasts [GNT, Hu, Ld, NTC, TH; CEV, NCV, TEV], the beasts and the false prophet [Wal].

DISCOURSE UNIT: 13:1–10 [BNTC, EC, Hu, Lns, NIC, NTC, Sw, TNTC; NAB]. The topic is the monster from the abyss [BNTC, EC], the first beast [Lns; NAB], the beast from the sea [Hu, NIC, TNTC, WBC].

13:1 And I-saw (a) beast[a] coming-up out-of the sea,
LEXICON—a. θηρίον (LN **4.4**): 'beast' [BNTC, EC, **LN**, WBC; all versions], 'wild beast' [Lns], 'monster' [BNTC]. See this word also at 6:8 and 11:7.
QUESTION—What is the function of εἶδον 'I saw'?
It introduces a new scene in the drama [EC].
QUESTION—Is this the same beast as the one referred to in 11:7 that came out of the Abyss?
It is the same beast [Be, BNTC, EC, Ld, NTC, Sw, TH, TNTC]. It is also referred to again in 17:8 [Be, EC].
QUESTION—What or whom does this beast symbolize?
1. It symbolizes the Roman Empire [Be, BNTC, ICC, NTC, Sw, WBC].

2. It symbolizes the Antichrist [Hu, Ld, NIGTC, TNTC]. This Antichrist has two expressions: it represents an individual who will lead the opposition against the people of God in the final days and it represents a corporate spirit that has inspired false teaching and persecution since the time of Christ [NIGTC]. The beast is the Antichrist of 1 John 2:18 or the man of lawlessness of 2 Thessalonians 2:3 [TNTC]. It symbolizes the spirit of antichristianity that has been in the world from the times of the Apostles and may be finally realized in a person at the final day [Hu].
3. It symbolizes the revived Roman Empire and the Antichrist [EC, Wal].
4. It symbolizes the deification of secular authority [NIC].
5. It symbolizes a composite of all the empires of the world that are opposed to Christ [Alf].

QUESTION—Where else is this beast described?

It is described in Daniel 7 [Alf, Be, EC, ICC, Ld, Lns, NIC, NIGTC, NTC, Sw, Wal, WBC]. This is not a repetition of the vision or prophecy in Daniel where four beasts appeared successively, but the descriptions of three of Daniel's four beasts are combined in this one beast [Lns].

QUESTION—What is symbolized by τῆς θαλάσσης 'the sea'?

It symbolizes a storehouse of evil [BNTC, NIC, NIGTC, TNTC]. It symbolizes unbelieving humanity [Hu, Sw]. To the Jewish people of ancient times, the sea was a source of satanic monsters [EC]. It probably symbolized both unbelieving humanity and the Mediterranean Sea, indicating that the beast will be a Gentile and come from near the Mediterranean [Wal]. It is written in 17:15 that the waters are 'peoples and multitudes and nations and languages' [Ld]. The sea as the source of the first beast mentioned here combined with the earth as the source of the second beast of 13:11, symbolize the whole earth [Lns]. Since the sea is synonymous with the abyss, the storehouse of evil, including wicked spirits and unbelievers, the beast may have its origin from unregenerate humanity [NIGTC].

having ten horns and seven heads and on its horns ten crowns[a] and on its heads names of-blasphemy.[b]

TEXT—Instead of ὀνόματα 'names', some manuscripts have ὄνομα 'name'. GNT reads ὀνόμα[τα] 'names' with (with the plural suffix in brackets) and with a C rating, indicating difficulty in deciding whether or not to include it in the text. The reading 'name' is taken by KJV and NET.

LEXICON—a. διάδημα (LN **6.196**): 'crown' [CEV, KJV, NCV, NIV, NLT, TEV, TNT], 'diadem' [BNTC, EC, **LN**, Lns, WBC; NAB, NRSV, REB], 'diadem crown' [NET]. A διάδημα is a symbol of power, worn on the head [LN]. See this word also at 12:3.

b. βλασφημία (BAGD 2.b. p. 143): 'blasphemy' [BAGD, EC, Lns; KJV]. This noun is also translated as a phrase: '(name) against God' [NCV]; as a clause: '(names) that were an insult to God' [CEV, TEV], '(names) that blasphemed God' [NLT]; and as an adjective: 'blasphemous' [BNTC, WBC; NAB, NET, NIV, NRSV, REB, TNT]. See this word also at 2:9.

QUESTION—What do τῶν κεράτων 'the horns' symbolize?
  They symbolize strength or power [Hu, Lns, NIGTC].
QUESTION—What is symbolized by διαδήματα 'crowns'?
  They symbolize royalty or kingly rule [Be, EC, NIC, NIGTC, NTC, TH, TNTC, Wal, WBC]. The seven crowns symbolize universal authority [NIGTC].
QUESTION—What is symbolized by the ten crowns on the ten horns?
  They indicate that the rule of the beast is maintained by its strength [Lns, TNTC].
QUESTION—How are the nouns related in the genitive construction ὀνόμα[τα] βλασφημίας 'names of blasphemy'?
  The word 'blasphemy' modifies 'names' [BAGD, BNTC, Lns, NIC, TH, WBC; all versions except KJV]: blasphemous names.
QUESTION—What is considered blasphemy in this context?
  It is blasphemous for a human being to take a divine name or title for him or herself and, by doing so, insult God [Alf, Be, BNTC, EC, ICC, Ld, Lns, NIC, NIGTC, NTC, Sw, TH]. The beast was claiming divine prerogatives and demanded that it be worshipped [Ld]. This was done by Roman Emperors [BNTC, ICC, NIGTC, NTC]. The beast claimed to be King of kings [BNTC].
QUESTION—In what manner does the beast have names of blasphemy on its heads?
  It has names (or a name) of blasphemy *on each* of its heads [Alf, BNTC; NCV, NIV, NLT, REB, TEV]. If the text has 'name' in the singular, all the heads have the same name, but if it is the plural form 'names', the heads have different names [TNTC]. It is not said how many names are found on each head [Lns].

13:2 And the beast I-saw was like (a) leopard[a] and its feet like (those of a) bear[b] and its mouth like (the) mouth of-(a)-lion.
LEXICON—a. πάρδαλις (LN **4.13**) (BAGD p. 624): 'leopard' [BAGD, BNTC, EC, **LN**, Lns, WBC; all versions]. If there is no word for 'leopard' in a given language, a phrase such as 'large, fierce, cat-like animal' may be used [LN].
  b. ἄρκος (LN **4.12**) (BAGD p. 107): 'bear' [BAGD, BNTC, EC, **LN**, Lns, WBC; all versions].
QUESTION—What is symbolized by the figure of a πάρδαλις 'leopard'?
  A leopard symbolizes: cruelty [EC, Sw], ferocity [EC, NIC, Sw], agility [EC, Lns, Sw], cunning [EC, Lns], vigilance [EC], quickness [Wal].
QUESTION—What is symbolized by the figure of a ἄρκος 'bear'?
  A bear symbolizes: strength [EC, Sw, Wal], ability to crush [EC, Lns, NIC], tenacity [Wal]. The bear's feet squeeze a person and crush him [Lns, NIC].

QUESTION—What is symbolized by the figure of a λέων 'lion'?
A lion symbolizes: the ability to devour [EC, TH], a terrifying roar [EC, Lns, NIC, Sw], strength [TH, Wal]. It is curious that although the beast has seven heads, the description uses the singular form for the lion's mouth [TNTC].

QUESTION—What is the significance of these three figures together?
They combine to signify a being that is: terrifying [Be, Hu, Lns, NIC, TNTC], extremely revulsive [TNTC], horrible [TNTC], extremely fierce [NIGTC], very strong [Be, EC], very brutal [EC], cruel and ungodly [Hu]. It shows that this beast personified all that was worldly and dictatorial [BNTC]. This figure combines the characteristics of three or four of the beasts depicted in Daniel 7 into one beast [Alf, EC, ICC, Ld, Lns, NIC, NIGTC, NTC, Sw, TNTC, Wal, WBC].

And the dragon gave it its power and its throne and great authority.

QUESTION—What is the source of the beast's strength?
The source of the beast's strength is the dragon or Satan [Be, Hu, Ld, Wal, WBC].

QUESTION—When the dragon gave his power, throne, and authority to the beast, was it then without these abilities?
The verse does not mean that he gave them so as to not retain them himself [Lns, TH]. It might be better to translate this as: 'the dragon shared its power and its throne and great authority with the beast' [TH].

QUESTION—What is symbolized by τὸν θρόνον 'the throne'?
It symbolizes dominion [Lns, NIC].

13:3 **And one of its heads as having-been-killed[a] to death, and the wound[b] of-its death was-healed.[c]**

TEXT—Following καί 'and', some manuscripts possibly include εἶδον 'I saw', although GNT does not mention this alternative. The reading 'I saw' is included by EC, ICC, TR; KJV, NAB, NLT.

LEXICON—a. perf. pass. participle of σφάζω (LN 20.7) (BAGD p. 796): 'to be killed' [LN; NCV, NET], 'to be slain' [EC, Lns], 'to be wounded' [KJV]. The phrase ὡς ἐσφαγμένην εἰς θάνατον 'as having been killed to death' is translated: 'that seemed to be mortally wounded' [BAGD], 'seemed to have been fatally wounded' [CEV, TEV], 'appeared to be fatally wounded' [WBC], 'appeared to have been killed' [NET], 'seemed to have received a death-blow' [NRSV, REB], 'seemed to have had a fatal wound' [NIV], 'looked as if it had been killed (by a wound)' [NCV], 'seemed wounded beyond recovery' [NLT], 'seemed to have been mortally smitten' [NAB, TNT], 'bore the deadly marks of slaughter' [BNTC]. See this word also at 5:6 and 6:4.

b. πληγή (LN **20.29 fn. 2**): 'wound' [EC, **LN**; NCV, TEV], 'stroke' [Lns], not explicit [CEV]. The phrase ἡ πληγὴ τοῦ θανάτου 'the wound of death' is translated: 'deadly wound' [BNTC; KJV], 'death wound' [NCV], 'lethal wound' [NET], 'fatal wound' [NIV, NLT], 'mortal wound'

[WBC; NAB, NRSV, REB, TNT], 'death blow' [Sw]. Πληγή does not typically include the sense of 'mortal' [**LN**].
   c. aorist pass. indic. of θεραπεύω (LN 23.139) (BAGD 2. p. 359): 'to be healed' [BAGD, BNTC, EC, LN, Lns, WBC; all versions except CEV], 'to be well' [CEV], 'to be cured, to be taken care of' [LN], 'to be restored' [BAGD].

QUESTION—Had the head of the beast really been killed or did it only appear to have been killed?
   1. The head had really been killed [Be, BNTC, EC, ICC, Ld, Lns, NIC, NIGTC, Sw]. The words ὡς ἐσφαγμένην 'as having been killed', are the same as those spoken of the Lamb in 5:6. It indicates that both had actually been killed [Ld, NIGTC]. This phrase, used also of the Lamb in 5:6, shows that the head is the Antichrist, the counterpart of Christ, who not only suffered a violent death but also came back to life [ICC]. The head was slain, but it was the beast who recovered from the death of one of its heads [NIC]. Or, the death blow on one of its heads killed the beast and then the beast became alive again [Lns]. The beast himself, in the person of one of its heads, was slain but later came alive again [Ld].
   2. The head only appeared or seemed to have been killed [Alf, Hu, Wal, WBC; all versions]. It only appeared to have been killed. Whether it really died is dependent on how one understands verse 14 [TH]. The wound refers to the phenomenal growth of the church and the conversion of Saul of Tarsus and the spread of the gospel. Its wound was mortal as it is without strength against Christ's death and resurrection [Hu].

QUESTION—To what does αὐτοῦ 'its', in the phrase ἡ πληγὴ τοῦ θανάτου αὐτοῦ 'the wound of its death' refer?
   1. It refers to the head of the beast [Be, EC, ICC]: the wound of the *head's* death was healed. Here it is the head that is healed, even though in 13:12 and 14 the entire beast is identified with the head [ICC]. This refers to the head itself, as the beast in 17:10, is seen as having survived the loss of five of its heads. However, as seen in v. 12, sometimes the Beast is associated with its head [Be].
   2. It refers to the beast itself [Hu, NIC, TNTC, WBC]: the wound of the *beast's* death was healed. The reference is to the beast as seen in verses 12 and 14 [WBC]. The text does not say that the head was healed, but the beast was healed [NIC].

QUESTION—Who is the implied actor of the passive verb ἐσφαγμένην 'having been killed'?
   God is the actor [NIGTC]: God killed one of the beast's heads. Elsewhere in Revelation the word πληγή 'wound' is a punishment that God administers. Here the head of the beast is killed by Christ's death and resurrection [NIGTC].

QUESTION—To what does the figure of the head of the beast refer?
   1. It refers to the Roman Emperor Nero [Be, BNTC, ICC, NTC, Sw]. The head refers to Nero and he will return but only reincarnated as another

emperor who persecutes God's people (see 17:11) [Be, BNTC]. There was a belief that Nero would rise from the dead. It came to be known as the *Nero redivivus* myth. Though it proved wrong, the expectation still remains that an Antichrist like Nero will arise with even increased cruelty [NTC].
2. It refers to the pagan Roman Empire [Alf, Wal]. The Roman Empire is the head that died and will be revived in the future [Wal].
3. It refers to a future king [EC]. This king will be controlled by Satan and will closely counterfeit Christ's death and resurrection [EC].
4. It refers to Satan himself. The wounding of Satan was Christ's victory over Satan when Christ died and was resurrected [NIGTC].

And all the earth marveled^a after^b the beast
LEXICON—a. aorist pass. indic. of θαυμάζω (LN **25.213**) (BAGD 2. p. 352): 'to marvel' [EC, **LN**; CEV], 'to wonder' [BAGD, LN; KJV], 'to gape in wonder' [Lns], 'to gape' [BNTC], 'to be amazed' [BAGD, LN; NCV, TEV], 'to be astonished' [WBC; NIV]. This verb is also translated as an adverbial phrase: 'full of wonder' [BAGD], 'in wonderment' [NAB], 'in amazement' [NET, NRSV], 'in astonishment' [TNT], 'in awe' [NLT], 'in wondering admiration' [REB]. Θαυμάζω here has the connotation of 'to worship' [BAGD].
b. ὀπίσω with genitive object (LN **36.35**) (BAGD 2.a.β. p. 575): 'after' [BAGD, BNTC, EC; KJV], '(to follow) after' [LN; NAB], '(went) after' [REB], 'behind' [Lns], 'at' [CEV]. This preposition is also translated as a verb: 'to follow' [BAGD, **LN**, WBC; NCV, NET, NIV, NLT, NRSV, TEV, TNT].
QUESTION—To whom does ὅλη ἡ γῆ 'all the earth' refer?
It refers to all the people on the earth [Hu, Lns, TH, WBC]. It refers to all the unbelievers on the earth [NIGTC].
QUESTION—What is the implied verb before the phrase 'after the beast'?
1. The implied verb is: 'followed' [Ld, Lns, NIC, WBC; NAB, NCV, NET, NIV, NLT, NRSV, TEV, TNT]: all the earth marveled and *followed* after the beast. The implied verb is: 'went' [WBC; REB].
2. Some make this phrase the object of 'marveled': 'Everyone on earth marveled at this beast' [CEV], 'the whole world gaped after the monster' [BNTC].

13:4 **And they-worshiped^a the dragon, because it-gave the authority to-the beast,**
TEXT—Instead of ὅτι 'because', some manuscripts possibly have ὅς 'which', although GNT does not mention this alternative. The reading 'which' is taken by TR; CEV, KJV.
LEXICON—a. aorist act. indic. of προσκυνέω (BAGD 3. p. 717): 'to worship' [BNTC, EC, WBC; all versions], '(to fall down and) worship, prostrate oneself before, do reverence to, welcome respectfully' [BAGD], 'to do

obeisance to' [BAGD, Lns]. Implied in the term 'to worship' is '(to worship) as God' [TH]. See this word also at 3:9 and 4:10.

QUESTION—What is the purpose of repeating the fact from verse 13:2 that the dragon gave the beast authority?

This fact is repeated to emphasize that Satan's power is concentrated in the beast [NIGTC].

and they-worshiped the beast saying, "Who (is) like the beast and who is-able to-wage-war with it?"

QUESTION—What reply is expected to the question, Τίς ὅμοιος τῷ θηρίῳ; 'who is like the beast?'

The expected reply is: 'No one is like the beast' [EC, Lns, NIGTC, TH; CEV].

QUESTION—What reply is expected to the question τίς δύναται πολεμῆσαι μετ' αὐτοῦ; 'who is able to wage war with it?'

The expected reply is: 'No one is able to wage war with the beast' [EC, Lns, NIGTC, TH]. Implied in the answer is that no one can make war *and win* [TH]. This rhetorical question is also translated as a statement: 'No one can fight against it' [CEV].

13:5 And (a) mouth speaking great[a] (things) and blasphemies[b] was-given to-it

LEXICON—a. μέγας (LN 59.22) (BAGD 2.b.β. p. 498): 'great' [LN; NLT], 'haughty' [WBC; NRSV], 'boastful' [TNT]. This adjective is also translated as a noun phrase: 'great things' [EC, Lns; KJV], 'proud words' [BAGD, Be; NCV, NET, NIV], 'proud claims' [TEV], 'proud boast' [NAB], 'boast' [BNTC], 'bombast' [REB]. The phrase 'a mouth speaking great things was given it' is translated 'the beast was allowed to brag' [CEV]. See this word also at 12:1 and 6:17.

b. βλασφημία (BAGD 2.b. p. 143): 'blasphemy' [BAGD, BNTC, LN, Lns; KJV, NAB, NET, NIV, NLT, REB], 'blasphemy against God' [EC], 'words against God' [NCV]. This noun is also translated as a verb: 'to claim to be God' [CEV]; and as an adjective or modifying phrase: 'blasphemous (words)' [WBC; NRSV, TNT], '(claims) insulting to God' [TEV]. Βλασφημία is speech of self-deification, not derogatory words about God [Ld]. It is to claim rights and authority that are only God's [TH]. Or, it is to insult or defame God [NIGTC, TH]. See the noun and verb forms of this word in 13:6 where it concerns blasphemies against God, his name, and his dwelling. See this word also at 2:9.

QUESTION—What other figure in Scripture is similar to the beast in this verse?

The little horn described in Daniel 7:8, 20, 25, is similar to the beast in this verse [Alf, BNTC, EC, ICC, Ld, NIC, NIGTC, NTC, Sw, TH, Wal, WBC].

QUESTION—What is the meaning of the figure 'to give a mouth'?

This is an idiom that means, 'to give someone something to say' [LN (33.105), WBC].

QUESTION—What is the relationship between μεγάλα 'great things' and βλασφημίας 'blasphemies'?
1. The καί 'and', before 'blasphemies', means 'even' so that 'blasphemy' further defines 'great things' [Be, EC, Lns, NIC]: speaking great things, *even* blasphemies.
2. The word 'blasphemies' modifies 'great things' [TEV]: speaking proud claims that were insulting to God.
3. The καί 'and' functions to join two separate things [EC, Lns, WBC; all versions except NLT, TEV]: speaking great things and speaking blasphemies.
4. The word 'great things' modifies 'blasphemies' [TH; NLT]: speaking great blasphemies.

QUESTION—Who is the implied actor of ἐδόθη 'was given'?
1. The implied actor is God [Lns, NIC, Sw, TH, WBC]: God gave it a mouth to speak. This is giving in the sense of God's permission [Lns, NIC, Sw, TH].
2. The implied actor is the dragon [Hu, Ld, TNTC]: the dragon gave it a mouth to speak. Although the dragon gave the beast this ability, God is the ultimate source [TNTC].

and authority was-given to-it to-do[a] forty and two months.

TEXT—Some manuscripts omit καί 'and' before δύο 'two'. GNT brackets this word in the text, indicating doubt about including it. 'And' is italicized in the KJV, indicating that it is omitted in its underlying Greek text.

LEXICON—a. aorist act. infin. of ποιέω (LN 42.7, 90.45) (BAGD I.2.c. p. 682): 'to do' [LN (42.7, 90.45)], 'to do (what one wants)' [NIC; NLT], 'to continue' [EC; KJV, REB], 'to operate' [Lns], 'to rule' [CEV], 'to use (its power)' [NCV], 'to exercise (authority)' [NET, NIV, NRSV], 'to have (authority)' [TEV], 'to act' [LN (42.7); TNT], 'to be active' [BAGD, NIC, WBC], 'to last' [NAB], 'to carry out, to accomplish' [LN (42.7)], 'to perform' [LN (42.7, 90.45)], 'to practice, to make' [LN (90.45)]. This verb is also translated as a noun phrase: '(to be given) free scope' [EC]. See this word also at 1:6 and 3:9.

QUESTION—Who is the implied actor of ἐδόθη 'was given'?
1. The implied actor is God [Lns, NIC, NIGTC, Sw, TH, WBC]: God gave it authority. This is giving in the sense of God giving permission [Lns, NIC, Sw, TH]. The set time limit indicates that it is God who is the source of the beast's authority [NIGTC].
2. The implied actor is the dragon [Hu, TNTC]: the dragon gave it authority. Although the dragon gave the beast this ability, God was the ultimate source [TNTC].

QUESTION—What does the period of forty-two months refer to?
It refers to the same period as the time that Jerusalem is trodden under the feet of the nations (11:2), the two witnesses prophecy (11:3) and the Woman lives in safety in the wilderness (12:6, 14) [Sw, WBC]. It refers to the period

of the great tribulation [Ld, Wal]. It refers to the rule of the Antichrist [Alf]. It refers to the time between the two comings of Christ [Hu]. It is the same length as the little horn's rule in Daniel 7 [NTC].

13:6 And it-opened its mouth in blasphemies against^a God to-blaspheme^b his name and his dwelling,^c

TEXT—Instead of the plural βλασφημίας 'blasphemies', some manuscripts read the singular βλασφημία 'blasphemy'. GNT does not mention this alternative. The reading 'blasphemy' is taken by KJV.

LEXICON—a. πρός with accusative object (LN 90.33) (BAGD III. 4.a. p. 710): 'against' [BAGD, BNTC, EC, LN, Lns, WBC; KJV, NAB, NCV, NET, NLT, NRSV, REB, TNT]. Some versions take πρός as a marker of the direct object: 'to blaspheme God' [CEV, NIV, TEV].

b. aorist act. infin. of βλασφημέω (LN 33.400) (BAGD 2.b.β. p. 142): 'to blaspheme' [BAGD, BNTC, EC, LN, Lns, WBC; KJV, NET, NRSV, TNT], 'to curse' [CEV, TEV], 'to slander' [NIV, NLT], 'to speak against' [NCV], 'to revile' [LN; NAB, REB], 'to defame' [LN]. Βλασφημέω means to injure or harm someone's reputation by what is said [LN].

c. σκηνή (LN 7.9, 7.17) (BAGD p. 754): 'dwelling' [BAGD, BNTC, WBC; NRSV, TNT], 'dwelling place' [NET, NIV, REB], 'the place where (God) lives' [CEV, NCV, TEV], 'heavenly household' [NAB], 'temple' [NLT], 'tabernacle' [EC, Lns; KJV], 'tent' [BAGD, LN (7.9, 7.17)], 'tabernacle tent' [LN (7.17)], 'booth, lodging' [BAGD].

QUESTION—What does βλασφημῆσαι τὸ ὄνομα αὐτοῦ 'to blaspheme his name' mean?

It is about the same as blaspheming the person since the person's name sums up who he is [Hu, NIC, TNTC]. It means to insult the names by which God is known [TH]. It means to say or do something that damages God's name or opposes God's glory and deity [Ld].

QUESTION—What is meant by τὴν σκηνὴν αὐτοῦ 'his dwelling'?

It means his heavenly, not his earthly tabernacle [Be]. It means his presence or his Shekinah [ICC]. Or, it refers to believers who are God's dwelling place [Hu]. 'God's dwelling' refers to those who dwell in heaven or whose citizenship is in heaven [Ld].

the-ones dwelling in heaven.

TEXT—Some manuscripts include καί 'and' before τούς 'the (ones)'. GNT rejects this addition with a B decision, indicating that the text is almost certain. The reading 'and' is included by ICC and KJV.

TEXT—The words τοὺς…σκηνοῦντες 'the ones…dwelling' do not occur in some manuscripts. GNT includes these words with a B decision, indicating that the text is almost certain.

QUESTION—What is the relationship between τὴν σκηνὴν αὐτοῦ, 'his dwelling', and τοὺς ἐν τῷ οὐρανῷ σκηνοῦντας 'the ones dwelling in heaven'?
1. The second noun phrase is *in apposition to* the first [Be, BNTC, EC, Ld, Lns, NIC, NIGTC, Sw, TH, TNTC, WBC; NAB, NET, NLT, NRSV, REB]: to blaspheme his dwelling, *that is*, the ones dwelling in heaven. This apposition shows that by God's dwelling, those who live there are indicated [Be].
2. The second noun phrase is *in addition to* the first so there are three objects of 'to blaspheme' indicated [ICC, Wal; CEV, KJV, NCV, NIV, TEV, TNT]: to blaspheme his name and his dwelling *and* the ones dwelling in heaven.

QUESTION—Who are 'the ones dwelling in heaven'?
1. They are angels [EC, ICC]. They are the angels who made up the army that with Michael evicted the dragon from heaven (see 12:7–9, 12) [EC].
2. They are God's people [BNTC, Hu, Ld, WBC]. They refer to those whose citizenship is in heaven (Philippians 3:20) [BNTC, Ld].
3. They are either angels or God's people [NIC, Sw]. They could be angels or the church that is viewed spiritually as seated in heavenly places (see Colossians 3:1 and Ephesians 2:6) [NIC].

13:7 And it-was-given[a] to-it to-make war with the-saints[b] and to-defeat them,

TEXT—Some manuscripts omit this entire clause. Other manuscripts include ἐξουσία 'authority' following αὐτῷ 'to it'. GNT includes this clause without the addition of ἐξουσία 'authority' with an A decision, indicating that the text is certain. The reading 'authority' is included by NCV and NIV.

LEXICON—a. aorist pass. indic. of δίδωμι (LN 13.42) (BAGD 1.b.β. p. 193): 'to be given' [BAGD, EC, Lns; KJV, NCV, NIV], 'to be allowed' [BNTC, LN; CEV, NAB, NLT, NRSV, REB, TEV], 'to be permitted' [WBC; NET, TNT], 'to be granted' [BAGD, LN].

b. ἅγιος (LN 11.27): 'holy'. The plural form τῶν ἁγίων 'the saints' [EC, Lns; KJV, NET, NIV, NRSV] is also translated 'God's people' [BNTC, LN, WBC; CEV, NAB, REB, TEV, TNT], 'God's holy people' [NCV, NLT]. See this phrase also at 5:8.

QUESTION—Where else in Scripture is this persecution prophesied?
It is prophesied in Daniel 7:21 [Alf, Be, EC, ICC, Ld, NIC, NIGTC, Sw, TH, TNTC, WBC].

QUESTION—Who is the implied actor of ἐδόθη 'was given'?
1. The implied actor is God [Ld, TH]: God gave the beast authority to make war.
2. The implied actor is Satan [NIC, Wal]: Satan gave the beast authority to make war. The beast is the dragon's instrument but even this authority is controlled ultimately by God [NIC].

and authority was-given to-it over every tribe and people and tongue and nation.

TEXT—Some manuscripts do not include καὶ λαόν 'and people'. GNT does not mention this alternative. The reading 'and people' is not included by KJV.

QUESTION—Where are the words 'tribe, people, tongue, and nation' treated previously?

This group of words is treated at 5:9 but occurs also at 7:9 and 11:9.

QUESTION—Who is the implied actor of ἐδόθη 'was given'?
1. The implied actor is God [TH]: God gave the beast authority.
2. The implied actor is the dragon or Satan [Hu, NIC, Wal]: Satan gave the beast authority. The beast is the dragon's instrument but even this authority is controlled ultimately by God [NIC].

QUESTION—What is the significance of the repetition of the verb ἐδόθη 'was given'?

It emphasizes the subordinate role of the beast [NIC].

13:8 And all the-ones dwelling on the earth will-worship it, the name of-whom not has-been-written in the book[a] of-life of-the Lamb the-one having-been-slain from (the) foundation[b] of-(the)-world.[c]

TEXT—Instead of the singular phrase οὗ...τὸ ὄνομα αὐτοῦ 'of whom...the name of him', some manuscripts read the plural ὧν...τὰ ὀνόματα 'of whom...the names'. GNT does not mention this alternative. The plural 'of whom...the names' is taken by KJV and NCV.

LEXICON—a. βιβλίον (LN 33.52): 'book' [BNTC, EC, LN (33.52), WBC; all versions], 'Book' [Lns]. See this word also at 1:11. See the phrase 'book of life' at 3:5.

b. καταβολή (LN 42.37) (BAGD 1. p. 409): 'foundation' [BAGD, BNTC, EC, Lns; KJV, NET, NRSV, REB], 'creation' [LN, WBC; NIV, TEV, TNT], 'beginning' [NAB, NCV]. This noun is also translated as a phrase: '(before the world) was made' [NLT]. The phrase καταβολῆς κόσμου 'foundation of the world' is also translated: 'creation' [CEV].

c. κόσμος (LN 1.1, 1.39) (BAGD 2. p. 445): 'world' [BAGD, BNTC, EC, LN (1.39), Lns; all versions except CEV], 'universe, cosmos' [LN (1.1)], 'earth' [LN (1.39)], not explicit [CEV].

QUESTION—To whom does the masculine pronoun αὐτόν 'it' as the object of 'will worship' refer?

It refers to the beast [Alf, EC, Hu, Lns, Sw; CEV, NAB, NCV, NET, NIV, NLT]. Although the word θηρίον 'beast' is neuter, John uses the masculine pronoun to refer to it since he is thinking of the beast as a real king [Alf, EC, Sw]. Or, if the masculine form is authentic, then the dragon is the antecedent [NIGTC].

QUESTION—How are the nouns related in the genitive construction τῷ βιβλίῳ τῆς ζωῆς 'the book of life'?

The *book* contains the names of those who will have eternal *life* [Hu, TH]. It contains the names of those who will be members of God's kingdom [Be]. It contains the names of those who believe in Christ [Ld, Lns]. The word 'life' modifies 'book' by telling the book's purpose—it clarifies the kind of security the book provides, they are given the protection of eternal life [NIGTC]. See a similar question at 3:5.

QUESTION—How are the nouns related in the genitive construction τῷ βιβλίῳ τῆς ζωῆς τοῦ ἀρνίου 'the book of life of the Lamb'?

The book of life *belongs to* the Lamb [Be, BNTC, EC, Ld, NIGTC, Sw, Wal; TEV]. Or, it could identify the Lamb as being the source of the life associated with the book [NIGTC].

QUESTION—How are the nouns related in the genitive construction καταβολῆς κόσμου 'foundation of the world'?

'The world' is the direct object of the verb 'to found' [NLT]: God founded the world.

QUESTION—The phrase 'from the foundation of the world' can modify either 'slain' or 'written'. Which one is indicated here?

1. It modifies 'slain' [Alf, BNTC, ICC, Lns, NIC, TNTC; KJV, NIV, NLT, REB]: the Lamb slain from the foundation of the earth. This interpretation is supported by 1 Peter 1:19, 20 where the death of Jesus is seen as predestined from the world's creation [Alf, BNTC, Lns, TNTC]. It is more natural to understand that this phrase modifies 'slain' as it immediately follows it while it is separated from the word 'written' by twelve words [BNTC, NIC].
2. It modifies 'written' [Be, EC, Hu, Ld, NTC, Sw, TH, Wal, WBC; CEV, NAB, NET, NRSV, TEV, TNT]: name not written in the book of life from the foundation of the world. In Revelation 17:8 this same phrase occurs modifying 'written' and there is no ambiguity [Be, Hu, NTC, Sw; NET]. This interpretation is also supported by Matthew 25:34 and Ephesians 1:4 [Sw].
3. It modifies 'people' [NCV]: all people since the beginning of the world whose names....

13:9 **If anyone has an-ear let-him-hear.**

QUESTION—Where is this phrase first treated?

It is treated at 2:7.

QUESTION—What is the function of this statement?

1. It calls for attention to what precedes [Ld, Lns, NIGTC, Wal]. This is the statement that concluded each of the letters to the churches [Ld].
2. It calls the reader's attention to the following statement in 13:10 [Alf, Be, BNTC, EC, Hu, NIC, NIGTC, Sw, TNTC, WBC; CEV, NCV]. This exhortation pertains to the situation described in 13:1–8 and includes the decree stated in 13:10 [NIGTC].

13:10 **If anyone (is-to-go/goes) into[a] captivity,[b] into captivity he-goes;**

TEXT—Following the first occurrence of αἰχμαλωσίαν 'captivity', some manuscripts include ἀπάγει 'he leads'. GNT rejects this inclusion with a B decision, indicating that the text is almost certain. The reading 'he leads' is included by KJV in its translation 'he that leadeth into captivity'.

TEXT—Instead of this entire clause, some manuscripts read εἴ τις εἰς αἰχμαλωσίαν, ὑπάγει 'if anyone (is-to-go) into captivity, he goes'. Other manuscripts read εἴ τις ἔχει αἰχμαλωσίαν, ὑπάγει 'if anyone has captivity, he goes'. GNT rejects both of these alternatives with a B decision, indicating that the text is almost certain.

LEXICON—a. εἰς with accusative object (LN 89.57, 90.59): 'into' [KJV], 'for the purpose of' [LN (89.57)], 'for' [LN (90.59)]. The clause 'if anyone into captivity' is translated: 'if anyone is for captivity' [EC, WBC], 'if anyone is for prison' [BNTC], 'if anyone is to go into captivity' [NIV], 'if anyone goes into captivity' [Lns], 'if anyone is meant for captivity' [LN (55.23); NET], 'if anyone is meant to be captured' [TEV], 'if anyone is doomed to be captured' [CEV], 'if anyone is to be a prisoner' [NCV], 'if anyone is to be taken captive' [NRSV, TNT], 'if anyone is to be made prisoner' [REB], 'if anyone is destined to/for captivity' [Be, NIGTC; NAB], 'if anyone is destined for prison' [NLT].

b. αἰχμαλωσία (LN **55.23**) (BAGD 1.a. p. 26): 'captivity' [BAGD, EC, **LN**, Lns, WBC; KJV, NAB, NET, NIV], 'prison' [BNTC; NLT]. This verb is also translated as a verb: 'to be captured' [CEV, TEV], 'to be taken captive' [NRSV, TNT], 'to be (made) prisoner' [NCV, REB].

QUESTION—What other Scripture is similar to this verse?

Jeremiah 15:2 is similar to this verse [Hu, NIGTC, Sw, TH, WBC].

QUESTION—Is this written to warn believers to be alert or to warn unbelievers of their fate?

1. It is written to warn believers about the coming persecution [Alf, Be, BNTC, Hu, ICC, Ld, NIC, NIGTC, Sw, TH, TNTC WBC; NLT]: if anyone is destined for captivity, into captivity he goes. The admonition, 'Anyone who has an ear, let him hear', is written to each of the churches in each of the seven letters. It is therefore likely to be written to believers here, not to unbelievers [BNTC]. This statement is meant to alert believers of their need to endure and be faithful [Be, ICC].

2. It is written to warn unbelievers [BAGD (1.a. p. 26), Lns, Wal]: if anyone goes into captivity, into captivity he goes. This means that anyone who persecutes believers must face the wrath of God [Wal]. Or, it means that if a person chooses to go into captivity to the beast, like those spoken of in verse 8 who worship the beast, into captivity they will go [Lns].

if anyone (is)-to-be-killed/kills by (a) sword he by (a) sword (is) to-be-killed.

TEXT—Instead of ἀποκτανθῆναι, αὐτόν 'to be killed, him', some manuscripts have ἀποκτενεῖ, δεῖ αὐτόν 'he will kill, it is necessary for him'; others have ἀποκτείνει, δεῖ αὐτόν 'he kills, it is necessary for him'; still others have this entire clause as follows: εἴ τις ἐν μαχαιρῃ, δεῖ αὐτὸν ἀποκτανθῆναι 'if anyone by sword, it is necessary for him to be killed'. GNT rejects all of these alternatives with a B decision, indicating that the text is almost certain. The reading 'he kills, it is necessary for him' is taken by KJV and NRSV.

QUESTION—Which text is authentic?
1. The text that reads the verb 'to kill' as passive is correct [Alf, EC, GNT, Hu, ICC, NIC, NIGTC, TH, Wal, WBC; all versions except KJV, NRSV]: if anyone is destined *to be killed* by a sword, by a sword he will be killed. In view of the fact that they may be killed, Christians need to endure and be faithful [ICC].
2. The text that reads the verb 'to kill' as active is correct [Be, BNTC, Ld, Lns, Sw, TNTC; KJV, NRSV]: he *who kills*/if *anyone kills*. This indicates that the persecutor who kills God's people, will be punished accordingly [Ld, Lns]. Or, it indicates that anyone who takes up the sword against his persecutor, will himself be killed (Matthew 26:52) [Be, BNTC, Sw, TNTC].

Here is the endurance and the faith^a of-the saints.

LEXICON—a. πίστις (LN 31.88) (BAGD 2.d.γ. p. 663): 'faith' [BAGD, BNTC, EC, Lns, WBC; KJV, NCV, NET, NLT, NRSV, TEV], 'faithfulness' [Be, LN, NIC, TH; NIV, REB], 'trustworthiness, dependability' [LN]. This noun is also translated as an adjective: 'faithful' [CEV, NAB, TNT]. See this word also at 2:13.

QUESTION—How is the phrase ⁿὯδέ ἐστιν 'Here is' translated?
It is translated: 'this calls for' [BNTC; NIV, NRSV, REB, TEV], 'this means that' [WBC; CEV, NCV], 'this requires' [Be; NET], 'such is the' [NAB], 'here is your opportunity' [NLT], 'it is here that there is need for' [TNT].

QUESTION—What is the meaning of this statement?
1. It means that the saints must *endure* and *be faithful* in the face of persecution [ICC, Ld, TH; CEV, NIV, REB, TNT].
2. It means that the saints must *endure* and *continue to believe* in the face of persecution [Be, BNTC, NIGTC, WBC; NCV, NET, NRSV, TEV].
3. It means that the saints now have a chance to *endure and believe* [NLT].
4. It means that the acceptance of persecution shows the *endurance* and *faith* of believers [Hu].
5. It means that *faithful endurance* characterizes the saints [NAB].

DISCOURSE UNIT: 13:11–18 [Alf, BNTC, EC, Hu, ICC, Lns, NIC, NTC, Sw, TNTC, WBC; NAB, NIV, NLT, NRSV]. The topic is the second beast [Alf, ICC, Lns; NAB, NRSV], the beast from the earth [BNTC, EC, Hu, NIC, NTC, Sw, TNTC, WBC; NIV, NLT].

13:11 **And I-saw another beast coming-up out-of the earth, and it-had two horns like (a) lamb^a and it-was-speaking like (a) dragon.**

LEXICON—a. ἀρνίον (LN 4.25): 'lamb' [BNTC, EC, LN, Lns; all versions except NAB], 'ram' [LN, WBC; NAB], 'sheep' [LN]. In the context in which horns are mentioned, the reference is undoubtedly to a ram [LN, WBC]. See this word also at 5:6.

QUESTION—What is indicated by the phrase καὶ εἶδον 'and I saw'?
It indicates the introduction to a new scene in the drama [EC, WBC].
QUESTION—What is this beast also known as in Revelation?
He is also referred to as the false prophet (see 16:13, 19:20, 20:10) [EC, Hu, Ld, NIGTC].
QUESTION—What is the significance of the earthly origin of this beast?
It may indicate inferiority in power to the first beast since the first beast rose out of the sea, which to the ancients is greater than the land [EC]. It indicates its earthly origin in contrast to a heavenly one [Wal]. It may indicate a closer connection with humanity [Hu]. It may indicate that this beast is of humbler origin than the first beast [Sw].
QUESTION—What is the significance of the lamb with two horns?
Its being a lamb with two horns may indicate its gentle appearance [EC, ICC, TH]. They may indicate an inferiority of power to the first beast which had ten horns [Be, EC, TNTC, WBC]. It gives the appearance of harmlessness [Lns, NIC, NTC]. It appears innocent and weak [Sw]. It indicates that it appears to be a savior like the Lamb of God [Hu].
QUESTION—What is the significance of the addition of this second beast?
It completes the trinity of evil beings that parallel the Holy Trinity [Hu]. As the Father gives authority to the Son (Matthew 11:27, 28:18; John 13:3), so the dragon gives authority to the first beast (Revelation 13:7). As the Holy Spirit honors the Son (John 16:14), so the second beast honors the first beast (Revelation 13:12) [NIC, NTC].
QUESTION—In what specific way(s) is the speech of the beast speech like a dragon's?
Its speech may be deceptive [Be, EC, Hu, NIC, NIGTC]. Its speech may resemble the roar of a dragon's speech [NIC, Sw] or its harshness and angry timbre [TH]. Its speech was evil like the dragon's [TNTC]. Its speech was empowered by Satan who is the dragon [Wal]. This beast is able to take the loud speech of the first beast and make its claims sound reasonable and persuasive [NIGTC]. That its speech was like a dragon's indicates that it is the agent of the first beast [WBC].
QUESTION—What is the role of the second beast?
It encourages the worship of the first beast [Hu]. Its role is priestly in that it represents the interests of the first beast to the people [Alf, TNTC]. It has a religious role since it is later called the false prophet [EC, Ld, NIGTC, Sw, Wal].

13:12 And it-exercises[a] all the authority of-the first beast before/on-behalf-of[b] it,

LEXICON—a. pres. act. indic. of ποιέω (BAGD I.1.c.α. p. 682): 'to exercise' [BAGD, EC, WBC; KJV, NET, NIV, NLT, NRSV,], 'to use' [CEV, NAB, NCV, TEV, TNT], 'to wield' [BNTC; REB], 'to operate' [Lns], 'to exert' [Wal]. See this word also at 13:5.

b. ἐνώπιον with genitive object (LN 83.33) (BAGD 5.c. p. 271): 'before' [EC, LN, Lns; KJV], 'in front of' [LN], 'stands before' [NCV], 'in presence of' [Alf, Be, BNTC, Ld, Wal; REB, TEV], 'on behalf of' [BAGD, WBC; NET, NIV, NRSV], 'by the authority of' [BAGD], not explicit [CEV, NAB, NLT]. This word is also translated as a clause: 'while the first beast looked on' [TNT]. See this word also at 3:2.

QUESTION—Does ἐνώπιον mean 'before' or 'on behalf of'?

1. It means 'before, in the presence of' [Alf, Be, BNTC, EC, Ld, Lns, NIC, Wal; KJV, NCV, REB, TEV]: it exercises the authority of the first beast in the presence of that beast. He carries out the will of the first beast as a prophet stands in readiness before God [NIC].
2. It means 'on behalf of' [BAGD, WBC; CEV, NET, NIV, NLT, NRSV]: it exercises the authority received from the first beast on behalf of that beast. The preposition ἐνώπιον literally means 'in the presence of the beast' and could hint that this second beast served as a priest for the false prophet, but here it is a Semitic idiom meaning 'by his authority, on his behalf' [WBC].

and it-makes[a] the earth and the-ones dwelling in it that they-will-worship the first beast, whose wound of-death was-healed.

LEXICON—a. pres. act. indic. of ποιέω (LN 13.9) (BAGD I.1.b.ι. p. 682): 'to make' [BAGD, BNTC, LN, WBC; NAB, NCV, NET, NIV, NRSV, REB, TNT], 'to cause' [KJV], 'to require' [NLT], 'to force' [CEV, TEV], 'to affect' [Lns]. The phrase ποιεῖ...ἵνα 'it makes...that' is translated: 'it causes...to' [KJV], 'it causes...that' [EC], 'it forces...to' [CEV, TEV], 'it requires...to' [NLT], 'it makes...to' [WBC], 'it affects...so that' [Lns], 'it makes' [BNTC; NAB, NET, NIV, NRSV, REB, TNT].

QUESTION—What is indicated by the redundant phrase τὴν γῆν καὶ τοὺς ἐν αὐτῇ 'the earth and the ones dwelling in it'?

It indicates the totality of the human race [NIC]. It may emphasize totality [TNTC]. The conjunction καί 'and' here means 'that is': the earth, *that is*, those who dwell in it [WBC]. The phrase 'the earth and the ones dwelling in it' is condensed to 'everyone living on earth' [NCV].

QUESTION—What is the significance of saying that the beast was healed of its death wound?

It signifies that the beast is identified with its head that was said to have been fatally wounded in verse 13:3 [Be, EC, ICC, Ld, NIC].

QUESTION—What is indicated by the change from the past tense of verse 11 to the present tense here through verse 18?

It indicates a more vivid way of expression [WBC]. Although the tense shifts to the present tense, some translations continue to use the past tense: [BNTC, WBC; CEV, NAB, NET, NIV, NLT, REB, TEV, TNT]. The translator needs to decide what the change will mean to his/her readers if they change to present tense [TH].

13:13 And it-does great signs,[a] so-that[b] it-makes even fire to-come-down out-of heaven to the earth before[c] men,

LEXICON—a. σημεῖον (LN 33.477) (BAGD 2.c. p. 748): 'sign' [EC, LN, Lns; NET, NRSV, TNT], 'portent' [BAGD], 'miracle' [BNTC, WBC; CEV, NCV, NLT, REB, TEV], 'miraculous sign' [NIV], 'wonder' [KJV], 'prodigy' [NAB]. See this word also at 12:1.
- b. ἵνα (LN 89.49, 91.15) (BAGD II.2. p. 378): 'so that' [BAGD, LN (89.49), Lns; KJV, NCV], 'that' [EC, LN (89.49, 91.15)], 'such as' [NLT], 'that is, namely, namely that' [LN (91.15)], 'so as a result' [LN (89.49)], not explicit [BNTC, WBC; all versions except KJV, NLT]. See this word also at 2:21.
- c. ἐνώπιον with genitive object (LN 83.33) (BAGD 2.a. p. 270): 'before' [EC, LN, Lns, WBC], 'before (one's) eyes' [BNTC; TNT], 'in the sight of' [BAGD; KJV, NRSV, TEV], 'in full view of' [NIV], 'in front of' [LN; NET], 'in the presence of' [BAGD]. This preposition is also translated as a clause: 'while people watched' [CEV, NAB, NCV, NLT], 'where people could see' [REB]. See this word also at 3:2.

QUESTION—What relationship is indicated by ἵνα 'that'?

It may indicate result [BAGD, NIGTC], or it may be epexegetical explaining what the great signs were [NIGTC]. It indicates an example of the signs [Lns, TNTC, WBC; NLT]: it does great signs, it even makes fire to come down. This is an example of the signs he performed [TNTC].

QUESTION—In what sense is the word ἀνθρώπων 'men' used here?

It is used to refer to people in general, not just to the male members of society [TH, WBC; CEV, NCV, NET, NLT, NRSV, REB, TEV].

QUESTION—What other Scripture records action similar to this ability of the beast?

2 Thessalonians 2:9–10 in its description of the 'lawless one' and his activity is similar to the action of this beast [Be, BNTC, EC, Hu, ICC, Ld, NIC, TNTC, WBC].

QUESTION—What OT prophet also called fire from heaven?

The prophet Elijah called fire from heaven to consume the sacrifice he had laid out (see 1 Kings 18:36–39; 2 Kings 1:10) [Alf, Be, EC, Hu, ICC, Lns, NIC, NIGTC, Sw, TH, Wal, WBC].

QUESTION—What would be the purpose of calling down fire?

This may be intended to show how this false prophet counterfeits Elijah [Alf, BNTC, Hu]. This kind of miracle would show God's approval of the beast [Sw]. It may just be to gain admiration [TNTC]. This was not destructive fire but a visible sign to show his power [Ld].

13:14 and it-deceives[a] the-ones dwelling on the earth by[b] the signs that were-given[c] to-it to-perform before[d] the beast,

LEXICON—a. pres. act. indic. of πλανάω (LN 31.8) (BAGD 1.b p. 665): 'to deceive' [BAGD, BNTC, EC, LN, Lns, WBC; KJV, NET, NIV, NLT,

NRSV, TEV], 'to delude' [REB], 'to fool' [CEV, NCV], 'to lead astray' [NAB, TNT]. See this word also at 2:20.
  b. διά with accusative object (BAGD B.II.4.a. p. 181): 'by' [BAGD, BNTC; CEV, NCV, NET, NRSV, REB, TNT], 'by means of' [KJV, TEV], 'through' [Be, WBC], 'with' [NLT], 'because of' [EC, ICC, LN, Lns; NAB, NIV], 'on account of' [NIGTC]. See this word also at 1:9.
  c. aorist pass. indic. of δίδωμι (LN 57.71) (BAGD 1.a. p. 539): 'to be given' [LN, Lns], 'to be given power' [NCV, NIV], 'to be allowed' [BNTC; NAB, NLT, NRSV, REB, TEV], 'to be permitted' [WBC; NET, TNT], 'to be granted' [EC], not explicit [CEV]. This verb is also translated: '(which) he had power (to do)' [KJV]. See this word also at 2:7.
  d. ἐνώπιον with genitive object (LN 83.33, 90.20) (BAGD 3. p. 270): 'before' [EC, LN (83.33), Lns], 'in the presence of' [BNTC, NIGTC, Sw, TH; REB, TEV, TNT], 'in front of' [LN (83.33)], 'in the sight of' [LN (90.20), Wal; KJV], 'on behalf of' [TNTC; NET, NIV, NLT, NRSV], 'by authority of' [WBC; NAB], 'for' [CEV]. This preposition is also translated as a verb: 'to serve (the first beast)' [NCV]. See this word at 3:2; 13:12, 13.
QUESTION—Who is the implied actor of ἐδόθη αὐτῷ ποιῆσαι 'were given to it to perform'?
  1. The implied actor is God [Lns, TH, WBC]: God gave/allowed him to perform.
  2. The implied actor is the dragon or Satan through the first beast [Hu].

telling[a] the-ones dwelling on the earth to-make[b] (an) image[c] to-the beast, who has the wound of-the sword and lived.[d]
TEXT—Instead of the masculine ὅς 'who', some manuscripts have the grammatically correct neuter ὅ 'which'. GNT does not mention this alternative. The reading 'which' may possibly be taken by KJV.
LEXICON—a. pres. act. participle of λέγω (LN 33.69) (BAGD II.1.c. p. 469): 'to tell' [BNTC, LN, WBC; NAB, NET, NRSV TEV, TNT], 'to say' [EC, LN, Lns; KJV], 'to order' [BAGD; NCV, NIV, NLT], 'to command' [BAGD, EC, NIGTC], 'to persuade' [REB], 'to talk someone into' [CEV], 'to direct, to enjoin, to recommend' [BAGD].
  b. aorist act. infin. of ποιέω (LN **42.29**) (BAGD I.1.a.α. p. 680): 'to make' [BAGD, BNTC, EC, **LN**, Lns, WBC; all versions except NIV, REB, TEV], 'to build' [TEV], 'to erect' [REB], 'to set up' [NIV], 'to fashion' [LN], 'to manufacture, to produce' [BAGD].
  c. εἰκών (LN 6.96) (BAGD 1.a. p. 222): 'image' [BAGD, EC, Lns; KJV, NET, NIV, NRSV, REB, TEV, TNT], 'cult image' [WBC], 'idol' [CEV, NAB, NCV], 'statue' [BNTC], 'great statue' [NLT], 'likeness' [BAGD, LN]. An εἰκών is an object made to look like a person, god, or animal [LN].
  d. aorist act. indic. of ζάω (LN 23.88): 'to live' [LN, Lns, WBC; KJV, NAB, NET, NIV, NRSV, REB, TEV], 'to come to life' [BNTC, EC], 'to

come back to life' [NLT], 'to spring to life again' [NCV], 'to live again' [Be], 'to survive' [TNT]. This word is also translated by negating its opposite: 'not to die' [CEV]. See this word at 1:18 and 2:8.

QUESTION—Who are τοῖς κατοικοῦσιν ἐπὶ τῆς γῆς 'the ones dwelling on the earth'?

They are those people on earth who do not believe in Christ [EC, ICC, Ld, NIC, TNTC].

QUESTION—What is indicated by the dative case in the phrase τῷ θηρίῳ 'to the beast'?

The dative case indicates: 'to the beast' [BNTC, Hu; KJV, NET], 'for the beast' [EC, Lns; NRSV, TNT], 'of the beast' [NIC; NLT], 'in honor of the beast' [Lns, TH, WBC; NAB, NCV, NIV, REB, TEV], or '(an idol) in the form of the beast' [CEV].

QUESTION—What relationship is indicated by καί 'and/but'?
1. It indicates a contrastive relationship [Hu, Lns, WBC; NAB, NCV, NET, NIV, NRSV, REB, TEV, TNT]: who has the wound of the sword *but* lived.
2. It indicates a conjoining relationship [BNTC, EC; NLT]: has the wound of the sword *and* lived.

QUESTION—Did just the head receive the wound, or the beast itself?

Here the beast is equated with the head [Be, EC].

13:15 **And it-was-given**[a] **to-it to-give spirit**[b] **to-the image of-the-beast,**

LEXICON—a. aorist pass. indic. of δίδωμι: 'to be given'. See this word at 13:7.

b. πνεῦμα (LN 23.186, 26.9) (BAGD 2. p. 675): 'spirit' [BAGD, LN (26.9)], 'breath' [BNTC, EC, LN (23.186), Lns, Sw; CEV, NIV, NRSV, REB, TNT], 'life' [WBC; KJV, NAB, NCV, NET, NLT], 'inner being' [LN (26.9)], '(life-) spirit' [BAGD]. This noun is also translated as a verb: 'to breathe life' [TEV]. Πνεῦμα here indicates that which gives life to the body [BAGD, Sw]. It probably means πνεῦμα ζωῆς 'spirit of life' as stated in 11:11 [NIC]. It is implied that he gave life to the image [Alf, Be, EC, TH].

QUESTION—Who is the implied actor of ἐδόθη 'it was given'?

The implied actor is God [EC, Lns, TH]: God gave to it. In this context, God gave in the sense permitting the action [EC, Lns, TH]: God *permitted* it to give spirit to the image of the beast. The verb 'was given' indicates 'was permitted' but does not specify who the actor is [BNTC, WBC].

QUESTION—What is the antecedent of αὐτῷ 'to it'?

The antecedent is the second beast [Be; NCV]: it was given *to the second beast* to give spirit to the image of the beast.

so-that the image of-the-beast (might) both[a] **speak and**[a] **might-cause**[b] **that as-many-as ever not would-worship the image of-the-beast should-be-killed.**

TEXT—Some manuscripts do not include ἵνα 'so that' before ὅσοι 'as many as', and some manuscripts include ἵνα 'so that' before ἀποκτανθῶσιν 'should be killed'. GNT selects the reading ἵνα 'so that' only before ὅσοι 'as many as' in brackets and with a C decision, indicating difficulty in deciding which alternative to place in the text.

LEXICON—a. καί...καί (LN 89.102): 'both...and' [EC, LN, Lns; KJV], 'even...and' [NRSV, REB, TNT], '...and' [BNTC, WBC; NAB, NET, NIV, TEV], not explicit [CEV, NCV, NLT].

b. aorist act. subj. of ποιέω (LN 13.9) (BAGD I.1.b.θ. p. 681): 'to cause' [BAGD, EC, LN, Lns, WBC; KJV, NET, NIV, NRSV, REB, TNT], 'to command' [NCV], 'to make to, to bring about' [BAGD, LN]. The phrase ποιήσῃ...ἣ ἀποκτανθῆσιν 'he might cause...they be killed' is translated: 'to have killed' [BNTC], 'was put to death' [CEV], 'he had the power of putting to death' [NAB]. See this word also at 12:15.

QUESTION—Who is the actor of ποιήσῃ...ἀποκτανθῶσιν 'he might cause...they be killed'?

1. The actor is the image of the beast [BNTC, EC, Lns, TH, WBC; KJV, NAB, NET, NIV, NLT, NRSV, REB, TEV, TNT]: the image of the beast might cause...that they be killed.
2. The actor is perhaps the second beast [TNTC; NCV]: the second beast enabled the image of the beast to speak and caused...that they be killed.

13:16 And it-causes all, the small and the great, and the rich and the poor, and the free and the slaves, that they-should-give to-them (a) mark[a] on their right hand or on their forehead

LEXICON—a. χάραγμα (LN 33.482) (BAGD 1. p. 876): 'mark' [BAGD, BNTC, EC, LN, Lns; CEV, KJV, NCV, NET, NIV, NLT, REB, TEV], 'stamped image' [NAB], 'brand' [LN, WBC]. This noun is also translated as a verb: 'to be marked' [NRSV], 'to be branded' [TNT]. A mark like this could be engraved, imprinted, branded [BAGD, LN], etched, or cut [BAGD]. It is a mark showing the receiver's relationship to the beast [LN].

QUESTION—Who is the antecedent of ποιεῖ 'it causes'?

It is the second beast [Alf, EC, NIC, Sw, TH, Wal, WBC; NAB, NCV, NET, TEV]: the second beast causes all. It is natural to take the antecedent as referring back to the dative αὐτῷ '(it was given) to it' of verse 15, where the reference is to the second beast [EC].

QUESTION—What is the purpose of the detailed listing of 'great-small', 'rich-poor' and 'free-slaves'?

It is a figure of speech used to stress totality, no one was exempt [Be, EC, Lns, NIC, Sw, TNTC, WBC].

QUESTION—Who are indicated by the pronoun in δῶσιν 'they should give'?

The agents of the beast are indicated [Lns, Sw, TH]: the agents of the beast should give. Those who have the responsibility to give should do so [Alf]. It is an indefinite plural and need not be equated with a specific group [EC].

QUESTION—What is symbolized by the mark?

It symbolized that those marked: were loyal to the beast [Alf, Be, Ld, NIC], were worshippers of the beast [Ld, Wal], were under the protection of the beast [ICC], were owned by the beast [EC], were identified spiritually with the beast [NIGTC].

QUESTION—What other group of people are similarly marked?

The servants of God are marked in their foreheads (see 7:3 and 9:4) [Ld, Sw, WBC].

13:17 **and that no-one should-be-able to-buy or sell except the-one having the mark, the name of-the beast or the number of-its name.**

TEXT—Some manuscripts do not include καί 'and' at the beginning of this verse. GNT includes it with an A rating, indicating that the text is certain.

TEXT—Some manuscripts include ἤ 'or' before τὸ ὄνομα 'the name'. GNT does not mention this alternative. The reading 'or' is included by KJV.

QUESTION—What is the relationship between τὸ χάραγμα 'the mark' and τὸ ὄνομα τοῦ θηρίου 'the name of the beast'?

The two are in apposition to each other [Alf, Be, Ld, Lns, WBC; NCV, NET, NIV, NLT, NRSV, TEV]: the mark, *that is*, the name of the beast.

QUESTION—Which beast is indicated by τὸ ὄνομα τοῦ θηρίου 'the name of the beast'?

The name of the first beast is indicated [TH; NAB]: the mark: the name of the first beast or the number of its name.

QUESTION—Is the mark: (1) either the name of the beast or the number of its name, or (2) simply the number of its name?

1. The mark is either the name of the beast or the number of its name [Alf, Be, BNTC, WBC; KJV, NAB, NCV, NET, NIV, NLT, NRSV, REB, TEV, TNT].
2. It is simply the number of its name [EC, Lns, NIC, Sw]. The ἤ 'or' after 'beast' means 'that is', making the number of its name and the name of the beast the same thing: having the mark: the name of the beast, *that is*, the number of its name [EC, Lns]. The mark is the beast's name written in its numerical equivalent [NIC].

QUESTION—What is meant by 'the number of its name'?

There was a system known as *gematria*, in which each letter of the alphabet was given a numerical value. The first nine letters had a value of 1 through 9 respectively, the second nine had a value of 10–90 and so on. The number of a person's name then would be the total numerical value of the letters comprising that person's name [Alf, BNTC, EC, ICC, Ld, NIC, NIGTC, Sw, TH, TNTC].

13:18 **Here is wisdom.**[a]

LEXICON—a. σοφία (BAGD 2. p. 759): 'wisdom' [BAGD, BNTC, EC, Lns, WBC; all versions except REB], 'skill' [Be, EC; REB], 'understanding' [Be, EC]. See this word also at 5:12.

QUESTION—What is the function of this statement?
It calls attention to or refers ahead to the rest of the verse [Alf, EC, ICC]. It advises believers not to be deceived by the beast's deception like the ones who dwell on earth are [NIGTC]. It should be taken as an imperative to the readers to be wise, not as a simple statement [TH]. It is a pause for emphasis before the important statement that follows [TNTC].

QUESTION—How is this clause translated?
This verse is also translated: 'this calls for wisdom' [BNTC; NET, NIV, NRSV, REB, TEV], 'this takes wisdom' [NCV], 'you need wisdom (to understand the number of the beast)' [CEV], 'wisdom is need to understand this' [NLT], 'here there is need for wisdom' [NAB, TNT].

The-one having understanding^a let-him-calculate^b the number of-the beast, for it-is (the) number of-(a)-man, and his number (is) six-hundred sixty six.

LEXICON—a. νοῦς (LN 26.14) (BAGD 1. p. 544): 'understanding' [BAGD, EC, WBC; KJV, NCV, NLT, NRSV, TNT], 'insight' [NET, NIV], 'intelligence' [BNTC; REB], 'ingenuity' [NAB], 'mind' [LN, Lns]. Νοῦς indicates the faculty of understanding, reasoning, thinking, and deciding [LN]. The phrase ὁ ἔχων νοῦν 'the one having understanding' is translated: 'if you are smart enough' [CEV], 'whoever is intelligent' [TEV].

b. aorist act. impera. of ψηφίζω (LN **32.15, 60.4**) (BAGD p. 892): 'to calculate' [BAGD, BNTC, LN (60.4), WBC; NAB, NET, NIV, NRSV, TNT], 'to solve' [NLT], 'to find the meaning' [NCV], 'to figure out' [LN (32.15, 60.4); CEV, TEV], 'to work out' [REB], 'to understand the meaning of' [**LN** (32.15)], 'to count' [EC, LN (60.4), Lns; KJV], 'to count up, to reckon' [BAGD], 'to add up' [**LN** (60.4)], 'to come to understand, to interpret' [LN (32.15)]. 'Calculating' involves adding up the total based on the numerical values of each letter of the name [**LN** (60.4)].

QUESTION—What relationship is indicated by γάρ 'for'?
It indicates that what follows stands as the reason a person could calculate the number of the beast [Alf]: let him calculate the number of the beast, *he can do this because* it is the number of a man. It indicates that what follows stands as the reason a person should calculate the number of the beast [EC]: let him calculate the number of the beast, *he should do this because* it is the number of a man.

QUESTION—What is meant by τὸν ἀριθμὸς ἀνθρώπου 'the number of a man'?
1. It refers to a specific historical person [Be, ICC, NIC, NTC, TH, TNTC, WBC]. The writer intended that the reader understand the number so as to be able to identify a specific person from it [EC]. If it refers only to 'a human number', what is to be understood as 'an inhuman number' [EC, NIC]? If the phrase is taken to mean merely a common number that humans use, it would not be a help to solve the problem [Be].

2. It refers to the type of mark, it is a human mark [Alf, Ld, Lns, NIGTC, Sw]. The genitive 'of man' should be understood as modifying 'number', a human number [Lns, NIGTC]. The phrase means 'as men usually count' [Alf]. Since it is a human number, it can be easily understood by an intelligent human [Lns].

QUESTION—What person is indicated by the number 666?
It may refer to the trinity composed of Satan, the antichrist, and the false prophet. Each have the number 6 symbolizing that they each fall short of divinity whose number is seven [Hu]. All other commentaries consulted simply listed the possibilities that have been suggested by authorities, but none committed themselves to a definite answer.

DISCOURSE UNIT: 14:1–20 [Alf, Hu, Ld, Lns, NTC, TH, Wal, WBC]. The topic is the song of the 144,000 [Alf; NET], Mount Zion and the vintage of the earth [Hu], visions of assurance [Ld], Zion—Babylon—the Sickles [Lns], first fruits, harvest, and vintage [NTC], interlude: three visions [TH], the victory of the Lamb and his followers [Wal; CEV], visions of eschatological salvation and judgment [WBC].

DISCOURSE UNIT: 14:1–5 [Alf, Be, BNTC, EC, GNT, Hu, Ld, Lns, NIC, NIGTC, NTC, Sw, TNTC, Wal, WBC; CEV, KJV, NAB, NCV, NET, NIV, NLT, NRSV, TEV]. The topic is the song of the 144,000 [GNT, Hu; KJV, NET], the song of the saved [NCV], the Lamb on mount Zion [Alf, Be, Ld, NIC, TNTC], the Lamb and the 144,000 [ICC, Wal, WBC; NAB, NIV, NLT, NRSV], the Lamb and his people [TEV], the victorious followers of the Lamb [EC], the soldiers of the cross [BNTC], first fruits [NTC], the vision of the 144,000 on Mount Zion [Sw], Mount Zion [Lns].

14:1 **And I-saw, and behold^a the Lamb standing on mount^b Zion^c**
TEXT—Some manuscripts do not include τό 'the' before ἀρνίον 'Lamb'. GNT includes this word with an A rating, indicating that the text is certain. The word 'the' is also not included by KJV.
LEXICON—a. ἰδού (LN 91:13) (BAGD 1.a. p. 370): 'behold' [EC, WBC], 'lo' [Lns; KJV], 'there was' [NAB, NCV, NIV, NRSV, TEV, TNT], 'there (stood)' [BNTC; REB], 'here was' [NET], not explicit [CEV, NAB, NLT]. This command calls the attention of the reader to what follows [EC, TH]. See this word also at 12:3.
  b. ὄρος (LN 1.46) (BAGD p. 582): 'mount' [BNTC; KJV], 'Mount' [BNTC, EC, Lns, WBC; CEV, NAB, NCV, NET, NIV, NLT, NRSV, REB, TEV, TNT], 'mountain' [BAGD, LN], 'hill' [BAGD]. A ὄρος is relatively higher than what is known as a hill [LN].
  c. Σιωᾶν (LN **93.582**) (BAGD 1. p. 752): 'Zion' [BAGD, BNTC, EC, LN, Lns, WBC; all versions except TNT], 'Sion' [TNT]. 'Mount Zion' refers to a hill in the city of Jerusalem [**LN**].

QUESTION—What is indicated by the words εἶδον, καὶ ἰδοὺ 'I saw, and behold'?

It indicates a new scene in the drama [EC, ICC, Lns, NIC, WBC]. It marks the beginning of very dramatic scenes in Revelation (see 4:1; 6:2; 6:5; 6:8; 7:9; and 14:14) [NIC].

QUESTION—Does 'Mount Zion' refer to a heavenly or earthly place?

1. It refers to an earthly place [Be, EC, ICC, Lns, TH, Wal, WBC]. Mount Zion refers to a geographical hill near Jerusalem, the hill on which the temple stood, the city of Jerusalem, or the land of Judah [EC]. Mount Zion is the earthly center of the Messianic Kingdom [Be, EC, ICC, TH]. This refers to the time when Christ returns to earth to set up his millennial reign [Wal]. It refers to Jerusalem [WBC].
2. It refers to a heavenly place [Ld, Lns, NIC, NTC, TNTC]. Mount Zion here refers to heavenly Jerusalem (see Hebrews 12:22 and Galatians 4:26) [Ld, NIC, NTC]. The heavenly city will descend to earth and God will live with men [Ld]. Zion is the highest elevation of Jerusalem but is used here symbolically to refer to heaven [Lns].

and with him one-hundred forty four thousand having his name and the name of-his Father written on their foreheads.

TEXT—Some manuscripts possibly do not include the words τὸ ὄνομα αὐτοῦ καὶ 'his name and'. GNT does not mention this alternative. The words 'his name and' are also not included by KJV.

QUESTION—Who are the 144,000? (See a similar question at 7:4).

1. The number symbolizes the total body of believers through all ages [Be, Hu, Ld, Lns, NIC, NIGTC, NTC, TH, TNTC]. They are the same as the 144,000 mentioned in 7:4 [Be, Hu, Lns, NIC, NIGTC, NTC, TH, TNTC], and/or the great multitude mentioned in 7:9 [Hu, Ld, NIC, NIGTC, NTC].
2. They are all believers living in the last days and are the same as those mentioned in 7:4 [ICC, WBC] and 7:9 [ICC].
3. They are all believers living on earth at one time and are the same as those mentioned in 7:4 but not those of 7:9 [Sw].
4. They are all the martyrs and are the same as those mentioned in chapter 7 [BNTC].
5. They are a select body of Jewish believers and are the same as those mentioned in chapter 7 [EC, Wal].
6. They are an elect group from within the whole body of believers and are the same as those of chapter 7 [Alf].

QUESTION—What is the significance of the number 144,000?

It symbolizes completeness [NIGTC, TNTC].

QUESTION—What is the significance of their having the names of the Lamb and his Father written on their foreheads?

It signifies their commitment and loyalty to the Lamb and his Father [Be, NIC, NIGTC]. It signifies that they belong to the Lamb and his Father [NIGTC]. It signifies ultimate victory [EC]. It is the same as the sealing of the 144,000 in chapter 7, and the seal there consisted of writing the names of the Lamb and his Father on their foreheads [Be, WBC].

14:2 And I-heard (a) sound out-of heaven as (a) sound of-many waters and as (a) sound of-great thunder, and the sound that I-heard as of-harpists[a] playing[b] on their harps.[c]

TEXT—Instead of ἡ φωνὴ ἣν ἤκουσα ὡς 'the sound that I heard as', some manuscripts have φωνὴν ἤκουσα 'I heard a sound'. GNT does not mention this alternative. The reading 'I heard a sound' is taken by KJV.

LEXICON—a. κιθαρῳδός (LN **6.85**) (BAGD p. 432): 'harpist' [BAGD, **Lns**; NAB, NET, NIV, NLT, NRSV, REB], 'lyre-player' [BAGD], 'harper' [BNTC, EC; KJV, TNT], 'zither player' [Lns], 'kitharist' [WBC], 'musicians' [TEV], 'people' [NCV]. It also refers to one who plays the lyre [Lns], not explicit [CEV].

b. pres. act. participle of κιθαρίζω (LN **6.84**) (BAGD p. 432): 'to play (a harp)' [BNTC, EC, WBC; all versions except CEV, KJV], 'to play a harp' [BAGD, LN], 'to harp' [KJV], 'to play a lyre' [BAGD, LN], 'to zither play' [Lns], not explicit [CEV].

c. κιθάρα (LN **6.83**) (BAGD p. 432): 'harp' [BAGD, BNTC, EC, LN; all versions except NLT], 'lyre' [BAGD, LN], 'zither' [Lns], 'kithara' [WBC]. A κιθάρα is a small stringed harp-like instrument that is held in the hands and plucked [LN]. The phrase κιθαρῳδῶν κιθαριζόντων ἐν ταῖς κιθάραις αὐτῶν 'harpists playing on their harps' is also translated: 'the music of harps' [CEV], 'harpists playing together' [NLT].

QUESTION—How is the sound like the sound of many waters and great thunder?

The comparison of the sound to many waters and great thunder indicate that it was a very loud sound [Be, EC, Lns, NIC, NIGTC, TH, TNTC, WBC].

QUESTION—What is the meaning of many waters?

It could indicate the ocean [NIC, WBC], rushing water [TNTC; CEV, NAB, NIV, REB] or a waterfall [NIC, TH; NLT, TEV].

QUESTION—What is indicated by the sound being like the sound of harp playing?

It indicates that the sound was melodious [EC, Hu, TNTC].

14:3 And they-sing[a] as[b] (it-were) (a) new song[c] before the throne and before the four living-creatures[d] and the elders;

TEXT—Some manuscripts do not include ὡς 'as'. GNT reads ὡς putting it in brackets with a C rating, indicating difficulty in deciding whether or not to include it in the text. Ὡς 'as' is also read by Alf, EC, Lns, WBC; KJV, NAB.

LEXICON—a. pres. act. indic. of ᾄδω (LN **33.109**): 'to sing' [BNTC, EC, **LN**, Lns, WBC; all versions]. See this word also at 5:9.

b. ὡς (LN 64.12): 'as it were' [Lns, WBC; KJV], 'what seemed to be' [NAB], 'like' [LN], 'something like' [EC], 'what sounded like' [Alf, EC],

not explicit [BNTC; all versions except KJV, NAB]. See this word also at 6:6.
   c. ᾠδή (LN **33.110**): 'song' [BNTC, EC, **LN**, Lns, WBC; all versions except NAB], 'hymn' [NAB]. See this word also at 5:9.
   d. ζῷον (LN 12.32) (BAGD 1. p. 341): 'living creature' [BNTC; all versions except KJV, NLT], 'living being' [EC; NLT], 'living one' [Lns], 'cherubim' [WBC], 'beast' [KJV]. See this word also at 4:6.
QUESTION—Who are the actors of 'they sing'?
   1. They are the 144,000 [Lns, NIC, NIGTC, TH, TNTC; TEV]. This is the innumerable multitude of 7:9 symbolized by the 144,000 [NIGTC]. Since only the 144,000 were able to learn the new song and thus sing it, they are ones singing it [Lns]. Without the experience of redemption no one could sing this song [NIC, TNTC]. They sing with God, the angels, and the living creatures as their audience [TNTC].
   2. They are angels [EC, Ld, Sw]. The new song must be about redemption since only those who have been redeemed can learn it, and although it was designed primarily for redeemed, this new song is now sung by angels [Ld].
   3. They are the harpists of verse 2 [Alf].
   4. They are those martyred believers of the tribulation [BNTC, Wal]. These are the martyrs of the tribulation who sing from heaven while the 144,000 saints preserved from the tribulation listen on earth [Wal].
QUESTION—What is meant by the phrase ἐνώπιον τοῦ θρόνου 'before the throne'?
   It is a figure of speech indicating 'before God' [WBC]. This indicates that it was sung in God's presence and by referring to his 'throne' there may be an emphasis on God's sovereignty [TNTC].

and no-one was-able to-learn[a] the song except the hundred forty four thousand, the-ones redeemed[b] from the earth.
LEXICON—a. aorist act. infin. of μανθάνω (LN 27.12) (BAGD 5. p. 490): 'to learn' [BAGD, BNTC, EC, LN, Lns, WBC; all versions], 'to understand' [BAGD]. The context seems to mean 'to hear' [BAGD].
   b. perf. pass. participle of ἀγοράζω (LN 37.131, 57.188) (BAGD 2. p. 13): 'to be redeemed' [EC, LN (37.131), WBC; KJV, NET, NIV, NLT, NRSV, TEV], 'to be bought' [BAGD, LN (57.188), Lns; NCV], 'to be purchased' [LN (57.188)], 'to be set free' [LN (37.131)], 'to be rescued' [CEV], 'to be ransomed' [BNTC; NAB, REB, TNT], 'to be acquired as property' [BAGD]. The word ἀγοράζω means to cause the release of someone by a means that is costly to the one doing the releasing [LN].
QUESTION—What is the significance of naming the 144,000 as those redeemed from the earth?
   It indicates that identifying the 144,000 of 14:1 with the total number of believers was the correct one (see 7:4 and 7:9) [Hu]. They were redeemed from worldly things and worldly men [TNTC].

14:4 These are the-ones (who) were- not -defiled[a] with women, for they-are virgins.[b] These (are) the-ones following the lamb where ever he-goes.

LEXICON—a. aorist pass. indic. of μολύνω (LN **53.34**) (BAGD 2. p. 527): 'to be defiled' [BAGD, BNTC, EC, LN, Lns; KJV, NAB, NET, NIV, NRSV, TNT], 'to be stained' [BAGD, LN], 'to be made impure, to be soiled' [BAGD]. This verb is also translated as an adjective phrase: '(to be) spiritually (un)defiled' [NLT]. It is also translated as an adjective of its positive counterpart: 'pure (virgins)' [CEV]. The passive is also translated actively: 'to do sinful things' [NCV], 'to defile oneself' [BNTC; REB], 'to pollute oneself' [WBC], 'to keep oneself pure by not having sexual relations' [TEV]. Μολύνω means to cause something to be ceremonially impure [LN]. See this word also at 3:4.

b. παρθένος (LN **9.33**) (BAGD 2. p. 627): 'virgin' [BNTC, EC, **LN**, Lns; CEV, KJV, NAB, NET, NRSV, TEV], 'chaste man' [BAGD]. This noun is also translated as a verb: 'to keep oneself pure' [NCV, NIV, TNT], 'to keep oneself chaste' [BNTC; REB]; and as an adjective phrase: '(they are) pure as virgins' [NLT], '(they are) chaste' [LN, WBC]. Παρθένος is used here in the sense of 'celibates' [EC].

QUESTION—Should the clause, μετὰ γυναικῶν οὐκ ἐμολύνθησαν 'they did not defile themselves with women' be taken literally or symbolically and what is meant by it?

1. It should be taken symbolically and it means that they remained faithful to God and did not enter into any defiling relationship with the pagan world system [BNTC, Hu, Ld, Lns, NIC, NIGTC, NTC, Sw, TNTC, Wal]. The 144,000 is used symbolically of the church or bride of Christ who have kept themselves pure for their marriage to Christ from relationships with the pagan world [NIC, NIGTC, TNTC]. In the OT, unfaithfulness to God was compared with engaging in immoral sexual relations [TNTC]. In Revelation, idolatrous worship of the beast was considered fornication (14:8; 17:2, 4; 18:3, 9; 19:2) [Ld]. The Scriptures do not view sexual relations between husband and wife as being defiling [Hu, Ld, NIC, Sw]. In the OT, Israel is referred to as 'the virgin daughter of Zion' (Lamentations 2:13) [NIC, Wal]. Also in 2 Corinthians 11:2, Paul refers to believers (including both men and women) as being a virgin presented to Christ [NIC, Wal], since the entire picture is to be understood figuratively [NIC].
2. It should be taken literally and indicates that they never had sexual relations with women [Alf, EC]. The emphatic position of the phrase μετὰ γυναικῶν 'with women' before the phrase, 'were not defiled', excludes a symbolical interpretation of this verse [Alf, EC]. Although marriage is the norm for a believer, because of the extreme persecution of this period, this group remained virgins so as to serve the Lord without distraction [EC].
3. It should be taken literally and indicates that they did not have *immoral* sexual relations with women [BAGD, Be, NTC, WBC]. The reference is probably to those who have been the husband of one wife [NTC, WBC].

QUESTION—What relationship is indicated by γάρ 'for'?

It indicates that what follows is the reason why they were undefiled with women [Be, EC]: they were undefiled with women *because* they were virgins. That they were virgins was part of their fixed character and therefore they were undefiled with women [EC].

These were-redeemed from men (as) firstfruits[a] to God and to-the Lamb,

LEXICON—a. ἀπαρχή (LN 53.23) (BAGD 1.b.α. p. 81): 'first-fruits' [BAGD, BNTC; CEV, KJV, NAB, NET, NIV, NRSV, REB], 'first fruits' [Lns], 'contribution' [EC] 'a special offering' [NLT], 'first ones to be offered' [TEV], 'servants devoted' [WBC], 'the most precious people' [CEV], 'first offering, first portion' [LN]. This noun is also translated as a verb: '(people) to be offered' [NCV], 'to offer as firstfruits' [NIV]. The word ἀπαρχή is the first portion of something that has been set aside and offered to God before the rest of that thing can be used [LN].

QUESTION—What is the primary sense of ἀπαρχή 'first-fruits'?

1. It indicates a smaller portion of a larger group to follow [Alf, BNTC, LN, NTC, TH, Wal]. They are like the first part of a harvest [TH].
2. It indicates a group that was set apart to God for his own possession with no implication of a larger group to follow [Be, EC, Hu, ICC, Ld, NIC, NIGTC, TNTC, WBC]. This group is singled out as a contribution to God with a special role and there is no idea of more like them to follow [EC]. Here ἀπαρχή indicates 'offering' or 'sacrifice' [ICC, NIC].

14:5 and in their mouth not was-found (a) lie,[a] they-are blameless.[b]

TEXT—Some manuscripts possibly include the words ἐνώπιον τοῦ θρόνου τοῦ θεοῦ 'before the throne of God' after ἄμωμοί εἰσιν 'they are blameless', although GNT does not mention this alternative. The reading 'before the throne of God' is included by TR and KJV.

LEXICON—a. ψεῦδος (LN 33.254) (BAGD p. 892): 'lie' [BAGD, BNTC, EC, LN, Lns; CEV, NCV, NET, NIV, NRSV, REB, TEV], 'falsehood' [BAGD, LN; NLT]. 'guile' [WBC; KJV], 'deceit' [NAB]. This noun is also translated as a verb: 'to lie' [TNT].

b. ἄμωμος (LN 88.34) (BAGD 2.a. p. 48): 'blameless' [BAGD, EC, LN, WBC; NET, NIV, NLT, NRSV, TNT], 'without blame' [BAGD], 'innocent' [CEV], 'faultless' [LN; TEV], 'without fault' [KJV, NCV, REB], 'unblemished' [NAB], 'without blemish' [BNTC], 'blemishless' [Lns], 'perfect' [LN].

QUESTION—What is meant by ἐν τῷ στόματι αὐτῶν οὐχ εὑρέθη ψεῦδος 'in their mouth a lie was not found'?

It means that they do not tell lies [TH; CEV, NCV, TEV, TNT] or that no falsehood can be charged against them [NLT]. This is a Semitic idiom meaning to tell the truth [WBC].

QUESTION—What sense of ἄμωμος 'blameless' is intended here?
1. It indicates acceptability as a sacrifice [EC, ICC, Ld, Sw, TNTC]. In seventy-five percent of its occurrences in the Septuagint this word has the sense of being without imperfection as a sacrifice [ICC].
2. It indicates moral or ethical purity [NIC, TH, WBC].
3. It indicates purity that was ascribed to them because they were forgiven [Hu, NTC]. A believer's purity is only one that is attributed to him because he has been made so by the blood of Christ [Hu].
4. It indicates that they, like Christ, were innocent of the world's accusations against them [NIGTC].

DISCOURSE UNIT: 14:6–20 [Be, NIC, TNTC; NET]. The topic is the three angels [NIV], three angels and three messages [NET], visions of final judgment [NIC], last judgment, warning, and promise [Be], the harvest of the earth [TNTC].

DISCOURSE UNIT: 14:6–13 [Alf, BNTC, EC, GNT, Hu, Lns, NIC, NIGTC, NTC, Sw; CEV, KJV, NAB, NCV, NIV, NLT, NRSV, TEV]. The topic is the three angels [NAB, NCV, NIV, NLT, TEV], the messages of the three angels [Alf, GNT, NTC, Sw; CEV, KJV, NRSV], the hour of divine judgment [Hu, NIC], Babylon [Lns], the eternal gospel [BNTC], four climactic announcements [EC].

DISCOURSE UNIT: 14:6-12 [TNTC, WBC]. The topic is three angelic speeches.

DISCOURSE UNIT: 14:6–7 [EC, Ld, NTC, Wal]. The topic is a call to repentance [Ld], an eternal gospel [NTC, Wal].

14:6 **And I-saw another[a] angel flying in midheaven,[b] having (the) eternal[c] good-news[d] to-announce[e] to the-ones living[f] on the earth and to every nation and tribe and tongue and people,**

TEXT—The word ἄλλον 'another' does not occur in some manuscripts. It is included by GNT with a B rating, indicating that the text is almost certain.

LEXICON—ἄλλος (LN 58.37) (BAGD p. 39): 'another' [BNTC, EC, LN, Lns, WBC; CEV, KJV, NAB, NCV, NET, NIV, NLT, NRSV, TEV], 'an' [BNTC; REB].
b. μεσουράνημα (LN 1.10) (BAGD p. 508): 'midheaven' [BAGD, BNTC, EC, Lns, WBC; NRSV, REB, TNT], 'the midst of heaven' [KJV], 'midair' [NIV], 'directly overhead' [NET], 'high overhead' [NAB], 'high in the air' [NCV, TEV], 'high in the sky, straight above in the sky' [LN]. The phrase ἐν μεσουρανήματι 'in midheaven' is translated: 'across the sky' [CEV], 'through the heavens' [NLT]. See this word also at 8:13.
c. αἰώνιος (LN 67.96) (BAGD 3. p. 28): 'eternal' [BAGD, BNTC, EC, LN, Lns, WBC; all versions except KJV, NAB, NLT], 'everlasting' [KJV, NAB, NLT].

d. εὐαγγέλιον (LN 33.217) (BAGD 2.a. p. 318): 'good news' [BAGD, LN; CEV, NAB], 'Good News' [NCV, NLT], 'message of Good News' [TEV], 'message of good news' [TNT], 'gospel' [BAGD, BNTC, EC, LN, Lns; KJV, NET, NIV, NRSV, REB], 'message' [WBC].
   e. aorist act. infin. of εὐαγγελίζω (LN 33.215) (BAGD 1. p. 317): 'to announce' [CEV, NAB, TEV], 'to announce the gospel' [LN]. 'to proclaim' [BAGD, BNTC, Lns, WBC; NET, NIV, NRSV, REB, TNT], 'to preach' [EC; KJV, NCV, NLT]. See this word also at 10:7.
   f. pres. mid. (deponent = act.) participle of κάθημαι (LN 85.63) (BAGD 1.b. p. 389): 'to live' [BAGD; NCV, NET, NIV, NRSV], 'to dwell' [WBC; KJV, NAB], 'to reside' [BAGD, LN], 'to sit' [EC, Lns], 'to be' [BAGD, LN; CEV, REB, TNT], 'to belong to' [NLT, TEV], 'to inhabit, to remain' [LN], 'to stay, to settle' [BAGD, LN]. This verb is also translated as a noun: 'inhabitant' [BNTC].

QUESTION—What relationship is indicated by the καί 'and' after τῆς γῆς 'the earth'?

It has the sense of 'that is' or 'even' [Be, EC, Hu, Lns, NIC; CEV, NCV, NLT]: to the ones living on the earth, *that is* to every nation and tribe....

QUESTION—With what is the word ἄλλον ἄγγελον 'another angel' contrasted since no other angel precedes it?

   1. It contrasts with the two angels mentioned in verses 8 and 9 that follow [Lns, NTC, TNTC, WBC; REB]. In Greek idiom ἄλλος, used in a sequence like this, indicates 'one' and 'another' [BNTC, NTC; REB]: I saw (ἄλλος) *an* angel...(ἄλλος) *another* angel followed. The occurrence of the phrase ἄλλος ἄγγελος δεύτερος 'another angel, a second' in verse 8 indicates that the phrase, ἄλλον ἄγγελον 'another angel' in verse 6 is the first of a series [WBC].
   2. It contrasts with other angels in general that have been mentioned so far in Revelation [Alf, Be, NIC, TH].
   3. It contrasts with the angels of 8:2 and 8:3 [Wal].
   4. It probably contrasts with Michael and his angels mentioned in 12:7 [EC].

QUESTION—Does the phrase εὐαγγέλιον αἰώνιον 'eternal good news' refer to the Good News about salvation through Jesus Christ, or something else?

   1. It refers to the Good News about salvation through Jesus Christ [Alf, BNTC, Ld, Lns, NIGTC; CEV, KJV, NCV, NIV, NLT]. This is the Good News that the church is commanded to proclaim to all nations. The words 'Good News' plus the verb 'announce good news' emphasize this fact [Lns]. The angel does not proclaim a different gospel but one that has emphasis on the consequences of rejection [NIGTC].
   2. It refers to a message of good news, but not the Gospel or Good News in the usual sense [Be, ICC, NIC, NTC, TH, TNTC, Wal, WBC; NAB, NET, NRSV, REB, TNT]. The lack of the article 'the' before 'good news' indicates that some other meaning is intended [Be, ICC, NIC, TNTC, Wal, WBC]. This is the only place in the New Testament that εὐαγγέλιον 'good news' occurs without the definite article [WBC]. The message of

good news is: good news in general [TH], judgment is near [Be, ICC, TNTC, Wal, WBC], the end of the world is imminent [ICC], God's eternal purpose is about to be realized [Be], worship belongs to the Creator [NIC, Wal], a plea for repentance [TNTC, WBC], the announcement of the defeat of evil [TNTC, Wal].

QUESTION—In what sense is the good news 'eternal'?

The good news is eternal in that it is permanently valid [ICC, NIGTC, TH, TNTC], unchangeable [NIGTC] or ageless—not meant for any particular time [Wal]. Or, it is eternal in that it has everlasting consequences [Hu].

QUESTION—What is the significance of the angel flying in 'midheaven'?

From there he can be seen and heard by all [Be, EC, NIC, WBC].

14:7 saying with (a) loud voice, "Fear[a] God and give him glory,[b] because the hour of-the judgment[c] of-him has-come;

LEXICON—a. aorist pass. (deponent = act.) impera. of φοβέομαι (LN 87.14) (BAGD 2.a. p. 863): 'to fear' [BAGD, BNTC, EC, LN, Lns, WBC; all versions except CEV, TEV], 'to honor' [TEV], 'to worship' [CEV], 'to reverence' [BAGD], 'to show great respect/reverence for' [LN]. See this word also at 11:18.

b. δόξα (LN 33.357) (BAGD 3. p.204): 'glory' [EC, Lns, WBC; KJV, NAB, NET, NIV, NLT, NRSV], 'praise' [BAGD, LN; NCV], 'honor, fame, renown' [BAGD]. The phrase δότε αὐτῷ δόξαν 'give him honor' is translated: 'honor him' [CEV], 'do/pay him homage' [BNTC; REB], 'praise him' [TNT], 'praise his greatness' [TEV]. See this word also at 1:6.

c. κρίσις (LN 30.110) (BAGD 1.a.α. p. 452): 'judgment' [BAGD, BNTC, EC, LN, WBC; KJV, NAB, NET, NIV, NRSV, REB, TNT], 'decision, evaluation' [LN]. This noun is also translated as a verb: 'to judge' [Lns; CEV, NCV, TEV], 'to sit as judge' [NLT]. The phrase τῆς κρίσεως αὐτοῦ 'the judgment of him' is translated: 'when he is to judge' [BAGD].

QUESTION—What is the significance of the angel using a loud voice?

He used a loud voice so as to be heard by all [EC, Lns, NIC, TNTC]. The loud voice also showed urgency and concern [EC].

QUESTION—How are the nouns related in the genitive construction τῆς κρίσεως αὐτοῦ 'the judgment of him'?

God is the one who judges [EC, TH; CEV, NAB, NCV, NLT, TEV, TNT]. The ones he will judge will be the people [TH; CEV, NCV, TEV].

QUESTION—What is the significance of the article in the phrase, 'the judgment of him'?

It signifies the final judgment [Ld, NIC, WBC].

QUESTION—What sense of φοβέομαι 'to fear' is intended here?

It means 'to fear' in the sense of 'to reverence', 'to respect' or 'to hold in awe' [Lns, NIC, TH, WBC]. It has the sense of 'to honor' [TH; TEV]. It has the sense of 'to worship' [CEV].

QUESTION—Does the phrase, 'give him glory' imply anything more?
It implies a turning away from sin [Be, EC, TH] as it does in 11:13 [Be]. It is an idiomatic phrase indicating repentance [Be].

and worship[a] the-(one) having-made the heaven[b] and the earth and sea and springs of-waters."
LEXICON—a. aorist act. impera. of προσκυνέω (LN 53.56) (BAGD 2.a. p. 717): 'to worship' [BAGD, BNTC, EC, LN, WBC; KJV, NAB, NCV, NET, NIV, NLT, NRSV, REB, TEV, TNT], 'to bow down and worship, to prostrate oneself in worship' [LN], 'kneel down before' [CEV], 'do obeisance to' [Lns]. See this word also at 4:10.
  b. οὐρανός (LN 1.5, 1.11) (BAGD 1.a.α. p. 593): 'heaven' [BAGD, BNTC, EC, LN (1.11), Lns, WBC; all versions except NCV, NIV], '(the) heavens' [NCV, NIV], 'sky' [LN (1.5)]. It refers to heaven as a part of the universe. Also when mentioned with the earth it refers to the totality of creation [BAGD]. Οὐρανός has two senses: (1) the dwelling place of God and heavenly beings; and (2) the space above the earth, including the sun, moon and stars [LN (1.11, 1.5)]. See this word also at 3:12.
QUESTION—What is meant by the phrase, 'the heaven and the earth and sea and springs of waters'?
It means the whole of creation [EC].

DISCOURSE UNIT: 14:8 [EC, Ld, NTC, Wal]. The topic is the fall of Babylon.

14:8 And another angel a-second (one) followed saying, "Fallen,[a] fallen (is) Babylon[b] the great,
TEXT—Instead of ἄγγελος δεύτερος 'second angel', some manuscripts have δεύτερος 'second'. Others have ἄγγελος 'angel'. GNT selects the reading 'second angel' with a B rating, indicating that the text is almost certain. The reading 'angel' is taken by KJV.
LEXICON—a. aorist act. indic. of πίπτω (LN 15.118, 20.60) (BAGD 2.a.α. p. 660): 'to fall' [BAGD, BNTC, EC, LN (15.118), Lns, WBC; all versions except NCV]. This is also translated with passive voice: 'to be destroyed' [BAGD, LN (20.60)], 'to be ruined' [NCV], 'to experience destruction' [LN (20.60)]. Πίπτω is used here in the extended sense of being ruined for commerce [TH]. See this word also at 2:5.
  b. Βαβυλών (LN 93.420) (BAGD p. 129): 'Babylon' [BAGD, BNTC, EC, LN, Lns, WBC; KJV, NAB, NIV, NRSV, REB, TEV, TNT], 'the city of Babylon' [CEV, NCV, NET, NLT]. Βαβυλών is literally the capital of Babylonia but occurs here as a symbol of demonic world power [LN].
QUESTION—What is the significance of repeating the verb ἔπεσεν 'fallen' twice?
It indicates that the verb is emphasized [BAGD, EC, TH, TNTC, Wal, WBC]. It indicates that her fall is certain [WBC]. It indicates that her fall will be complete [TH].

QUESTION—What is indicated by the aorist tense of the verb ἔπεσεν 'fallen'?
It indicates an event that will take place in the future but that is referred to as though it had already happened [EC, Ld, Lns, Wal, WBC].

QUESTION—To what does Babylon refer?
1. It refers to the city Babylon located on the river Euphrates [EC, Wal]. This city symbolized the final civilization opposed to God [EC].
2. It refers to Rome [Alf, Be, ICC, Sw, WBC]. Both Babylon and Rome were centers of world empires and both captured Jerusalem and destroyed the Temple, Babylon in 587 B.C. and Rome in A.D 70 [WBC]. It symbolizes primarily papal but also pagan Rome [Alf]. The reference to Rome is supported by Revelation 17 and 18 [Be].
3. It refers to a city or system that like Babylon and Rome stands in opposition to God [Hu, Ld, LN, Lns, NIC, NIGTC, TNTC]. It refers to an anti-Christian empire [Lns].

who has-made-to-drink[a] **all the nations from the wine of-the passion**[b] **of-her immorality."**[c]

LEXICON—a. perf. act. indic. of ποτίζω (LN 23.35) (BAGD 1. p. 695): 'to make to drink' [BNTC, EC, Lns; all versions except CEV], 'to give to drink' [BAGD, LN, WBC], 'to cause to drink' [BAGD, LN]. The verb πεπότικεν 'has made to drink' is also translated: 'made drunk' [CEV].

b. θυμός (LN **25.19**, 88.178) (BAGD 1. 2. p. 365): 'passion' [BAGD, Lns, WBC; NAB, NET], 'overwhelming passion' [LN (25.19)], 'lust' [TEV], 'intense desire' [LN (25.19), WBC], 'intoxication' [NTC], 'anger' [EC, LN (88.178); NCV, REB, TNT], 'wrath' [BNTC, LN (88.178); KJV, NRSV], 'fury, rage' [LN (88.178)]. This noun is also translated as an adjective: 'maddening (wine)' [NIV], 'passionate (immorality)' [BAGD (1.); NLT], 'passionate (lust)' [**LN** (25.19)], '(Now God is) angry' [CEV]. Here the wine of Babylon's harlotry, that intoxicates the nations, becomes the wine of God's wrath for them [BAGD (2.)].

c. πορνεία (LN 88.271) (BAGD 2. p. 693): 'immorality' [BAGD; NLT], 'sexual immorality' [LN], 'sexual vice' [TNT], 'fornication' [BAGD, BNTC, EC, LN; KJV, NRSV, REB], 'adultery' [NCV, NIV], 'whoring' [Lns], 'prostitution' [BAGD, LN], 'unchastity' [BAGD]. This noun is also translated as an adjective: 'licentious (passion)' [NAB], 'immoral (passion/lust)' [WBC; NET, TEV], '(made all nations drunk and) immoral' [CEV]. The phrase τοῦ θυμοῦ τῆς πορνείας αὐτῆς 'of the passion of her immorality' is translated: 'of her passionate immorality' [BAGD]. Πορνεία refers to all kinds of unlawful sexual intercourse [BAGD, TH]. It not only refers to sexual immorality, but to all excesses that show unfaithfulness to God [Hu]. It refers to the extreme corruptibility of the city [Sw]. See this word also at 2:21.

QUESTION—What is meant by the verb 'to drink' something?
It means participation in an action [Ld, NIGTC, Wal; CEV]: all the nations *participated in* her immorality. See 18:3 where the nations committed immorality with Babylon [NIGTC].

QUESTION—Should θυμός be taken to mean 'passion' or 'anger'?
1. It means 'passion' [LN, Lns, NIGTC, NTC, WBC; NAB, NET, NIV, NLT, TEV]. The primary meaning of θυμός is 'passion' [Lns, NIC], while its secondary meaning is 'anger'. Further, there is only one feminine pronoun, αὐτῆς 'her', so the figure only refers to Babylon's passion, not to God's anger as well [Lns].
2. It means 'anger' [Alf, BNTC; CEV, KJV, NCV, NRSV, REB, TNT].
3. Perhaps both meanings should be taken here [BAGD, Be, EC, Hu, ICC, Ld, NIC, Sw, TH, TNTC, Wal]. This may mean that the passion of Babylon's immorality will inevitably result in the anger of God [EC, NIC, Wal]. On the one hand, Babylon intoxicates the nations with the wine of her fornication, and on the other, God's cup of wrath is given to the nations to drink to punish them by its maddening effects [Be]. To drink the wine of Babylon's immorality was to drink the wine of God's wrath (see 14:10) [Hu].

QUESTION—How are the nouns related in the genitive construction τοῦ οἴνου τοῦ θυμοῦ 'the wine of the passion'?
1. The second noun modifies the first [Be, BNTC, EC, ICC, Ld, NIC, NIGTC, NTC, Sw]: intoxicating wine or wine *that causes* passion. The wine shows the intoxicating strength of Rome's influence [ICC].
2. The second noun restates the first: wine, *that is*, immoral passion [WBC].

QUESTION—How are the nouns related in the genitive construction τοῦ θυμοῦ τῆς πορνείας 'the passion/anger of her immorality'?
1. 'Passion' modifies the noun 'immorality' [BAGD, LN; NLT]: 'passionate immorality' [BAGD; NLT], 'passionate lust' [LN].
2. 'Passion' causes or results in 'immorality' [NIGTC]: passion *resulting in* immorality.
3. 'Immorality' modifies 'passion' [Lns, WBC; NAB, NET, TEV]: 'licentious passion' [NAB], 'immoral passion' [WBC; NET], 'immoral lust' [TEV].
4. 'Immorality' causes God's 'anger' [CEV, REB, TNT]: God's anger roused by her fornication [REB], 'sexual vice…that brings God's anger' [TNT].

QUESTION—How are the nouns related in the genitive construction τῆς πορνείας αὐτῆς 'her immorality'?
1. The second noun describes the first [Lns]: she is immorally passionate.
2. The first noun possesses the second [WBC]: she possesses immoral passion.
3. The first noun names the one with whom the second occurs [NIGTC]: immorality *with* her.

QUESTION—If the word θυμός is taken to mean 'anger', who is the implied actor?

The actor is God [Be, Ld, NIC, TH, TNTC; CEV, REB, TNT]: God is angry.

DISCOURSE UNIT: 14:9-12 [EC, Ld]. The topic is the doom of the worshipers of the beast.

DISCOURSE UNIT: 14:9-11 [NTC, Wal]. The topic is the doom of the apostates.

14:9 **And another angel a-third (one) followed them saying with (a) loud voice, "If anyone worships the beast and his image, and receives (a) mark[a] on his forehead or on his hand,**

TEXT—Instead of ἄλλος ἄγγελος τρίτος 'another angel third', some manuscripts possibly read τρίτος ἄγγελος 'third angel', although GNT does not mention this alternative. The reading 'third angel' is taken by TR and KJV.

LEXICON—a. χάραγμα (LN 33.482) (BAGD 1. p. 876): 'mark' [BAGD, BNTC, EC, LN, Lns; all versions except TNT], 'brand-mark' [TNT], 'brand' [WBC]. See this word also at 13:16.

QUESTION—Who does the pronoun αὐτοῖς 'them' refer to?

It refers to the two angels who preceded this angel [Lns, TH].

QUESTION—What is the significance of φωνῇ μεγάλῃ 'a loud voice'?

It signifies the importance of the warning [EC, Lns].

QUESTION—Which beast does this refer to?

It refers to the first beast, the one that came up out of the sea (see Revelation 13:1) [EC, TH]. The second beast caused the people to make an image of the first beast in 13:14.

QUESTION—Whose mark does this refer to?

It refers to the mark of the first beast as seen in Revelation 13:15–17 [EC, ICC, NIC, NTC].

QUESTION—On which hand would be the mark be placed?

If it is necessary to specify the hand, it would probably be the right hand [TH].

14:10 **(he) himself also will-drink from the wine of-the anger[a] of-God the (wine) poured/mixed[b] undiluted[c] into[d] the cup of-his wrath,[e]**

LEXICON—a. θυμός (LN 88.178) (BAGD 2. p. 365): 'anger' [EC, Lns; NCV, NET, REB, TNT], 'wrath' [BAGD, BNTC, LN; KJV, NLT, NRSV], 'fury' [LN, WBC; NAB, NIV, TEV], 'rage' [LN]. Θυμός indicates a state of intense anger [LN, Lns, NIC, Sw]. This noun is also translated as an adjective: 'angry' [CEV]. Θυμός may indicate a more vehement outburst of emotion than ὀργή 'wrath' [Be, EC, Ld, NIC]. See this word also at 14:8.

b. perf. pass. participle of κεράννυμι (LN **47.3, 63.9**) (BAGD 1. p. 429): 'to be poured' [LN (47.3), WBC; NAB, NIV, NRSV, REB, TEV], 'to be mixed' [BNTC, EC, **LN** (63.9); NET, TNT], 'to be poured out' [BAGD,

LN (47.3); KJV, NLT], 'to be prepared' [NCV], 'to be served' [Lns], not explicit [CEV]. The phrase τοῦ κεκερασμένου ἀκράτου 'poured out undiluted' can also be translated: 'mixed at full strength' [**LN** (63.9)], or 'poured out undiluted' [**LN** (47.3)].

c. ἄκρατος (LN **79.99**) (BAGD p. 33): 'undiluted' [BNTC, LN; NET, NLT, REB], 'full strength' [NAB, NIV], 'with all its strength' [NCV], 'at full strength' [**LN**; TEV], 'in full strength' [BAGD; TNT], 'unmixed' [BAGD (1. p. 429), EC, Lns, WBC; NRSV], 'without mixture' [KJV], 'pure' [LN], not explicit [CEV]. The word ἄκρατος indicates that the wine contains no water to weaken it [TH]. In this case this wine of wrath would not be diluted by God's kindness and favor [NIC, Wal].

d. ἐν with dative object (LN 83.13, 84.22): 'into' [LN (84.22), WBC; KJV, NAB, NIV, NLT, NRSV, REB, TEV], 'in' [BNTC, EC, LN (83.13), Lns; NCV, NET, TNT], not explicit [CEV].

e. ὀργή (LN 88.173) (BAGD 2.b. p. 579): 'wrath' [BAGD, EC, Lns; NAB, NET, NIV, NLT, REB, TNT], 'indignation' [KJV], 'anger' [BNTC, LN, WBC; CEV, NCV, NRSV, TEV], 'fury' [LN]. Ὀργή may indicate a more settled indignation than θυμός 'anger' [Be, EC, Ld, NIC]. See this word at 6:16 and 11:18.

QUESTION—What is indicated by καί 'also'?

1. It introduces the consequence clause in this conditional sentence [Alf, Be, ICC, NIC, NIGTC, Sw, WBC]: If anyone worships...*then* he will drink.
2. It emphasizes the person who worships [EC]: If anyone worships...*even* he himself will drink.
3. It indicates *in addition to* someone or something else [BNTC, Lns, WBC; NAB, NIV, NRSV, REB, TNT]: he *also* will drink or he will *also* drink. The one who participates in worship of the beast will *also* participate in God's anger [Lns].

QUESTION—What is indicated by the inclusion of αὐτός 'he'?

It emphasizes the subject [EC, WBC; TEV]: he himself. There are eleven occurrences of the phrase καὶ αὐτός 'and he' in Revelation, and all of them are emphatic [WBC].

QUESTION—How are the nouns related in the genitive construction τοῦ οἴνου τοῦ θυμοῦ 'the wine of the anger'?

1. The second noun restates the first [NIGTC, TH]: he will drink from the wine, *that is*, the anger of God. It may be wine *that represents* God's anger [TH].
2. The first noun may cause the second [TH]: he will drink from the wine *that brings* the anger of God.
3. The second results in God giving the first [CEV]: God gives this wine to those who make him angry.

QUESTION—What is the point of similarity in the metaphor of drinking?

The point of similarity is experience [EC, Hu, Ld]: he will experience the anger of God. Drinking this cup is the same as being tormented in fire and sulfur [EC, Hu].

QUESTION—What does a cup sometimes symbolize in Scripture?
It can symbolize destiny, violent death, or God's punishment resulting in violent death (See Isaiah 51:17, 22; John 18:11; Matthew 20:22-23; Mark 14:36; and Luke 22:42) [WBC]. In some places in the OT a cup of wine symbolized God's punishment (See Jeremiah 25:15-29; 49:12; Psalm 75:8; Obadiah 16; Habakkuk 2:16) [TH].

QUESTION—How should κεράννυμι 'to pour/mix' be translated?
1. It should be translated 'poured, poured out', or 'served' [Alf, Be, Ld, LN, Lns, NIC, WBC; KJV, NAB, NCV, NIV, NLT, NRSV, REB, TEV]. The primary meaning of κεράννυμι is 'to mix' and refers to the custom of mixing wine with spices [Ld, WBC] or water [Alf, Be, NIC] to prepare it for pouring into cups for serving. This idea of 'mixing' then was lost and subsumed under the more general term of 'pouring' [Alf, Be, Ld, NIC].
1. It should be translated 'mixed' [BNTC, EC, Hu, ICC, LN, NIGTC, Sw, TNTC; NET, TNT]. Wine was mixed with spices and served. This wine was mixed with a substance to make it harmful or poisonous [ICC]. 'Mix' implies the preparation of wine for drinking [NIGTC]. The wine in this cup was mixed with God's wrath [Hu].

and he-shall-be-tormented[a] with[b] fire and sulfur[c] before holy angels and before the Lamb.

TEXT—Before ἀγγέλων ἁγίων 'holy angels', one manuscript includes τῶν 'the'. GNT does not mention this alternative. 'The' is included by BNTC, EC, WBC; CEV, KJV, NAB, NCV, NET, NIV, NLT, NRSV, REB, TEV, TNT.

LEXICON—a. fut. pass. indic. of βασανίζω (LN 38.13) (BAGD 2.a. p. 134): 'to be tormented' [BAGD, BNTC, EC, LN, Lns, WBC; KJV, NAB, NIV, NLT, NRSV, REB, TEV], 'to suffer torment' [TNT], 'to be tortured' [BAGD, LN; CEV, NET], 'to be put in pain' [NCV]. Βασανίζω carries the sense of torture in order to punish [LN].

b. ἐν with dative object (LN 89.76, 90.10): 'with' [LN (90.10); CEV, KJV, NCV, NET, NIV, NLT, NRSV], 'by' [LN (89.76, 90.10); TNT], 'in' [BNTC, EC, Lns, WBC; NAB, REB, TEV], 'by means of, through' [LN (89.76)]. See this word also at 6:8.

c. θεῖον (LN 2.26) (BAGD p. 353): 'sulfur' [BAGD, LN, WBC; NET, NRSV, TEV, TNT], 'burning sulfur' [CEV, NAB, NCV, NIV, NLT], 'sulphurous flames' [REB], 'brimstone' [BNTC, EC, LN, Lns; KJV]. Θεῖον refers to the kinds of burning hot rocks issuing from volcanic eruptions [LN]. Sulfur is a yellow chemical element [TH]. It is a combustible element [EC]. It burns with intense heat and has a bad odor [EC, TH]. See this word also at 9:17.

QUESTION—What is the significance of being tormented before the angels and the Lamb?

The presence of the angels and the Lamb increases the effect of their punishment [Be, EC, Ld, NIC, Sw, TNTC]. When believers suffered persecution, their suffering was intensified by the humiliation they had to face before their persecutors [EC].

14:11 And the smoke of-their torment[a] goes-up into ages[b] of-ages, and the-ones worshiping the beast and its image, and if anyone receives the mark of-its name, not they-have relief[c] day and night."

LEXICON—a. βασανισμός (LN **24.90**): 'torment' [BNTC, EC, LN, Lns, WBC; KJV, NIV, NLT, NRSV, REB, TNT], 'burning pain' [NCV], 'torture' [NET], 'severe suffering' [**LN**], 'severe pain' [LN]. This noun is also translated as a verb: 'to be tortured' [CEV], 'to torment' [NAB, TEV]. Βασανισμός indicates severe pain associated with torture and torment [LN]. It is the fire, not the smoke, that causes the torment as seen in 14:10 [LN]. It may be necessary to translate: 'the smoke of the fire that torments them' [**LN**, TH; TEV]. See this word also at 9:5.

b. αἰών (LN 67.95, 67.143) (BAGD 1.b. p. 27): 'age, era, eon' [LN]. The phrase εἰς αἰῶνας αἰώνων 'into ages of ages' is translated: 'forever and ever' [BNTC, EC, LN (67.95); all versions except REB], 'forever' [WBC; REB], 'for the eons of the eons' [Lns], 'for evermore' [BAGD]. See this word at 1:6.

c. ἀνάπαυσις (LN 22.37): 'relief' [LN, WBC; NAB, NLT, TEV], 'rest' [EC; KJV, NCV, NET, NIV, NRSV], 'respite' [BNTC, Lns; REB, TNT]. This noun is also translated as a verb: 'to rest' [CEV]. See this word also at 4:8.

QUESTION—How are the nouns related in the genitive construction ὁ καπνὸς τοῦ βασανισμοῦ αὐτῶν 'the smoke of their torment'?

The first noun commemorates the second [EC, NIGTC]: the smoke *that commemorates* their torment.

QUESTION—How are the nouns related in the genitive construction τὸ χάραγμα τοῦ ὀνόματος αὐτοῦ 'the mark of its name'?

The second noun is in apposition to the first [WBC]: the mark, *that is*, its name. It means that they are marked with the name of the beast [TH]. The mark is 666 [WBC].

QUESTION—What is indicated by the phrase ἡμέρας καὶ νυκτὸς 'day and night'?

It is a figure that means 'continually' or 'unceasingly' [TH, WBC].

DISCOURSE UNIT: 14:12-13 [NTC, Wal]. The topic is the blessing of the saints.

14:12 Here is the endurance[a] of-the saints,[b] the-ones keeping[c] the commandments[d] of-God and the faith[e] of-Jesus."
TEXT—Some manuscripts include ὧδε 'here' before οἱ 'the ones'. GNT does not mention this alternative. 'Here' is included by KJV.
LEXICON—a. ὑπομονή (LN 25.174) (BAGD 1. p. 846): 'endurance' [BAGD, BNTC, EC, LN, Lns; NRSV, REB, TEV], 'steadfast endurance' [NET], 'patient endurance' [NIV], 'patience' [BAGD; KJV], 'steadfastness' [TNT], 'perseverance' [BAGD, WBC]. This noun is also translated as a verb: 'to endure' [CEV], 'to be patient' [NCV], 'to endure patiently and remain firm' [NLT], 'to sustain' [NAB]. See this word also at 1:9 and 2:2
   b. ἤγιος (LN 11.27): 'holy' [LN]. The plural form τῶν ἁγίων 'the saints' [EC, Lns; KJV, NET, NIV, NRSV], 'God's people' [BNTC, LN, WBC; CEV, REB, TEV, TNT], 'God's holy people' [NCV, NLT], 'holy ones' [NAB]. See this word also at 5:8, 13:7.
   c. pres. act. participle of τηρέω (LN 36.19, 13:32) (BAGD 5. p. 815): 'to keep' [BAGD, BNTC, EC, LN (13.32), Lns, WBC; KJV, NAB, NRSV, REB, TNT], 'to obey' [LN (36.19); CEV, NCV, NET, NIV, NLT, TEV]. See this word also at 1:3.
   d. ἐντολή (LN 33.330) (BAGD 2.b. p. 269): 'commandment' [BAGD, BNTC, EC, LN, Lns, WBC; KJV, NAB, NET, NIV, NRSV, TEV, TNT], 'command' [BAGD; CEV, NCV, NLT, REB]. See this word also at 12:17.
   e. πίστις (LN 31.88) (BAGD 2.dγ. p. 663): 'faith' [BAGD, BNTC, EC, Lns; CEV, KJV, NAB, NCV, NET, NRSV, TNT], 'faithfulness' [LN, WBC]. This noun is also translated as a verb: 'to remain faithful/loyal' [NIV, REB], 'to be faithful' [TEV], 'trust' [NLT]. See this word also at 2:13 and 13:10.
QUESTION—How is the phrase Ὧδε ἐστίν 'here is' translated?
   It is translated: 'this calls for' [Be, BNTC; NIV, NRSV, REB, TEV], 'this requires' [Be; NET], 'this means that' [WBC; CEV, NCV], 'such is the' [NAB], 'here is your opportunity' [NLT], 'it is here that there is need for' [TNT].
QUESTION—To what does the word ὧδε 'here' refer?
   1. It refers to the previous context [Alf, Be]. It refers to the trials the saints will have to undergo from the beast [Be]. It refers to the terrible destiny of the worshipers of the beast [Alf].
   2. It refers to the following context [WBC]. It refers to keeping God's commands and being loyal to Jesus, these are the endurance of the saints [WBC].
QUESTION—What is the meaning of this verse (see also 13:10)?
   1. It means that in the face of persecution the saints must endure [Alf, Be, BNTC, EC, NIC, NIGTC, TH, Wal, WBC]. This is a warning to the weak not to defect and an encouragement to the saints to endure [EC]. It was for this unrepentant world that Jesus gave his life and bore witness to it. Now the saints are called on to suffer and bear witness to the same world

[BNTC]. Endurance will mean that the saints will avoid the eternal punishment of the beast and gain an eternal reward [NIGTC].
2. It means that the saints will be encouraged to endure when they think of the fate awaiting the beast and his followers [Hu, Ld, Lns, NIGTC, TNTC, Wal; NAB, NCV]. The sureness of God's victory and final judgment are a strong incentive to endure persecution [Hu].
3. It means that the saints will be given the opportunity to endure in their struggle with the beast [Sw].
4. It means that for the saints, endurance is obeying God's commands and remaining loyal to Jesus [WBC].

QUESTION—How are the nouns related in the genitive construction ἡ ὑπομονὴ τῶν ἁγίων 'the endurance of the saints'?
1. The second noun does the action of the first [BNTC, EC; CEV, NCV, NET, NIV, NLT, TEV]: the saints endure.
2. The second noun receives the action of the first [TNTC; NAB]: the saints are sustained.

QUESTION—How are the nouns related in the genitive construction τὴν πίστιν Ἰησοῦ 'the faith of Jesus'?
1. Jesus is the object of people's faith [Alf, BAGD, Be, BNTC, EC, Hu, Ld, Lns, Sw; CEV, NAB, NCV, NET, NLT, TNT]: people believe in Jesus.
2. Jesus is the object of people's loyalty [NIC, TH, WBC; NIV, REB, TEV]: people are loyal to Jesus.
3. Jesus is the source of the faith [Lns, NIGTC]: the faith Jesus taught. This is the faith that Jesus taught and which his followers keep [Lns]. Faith refers to the doctrinal content Jesus taught [NIGTC].

DISCOURSE UNIT: 14:13 [EC, Ld, TNTC, WBC]. The topic is a beatitude on the martyrs [EC, Ld, WBC], the dead who die in the Lord [TNTC].

14:13 And I-heard (a) voice from heaven saying, "Write: Blessed[a] (are) the dead the-ones dying in (the) Lord from now-on."[b]

TEXT—Some manuscripts include μοι 'to me' after λεγούσης 'saying'. GNT does not mention this alternative. The word 'to me' is also included by KJV.

LEXICON—a. μακάριος (LN 25.119) (BAGD 1.b. p. 486): 'blessed' [BAGD, BNTC, EC, Lns; KJV, NAB, NET, NIV, NLT, NRSV], 'happy' [BAGD, LN; NCV, REB, TEV, TNT], 'how fortunate' [BAGD, WBC]. This adjective is also translated as a verb: 'God will bless' [CEV]. See this word also at 1:3.
b. ἄρτι (LN 67.38) (BAGD 3. p. 110): 'now on' [BAGD, Lns; CEV, NAB, NCV, NIV, NLT, NRSV, TEV, TNT], 'henceforth' [BNTC; KJV, REB], 'this moment on' [NET], 'now' [EC, LN], not explicit [WBC].

QUESTION—What is the significance of the command to write?
It emphasizes the importance of the statement that follows [Be, EC, Lns, NIC].

QUESTION—To what class of people does the clause οἱ ἐν κυρίῳ ἀποθνῄσκοντες ῳ 'the ones dying in the Lord' refer.
1. It refers primarily to martyrs [BAGD (1.a.α. p. 91), EC, Ld, WBC, NIC, NTC, TH, Wal, WBC].
2. It refers to believers in general and not only to martyrs [Alf, Be, Lns, NIGTC]. It refers to all who die as believers, by whatever means [Alf, NIGTC]. It refers to all who die, but especially to martyrs [Be]. The emphasis is not on the means of death but on the phrase 'in the Lord' [NIGTC].

QUESTION—What is indicated by the words ἐν κυρίῳ 'in (the) Lord'?
It indicates that they are believers in the Lord [Be, Ld, NIC; CEV, REB]: who die believing in the Lord. It indicates that they are in the service of the Lord [TEV]: who die serving the Lord. It indicates 'in union with the Lord' [Be, EC, NIC, TH]: who die in union with the Lord.

QUESTION—Whose voice did John hear?
It was the voice of God [EC, Wal]. It was the voice of God or Christ [Be]. It was the voice of God or an angel [TH].

"Yes,"[a] says the Spirit, "that[b] they-will-rest[c] from their labors,[d] for their works follow after[e] them."

TEXT—Instead of ναί, λέγει 'Yes, he-says', some manuscripts have λέγει ναί 'he-says Yes', and other manuscripts have λέγει 'he-says'. GNT has ναί, λέγει 'Yes, he-says' with an A decision, indicating that the text is certain.

TEXT—Instead of ναί, λέγει 'Yes, he-says', some manuscripts have απαρτι λεγει 'truly, he-says'. GNT does not mention this alternative. The reading 'truly, he-says' is taken by WBC.

TEXT—Instead of the future indicative ἀναπαήσονται 'they shall rest', some manuscripts have the aorist subjunctive ἀναπαύσωνται 'they may rest'. GNT does not mention this alternative. The reading 'they may rest' is taken by KJV.

TEXT—Instead of γάρ 'for', some manuscripts read δέ 'and'. GNT does not mention this alternative. The reading 'and' is taken by KJV.

LEXICON—a. ναί (BAGD 2. p. 533): 'yes' [BNTC, EC; all versions except KJV, NLT, TEV], 'yes indeed' [TEV], 'yes...they are blessed indeed' [NLT], 'yea' [Lns; KJV], 'indeed, certainly, quite so' [BAGD], not explicit [WBC]. See this word also at 1:7.
b. ἵνα (LN 89.49) (BAGD III.2., p. 378): 'that' [EC, Lns, WBC; KJV], 'so' [NET], 'so that, so as a result' [LN (89.49)]. The phrase ἵνα ἀναπαήσονται 'that they will rest' is translated: 'let them rest' [BAGD], not explicit [BNTC; all versions except KJV, NET]. See this word also at 2:10.
c. fut. pass. (deponent = act.) indic. of ἀναπαύω (LN 23.84) (BAGD 2. p. 59): 'to rest' [BAGD, BNTC, EC, Lns, WBC; all versions except NAB], 'to find rest' [NAB], 'to take one's rest' [BAGD], 'to be given rest, to be caused to rest' [LN]. See this word also at 6:11.

d. κόπος (LN 42.47, 22.7) (BAGD 2. p. 443): 'labor' [BAGD, BNTC, EC, WBC; KJV, NAB, NIV, NRSV, REB], 'work' [BAGD], 'hard work' [LN (42.47); CEV, NCV, NET, TEV], 'toil' [BAGD, LN (42.47), Lns; NLT], 'trouble' [LN (22.7); TNT], 'distress' [LN (22.7)]. Κόπος is hard work that implies difficulties and trouble [LN (22.7)].

e. μετά with genitive object (LN 67.48) (BAGD A.II.1.a. p. 508): 'after' [BAGD, LN, WBC], 'with' [BNTC, EC, Lns; REB, TEV, TNT], not explicit [CEV, KJV, NAB, NCV, NET, NIV, NLT, NRSV]. See this word also at 1:7.

QUESTION—What relationship is indicated by ἵνα 'that'?

1. It indicates the complement or explanation of the previous statement [Alf, Be, EC, ICC, Ld, Lns, NIC, NIGTC, Sw, TH; NLT]: Blessed are the dead...*in that* they will rest from their labors.
2. It indicates that the following statement should be taken as an imperative [BAGD, BNTC; NAB, REB]: Blessed are the dead...let them rest from their labors.

QUESTION—What is the difference between κόπος 'labor' and ἔργον 'work'?

1. Κόπος refers to the physical toil of working, while ἔργον refers to accomplishment [Lns, NTC, Sw, TH, TNTC]. Κόπος refers to enduring persecution and difficulties while ἔργον refers to the things accomplished that will form the basis of future reward [TH]. Κόπος ends at death but ἔργον goes with the saint beyond the grave [Sw]. Κόπος refers specifically to the stress of continuing to remain faithful in the face of opposition, while ἔργον is a more general word that includes κόπος. Both of these 'works' God will use as evidence when he judges [Lns]. Κόπος refers to work to the point of exhaustion while ἔργον refers to their endurance, obedience and faith in Jesus (See 14:12) [Ld].
2. There is no difference, they are synonymous [NIC, NIGTC]. Both refer to acts of faith under persecution [NIGTC]. Both words refer to enduring persecution and trouble, sometimes even to death. It is these deeds that God will remember after they die [NIC].

QUESTION—What relationship is indicated by γάρ 'for'?

It indicates that what follows is the reason why they will be blessed [Be, NIC]: They will be blessed *because* their works will follow them (and gain them approval at the judgment). There is an ellipsis here that needs to be supplied: they will rest from their labors, *not from their works*, because their works will follow them [Sw].

DISCOURSE UNIT: 14:14–20 [Alf, BNTC, EC, GNT, Hu, Lns, NIGTC, Sw; CEV, KJV, NAB, NCV, NIV, NLT, NRSV, TEV]. The topic is the harvest of the earth [Alf, BNTC, EC, GNT, Sw; CEV, KJV, NAB, NCV, NIV, NLT, NRSV, TEV], the winepress of God's wrath [Hu], the two sickles [Lns].

DISCOURSE UNIT: 14:14–16 [Ld, NIC, NTC, TNTC, Wal, WBC]. The topic is the harvest [Ld, NIC, NTC], the reaper on the cloud [TNTC], the judgment of the Son of Man [Wal], vision of angelic reapers of the earth [WBC].

14:14 And I-saw, and behold[a] (a) white cloud, and on the cloud (one) sitting like (a) son-of-man,[b]

LEXICON—a. ἰδού (LN 91:13) (BAGD 1.a. p. 370): 'behold'. See this word also at 12:3 and 14:1.
  b. υἱός ἄνθρωπου: This phrase is translated 'son of man' [BNTC, WBC; NAB, NIV], 'Son of man' [EC, Lns; CEV, KJV, NCV, NET, NLT, NRSV], 'man' [REB, TNT], 'human being' [TEV]. See this phrase at 1:13.

QUESTION—What is the significance of the phrase καὶ εἶδον 'and I saw'?
  It indicates a significant transition in the flow of the document (see also 5:1) [EC, Wal, WBC]. It indicates that John is seeing a vision [TH].

QUESTION—To whom does υἱὸν ἀνθρώπου 'son of man' refer (see this question also at 1:13)?
  1. It refers to Jesus Christ, the Son of God [Alf, Be, BNTC, Hu, Ld, Lns, NIC, NIGTC, NTC, Sw, TH, Wal; probably CEV, KJV, NCV, NET, NLT, NRSV]. The similarity of this phrase to Revelation 1:13 and Daniel 7:13 show that it is referring to the Messiah [Be]. Jesus referred to himself as the Son of man who would return in judgment (Matthew 13:37ff.) and as the one who would separate the righteous from the wicked (Matthew 25:31ff.). Further, the Second Coming of Christ is often seen as being with the clouds (Matthew 24:30; Revelation 1:7) [Ld].
  2. It refers to an angel [TNTC, WBC]. This must not be a reference to Jesus Christ since the next verse refers to 'another *angel*', and since the angel commands the first to reap he probably would not be giving a command to Christ himself [TNTC].

having on his head (a) golden crown[a] and in his hand (a) sharp[b] sickle.[c]

LEXICON—a. στέφανος (BAGD 1. p. 767): 'crown' [BAGD, BNTC, EC, Lns; all versions], 'wreath' [BAGD, WBC]. In Revelation the golden crown is worn by beings of high rank [BAGD]. See this word also at 2:10.
  b. ὀξύς (LN **79.95**): 'sharp' [BNTC, EC, **LN**, Lns, WBC; all versions]. Ὀξύς is sharp in the sense of having a thin cutting edge [LN]. See this word also at 1:16.
  c. δρέπανον (LN 6.5) (BAGD p. 206): 'sickle' [BAGD, BNTC, EC, LN, Lns, WBC; all versions]. A δρέπανον is a curved blade [Lns, NIC] with a handle and is used to cut grain, plants and grass [TH].

QUESTION—What is symbolized by στέφανος 'crown'?
  1. It symbolizes victory or triumph [Alf, EC, ICC, Ld, NIC, Sw].
  1. It symbolizes royalty [Be, Hu, NIGTC, TH, Wal].

QUESTION—What is symbolized by δρέπανον 'sickle'?
  It symbolizes harvest [Ld, Lns, NIC, Wal]. It symbolizes harvest and therefore an ingathering of people into God's Kingdom [BNTC, Ld]. It symbolizes judgment [NIGTC]. It symbolizes harvest and therefore judgment [NIC, Wal].

14:15 And another angel came-out of the temple[a] calling[b] with (a) loud voice to-the-one sitting on the cloud,

LEXICON—a. ναός (LN 7.15) (BAGD 1.b p. 533): 'temple' [BAGD, BNTC, EC, LN, Lns, WBC; all versions except NLT, TNT], 'sanctuary' [TNT], 'Sanctuary' [LN, Lns], 'Temple' [NLT]. See this word also at 3:12.

    b. pres. act. participle of κράζω (LN 33.83) (BAGD 2.a. p. 447): 'to call' [BNTC; NIV, NRSV, REB], 'to call out' [BAGD; NCV, NLT], 'to cry out' [NAB, TEV, TNT], 'to cry' [EC, Lns; KJV], 'to shout' [LN; CEV, NET], 'to exclaim' [WBC]. See this word also at 7:2.

QUESTION—What 'other' angel(s) does ἄλλος ἄγγελος 'another angel' refer to?

    1. It refers to the three angels of 14:6, 8, 9 [Be, EC, Hu, Lns, NIGTC, Sw, TH].

    1. It refers to the 'one like a son of man' of the previous verse [ICC, TNTC, WBC].

QUESTION—What is the significance of the angel coming out of the temple?

That he comes out of the temple indicates that he comes from the presence of God [Be, EC, Ld, Lns, NIC, NIGTC, Sw, TNTC, Wal, WBC], and this gives a divine character to his command [Be, Ld, Lns, NIGTC, WBC].

QUESTION—To which temple does this refer?

It refers to the temple in heaven rather than the one in Jerusalem [ICC, Lns, TH, WBC]. It may be necessary to make this explicit [TH].

"Put-in[a] your sickle and reap,[b] because the hour came to-reap, because the harvest[c] of-the earth is-ripe."[d]

TEXT—Some manuscripts include σοι 'for you' after ἦλθεν 'has come'. GNT does not mention this alternative. The reading 'for you' is taken by KJV.

LEXICON—a. aorist act. impera. of πέμπω (LN 15.66, **43.17**) (BAGD 2. p. 642): 'to put in' [BAGD; KJV, REB], 'to thrust in' [KJV], 'use' [WBC; NAB, NET, NLT, NRSV, TEV], 'to take' [NCV, NIV, TNT], 'to ply' [BNTC], 'to send' [BAGD, EC, LN (15.66), Lns]. This word is also translated by making the sickle the instrument [CEV]. The phrase πέμψον τὸ δρέπανον 'send the sickle' is an idiom meaning 'to use a sickle, to swing a sickle, to begin to harvest.' [**LN (43.17)**].

    b. aorist act. impera. of θερίζω (LN 43.14) (BAGD 2.b. p. 359): 'to reap' [BAGD, BNTC, EC, LN, Lns; all versions except CEV, NCV, NLT], 'to harvest' [BAGD, LN, WBC; CEV, NCV, NLT]. Θερίζω means to cut ripe grain and gather bundles of such grain together [LN]. The aorist tense is inceptive 'begin to reap' [Be, EC; CEV, NET, TNT].

    c. θερισμός (LN 43.15) (BAGD 2.b. p. 359): 'harvest' [BAGD, BNTC, EC, LN, Lns, WBC; KJV, NAB, NET, NIV, NRSV, TEV, TNT], 'all grapes on earth' [CEV], 'crop' [NLT], 'earth's crop' [REB], 'reaping' [LN]. This noun is also translated as a verb: 'to harvest' [NCV].

    d. aorist pass. (deponent = act.) indic. of ξηραίνω (LN 79.81, **23.198**) (BAGD 2.a. p. 548): 'to be ripe' [BNTC, **LN (23.198)**, WBC; CEV, KJV,

NCV, NET, NIV, NLT, TEV], 'to be fully ripe' [NAB, NRSV, REB, TNT], 'to become ripe' [EC, LN (23.198)], 'to be dried out' [Lns], 'to dry up' [BAGD, LN (79.81)], 'to become dry, wither' [BAGD].

QUESTION—What is symbolized by the earth?

It is a symbol for mankind [TH].

QUESTION—Is this reaping a reference to judgment or to the gathering of God's people into the Kingdom?

1. It refers to the gathering of God's people [Alf, BNTC, Hu, Ld, Lns, Sw]. This reaping probably refers to the ingathering of God's elect, while the next, 14:18 refers to the judgment of the evil ones [Alf, Ld]. In Mark 4:29 Jesus refers to the Kingdom of God being like the sowing, growth and harvesting of grain [Alf, Hu]. In the figure of reaping, there are two aspects, the harvesting of the wheat and harvesting of the tares. That this first figure refers to the harvesting of the wheat, that is, the ingathering of the elect, is seen in how specifically the following judgment of the wicked is described in the following context [Hu]. That this refers to the ingathering of God's people into the Kingdom is supported by the following NT verses: Matthew 9:37f.; Luke 10:2; and John 4:35-38 [Ld]. Both verses, 15 and 16, and the following, 17 and 18, refer to the ingathering of the people of God [BNTC].
2. It refers to the judgment [NIGTC, NTC, TNTC, Wal, WBC]. It is best to see 14–16 as reference to a general judgment and 17–18 as the final one [Wal]. There is no basis for seeing verses 14–16 as referring to the gathering of God's people [WBC]. The repetition of reference to judgment in both 14–16 and 17–18 functions to emphasize it [EC, NIGTC]. Part of this figure of the grain harvest is that the tares and the chaff are burned [NTC].
3. It refers to both of the above [EC, NIC]. These verses refer to judgment. In one aspect we see the ingathering of the elect and in the other the judgment of the wicked [EC, NIC].

14:16 And the-(one) sitting on the cloud swung[a] his sickle on the earth and the earth was-harvested.

LEXICON—a. aorist act. indic. of βάλλω (LN **43.17**) (BAGD 2.b., p. 131): 'to swing' [BAGD, BNTC, **LN**, WBC; all versions except KJV, REB, TNT], 'to sweep' [REB], 'to thrust in' [KJV], 'to take' [TNT], 'to throw' [Lns], 'to cast' [EC]. The phrase ἔβαλεν τὸ δρέπανον 'swung the sickle' is an idiom meaning, 'swing a sickle, use a sickle, begin to harvest' [LN]. The aorist tense has an inceptive aspect 'to begin to swing' [WBC]. See this word also at 2:24.

QUESTION—What is the meaning of καὶ ἐθερίσθη ἡ γῆ 'and the earth was harvested'?

It means that *the harvest* on the earth was reaped [TH].

DISCOURSE UNIT: 14:17-20 [Ld, NIC, NTC, TNTC, Wal, WBC]. The topic is the vintage [Ld, NIC, NTC, TNTC, WBC], the angel with the sharp sickle [Wal].

14:17 **And another angel himself[a] also having (a) sharp sickle came-out of the temple the-one in the heaven.**

LEXICON—a. αὐτός (LN 92.37): 'himself' [EC, LN], 'he' [BNTC, Lns, WBC; KJV, NCV, NET, NIV, NLT, NRSV, REB, TEV, TNT], not explicit [CEV, NAB]. Αὐτός is a marker that emphasizes the distinctiveness of the word to which it refers [LN].

QUESTION—To whom does ἄλλος ἄγγελος 'another angel' stand in comparison?

> It stands in comparison with the angel who had just given the command to reap [TH, TNTC, Wal]. He stands in comparison to the one sitting on a cloud who had just swung his sickle [Alf].

QUESTION—The phrase καὶ αὐτός 'himself also' compares this angel with which other one?

> It compares him with the 'one like a son of man' who also had a sickle [Alf, Be, EC, Hu, NIC, Sw, TNTC, Wal].

QUESTION—What is the significance of this angel's coming out of the temple?

> It signifies the divine authority of his mission [Alf, Be, Ld, Lns, NIC, WBC].

14:18 **And another angel the-one having authority[a] over the fire came-out of the altar,[b]**

TEXT—Some manuscripts do not include ἐξῆλθεν 'came out'. GNT includes this word in brackets with a C rating, indicating difficulty in deciding whether or not to include it in the text.

TEXT—Some manuscripts omit the definite article ὁ 'the-one' before ἔχων 'having'. GNT includes this word in brackets with a C rating, indicating difficulty in deciding whether or not to include it in the text.

LEXICON—a. ἐξουσία (LN 37.35, 37.36, 76.12) (BAGD 3. p. 278): 'authority' [BAGD, BNTC, EC, Lns, WBC; NRSV, REB, TNT], 'authority to rule' [LN (37.35)], 'jurisdiction' [LN (37.36)], 'power' [LN; CEV, KJV, NCV]. The phrase ἔχων ἐξουσίαν 'having authority' is translated: 'to have/be in charge of' [NAB, NET, NIV, TEV]. The phrase ἔχων ἐξουσίαν ἐπὶ τοῦ πυρός 'having authority over the fire' is translated: 'to have power to destroy (the earth) with fire' [NLT]. The phrase 'to have authority over' means: 'to look after, to take care of' or 'to be responsible for' [TH].

b. θυσιαστήριον (LN 6.114) (BAGD p. 366): 'altar' [BAGD, BNTC, EC, LN, Lns; all versions], 'sanctuary' [WBC]. See this word also at 6:9.

QUESTION—What does fire symbolize?

> Fire symbolizes judgment [Hu, Ld, NIC, NIGTC, NTC]. The word fire occurs 24 times in Revelation and 23 of these have reference to judgment [NIGTC]. That the angel has authority over fire indicates that he is God's agent for punishing the wicked [WBC].

QUESTION—What specific fire is in focus here?
It is the fire that burns on the altar [Alf, Be, EC, Ld, Lns, TH]. Or, it may not refer to any specific fire but simply results from the fact that fire is associated with judgment [Ld, TNTC, WBC].

QUESTION—Where and what is this altar?
It is an altar in heaven [EC]. It is the altar of incense [Be, EC, Hu, Ld, Lns, TH].

QUESTION—What does the angel's coming out of the altar refer to?
It may refer back to 6:9–10 and/or 8:3–5 and indicate that the prayers for vengeance of the saints under the altar are about to be answered [Alf, Be, EC, Ld, NIC, NIGTC, TH, TNTC]. It refers back to 8:3-5 but not to 6:9 [Lns].

and he-called with-(a)-loud voice to-the-one having the sharp sickle saying, "Use your sharp sickle and gather[a] the bunches-of-grapes[b] of-the vine[c] of-the earth, because its grapes[d] have-ripened."[e]

TEXT—Instead of φωνῇ 'voice', some manuscripts have κραυγῇ 'cry'. GNT does not mention this alternative. The reading 'cry' is taken by KJV.

LEXICON—a. aorist act. impera. of τρυγάω (LN 43.18) (BAGD p. 828): 'to gather' [BNTC, EC, LN, Lns, WBC; all versions except CEV, TEV], 'to pick' [BAGD, LN], 'to harvest' [CEV], 'to cut' [TEV].

b. βότρυς (LN **3.38**) (BAGD p. 145): 'bunch of grapes' [BAGD, LN; NCV NLT], 'cluster of grapes' [NET, NIV, NRSV], 'grape cluster' [Lns, WBC], 'cluster' [EC; KJV, NAB], 'grape' [BNTC, **LN**; CEV, TEV]. The phrase τοὺς βότρυας τῆς ἀμπέλου τῆς γῆς 'the bunches of grapes of the vine' is translated: 'grape harvest' [REB, TNT].

c. ἄμπελος (LN 3.27) (BAGD 1. p. 46): 'vine' [BAGD, BNTC, Lns; KJV, NAB, NCV, NET, NIV NLT, NRSV], 'vineyard' [EC, WBC; TEV] 'grapevine' [BAGD, LN], not explicit [CEV, REB, TNT].

d. σταφυλή (LN **3.38**) (BAGD p. 765): 'grape' [BAGD, **LN**, Lns; all versions except NLT, REB], 'cluster' [BNTC; REB], 'cluster of grapes' [NLT], 'bunch of grapes' [BAGD, EC, LN], not explicit [WBC]. Some scholars have contended that βότρυς means primarily a bunch of grapes, while σταφυλή designates individual grapes. In Revelation 14:18 this difference might seem plausible, but there is scarcely any evidence for such a distinction, since both words may signify grapes as well as bunches of grapes [LN].

e. aorist act. indic. of ἀκμάζω (LN **23.197**) (BAGD p. 30): 'to be ripe' [BAGD, BNTC, EC, LN; all versions except KJV, NLT], 'to be fully ripe' [KJV], 'to be fully ripe for judgment' [NLT], 'to reach one's prime' [Lns], 'to ripen' [**LN**], not explicit [WBC].

QUESTION—How are the nouns related in the genitive construction τῆς ἀμπέλου τῆς γῆς 'the vine of the earth'?

The earth is in apposition to the vine [BAGD, WBC]: the vine, that is, the earth. 'The vine of the earth' is the same as 'the harvest of the earth' referred to in 14:15 where earth was a figure for humanity [TH].

QUESTION—What is symbolized by the grape harvest?

The grape harvest is a symbol of God's judgment (see Isaiah 63:2, 3 and Joel 3:13) [Ld, WBC].

QUESTION—What is symbolized by the clusters of grapes?

Clusters of grapes here symbolize evil people [TH].

QUESTION—What is indicated by the harvest's being ripe?

It indicates that the time for judgment has come [NIC].

14:19 And the angel swung[a] his sickle on the earth and gathered the vine[b] of-the earth and he-threw (it) into the winepress[c] of-the wrath of-God the great.

TEXT—Instead of the masculine accusative τὸν μέγαν 'the great', some manuscripts have the feminine accusative τὴν μεγάλην 'the great' agreeing with ληνός 'winepress'. Other manuscripts read the masculine or neuter genitive τοῦ μεγάλου 'the great' agreeing with either θυμοῦ 'wrath' or θεοῦ 'God'. GNT has the masculine accusative τὸν μέγαν 'the great'. BNTC, EC, Lns, WBC and all versions except CEV, TEV translate 'great winepress' either accepting the feminine reading or making the masculine reading modify the feminine ληνός 'winepress'.

LEXICON—a. aorist act. indic. of βάλλω (LN **43.17**): 'to swing' [BAGD, BNTC, **LN**, WBC; all versions except KJV, REB, TNT], 'to thrust in' [KJV], 'to sweep (over)' [REB], 'to take' [TNT], 'to throw' [Lns], 'to cast' [EC]. See this word also at 14:16.

b. ἄμπελος (LN 3.27) (BAGD 1. p. 46): 'vine' [Lns; KJV], 'fruit of the vine' [TNT], 'grapes from the vineyard' [NET], 'grape' [CEV, NCV, NIV, NLT, REB, TEV], 'vintage' [BNTC, WBC; NAB, NRSV], 'vineyard' [EC]. See this word also at 14:18.

c. ληνός (LN 7.66) (BAGD p. 473): 'winepress' [BAGD, BNTC, EC, LN, Lns, WBC; all versions except CEV], 'pit where (the grapes) were trampled on' [CEV]. A ληνός is an instrument for pressing the juice out of grapes to make wine. Ancient winepresses were large vats into which grapes were placed and then trampled on to extract the juice [LN].

QUESTION—What is indicated by τὴν ἄμπελον τῆς γῆς 'the vine of the earth'?

Vine is used to indicate what is harvested from the vine of the earth, the vintage [BNTC, NIC, Sw, TH, WBC; CEV, NAB, NCV, NIV, NLT, REB, TEV, TNT]. The vintage is what the earth has produced [Sw]. The vintage is Babylon [Lns]. The vintage is all who reject God's way and so make themselves his enemies [NIC].

QUESTION—What does τὸν μέγαν 'the great' modify?
1. It modifies 'winepress' [Alf, Be, BNTC, EC, ICC, Lns, NIC, NTC, Sw, TH, TNTC, WBC; all versions except CEV, TEV]: the great winepress. The word ληνός 'winepress' is sometimes masculine in classical Greek and this would account for its being modified by the masculine τὸν μέγαν 'great' here [ICC].
2. It modifies 'anger' [TEV]: the winepress of God's fierce anger.

QUESTION—How are the nouns related in the genitive construction τὴν ληνὸν τοῦ θυμοῦ τοῦ θεοῦ 'the winepress of God's wrath'?
'God's wrath' is in apposition to 'the winepress' [EC, Lns, NIGTC, TH]: the great winepress, *that is*, God's anger.

QUESTION—What is symbolized by the treading out of grapes in a winepress?
1. It symbolizes judgment [EC, Hu, Ld, Lns, NIC, NIGTC, NTC, TNTC, Wal, WBC]. In the OT the treading out of grapes in a winepress is always a figure of judgment [NIGTC]. See especially Isaiah 63:1–6 [Lns, NIC, WBC]. In Revelation 19:15 it symbolizes Christ's judgment on evil nations [NIGTC].
2. Here the figure is symbolic of the death of the martyrs [BNTC]. Both of these figures depict God's people. The first, the figure of the harvest, depicts the ingathering of God's people into the Kingdom. The second, the figure of the vintage, depicts the death of the martyrs.

14:20 And the wine-press was-trodden[a] outside the city and blood came-out of the wine-press up-to[b] the bridles[c] of-the horses for (a) thousand six-hundred stadia.[d]

LEXICON—a. aorist pass. indic. of πατέω (LN 19.51) (BAGD 1.a.α. p. 634): 'to be trodden' [BAGD, BNTC, Lns, WBC; KJV, NAB, NLT, NRSV, REB, TNT], 'to be trodden down' [EC], 'to be trampled' [LN; NCV, NIV], 'to be mashed' [CEV], 'to be stomped' [NET], 'to be squeezed out' [TEV]. Πατέω indicates the practice of squeezing out the juice from grapes by trampling on them in a large vat or container that had an opening at the bottom through which the grape juice could flow [LN].
b. ἄχρι with genitive object (LN **84.19**): 'up to' [EC, **LN**, Lns], '(up) to the height of' [WBC; NAB, NET, REB, TNT], 'as high as' [NCV, NIV, NLT, NRSV], 'even unto' [KJV], not explicit [CEV, TEV]. This preposition is also translated as a verb: 'to reach to' [BNTC]. See this word also at 2:10.
c. χαλινός (LN **6.7**) (BAGD p. 874): 'bridle' [BAGD, BNTC, EC, LN, Lns, WBC; all versions except CEV, TEV], 'bit' [BAGD, LN]. The phrase ἄχρι τῶν χαλινῶν τῶν ἵππων 'up to the bridles of the horses' is an indication of height from the ground up, about 1.5 meters or five feet [**LN**]. This phrase is translated: 'almost deep enough to cover a horse' [CEV], 'about five feet deep' [TEV].
d. στάδιος (LN 81.27) (BAGD 1. p. 764): 'stade' [BAGD, EC, LN, Lns, WBC; NIV, TNT], 'furlong' [BNTC; KJV]. A στάδιον is a measure of distance equal to about 600 feet or 185 meters [BAGD, LN]. The phrase

σταδίων χιλίων ἑξακοσίων 'a thousand six hundred stadia' is translated: '(about) two hundred miles' [CEV, NAB, NET, NRSV, REB, TEV], 'about one hundred eighty miles' [NCV, NLT]. 1600 stadia is equal to about 184 miles [Ld, NIC, TH, TNTC].

QUESTION—Who is the implied actor of the passive verb ἐπατήθη 'was trodden'?

It may be that God is the actor, although in 19:15 it is Christ who treads the winepress [WBC]. If an actor needs to be supplied one could say, "God's angels trod" [TH].

QUESTION—Which city is intended here?

The city of Jerusalem is indicated [Alf, Be, EC, Hu, ICC, Ld, Lns, NIC, NIGTC, Sw, TH, Wal, WBC]. Specifically the New Jerusalem is indicated (see Revelation 21) [Hu, ICC, Ld, Lns, NIGTC, Sw]. The definite article may indicate that Jerusalem is intended [WBC].

QUESTION—What is the meaning of ἐπατήθη ἡ ληνὸς 'the winepress was trodden'?

It means that the grapes in the winepress were trodden [TH].

QUESTION—What is the relationship between grape juice and blood?

As grape juice comes out of a winepress, so blood results from God's judgment [NIC].

QUESTION—Should the quantity of blood here be taken literally?

This is an hyperbole emphasizing an enormous quantity of blood [Be, EC, NIC, NIGTC, WBC]. It indicates a liberal splattering of blood [Wal].

QUESTION—What does this figure indicate?

It indicates that there will be a radical act of judgment [Alf, Ld, Wal], that crushes all opposition to God [Ld]. It indicates that the judgment will be severe and unrestricted [NIGTC]. It indicates that this is the final decisive defeat of God's enemies [Sw]. It indicates a massacre of extraordinary proportions [EC, TNTC, WBC]. It indicates that unbelievers will be destroyed forever [Lns]. It indicates that judgment is sure [NIC].

DISCOURSE UNIT: 15:1–16:21 [Alf, Be, EC, Hu, Ld, Lns, NIC, NTC, TH, TNTC, Wal, WBC; NLT]. The topic is the seven plagues [Alf, Be, EC, Hu, Ld, Lns, NIC, NTC, TNTC, Wal, WBC], the song of Moses and of the Lamb [NLT].

DISCOURSE UNIT: 15:1–16:18 [REB]. The topic is the seven bowls.

DISCOURSE UNIT: 15:1–8 [Alf, BNTC, GNT, Ld, NIC, NTC, Sw, TNTC; CEV, KJV, NAB, NCV, NET, NIV, NRSV]. The topic is the seven angels with the last plagues [GNT; KJV, NIV, NRSV, TEV], the last of the terrible troubles [CEV, NAB, NCV, NET], the exodus [BNTC], the seven angels and the song of the redeemed [NTC], the preparation [Ld, NIC, Sw], the preface [Alf, TNTC].

DISCOURSE UNIT: 15:1–4 [EC, NIGTC, WBC; NLT]. The topic is rejoicing over the seven last plagues [EC], the prologue [WBC], the song of Moses and the Lamb [NLT].

15:1 And I-saw another great and marvelous[a] sign in heaven, seven angels having seven last plagues[b] because by them the wrath of God was-completed[c].

LEXICON—a. θαυμαστός (LN 25.215) (BAGD 2. p. 353): 'marvelous' [BAGD, BNTC, EC, LN; KJV, NIV, NLT], 'amazing' [NCV, NRSV, TEV], 'wonderful' [BAGD, LN, Lns, WBC; TNT], 'astounding' [NET], 'awe-inspiring' [NAB], 'astonishing' [REB], 'strange' [CEV], 'remarkable' [BAGD, LN]. See θαυμάζω the verb form of this word at 13:3.

b. πληγή (LN 22.13) (BAGD 3. p. 668): 'plague' [BAGD, BNTC, EC, LN, Lns, WBC; all versions except CEV, NCV], 'disaster' [NCV], 'terrible trouble' [CEV]. See this word also at 9:18.

c. τελέω aorist pass. indic. (LN 68.22) (BAGD 1. p. 811): 'to be completed' [BAGD, EC, LN; NET, NIV, REB], 'to be ended' [CEV, NRSV], 'to be accomplished' [BNTC, LN], 'to be filled up' [KJV], 'to be finished' [NCV], 'to be brought to a finish' [Lns], 'to be consummated' [TNT], 'to be spent' [WBC]. This word is also translated actively: 'to bring to a climax' [NAB], 'to bring to completion' [NLT], 'to be an expression of (God's anger)' [TEV]. See this word also at 10:7 and 11:7.

QUESTION—What is the significance of the phrase καὶ εἶδον 'and I saw'?

It introduces a new vision in the narrative [EC, WBC] or a new major section [ICC, NIGTC].

QUESTION—Since this is ἄλλο σημεῖον 'another sign', what other signs are there?

There are two other signs—12:1, 'a woman clothed with the sun', and 12:3, 'an enormous red dragon' [EC, Hu, Lns, NTC, Sw, TH, Wal, WBC].

QUESTION—In what sense did the angels *have* the plagues?

The angels *had* the plagues in the sense that they were responsible for causing them [Be, EC, TH].

QUESTION—In what sense were these plagues 'the last'?

They were last in the sense that they are the final judgments before Christ's Second Coming [Wal]. They were last in that they occur in the last days of the earth [NIGTC]. They were last in the sense that they conclude the warnings to an unrepentant people [Ld, NIC]. They were the last of the preliminary judgments [Lns].

QUESTION—What relationship is indicated by ὅτι 'because'?

It indicates that the following clause gives the reason the plagues were the last ones [Alf, Be, BNTC, EC, Lns, Sw; NCV, NET, NIV, NRSV, REB, TEV, TNT]: seven last plagues—last *because* in them the wrath of God is completed.

QUESTION—What is meant by ἐτελέσθη 'was completed'?

God's wrath was completed in the sense that it completely expressed God's anger at sinners [TH]. The verb ἐτελέσθη is used in the sense of 'to be filled up' and refers to the figure of the bowls *being full* of God's anger. As such the figure indicates that this vision displays God's anger in a more intense manner than the previous woe visions [NIGTC]. 'Was completed' is not used in the sense that God's wrath is exhausted [Alf, Be, Ld, Sw].

QUESTION—Who is the implied actor of ἐτελέσθη 'was completed'?

The implied actor is God [Lns]: by them God completed his anger.

QUESTION—How are the nouns related in the genitive construction ὁ θυμὸς τοῦ θεοῦ 'the wrath of God'?

God experiences the wrath [Lns; CEV].

QUESTION—With what are these seven last plagues associated?

They are the third woe of 11:14 [EC, Hu, Ld]. They are the contents of the seventh trumpet of 11:15 [Hu, Ld, Wal].

15:2 **And I-saw something-like^a (a) sea of-glass^b mixed^c with-fire and the-ones (who) overcame from the beast and its image and the number of its name standing on^d the glassy sea having harps of God.**

TEXT—Some manuscripts include ἐκ τοῦ χαράγματος αὐτοῦ 'over its mark' after τῆς εἰκόνος αὐτοῦ 'its image' GNT does not mention this alternative. The reading 'over its mark' is included by TR and KJV.

LEXICON—a. ὡς(LN 64.2) (BAGD II.3.a.α. p. 897): 'something like' [BAGD, EC, WBC; NAB, NET], 'something that looked like' [CEV], 'what looked like' [NCV, NIV, REB, TEV], 'what seemed (to be)' [BNTC; NLT, TNT], 'what appeared to be' [NRSV], 'as it were' [Lns; KJV], 'as, like' [LN]. See this word also at 4:6.

b. ὑάλινος (LN 6.223) (BAGD p. 831): 'of glass' [BAGD, BNTC, EC, LN, WBC; all versions except CEV, NLT], 'glassy' [LN], 'glass' [CEV], 'crystal' [NLT], 'transparent' [Lns]. See this word also at 4:6.

c. perf. pass. participle of μίγνυμι (LN 63.10) (BAGD 1. p. 499): 'to be mixed' [BAGD, EC, LN, Lns; all versions except KJV, REB], 'to be mingled' [BAGD, BNTC, LN, WBC; KJV], 'to be shot through' [REB]. See this word also at 8:7.

d. ἐπί with accusative object (LN 83.23, 83.46): 'on' [Be, EC, LN (83.46), Lns; CEV, KJV, NAB, NLT], 'by' [LN (83.23); NCV, NET, TEV, TNT], 'beside' [BNTC; NIV, NRSV, REB], 'near' [WBC], 'at' [LN (83.23)], 'upon' [EC, LN (83.46)].

QUESTION—To which 'sea of glass' does this refer?

It probably refers to the sea of glass described in 4:6 that stood before the throne of God [Alf, Be, BNTC, EC, Hu, Ld, Lns, NIC, NTC, Sw, TH, TNTC, Wal, WBC]. The fact that this reference to the sea of glass and the one in 4:6 both include the presence of the four living creatures makes the identity unmistakable (see 15:7) [Alf, Wal].

QUESTION—What is symbolized by its appearing to be 'mixed with fire'?

It probably symbolizes the approaching judgment that the angels were about to bring [EC, Ld, Lns, NTC, Sw, TNTC, Wal, WBC]. It symbolizes God's holiness and justice [BNTC]. It symbolizes dazzling purity [Hu]. It does not symbolize anything special [Be, NIC], but is only included to enhance the beauty of the scene [NIC].

QUESTION—What is the function of ἐκ 'from' in the phrase τοὺς νικῶντας ἐκ τοῦ θηρίου 'the ones overcoming from the beast'?
It probably has reference to escaping *from* the grasp of the beast and its image and the number of its name [Alf, BNTC, EC, Lns, NIGTC, Sw]: the ones overcoming *and escaping from* the beast. It means that they prevailed *over* the beast and its image and the number of its name [NIC, NIGTC, NTC, WBC]. They have come as victors out of the battle with the beast [Lns].

QUESTION—What relationship is indicated by the first καί 'and' in the clause, 'overcame the beast *and* its image and the number of its name'?
1. It simply indicates a conjoining relationship [BNTC, EC, Lns; all versions]: they overcame the beast *and* its image and the number of its name.
2. It indicates that the two phrases that follow further define the first [EC, NIC, WBC]: they overcame the beast, *that is*, its image and the number of its name. The two phrases explain and bring out what is entailed in overcoming the beast [NIC].

QUESTION—Were these overcomers standing *on* or *beside* the sea of glass?
1. They were standing *on* the sea of glass [Be, EC, LN, Lns, NIC, NIGTC, Sw, Wal; CEV, KJV, NAB, NLT].
2. They were standing *beside* the sea of glass [Alf, BNTC, WBC; NCV, NET, NIV, NRSV, REB, TEV, TNT].

QUESTION—How are the nouns related in the genitive construction κιθάρας τοῦ θεοῦ 'harps of God'?
1. God gave them the harps [BNTC, Lns, TH; CEV, NCV, NET, NIV, NLT, REB, TEV]: the harps God *gave* them.
2. The harps were used to worship God [EC, ICC, NIGTC]: harps *for worshiping* God.

15:3 And they-sing the song of God's servant Moses and the song of-the Lamb saying, "Your works (are) great and marvelous, Lord God almighty; your ways (are) just[a] and true,[b] King of-the nations;

TEXT—Instead of τῶν ἐθνῶν 'of the nations', some manuscripts have πάντων τῶν ἐθνῶν 'of all of the nations', others have τῶν αἰώνων 'of the ages', and one manuscript has τῶν ἁγίων 'of the saints'. GNT selects the reading 'of the nations' with a B decision, indicating that the text is almost certain. The reading 'of the nations' is also taken by BNTC, EC, Lns, Sw, Wal, WBC; NAB, NCV, NET, NLT, NRSV, TEV, TNT. The reading 'of the ages' is taken by Ld, NTC; NIV, REB. The reading 'of all the nations' is taken by CEV. The reading 'of the saints' is taken by TR and KJV.

LEXICON—a. δίκαιος (LN 88.12) (BAGD 4. p. 196): 'just' [BNTC, LN; all versions except CEV, NCV, TEV], 'righteous' [BAGD, EC, LN, Lns, WBC], 'right' [CEV, NCV, TEV].
  b. ἀληθινός (LN 73.2) (BAGD 1. p. 37): 'true' [BAGD, BNTC, EC, Ld, LN, WBC; all versions except CEV], 'genuine' [Lns], 'fair' [CEV]. See this word also at 3:7.

QUESTION—How are the nouns related in the genitive construction τὴν ᾠδὴν Μωϋσέως 'the song of Moses'?
1. Moses sang the song [Alf, BNTC, EC, Hu, Ld, NIC, NIGTC, Sw, TH, TNTC, WBC] or composed it [Be, TH, Wal]. It refers to the song of Moses in Exodus 15 in which Moses celebrates God's deliverance of the people of Israel from the Egyptians [Alf, BNTC, EC, Hu, Ld, Lns, NIC, Sw, TH, WBC]. Or, it refers to the song of Moses in Deuteronomy 32 that he wrote and presented to the people of Israel at the end of his career [Be, Wal]. Or, it could refer to the songs in both Exodus and Deuteronomy [NIGTC, NTC].
2. The song was about Moses, specifically about what God had done through Moses [Lns].

QUESTION—How are the nouns related in the genitive construction τὴν ᾠδὴν τοῦ ἀρνίου 'the song of the Lamb'?
1. The Lamb sang the song [NIGTC, TH] or composed it [Be, EC, Wal]. The Lamb was responsible for the song [EC].
2. The song was about the Lamb [EC, Hu, Lns, WBC], specifically about what God had done through the Lamb [Lns]. An example is Rev. 5:9–12 [WBC]. It is a song of deliverance from the hatred and opposition of the beast [Ld].

QUESTION—Are these two songs or one?
1. They are one song [Alf, BNTC, Ld, Lns, NIC, NIGTC, TNTC, WBC]. The καί 'and', before 'of the Lamb' is explanatory, the song of Moses, *that is*, the song of the Lamb [NIGTC]. The two are the same song because they both talk about a victory without weapons other than the Cross of Christ and the witness of His followers [BNTC].
2. They are two separate songs [EC, Sw, Wal]. The fact that the definite article before 'song' is repeated shows that two songs are intended [Wal]. Although there are two songs, they form a harmony [Sw].

QUESTION—Where should the vocatives, 'Lord God Almighty' and 'King of the nations' be placed?
It might be better to place them at the beginning of their statements [TH; TEV]: Lord God Almighty, your works are great and marvelous. King of the nations, your ways are just and true.

QUESTION—How are the nouns related in the genitive construction ὁ βασιλεὺς τῶν ἐθνῶν 'king of the nations'?
That God is king of the nations means that he rules the nations [Lns].

QUESTION—How are the nouns related in the genitive construction ὁ βασιλεὺς τῶν ἐθνῶν 'king of the ages'?
That God is king of the ages means that he rules forever [Lns].

15:4 Who would- not^a -fear^b (you), Lord, and glorify^c your name? For (you) only (are) holy,^d for all the nations will-come and worship before you, for your righteous-acts^e were-revealed.

LEXICON—a. οὔ (LN 69.5) (BAGD D.1.a. p. 517): 'not' [BNTC, EC, Lns, WBC; all versions except NCV]. This phrase is taken as a litotes and translated positively: 'everyone will respect you' [NCV]. This is a marker of emphatic negation [LN]. The use of οὐ μή 'not ever' with the aorist subjunctive indicates emphatic future [Be]. See this word also at 2:11.
- b. subj. aorist pass. of φοβέομαι (LN 53.58, 87.24) (BAGD 2.a. p. 863): 'to fear' [BNTC, EC, Lns, WBC; all versions except CEV, NCV, TEV], 'to honor' [CEV], 'to stand in awe of' [TEV], 'to reverence' [BAGD, LN (53.57)], 'to respect' [NCV]. See this word also at 11:18 and 14:7.
- c. fut. act. indic. of δοξάζω (LN 87.8, 87.24, 33.357): 'to glorify' [EC, LN (87.24, 33.357), Lns, WBC; KJV, NAB, NET, NLT, NRSV, TNT], 'to honor' [LN (87.8); NCV], 'to do homage to' [BNTC; REB], 'to respect' [LN (87.8)], 'to bring glory to' [NIV], 'to declare one's greatness' [TEV], 'to make gloriously great' [LN (87.24)], 'to praise' [LN (33.357); CEV].
- d. ὅσιος (LN **88.24**) (BAGD 1.b. p. 585): 'holy' [BAGD, BNTC, EC, **LN,** Lns, WBC; all versions], 'pure, divine' [LN]. The word ὅσιος means to possess superior moral qualities and certain essentially divine qualities in contrast with what is human [LN]. It refers not to his purity from sin but to his unique majesty and power [Be, EC, NIC]. It refers to his perfect purity [TNTC].
- e. δικαίωμα (LN 88.14) (BAGD 2. p. 198): 'righteous act' [EC, LN; NAB, NET, NIV, TNT], 'righteous deed' [BAGD; NLT], 'righteous verdict' [Lns], 'right thing' [NCV], 'judgment' [KJV, NRSV], 'righteous judgment' [WBC], 'just decree' [REB], 'just actions' [TEV], 'justice of one's deeds' [BNTC]. This noun is also translated as a clause: 'you judge with fairness' [CEV]. A δικαίωμα is an act that is in accordance with what God requires [LN]. These acts could either be righteous acts or verdicts [Lns, Sw]. They are judicial sentences in favor of or against those judged [ICC, TNTC]. They are judicial sentences against those judged [EC].

QUESTION—Is this question real or rhetorical?

It is rhetorical [EC, Lns, NIC, NIGTC, TH, TNTC, WBC; NCV], meaning everyone will fear you and honor your name [Lns, NIGTC, TH; NCV].

QUESTION—What does it mean to honor someone's name?

It means to honor the person themselves [EC, NIC, TNTC; TEV]. A person's name implies who they are and what they have done [NIC].

QUESTION—What relationship is indicated by the three occurrences of ὅτι 'for/because'?
1. The first because-clause is the grounds for the initial question. The second is a statement for which the third is the grounds [BNTC; NAB, NET, NIV, NLT, NRSV, REB, TNT]: Who will not fear you...*because* you

alone are holy. All the nations will come and worship before you, *because* your righteous acts have been revealed.
2. The first two because-clauses are the grounds for the initial question, the third is the grounds for second [Alf, Be, EC, Lns]: Who will not fear you…*because* you alone are holy, and *because* all the nations will come and worship before you. All the nations will come… *because* your righteous acts have been revealed.
3. The first two are merely statements while the third is the grounds of the second [CEV, NCV, TEV]: Who will not fear you…? You alone are holy. All the nations will come and worship before you *because* your righteous acts have been revealed.
4. All three are the grounds for the initial question [NIC; KJV]: Who will not fear you…? *because* you alone are holy, *because* all the nations will come and worship before you, *because* your righteous acts have been revealed.
5. The first and third clauses are the grounds for the initial question. The second clause is the result of the first [NIGTC]: Who will not fear you…? *Because* you alone are holy *so that* all the nations will come and worship before you. All will fear you *because* your righteous acts have been revealed.

QUESTION—What is the meaning of 'all the nations will come and worship before you'?

It means that *people from all* nations will come and worship [Ld, TH]. By the figure of metonymy it means that not all, but *many* will come and worship before God [NIGTC].

DISCOURSE UNIT: 15:5–8 [EC, NIGTC, WBC]. The topic is preparation for the seven last plagues [EC, NIGTC; NLT], the commission of the seven angels [WBC].

15:5 And after these-things I-looked, and the temple[a] of-the tent[b] of testimony[c] in heaven was-opened,

TEXT—Some manuscripts include ἰδού 'behold', after εἶδονκαί 'I looked, and'. GNT does not mention this alternative. The reading 'behold' is included by TR and KJV.

LEXICON—a. ναός (LN 7.15) (BAGD 1.b. p. 533): 'temple' [BAGD, EC, LN, WBC; all versions except NLT, REB TNT], 'Temple' [NLT], 'sanctuary' [LN; REB, TNT], 'Sanctuary' [Lns], 'shrine' [BNTC]. See this word also at 3:12.
  b. σκηνή (LN 7.17, 7.9) (BAGD p. 754): 'tent' [BAGD, LN (7.17, 7.9), WBC; NAB, NCV, NET, NRSV, TNT], 'Tent' [BNTC; REB, TEV], 'heavenly sacred tent' [CEV], 'tabernacle tent' [LN (7.17)], 'tabernacle' [EC; KJV, NIV], 'Tabernacle' [Lns; NLT], 'booth' [BAGD]. A σκηνή is a portable dwelling of cloth and/or skins, held up by poles and fastened by cords to stakes. It also refers to the relatively large tent used as a central place of worship by the Jews prior to the building of the Temple [LN].

c. μαρτύριον (LN 33.262, 33.264) (BAGD 2. p. 494): 'testimony' [BAGD, EC, LN (33.264), WBC; KJV, NAB, NET, TNT], 'Testimony' [BNTC, Lns; NIV, REB], 'witness' [LN (33.262, 33.264); NRSV], 'Agreement' [NCV]. This noun is also translated as an adjective: 'sacred' [TEV]. The phrase τῆς σκηνῆς τοῦ μαρτυρίου is translated: 'God's Tabernacle' [NLT], 'the sacred tent used for a temple' [CEV], 'the temple in heaven…with the sacred Tent in it' [TEV].

QUESTION—What is the significance of the phrase μετὰ ταῦτα εἶδον 'after these things I saw'?

It signifies an important transition to a new vision [EC, ICC, NIGTC, Sw, Wal, WBC].

QUESTION—Does the ναός 'temple' refer to the Tabernacle in the wilderness or to the temple in Jerusalem?

1. It refers to the Tabernacle in the wilderness [Be, BNTC, EC, Hu, Lns, NIC, NIGTC, Sw, TH, TNTC, Wal]. Although the reference is to the Tabernacle in the wilderness, it represents its heavenly reality [BNTC, EC, Hu, Lns, NIGTC, Sw, Wal].
2. The temple in heaven was patterned after the Temple in Jerusalem, which was in turn patterned after the Tabernacle in the wilderness [Ld].

QUESTION—How are the nouns related in the genitive construction ὁ ναὸς τῆς σκηνῆς τοῦ μαρτυρίου 'the temple of the tent of testimony'?

1. The tent is in apposition to the temple [Be, EC, NIC, NIGTC, WBC; NAB, NCV, NET, NIV, NLT]: the temple, *that is*, the tent of testimony. The tent was used for a temple [CEV]. Ναός is never used for the most holy place [WBC].
2. The temple was located in the tent of testimony [Alf, Hu, Lns, TH, Wal; REB, TNT]: the temple in the tent of testimony. Ναός is not the temple itself, but the Holy of Holies that formed the inner room of the Tabernacle in the Wilderness [Lns, Wal]. The ναός was the holy place in the tabernacle [Alf, Hu, TH, Wal].
3. The tent of testimony was in the temple [TEV]: the temple with the Sacred Tent in it.

QUESTION—How are the nouns related in the genitive construction τῆς σκηνῆς τοῦ μαρτυρίου 'the tent of the testimony'?

1. The tent contained the testimony, that is, the ten commandments inscribed on stone (see Exodus 32.15) [Be, BNTC, EC, NIC, NIGTC, Wal].
2. Testimony modifies tent [WBC]: the testimony tent or the tent that testifies.

QUESTION—What is the significance of the temple being opened?

It signifies that the seven angels with the seven bowls come from the very presence of God [Be, EC, Ld, Lns, NIC]. It signifies that God's purpose will unfold and be fulfilled [NTC].

15:6 And the seven angels [the-ones] having the seven plagues came-out of the temple dressed[a] in clean shining[b] linen[c] and golden belts[d] tied[e] around (their) chests.[f]

TEXT—Some manuscripts have ἔχοντες 'having' instead of οἱ ἔχοντες 'the ones having'. GNT does not treat this alternative in the apparatus, but brackets it in the text. The reading 'having' is taken by TR and KJV.

TEXT—Instead of λίνον 'linen', some manuscripts have the plural λινούς and make the two following adjectives plural, and others have λίθον 'stone'. GNT selects the reading 'linen' with a B rating, indicating that the text is almost certain.

TEXT—Some manuscripts possibly include καί 'and' after καθαρόν 'clean', although GNT does not mention this alternative. This word 'and' is included by TR and KJV.

LEXICON—a. perf. mid. participle of ἐνδύω (LN 49.1) (BAGD 2.a. p. 264): 'to be dressed' [LN; CEV, NAB, NCV, NET, NIV, TEV], 'to be clothed' [BAGD, EC, LN, Lns, WBC; KJV, NLT, TNT], 'to be robed' [BNTC; NRSV, REB]. See this word also at 1:13.
  b. λαμπρός (LN 14.50, 79.25) (BAGD 3. p. 465): 'shining' [BAGD, BNTC, LN (14.50), WBC; NCV, NIV, REB, TEV, TNT], 'bright' [BAGD, EC, LN (14.50, 79.25); NET, NRSV], 'white' [CEV, KJV, NAB, NLT], 'brilliant' [Lns], 'sparkling' [LN (79.25)], 'radiant' [LN (14.50)].
  c. λίνον (LN **6.165**) (BAGD 2. p. 475): 'linen' [BNTC, EC, LN, Lns, WBC; all versions except CEV, REB], 'linen garment' [BAGD, **LN**], 'linen robe' [CEV], 'fine linen' [REB]. Λίνον is made from the flax plant [TH]. What is important here is the quality of the garments, not so much the fact that they were made of linen [LN]. If there is no word for linen, it would be appropriate to simply translate: 'clean shining clothes' [TH].
  d. ζώνη (LN 6.178) (BAGD p. 341): 'belt' [BAGD, LN; CEV, NLT], 'wide belt' [NET], 'band' [NCV, TEV, TNT], 'sash' [WBC; NAB, NIV, NRSV], 'girdle' [BAGD, BNTC, EC, Lns; KJV, REB]. See this word also at 1:13.
  e. perf. mid. participle of περιζώννυμαι (LN 49.15) (BAGD 1., 2.b. p. 649): 'to be tied' [NCV, TEV], 'to be girded' [BAGD, EC, LN; KJV], 'to be girdled' [Lns], not explicit [BNTC; NAB, NLT, NRSV, REB, TNT]. This word is also translated actively: 'to wear' [CEV, NCV, NET, NIV], 'to encircle' [WBC]. See this word also at 1:13.
  f. στῆθος (LN **8.36**) (BAGD p. 767): 'chest' [BAGD, **LN**; NAB, NCV, NET, NIV, NLT, NRSV, TEV], 'breast' [BAGD, BNTC, EC, Lns; KJV, REB, TNT], 'waist' [WBC], not explicit [CEV]. Στῆθος indicates the trunk of the body from the neck to the abdomen [LN].

QUESTION—What is indicated by the definite articles in the phrases οἱ ἑπτὰ ἄγγελοι '*the* seven angels' and τὰς ἑπτὰ τὰς ἑπτά '*the* seven plagues'?
  It indicates that these are the same angels and plagues that were mentioned in 15:1 [EC].

QUESTION—What is symbolized by the 'clean shining linen' clothing of the angels?
It symbolizes that they are heavenly beings [Be, EC, Sw]. It symbolizes purity and shows that their work is one of purification [EC]. It symbolizes holiness and marks them as being from God [Lns]. It symbolizes the noble and holy nature of their roles [NIC].

QUESTION—What is symbolized by the golden belts around their chests?
It symbolizes the dignity and authority of the Lord (see 1:13) [Alf, Hu]. It symbolizes that their work is of a royal and kingly nature [NIC]. It symbolizes that their mission is disciplinary [EC].

QUESTION—What is symbolized by their overall appearance?
It symbolizes priestly attire [BNTC, NTC]. It merely enhances the magnificence of their appearance [Ld].

15:7 And one of the four living-creatures gave to-the seven angels seven golden bowls[a] filled[b] with-the wrath of God who lives for-ever-and-ever.[c]

LEXICON—a. φιάλη (LN 6.124) (BAGD p. 858): 'bowl' [BAGD, BNTC, EC, LN, Lns; all versions except KJV], 'vial' [KJV], 'libation bowl' [WBC]. A φιάλη is a (wide) shallow bowl [Alf, Be, EC, Ld, LN, NIC, NTC]. It was used for libations [Be, Ld, WBC]. See this word also at 5:8.

b. perf. act. participle of γέμω (LN 59.41) (BAGD 1. p. 153): 'to be full' [BNTC, Lns, WBC; KJV, NRSV, REB, TEV, TNT], 'to be filled' [EC; CEV, NAB, NCV, NET, NIV, NLT]. See this word also at 4:6.

c. εἰς τοὺς αἰῶνας τῶν αἰώνων: This phrase is translated: 'forever and ever' [BNTC, EC, WBC; all versions except NLT, REB], 'forever and forever' [NLT], 'for ever' [REB], 'for the eons of the eons' [Lns]. See this phrase also at 1:18, 4:9 and 11:15.

QUESTION—Who are the four living creatures and what is their significance here?
They are the same four living creatures that were referred to in 4:6–8 [TH]. Since the living creatures come from near God's throne they signify that the bowls have the full approval of God [Ld, TNTC].

QUESTION—What is the significance of the giving of these bowls to the angels?
It may signify that the angels are now commissioned and enabled to use them [Sw, Wal, WBC].

QUESTION—How are the bowls distributed?
Each angel is given a bowl [CEV, NLT].

QUESTION—What is the significance of the phrase 'forever and ever'?
It adds solemnity to the verse [Alf, EC, Wal].

QUESTION—What does it mean that the bowls are full of the wrath of God?
It means that the contents of the bowl *represent* the wrath of God [TH].

15:8 And the temple was-filled with-smoke from the glory[a] of God and from his power, and no-one could enter the temple until the seven plagues of the seven angels were-completed. [b]

LEXICON—a. δόξα (LN **14.49**) (BAGD 1.a. p. 203): 'glory' [BNTC, EC, Lns, WBC; all versions], 'brightness' [BAGD, **LN**], 'splendor' [BAGD], 'radiance' [BAGD, LN]. The reference to δόξα here is evidently to the Shekinah. The Shekinah, which filled the Temple when it was first constructed (1 Kings 8:11), was regarded to be a bright, cloud-like object that represented the personal presence of God [LN]. Δόξα here indicates the brilliant light resulting from the presence of God [TH].

b. aorist pass. subj. of τελέω (LN **68.22**): 'to be completed' [LN, WBC; NET, NIV, REB, TNT], 'to come to an end' [**LN**; TEV], 'to be ended' [NRSV], 'to be accomplished' [BNTC; NAB], 'to be finished' [EC; NCV], 'to be brought to a finish' [Lns], 'to be fulfilled' [KJV]. This verb is also translated actively: 'to finish (pouring)' [CEV], 'to complete (pouring)' [NLT]. See this word also at 10:7.

QUESTION—What is indicated by the καπνοῦ ἐκ τῆς δόξης τοῦ θεοῦ καὶ ἐκ τῆς δυνάμεως αὐτοῦ 'smoke from the glory of God and from his power'?

It indicates the presence of God [Alf, Be, EC, LN, NIC, NIGTC, NTC, Sw, TH, WBC]. In Isaiah 6:4 there is a close connection between the cloud of smoke and the presence of God. Also frequently in the OT, the phrase 'the glory of God' or 'the glory of the Lord' is a reference to God's presence [WBC].

QUESTION—In what other Scriptures is God's presence accompanied by smoke or a cloud?

Isaiah 6:4 [Be, BNTC, ICC, Ld, Lns, NIGTC, NTC, Sw, TH, TNTC], Exodus 40:34 [Ld, NTC, Sw, TH, TNTC, Wal], 1 Kings 8:10, 11 [Ld, NIC, NTC, TH, TNTC], Exodus 19:18 [Be, NIC, Sw] and Ezekiel 10:4 [Be, NIGTC, TNTC] tell of God's presence being accompanied either by a cloud or smoke.

QUESTION—What is the significance of entry to the temple being barred at this time?

It may signify that these plagues are unstoppable until completed [Sw, TNTC]. It may indicate that the time for intercession is past [NIGTC, NTC].

QUESTION—How would this 'smoke from the glory of God' keep anyone from entering the temple?

When the cloud from the glory of God filled the Tabernacle and the Temple it made it impossible for anyone to enter them (see Exodus 40:34, 35; 1 Kings 8:10, 11) [TH].

DISCOURSE UNIT: 16:1–21 [Alf, GNT, Hu, Ld, Lns, NIC, NTC, Sw, Wal, WBC; CEV, KJV, NAB, NCV, NET, NIV, NRSV, TEV]. The topic is the seven bowls.

DISCOURSE UNIT: 16:1–9 [BNTC]. The topic is the natural plagues.

DISCOURSE UNIT: 16:1–2 [EC, Ld, TNTC]. The topic is the first bowl.

DISCOURSE UNIT: 16:1 [NIGTC, WBC]. The topic is the command to pour out the bowls [NIGTC].

16:1 **And I-heard (a) loud voice from the temple saying to-the seven angels, "Go and pour-out^a the seven bowls of God's wrath on the earth."**

TEXT—Instead of τὰς ἑπτὰ φιάλας 'the seven bowls', some manuscripts have τὰς φιάλας 'the bowls'. GNT does not mention this alternative. The reading 'the bowls' is taken by TR and KJV.

LEXICON—a. ἐκχέω (LN **47.4**) (BAGD 1. p. 247): 'to pour out' [BAGD, EC, **LN**, WBC; all versions except CEV, NLT], 'to empty' [BNTC; CEV, NLT].

QUESTION—What is the significance of the phrase μεγάλης φωνῆς 'a loud voice'?

Everywhere else in Revelation where this phrase occurs, the adjective follows the noun [ICC, WBC]. Here the adjective precedes the noun and indicates that there is emphasis on the adjective [NIC, TNTC]: a *very loud* voice.

QUESTION—Whose voice does John hear?

John hears the voice of God [Alf, Be, BNTC, Ld, NIC, NIGTC, NTC, Sw, TH, TNTC, Wal, WBC], since according to 15:8, no one was allowed to enter the temple until the plagues had been poured out [Alf, Be, BNTC, Ld, NIC, Sw, TH, TNTC].

DISCOURSE UNIT: 16:2–11 [NIGTC]. The topic is the first five bowls.

16:2 **And the first (angel) went and poured-out his bowl into the earth, and (a) terrible^a and painful^b sore^c came^d on the men who had the mark of-the beast and who worshiped its image.**

TEXT—Instead of εἰς τὴν γῆν 'into the earth', some manuscripts have ἐπὶ τὴν γῆν 'on the earth'. GNT does not mention this alternative. The reading 'on the earth' is taken by TR and KJV.

TEXT—Instead of ἐπὶ οὺς ἀνθρώπους 'on men', some manuscripts have εἰς τοὺς ἀνθρώπους 'into men'. GNT does not mention this alternative. The reading 'into men' is read by TR.

LEXICON—a. κακός (LN 65.26) (BAGD 2. p. 398): 'terrible' [TEV], 'foul' [NRSV, REB, TNT], 'ugly' [CEV, NCV, NET, NIV], 'pernicious' [BAGD, EC], 'horrible' [NLT], 'harmful' [WBC], 'festering' [NAB], 'noisome' [KJV], 'bad' [LN, Lns], 'harsh, difficult' [LN], 'evil, injurious, dangerous' [BAGD].

b. πονηρός (LN 88.110) (BAGD 1.a.β.): 'painful' [BAGD; CEV, NCV, NET, NIV, NRSV, TEV, TNT], 'malignant' [EC; NLT, REB], 'grievous' [KJV], 'ugly' [NAB], 'festering' [WBC], 'evil' [LN], 'wicked' [LN, Lns], 'serious, virulent' [BAGD]. The phrase κακὸν καὶ πονηρὸν 'terrible and painful' is translated: 'foul' [BNTC].

c. ἕλκος (LN 23.179) (BAGD p. 251): 'sore' [BAGD, BNTC, EC, LN, Lns, WBC; all versions], 'ulcer' [BAGD, LN, Lns], 'abscess' [BAGD]. An ἕλκος is an ulcer, a suppurating wound [BNTC, EC, Lns].
  d. aorist mid. (deponent = act.) indic. of γίνομαι (LN 13.80) (BAGD I.4.c.γ. p. 160): 'to come' [EC, LN; NCV, NRSV], 'to occur' [Lns], 'to appear' [NET, REB, TEV], 'to break out' [BAGD, BNTC; CEV, NAB, NIV, NLT, TNT], 'to afflict' [WBC], 'to fall' [KJV].

QUESTION—In what sense did the angel 'pour out his bowl'?
  He poured out the contents of his bowl [TH].
QUESTION—What sense of ἀνθρώπους 'men' in indicated here?
  It should be an inclusive sense of mankind in general [ICC, Lns, TH, WBC; CEV, NAB, NCV, NET, NIV, NLT, NRSV, TEV]: people.
QUESTION—Which of the plagues on the Egyptians in the time of Moses does this plague resemble?
  It resembles the sixth plague of boils (see Exodus 9:8–12) [Be, Ld, Lns, NIC, NTC, Sw, TH, TNTC, Wal, WBC].
QUESTION—Should this plague be taken literally or figuratively?
  1. It should be taken literally [EC, Wal]. Since the plagues on the Egyptians were literal, this should be taken in the same way [EC].
  2. It should be taken figuratively [Lns, NIGTC]. It indicates that there will be serious trouble in society, in the economy, in education and in politics, wherever antichristian power rules [Lns]. It indicates that there will be suffering of some kind like the spiritual and psychological harm of the fifth trumpet (see 9:4–6, 10) [NIGTC].

DISCOURSE UNIT: 16:3 [EC, Ld, TNTC]. The topic is the second bowl.

16:3 And the second (angel) poured-out his bowl onto the sea, and it-became[a] blood like (that) of-a-dead-man,[b] and every soul[c] of-life died, the (things) in the sea.

TEXT—Some manuscripts include ἄγγελος 'angel' after δεύτερος 'second'. GNT does not mention this alternative. The reading 'angel' is included by TR and possibly all versions.
TEXT—Instead of ζωῆς 'of life', some manuscripts have ζῶσα 'living'. GNT does not mention this alternative. The reading 'living' is taken by TR and possibly KJV.
TEXT—Some manuscripts do not include τά 'the things' before ἐν τῇ θαλάσσῃ 'in the sea'. GNT does not mention this alternative. The reading 'the things' is also not included by TR and KJV.
LEXICON—a. aorist mid. (deponent = act.) indic. of γίνομαι (LN 13.48): 'to become' [EC, LN, WBC; KJV, NCV, NLT, NRSV, REB], 'to turn to/into' [BNTC; CEV, NAB, NET, NIV, REB, TNT], 'to occur' [Lns].
  b. νεκρός (LN 23.121) (BAGD 2.a. p. 535): 'dead man' [BAGD, LN; KJV, NCV, NIV], 'dead person' [EC; CEV, TEV], 'dead body' [REB], 'corpse' [BNTC WBC; NAB, NET, NLT, NRSV, TNT], 'one dead' [Lns]. See this word also at 1:5.

c. ψυχή (LN **4.1**) (BAGD 2. p. 894): 'soul' [BAGD], 'life' [LN]. It signifies 'that which possesses life' [BAGD]. The phrase ψυχὴ ζωῆς 'soul of life' [Lns] is also translated 'living soul' [EC; KJV], 'living creature' [BAGD, **LN**, WBC; NET, TEV], 'living thing' [BNTC; CEV, NCV, NIV, NRSV, REB, TNT], '(every) thing' [NLT]. This is also translated: 'creature living (in the sea)' [NAB]. The phrase ψυχὴ ζωῆς 'soul of life' is an idiom. It means any living creature whether animal or human [LN].

QUESTION—Which of the plagues on the Egyptians in the time of Moses does this plague resemble?

It resembles the first plague of turning the water of the Nile to blood (see Exodus 7:14–24) [Be, EC, Hu, ICC, Ld, NIC, NIGTC, Sw, TH, TNTC, Wal, WBC].

QUESTION—Which of the trumpet plagues of Revelation 8 does this plague resemble?

It resembles the sounding of the second trumpet when something like a mountain was thrown into the sea and one-third of the water turned into blood (see Revelation 8:8–9) [Hu, Ld, NIC, NIGTC, NTC, Sw, TNTC, Wal].

QUESTION—How are the nouns related in the genitive construction ψυχὴ ζωῆς 'soul of life'?

The second noun modifies the first [Be, BNTC, EC, NIGTC, WBC; all versions except NAB]: living soul.

QUESTION—What is the blood of a dead man like?

It is clotted and thick [Be, EC, Lns, NIC, TH]. It is in a state of decay or rot [Be, EC, Lns, NIC]. It has a bad odor [EC, Lns]. It is dark red [TH].

QUESTION—Should this plague be taken figuratively or literally?

1. It should be taken literally [EC, Wal].
2. It should be taken figuratively [Lns, NIGTC]. As the disgusting odor of death comes from the blood of a dead man, so one can sense the 'smell' of death coming from the antichristian world [Lns]. The sea being symbolical of ungodly humanity, this may indicate the collapse of the world's economic system [NIGTC].

DISCOURSE UNIT: 16:4–7 [EC, Ld, TNTC]. The topic is the third bowl.

16:4 **And the third (angel) poured-out his bowl into the rivers and the springs**[a] **of-the waters, and it became blood.**

TEXT—Some manuscripts include ἄγγελος 'angel' after τρίτος 'third'. GNT does not mention this alternative. It is included by TR and possibly all versions.

TEXT—Some manuscripts include εἰς 'into' after ποταμοὺς καί 'rivers and'. GNT does not mention this alternative. 'Into' is included by and TR and KJV.

LEXICON—a. πηγή (LN 1.78) (BAGD 1. p. 655): 'spring' [BAGD, BNTC, LN, Lns, WBC; NAB, NCV, NET, NIV, NRSV, TEV, TNT], 'fountain' [EC; KJV]. The phrase τὰς πηγὰς τῶν ὑδάτων 'the springs of the waters' is translated: 'streams' [CEV], 'springs' [NLT, REB], 'freshwater springs' [BNTC]. See this word at 8:10.

QUESTION—Which of the plagues on the Egyptians in the time of Moses does this plague resemble?
> It resembles the first plague of turning the water of the streams and canals and ponds and reservoirs to blood (see Exodus 7:14–24) [Hu, NIC, NIGTC, NTC, WBC].

QUESTION—Which of the trumpet plagues of Revelation 8 does this plague resemble?
> It resembles the sounding of the third trumpet when a large star fell on the springs of water and one-third of the water became bitter (see Revelation 8:10–11) [Be, EC, Ld, NIC, NIGTC, Sw, TH, TNTC]. In Revelation 8 only one-third of the water is affected, but here it all is. There the water becomes bitter, here it becomes blood [Sw, TNTC].

QUESTION—Should this plague be taken figuratively or literally?
> 1. It should be taken literally [EC, Wal]. The blood here is just as literal as the blood of the saints in 16:6 [EC].
> 2. It should be taken figuratively [Lns, NIGTC]. Springs of water should be taken to symbolize the supply of natural good sense that if taken away has disastrous results [Lns]. Blood here should be taken to indicate severe economic suffering possibly resulting in literal death [NIGTC].

QUESTION—What kind of water is indicated here?
> It indicates fresh water for drinking [Alf, Be, BNTC, EC, ICC, Lns, Sw, TH].

16:5 And I-heard the angel of-the waters saying, "You-are just,[a] the-one (who) is and the-one (who) was, the holy-one,[b] because you-judged[c] these-things,

TEXT—Some manuscripts possibly include κύριε 'Lord' after δίκαιος 'just,' although GNT does not mention this alternative. The reading 'Lord' is included by TR and KJV.

LEXICON—a. δίκαιος (LN 88.12) (BAGD 2. p. 196): 'just' [BAGD, BNTC; all versions except CEV, KJV, NCV], 'righteous' [BAGD, EC, LN, Lns, WBC; KJV], 'right' [NCV]. This adjective is also translated: 'to have the right (to judge)' [CEV]. See this word also at 15:3.
> b. ὅσιος (BAGD 2.b. p, 585): 'holy one' [BAGD, EC, WBC], 'Holy One' [BNTC; all versions except CEV, KJV], 'Sacred One' [Lns], 'holy God' [CEV]. See this word also at 15:4.
> c. aorist act. indic of κρίνω (LN 30.75): 'to judge' [EC, Lns; CEV, KJV, NIV, NRSV], 'to decide to punish' [NCV], 'to decide to inflict punishment' [WBC], 'to decide' [LN], 'to pass judgment' [NET], 'to send a judgment' [NLT], 'to make a judgment' [TEV], 'to pronounce a sentence' [BNTC], 'to pass a sentence' [NAB]. This verb is also translated as a noun: 'judgment' [REB, TNT]. See this word also at 6:10.

QUESTION—How are the nouns related in the genitive construction τοῦ ἀγγέλου τῶν ὑδάτων 'the angel of the waters'?
>The angel has authority over, rules over, or has jurisdiction over the waters [Alf, EC, Hu, Ld, NIGTC, TH, Wal].

QUESTION—What waters are indicated?
>Both salt and fresh water are indicated [EC, Hu, TH].

QUESTION—What relationship is indicated by ὅτι 'because'?
>It indicates that the following action is the grounds or reason for saying that God is just [EC, NIGTC]: you are just...*because* you have judged these things. If 'holy' is synonymous for 'just' it also gives the reason why God is holy [NIGTC].

QUESTION—What is the antecedent of ταῦτα 'these things'?
>'These things' refers back to the turning of the water into blood in verse 4 [Alf, EC, Lns]. It refers to the plagues that were being sent onto the world [TH].

16:6 Because they-poured-out[a] (the) blood of (the) saints and prophets and you-have-given them blood to-drink, they-are worthy[b] (of punishment)."

TEXT—Some manuscripts have ἔδωκας 'you gave' instead of δέδωκας 'you have given'. GNT does not treat this alternative in the apparatus, but reads [δ]έδωκας 'have given' in the text.

TEXT—Some manuscripts include γάρ 'for' after ἄξιοι 'worthy'. GNT does not mention this alternative. TR and KJV also include this word.

LEXICON—a. aorist act. indic. of ἐκχέω (LN 47.4) (BAGD 1. p. 247): 'to pour out' [BAGD, EC, LN, Lns, WBC; CEV, NCV, NET, TEV, TNT], 'to shed' [BNTC; KJV, NAB, NIV, NRSV, REB]. This active verb is also translated passively: 'to be poured out' [NLT]. To pour out someone's blood means to murder them [TH, WBC]. See this word also at 16:1.

b. ἄξιος (LN 66.6) (BAGD 2.a. p. 77): 'worthy' [EC, Lns, WBC; KJV], 'proper, fitting, worthy of, corresponding to' [LN]. The word ἄξιος means pertaining to being fitting or proper in correspondence to what should be expected [LN]. This adjective is also translated as a verb: 'to deserve' [BAGD; all versions except KJV]. It is also translated as a clause: '(they have their) just deserts' [BNTC], '(it is their) just reward' [NLT].

QUESTION—What relationship is indicated by ὅτι 'because'?
>1. It indicates a new reason for saying that God is just [NIC]. (You are just...because you judged these things), And also because you have given them blood to drink *because* they poured out the blood of the saints.
>2. It indicates a new reason for saying that God is just; this reason further explains the first reason given in the previous verse [EC, Lns, NIGTC]: (You are just...because you judged these things), *that is, because* they poured out the blood of the saints...you also have given them blood to drink. Here God's judging these things is further defined as His giving

them blood to drink in response to their pouring out the blood of the saints and prophets [EC].

3. It indicates that the first clause of this verse as it appears in the text above is the reason for the second, making this a separate sentence from the previous verse [Sw]: You have also given them blood to drink *because* they poured out the blood of the saints and prophets.

QUESTION—What is the relationship of the two nouns ἁγίων καὶ προφητῶν 'saints and prophets'?

'Saints' is a general term for all Christians while 'prophets' is a group of people within that group [Be, EC, NIC, Sw].

QUESTION—What is the significance of the word αἷμα 'blood' being repeated and being placed in a forward position in each clause?

It places emphasis on the word 'blood' [EC, Lns], and brings out the fact that the punishment fits the crime [EC].

QUESTION—Who is the antecedent of the pronoun in the verb εἰσιν 'they are'?

The antecedent is the same as the subject of 'they poured out the blood' [EC, NIC, NIGTC, Wal, WBC]: *they* poured out the blood of the saints and the prophets...*they* are worthy.

QUESTION—In what sense is the adjective ἄξιος 'worthy' used here?

It is used in the sense that they *deserve* this punishment [BAGD, EC, NIC, NIGTC, NTC, TH, TNTC, Wal, WBC; all versions except KJV]. 'Worthy' is used ironically here [WBC]. The use of worthy here evokes a remarkable antithesis to its use in 3:4 where it means 'worthy of a good reward' [EC, NIGTC, NTC, Sw, WBC].

QUESTION—What is the significance of the use of ἐκχέω 'to pour out' both to describe the 'pouring out of blood' and the angels 'pouring out of the bowls'?

It emphasizes the principle that God makes the punishment fit the crime [NIGTC].

QUESTION—Why is God 'just' to have turned the water into blood?

God is just in doing this because the punishment fits the crime—they shed the blood of the believers, therefore they should be given blood instead of water to drink [Hu, TNTC, Wal].

QUESTION—How should καί 'and' be translated here?

1. It should be translated 'and' [BNTC, EC, Lns, WBC; KJV, NAB, NIV, REB]: they poured out the blood...*and* you have given them blood.
2. It should be translated 'so' [CEV, NCV, NET, NLT, TEV]: they poured out the blood...*so* you have given them blood.
3. It should be translated 'also' and is construed with the pronoun 'you' referring to God [NIGTC]: because they poured out the blood... you *also* have given them blood.
4. It should be left untranslated [NRSV, TNT].

16:7 And I heard the altar saying, "Yes,[a] Lord God Almighty, true[b] and just[c] (are) your judgments.[d]

TEXT—Some manuscripts include ἐκ 'from' before τοῦ θυσιαστηρίου 'the altar'. GNT does not mention this alternative.

TEXT—Some manuscripts possibly include ἄλλου ἐκ 'another from', although GNT does not mention this alternative. The reading 'another from' is included by TR and KJV.

LEXICON—a. ναί (BAGD 4. p. 533): 'yes' [BNTC, EC, WBC; all versions except KJV, TEV], 'indeed' [BAGD; TEV], 'even so' [KJV], 'yea' [Lns], 'certainly, quite so' [BAGD]. Ναί indicates agreement with the statement of the angel in verses 5 and 6 [EC, NIGTC, NTC, TNTC, WBC]. See this word also at 1:7

b. ἀληθινός (BAGD 2. p. 37): 'true' [BAGD, BNTC, EC, WBC; all versions except CEV, NCV], 'honest' [CEV], 'right' [NCV], 'genuine' [Lns]. This indicates that God's judgments are in keeping with the truth [NIC]. It indicates a norm of right [Lns]. See this word also at 3:7.

c. δίκαιος (LN 88.12) (BAGD 2. p. 196): 'just' [BAGD, BNTC, WBC; all versions except CEV, KJV, NCV], 'righteous' [BAGD, EC, LN, Lns; KJV], 'fair' [CEV, NCV]. This indicates that his judgments are absolutely fair [NIC]. See this word also at 15:3 and 16.5.

d. κρίσις (BAGD 1.a.β. p. 452): 'judgment' [BAGD, BNTC, EC, WBC; all versions except NCV, NLT], 'judging' [Lns], 'punishment' [TH; NLT]. This word is also translated as a clause: 'the way to punish people' [NCV]. Κρίσις more often indicates 'the act of judging', while κρίμα tends to indicates 'judicial verdict' [NIC]. Here κρίσις indicates judgment that goes against a person [BAGD]. See this word also at 14:7.

QUESTION—What is indicated by the genitive construction ἤκουσα τοῦ θυσιαστηρίου λέγοντος 'I heard of the altar saying'?

1. It indicates that someone associated with the altar speaks [Hu, Lns, NIGTC, TH, Wal, WBC; KJV, NCV, NLT, REB, TEV]. 'I heard a voice coming from the altar' [NCV, NLT]. This is the angel who came from the altar (see 14:18) [Lns]. It may be the voice of one of the martyrs under the altar (see 6:10) [WBC]. It is either the voice of the souls of the martyrs under the altar or the prayers of the saints going up from altar of incense (see 6:9, 5.8 and 8.3) [Hu]. The voice may represent all the martyrs who were under the altar crying out for vengeance [NIGTC].

2. It is the figure of personification in which the altar is treated as a person [Alf, Be, BNTC, EC, Ld, Lns, NIC, NTC, TNTC; CEV, NAB, NET, NIV, NRSV, TNT]. 'I heard the altar shout' [CEV]. The altar speaks as though it were the combination of the prayers of the saints that were offered on the altar and the cry for revenge of the souls of the martyrs under the altar (see 5:8, 8:3 and 6:9) [Alf, Be, NIC]. The altar represents the prayers of the saints for revenge (see 6:10) [EC, NTC]. The altar brings to mind the prayers of the saints (see 8:3) that resulted in the judgments of 8:5 [TNTC].

DISCOURSE UNIT: 16:8–9 [EC, Ld, TNTC]. The topic is the fourth bowl.

16:8 **And the fourth (angel) poured-out his bowl on the sun, and it-was-given to-it to-burn^a men with fire.**

TEXT—Some manuscripts include ἄγγελος 'angel' after ὁ τέταρτος 'the fourth'. GNT does not mention this alternative. The reading 'angel' is included by TR and KJV and possibly by WBC and all versions.

LEXICON—a. aorist act. infin. of καυματίζω (LN 14.68) (BAGD p. 425): 'to burn' [BAGD, EC, Lns, WBC; NAB, NCV, REB, TEV], 'to scorch' [BNTC, LN; CEV, KJV, NET, NIV, NLT, NRSV, TNT], 'to harm by heat' [LN].

QUESTION—What is the implied object of the passive ἐδόθη 'it was given'?
1. The implied object is 'power' [KJV, NAB, NCV, NIV]: it was given power to burn men.
2. The implied object is 'permission' [BNTC, WBC; NET, NRSV, REB, TEV, TNT]: permission was given for the sun to burn men.
3. The implied object is 'command' [NLT]: it was commanded to burn men.

QUESTION—Who is the implied agent of ἐδόθη 'it was given'?
God is the authority behind this action [EC, Ld, NIGTC, TH, TNTC]. This is seen in the following verse where people blame God for the scorching [EC].

QUESTION—What is the antecedent of αὐτῷ 'to it'?
1. The antecedent is the sun, not the angel [Alf, Be, BNTC, EC, Lns, NIC, Wal, WBC; all versions except KJV, NCV]: to the sun.
2. The antecedent may be the angel [KJV, NCV]: to him.
3. The antecedent could be either the angel or the sun [NIGTC].

QUESTION—In what sense is τοὺς ἀνθρώπους 'the men' used here?
It is used in the sense of 'people' [Lns, Sw, WBC; all versions except KJV, NRSV, TNT]: to burn people.

QUESTION—To whom does the definite article refer in the phrase τοὺς ἀνθρώπους '*the* men'?
It probably refers to the men who received the effects of the first bowl in 16:2 [EC, Lns, Wal]. There is reference to the same men in 16:9 [Wal]. It does not include believers [EC, Lns, Wal], since verse 7:16 show that believers are exempt [EC]. It refers to the worshipers of the beast [EC, Hu, Lns]. It refers to men in general [Alf].

QUESTION—To what does ἐν πυρί 'with fire' refer and what is its function?
It refers to the heat of the sun, not a different fire [Alf, TH]. It functions to intensify the burning action of the sun [EC, Lns, TNTC].

16:9 **And the men were burned (with) great heat and they-cursed^a the name of God the-one having the authority over these plagues and they-repented^b not to-give him glory.**

TEXT—Some manuscripts, have ἐξουσίαν 'authority' instead of τὴν ἐξουσίαν 'the authority'. GNT does not mention this alternative. The reading 'authority' is taken by TR and KJV.

LEXICON—a. aorist act. indic. of βλασφημέω (LN 33.400) (BAGD 2.b.β. p. 142): 'to curse' [CEV, NCV, NIV, NLT, NRSV, REB, TEV], 'to blaspheme' [BAGD, BNTC, EC, LN, Lns; KJV, NAB, NET, TNT], 'to revile' [WBC]. See this word also at 13:6.
b. aorist act. indic. of μετανοέω (LN 41.52) (BAGD p. 512): 'to repent' [BAGD, BNTC, EC, LN, Lns, WBC; all versions except CEV, NCV, TEV], 'to turn to God' [CEV], 'to turn from one's sins' [TEV], 'to change one's ways' [LN], 'to change one's heart and life' [NCV]. See this word also at 2:5 and 3:19.

QUESTION—What is meant by ἐκαυματίσθησαν...καῦμα μέγα 'they were burned...great heat'?
1. It means that they were burned by the great heat [EC, Lns, NIC, TNTC, WBC; all versions except REB, TNT]. The cognate accusative construction 'burned great heat' serves to intensify the suffering [EC, NIC, TNTC].
2. It means that they were very badly burned [BNTC, NIGTC, TH; REB, TNT]. This is the best way to translate this cognate accusative [NIGTC].

QUESTION—What relationship is indicated by the infinitive δοῦναι 'to give'?
1. It indicates a conjoining relationship [all versions except KJV, NAB]: they did not repent *and* give him glory.
2. It indicates an alternative relationship [BNTC; NAB]: they did not repent *or* give him glory.
3. It indicates a relationship of result [Be, EC, Lns]: they did not repent *so as to* give him glory.
4. It indicates a relationship of explanation [Alf]: they did not repent, *that is*, give him glory.
5. It indicates both explanation and result [NIGTC]: they did not repent, *that is, so as to* give him glory.

QUESTION—What is the meaning of cursing the name of God?
It means to tell lies about His character [NIGTC].

DISCOURSE UNIT: 16:10–21 [BNTC]. The topic is the political plagues.

DISCOURSE UNIT: 16:10–11 [EC, Ld, TNTC]. The topic is the fifth bowl.

16:10 **And the fifth (angel) poured-out his bowl on the throne of-the beast, and its kingdom became darkened,[a] and they-were-biting[b] their tongues from the pain,[c]**

TEXT—Some manuscripts include ἄγγελος 'angel' after ὁ πέμπτος 'the fifth'. GNT does not mention this alternative. The reading 'angel' is included by TR and KJV and possibly all versions.

LEXICON—a. perf. pass. participle of σκοτόομαι, σκοτόω (LN 14.55) (BAGD 1. p. 758): 'to be darkened' [BAGD, EC, LN, Lns, WBC; TNT]. This verb is also translated as a noun: 'darkness' [BNTC; all versions except TNT]. See this word also at 9:2.

b. imperfect mid. (deponent = active) indic. of σκοτόομαι (LN **23.40**) (BAGD p. 495): 'to bite' [BAGD, **LN**, WBC; CEV, NAB, NET, TEV], 'to gnaw' [BNTC, EC, Lns; KJV, NCV, NIV, NRSV, REB, TNT], 'to grind (one's teeth)' [NLT]. The imperfect tense indicates a continuous aspect: 'they kept biting' [EC, Lns]. Or, it indicates an inchoative aspect: 'they began to bite' [CEV, NET].

c. πόνος (LN 24.77) (BAGD 2. p. 691): 'pain' [BAGD, BNTC, EC, LN, Lns, WBC; CEV, KJV, NAB, NCV, NET, TEV, TNT], 'agony' [NIV, NRSV, REB], 'anguish' [NLT], 'suffering' [LN].

QUESTION—What is signified by τὸν θρόνον 'the throne'?

It signifies the center of the beast's power or rule [Alf, EC, Ld, Lns, NIC, NIGTC, Sw].

QUESTION—Which beast is indicated here?

It is probably the first beast, the one coming up out of the sea, introduced in chapter 13 [BNTC, TH, Wal]. The throne of the beast is mentioned in 13:2.

QUESTION—Who is the antecedent of the pronoun in ἐμασῶντο 'they were biting'?

It is the adherents of the beast [Alf, EC, Hu, TNTC, WBC].

QUESTION—What was the source of the pain?

1. The source of the pain was the darkness itself [Be, EC, Lns]. The definite article plus the singular of the word τοῦ πόνου 'the pain' (note the plural in the next verse), indicates that the specific pain from the darkness itself is indicated [Be]. The singular points to the specific pain of that caused by the darkness. Perhaps this refers to a type of darkness that the world has never yet experienced [EC].

2. The source of the pain was the previous plagues [Alf, Be, Hu, Ld, NIC, Sw, TH, TNTC, Wal]. The pain of the previous plagues is aggravated by the darkness [Be, NIC]. The pain is from the first plague which is aggravated by the darkness [Ld, TH, Wal]. The pain of the previous plague is now aggravated by the darkness [NTC].

QUESTION—What is the significance of 'biting the tongue in pain'?

It signifies severe agony [EC, Wal].

16:11 And they-cursed the God of Heaven because-of[a] their pains and because-of[a] their sores and they repented not of their works.

LEXICON—a. ἐκ (LN 89.25) (BAGD 3.f. p. 235): 'because of' [BAGD, BNTC, EC, LN, WBC; all versions except NLT, REB, TEV], 'due to' [Lns], 'for' [BNTC; NLT, REB, TEV], 'by reason of' [Alf, BAGD], 'as a result of' [BAGD].

DISCOURSE UNIT: 16:12–21 [NIGTC]. The topic is the sixth and seventh bowls.

DISCOURSE UNIT: 16:12–16 [EC, Ld, NIGTC, TNTC]. The topic is the sixth bowl.

16:12 And the sixth (angel) poured-out his bowl on the great river Euphrates, and its water was-dried-up,ᵃ so-that the way of-the kings from-the risingᵇ of-the-sun might-be-prepared.

TEXT—Some manuscripts include ἄγγελος 'angel' after ὁ ἕκτος 'the sixth'. GNT does not mention this alternative. The reading 'angel' is included by TR and KJV and possibly all versions.

LEXICON—a. aorist pass. indic. of ξηραίνομαι (LN **79.81**): 'to be dried up' [EC; KJV, NAB, NCV, NIV, NRSV, REB], 'to dry up' [BNTC, **LN**, Lns, WBC; CEV, NET, NLT, TEV, TNT]. See this word also at 14:15.

   b. ἀνατολή (LN 15.104, 82.1) (BAGD 2.a. p. 62): 'rising' [BAGD, EC, LN (15.104)] 'east' [LN (82.1)]. The phrase ἀπὸ ἀνατολῆς ἡλίου 'from the rising of the sun' is translated: 'from the east' [BAGD, WBC; all versions], 'from the sunrise' [BNTC], 'from the sunrising' [Lns]. See this word also at 7:2.

QUESTION—To which of the trumpet judgments is this bowl similar?

It is similar to the sixth trumpet in which four angels are released from the Euphrates River resulting in the death of one-third of mankind (see 9:13–21) [Alf, Hu, NIC, Sw, TNTC].

QUESTION—What relationship is indicated by ἵνα 'so that'?

1. It indicates a relationship of result [Lns, NIC; TNT]: its water was dried up *with the result that* the way...was prepared.
2. It indicates a relationship of purpose [BNTC; CEV, NAB, NCV, NET, NIV, NRSV, REB, TEV]: its water was dried up *in order to* make a road.

QUESTION—What is signified by this verse?

1. It signifies the release of a group of Eastern Kings to engage in a final battle against the forces of God (see verse 12:14) [Alf, Be, EC, Hu, Ld, Wal]. The kings will join with the kings of the world in this effort [Alf, EC, Ld, Wal].
2. It signifies the release of the Parthian army [BNTC, NIC, NTC], under the leadership of a revived Emperor Nero [Be]. There is a difference between the kings of the east and the kings of the world of verse 14. The former will lay siege to Rome while the latter (verse 14) will fight the forces of Christ [NIC].

QUESTION—Would these kings gather to attack the forces of God or of those opposed to God?

1. They would gather to attack the forces of God [Alf, EC, Hu, Ld, Wal].
2. They would gather to attack the forces opposed to God [Be, BNTC, NIC, NTC, TH, TNTC]. They would gather to attack Rome [Be, BNTC, NIC, NTC]. They would gather to attack the beast [TH].

16:13 And I-saw three unclean[a] spirits like[b] frogs[c] (come) from the mouth of-the dragon and from the mouth of-the beast and from the mouth of-the false-prophet;[d]

TEXT—Some manuscripts possibly read ὅμοια 'like' instead of ὡς 'as' although GNT does not mention this alternative. The reading 'like' is taken by TR.

LEXICON—a. ἀκάθαρτος (LN 12.39, 53.39) (BAGD 2. p. 29): 'unclean' [BAGD, EC, LN (12.39), Lns, WBC; KJV NAB, NET, TEV, TNT], 'evil' [CEV, NCV, NIV, NLT], 'foul' [BNTC; NRSV, REB], 'ritually unclean, defiled' [LN (53.39)], 'impure, vicious' [BAGD].

b. ὡς (LN 64.12) (BAGD II.3.b. p. 897): 'like' [BAGD, BNTC, EC, LN, WBC; KJV, NAB, NRSV, REB, TNT], 'as' [LN], 'that looked like' [CEV, NCV, NET, NIV, NLT, TEV], 'as it were' [Lns].

c. βάτραχος (LN **4.55**) (BAGD p. 137): 'frog' [BNTC, EC, **LN**, Lns, WBC; all versions].

c. ψευδοπροφήτης (LN 53.81) (BAGD p. 892): 'false prophet' [BAGD, BNTC, EC, LN, WBC; all versions], 'pseudo-prophet' [Lns].

QUESTION—What verb is implied about the action of the frogs here?

The verb 'coming' or 'emerging' is implied [Be, BNTC, EC, WBC; all versions]: spirits like frogs *coming* from the mouth of the dragon. The verb 'leaping' is implied [NLT].

QUESTION—What is signified by the spirits coming out of the mouths of the dragon, the beast, and the false prophet?

It signifies that their activity will be one of speaking [EC, Lns]. The mouth as a speech organ is the main tool of human influence [Sw].

QUESTION—What is the point of similarity in the simile πνεύματα…ὡς βάτραχοι 'spirits…like frogs'?

The point of similarity is: uncleanliness [Alf, EC, Hu, NIC], persistent noise [Alf, NIC, NIGTC, TNTC], shape [Alf, Be, TH] or character [Alf]. The frog was classified as unclean in Hebrew law (see Leviticus 11:10) [EC, NIC, Sw].

QUESTION—Who is τοῦ δράκοντος 'the dragon'?

He is the dragon referred to in 12:3, 9 [Hu, ICC, Lns, NIC, NIGTC, Sw, Wal]. He is also identified as Satan [ICC, Lns, NIC, NIGTC, Sw, Wal].

QUESTION—Who is τοῦ θηρίου 'the beast'?

He is the same as the first beast, the one that came out of the sea (see 13:1) [EC, Hu, NIC, Sw, Wal]. He is the Antichrist [Hu]. Mark 13:22, in which Jesus refers to 'false messiahs and false prophets', may very well imply that he is the 'Antichrist' [BNTC, EC].

QUESTION—Who is τοῦ ψευδοπροφήτου 'the false prophet'?

He is the same as the second beast, the beast that came out of the earth (see 13:11) [Alf, BNTC, EC, Hu, ICC, Ld, Lns, NIC, NIGTC, Sw, TH, TNTC, Wal]. Verse 19:20 makes this identification clear [Sw, TH, TNTC]. This shows that he was the spokesman of the first beast [TH].

QUESTION—In what manner did the unclean spirits emerge from the mouths of the dragon, the beast and the false prophet?
One spirit came out of the dragon, one out of the beast, and another out of the false prophet [NIGTC, Sw, WBC; CEV].

16:14 For they-are spirits of-demons performing signs,[a] that go-out to the kings of-the whole inhabited-earth[b] to-gather them to the battle of-the great day of-God the Almighty.

TEXT—Instead of ἃ ἐκπορεύεται 'which go forth', some manuscripts have ἐκπορεύεσθαι 'to go forth'. GNT does not mention this alternative. The reading 'to go forth' is taken by TR and probably KJV.

TEXT—Some manuscripts possibly include τῆς γῆς καί 'of the earth and' after βασιλεῖς 'kings', although GNT does not mention this alternative. The reading 'of the earth and' is included by TR and KJV.

TEXT—Instead of τὸν πόλεμον 'the war', some manuscripts have πόλεμον 'war'. GNT does not mention this alternative. The reading 'war' is taken by TR.

TEXT—Some manuscripts include ἐκείνης 'that' after ἡμέρας 'day'. GNT does not mention this alternative. The reading 'that' is included by TR and KJV.

LEXICON—a. σημεῖον (BAGD 2.b. p. 748): 'sign' [EC, Lns, WBC; NAB, NET, NRSV, TNT], 'miraculous sign' [TNTC; NIV], 'miracle' [BNTC; CEV, KJV, NCV, REB, TEV]. This noun is also translated as an adjective: 'miracle-working (demons)' [NLT]. A σημεῖον is a miracle that has meaning [TNTC]. See this word also at 12:1 and 13:13.

b. οἰκουμένη (LN 1.39) (BAGD 1.a. p. 561): 'inhabited earth' [BAGD, Lns, NIGTC, Wal], 'inhabited world' [EC], 'world' [BAGD, BNTC, LN, WBC; all versions except CEV, NET], 'earth' [LN; CEV, NET]. See this word also at 3:10 and 12:9.

QUESTION—Is the γάρ-clause εἰσὶν γὰρ πνεύματα δαιμονίων ποιοῦντα σημεῖα 'for they are spirits of demons performing signs' parenthetical?

1. This clause is parenthetical and the relative clause that follows it should be connected with the phrase 'three unclean spirits' of verse 13 [Be, EC, NIC]: three unclean spirits...(for they are spirits of demons performing signs) that go out to the kings of the whole inhabited earth.
2. This clause is parenthetical but ends at δαιμονίων 'demons' and the remainder of the verse beginning with 'performing miracles' should be connected with the phrase 'three unclean spirits' of verse 13 [Sw]: three unclean spirits...(for they are spirits of demons) performing signs that go out to the kings of the whole inhabited earth.

QUESTION—What relationship is indicated by γάρ 'for'
1. It indicates that this verse is the grounds telling why these unclean spirits are like frogs [Alf, NIGTC]: three unclean spirits like frogs *because* they are spirits of demons.
2. It indicates that this γάρ-clause explains the power of the spirits [Be, EC]: three unclean spirits, *that is*, spirits of demons that perform signs.

3. It indicates that this γάρ-clause explains why the unclean spirits are evil [NIC, Sw]: three unclean spirits, *that is*, spirits of demons.

QUESTION—How are the nouns related in the genitive construction πνεύματα δαιμονίων 'spirits of demons'?
1. Demons modifies spirits [BNTC, Ld, TH, TNTC; CEV, NAB, NRSV, REB]: demonic spirits.
2. Spirits are the same as demons [WBC; NLT]: spirits, *that is*, demons.

QUESTION—What relationship is indicated by the infinitive συναγαγεῖν 'to gather'?

It indicates purpose [EC]: that go out to the kings of the whole inhabited earth *in order to* gather them to the battle.

QUESTION—What does the phrase τῆς ἡμέρας τῆς μεγάλης τοῦ θεοῦ τοῦ παντοκράτορος 'the great day of God Almighty' refer to?

It refers to the final battle between the forces of the ungodly nations and the forces of God [EC, ICC, Ld, NIGTC, Sw, TH, WBC]. It is the same day that is further described in Revelation 19:11–21 [Alf, NIC, NIGTC, Sw, TH, WBC]. It is the same as the day described in Revelation 20:8 [NIGTC, WBC]. It is the same day that is elsewhere referred to in Scripture as: 'the last day' (John 6:39, 11:24, 12:48); 'the day of God' (2 Peter 3:12); 'the day of the Lord' (1 Thessalonians 5:2); 'the day of Christ' (Philippians 1:10); 'the day of the Lord Jesus Christ' (1 Cor. 1:8); 'the day' or 'that day' (1 Corinthians 3:13, 2 Thessalonians 1:10) [Ld]. It is referred to in Joel 2:31 [EC, NIGTC] and Joel 2:11 [NIC, Sw]. It is also referred to in Psalm 2:1–3 [EC, Hu]. It refers to the climax of military engagements described in Daniel 11:40–45. The reference to 'news from the east' (in Daniel 11:44) may be the same as the reference to the 'kings of the east' of 16:12 here [Wal].

16:15 "Look,[a] I-come like a-thief. Blessed[b] (is) the-one staying-awake[c] and keeping[d] his clothes, lest he walk-around[e] naked and they-see his shame."[f]

LEXICON—a. ἰδού (LN 91.13, 91.10) (BAGD 1.a. p. 370): 'look' [BAGD, LN (91.13); NET], 'see' [BAGD, BNTC; NRSV, REB], 'listen' [NCV, TEV], 'take note' [NLT], 'pay attention' [LN (91.13)], 'behold' [BAGD, EC; KJV, NAB, NIV], 'remember that Christ says' [CEV], 'indeed (says Jesus)' [WBC], 'lo' [Lns], not explicit [TNT]. See this word also at 1:7.

b. μακάριος (LN 23.119) (BAGD 1.b. p. 486): 'blessed' [BAGD, BNTC, EC, Lns; KJV, NAB, NET, NIV, NLT, NRSV], 'happy' [BAGD, LN; NCV, REB, TEV, TNT], 'fortunate' [BAGD], 'how fortunate' [WBC]. This adjective is also translated as a verb: 'to bless' [CEV]. See this word also at 1:3.

c. pres. act. participle of γρηγορέω (LN 23.72, 27.56) (BAGD 2. p. 167): 'to stay awake' [BNTC, LN (23.72), TH; NCV, NIV, NRSV, REB, TEV], 'to be awake' [CEV], 'to stay alert' [LN (27.56); NET], 'to watch' [EC, Lns, WBC; KJV, NAB, NLT], 'to be watchful' [BAGD, LN (23.72, 27.56); TNT]. See this word also at 3:2.

d. pres. act. participle of τηρέω (BAGD 3. p. 815): 'to keep' [BAGD, EC, Lns; KJV]. The phrase τηρῶν τὰ ἱμάτια αὐτοῦ 'keeping his clothes' is translated: 'to be ready' [CEV], 'to keep one's clothes ready' [NAB, NLT], 'to keep one's clothes with one' [NIV], 'to keep one's clothes at hand' [BNTC; REB], 'to keep one's clothes on' [NCV, TNT], 'to remain fully clothed' [WBC], 'to be clothed' [NRSV], 'to guard one's clothes' [TEV]. Τηρέω is used here in the sense of 'not to lose' [BAGD; NET]. See this word also at 1:3.

e. pres. act. subj. of περιπατέω (BAGD 1.c. p. 649): 'to walk around' [CEV, NCV, NET, TEV], 'to walk' [BNTC, EC, Lns; KJV, NLT], 'to go about' [WBC; NRSV, TNT]. The phrase γυμνὸς περιπατῇ 'he walk around naked' is translated: 'he (not) go naked' [BAGD; NAB, NIV, REB]. See this word also at 2:1.

f. ἀσχημοσύνη (LN **25.202**) (BAGD 2. p. 119): 'shame' [BAGD, EC, Lns; KJV, NCV, NRSV], 'shameful condition' [**LN**; NET], 'shameful state' [LN, WBC]. This word refers to private parts [BAGD]. This word is a euphemism for private parts (see Exodus 20:26) [EC, TH]. This noun is also translated as a verb: 'to be ashamed' [CEV, TEV], 'to be exposed' [NAB]. It is also translated as an adverb: 'ashamed' [BNTC; NLT, REB, TNT], 'shamefully (exposed)' [NIV].

QUESTION—Is this verse parenthetical?

It is parenthetical to the flow of thought [Be, EC, Hu, ICC, NIGTC]. The following commentaries and versions treat it as parenthetical in their translations: BNTC, EC; NAB, NET, NRSV, TNT.

QUESTION—Who is the implied speaker of this verse?

The implied speaker is Jesus Christ [Alf, Be, EC, Hu, Ld, Lns, NIC, Sw, TH, TNTC, WBC; CEV].

QUESTION—What is the point of similarity in the simile 'to come as a thief'?

The point of similarity is unexpectedness [Alf, Be, BNTC, Ld, Lns, NIC, NIGTC, TNTC, Wal, WBC; CEV, NLT]: I come *unexpectedly like* a thief. The point of similarity is suddenness [Hu, TH, Wal, WBC]: I come *suddenly* like a thief. A thief's coming is also unannounced [Hu, TH, TNTC].

QUESTION—To what does the figure of 'keeping one's clothes' refer?

It either refers to remaining dressed [Alf, NIGTC, WBC; NCV, TNT] or of keeping one's clothes handy [Be, BNTC, EC, NIC, TH, TNTC; NAB, NIV, NLT, REB]. In practical terms it amounts to refusing to give in to the idolatrous demands to worship the beast [NIGTC]. It is making sure that one's faith is genuine [EC].

QUESTION—What is the point of similarity in the figure to stay awake and keep one's clothes?

The point of similarity is preparedness [BNTC, Ld, NIC, TNTC, Wal].

QUESTION—What do ἱμάτια 'clothes' symbolize here?

They symbolize the righteousness of Christ [Alf, Lns, TNTC]. They symbolize the righteous deeds of believers [NIGTC, Wal].

QUESTION—What is symbolized by 'nakedness'?

It symbolizes the lack of righteousness [Alf, NIGTC]. It symbolizes spiritual poverty [EC].

16:16 **And he-gathered them to the place called in-Hebrew Armageddon.**[a]

LEXICON—a. Ἀρμαγεδών (LN 93.414) (BAGD p. 107): 'Armageddon' [BAGD, BNTC, LN, WBC; all versions except NRSV, TNT], 'Harmagedon' [EC; NRSV], 'Har-Magedon' [Lns; TNT]. Ἀρμαγεδών is the mystic name of a place that will be the scene of the final battle of the forces of good and evil [LN].

QUESTION—Who is the antecedent of the pronoun 'he' in συνήγαγεν 'he gathered'?

1. The pronoun 'he' may refer to God himself [Wal]. KJV also translates 'he'.
2. The neuter singular should be taken to indicate 'they' rather than 'he' and refers to the 'the spirits' of verse 13 and 14 [Be, EC, Hu, Ld, Lns, NIGTC, NTC, Sw, TH, TNTC, WBC; NAB, NCV, NET, REB, TEV]: *the spirits* gathered them. The following versions also translate 'they': NIV, NLT, and NRSV.

QUESTION—Who is the antecedent of the pronoun αὐτούς 'them'?

The antecedent is 'the kings of the whole earth' of verse 14 [Be, EC, Hu, Ld, NIC, NIGTC, Sw, TH, TNTC, Wal]: they gathered *the kings*.

QUESTION—What is Armageddon and what does it symbolize?

No satisfactory explanation has yet been found as to what it specifically refers [BAGD, Be, ICC, Lns, NIC, TNTC]. It is a mystical name that symbolizes the place where the final battle between the forces of good and evil will take place [Alf, Be, Ld, LN, Lns, NIC, TNTC, WBC]. Armageddon in Hebrew means 'the hill of Megiddo'. At the plain of Megiddo in Northern Palestine several important battles took place (Judges 5:19; 2 Kings 23:29; 2 Chronicles 35:22) [TH]. The Mount of Megiddo was east of the plain of Megiddo and southwest of the large plain of Esdraelon [Wal]. It symbolizes the whole world where the last battle against Christ and his followers will take place [NIGTC]. It symbolizes worldwide revolt [Hu]. It symbolizes Rome [BNTC].

DISCOURSE UNIT: 16:17–18:24 [EC]. The topic is the seventh bowl: Babylon's destruction [EC].

DISCOURSE UNIT: 16:17–21 [EC, Ld, NIGTC, TNTC]. The topic is the seventh bowl.

16:17 **And the seventh (angel) poured-out his bowl on the air, and (a) loud voice came out-of the temple from the throne saying, "It has happened."**

TEXT—Some manuscripts include ἄγγελος 'angel' after ὁ ἕβδομος 'the seventh'. GNT does not mention this alternative. The reading 'angel' is included by TR and KJV and possibly all versions.

TEXT—Instead of ἐπί 'on', some manuscripts have εἰς 'into'. GNT does not mention this alternative. The reading 'into' is taken by TR and KJV and possibly NAB, NCV, NET, NIV, NLT, NRSV, TNT.

TEXT—Instead of ναοῦ ἀπὸ τοῦ θρόνου 'temple from the throne', some manuscripts have οὐρανοῦ 'heaven', others have οὐρανοῦ ἀπὸ τοῦ θρόνου 'heaven from the throne', still others have ναοῦ τοῦ οὐρανοῦ ἀπὸ τοῦ θρόνου 'temple of heaven from the throne'. One important manuscript has ναοῦ τοῦ θεοῦ 'temple of God', another has ναοῦ τοῦ οὐρανοῦ ἀπὸ τοῦ θρόνου τοῦ θεοῦ 'temple of heaven from the throne of God'. GNT selects the reading ναοῦ ἀπὸ τοῦ θρόνου 'temple from the throne' with an A decision, indicating that the text is certain. The reading 'temple of heaven from the throne' is taken by TR and KJV and possibly NLT.

QUESTION—Whose voice does John hear?
He hears the voice of God [Alf, Be, EC, Ld, NIC, TH, Wal] as the phrase ἀπὸ τοῦ θρόνου 'from the throne' confirms [Alf, Be, EC, Ld, TH]. The same voice had commanded the seven angels to empty their bowls in 16:1 [Alf, Be, EC, Ld]. It is either the voice of God or the voice of Christ as it was in 16:1 [NIGTC]. It is a divine voice as it was in 16:1 [ICC]. Since it comes from the throne we can conclude it has God's approval [TNTC].

QUESTION—To what does γέγονεν 'it has happened' refer?
It refers to these seven bowl judgments and with them the wrath of God as seen in 15:1 [Alf, Be, EC, ICC, NIC, NIGTC, Sw, TH, WBC]. Since they are the last plagues, if they are finished, all is finished [Alf]. It refers to God's judgment [Hu].

QUESTION—In what sense should γέγονεν 'it has happened' be taken?
It should be taken proleptically, that is, as referring to future action as though it were already finished. The details of this action will in fact be spelled out in the following context [Alf, Be, EC, Ld, NIGTC].

16:18 And there-came lightning and sounds and thunder and (a) great earthquake, such-as[a] not occurred since man was on the earth, so-mighty[b] (an) earthquake, so[c] great.

TEXT—Instead of ἀστραπαὶ καὶ φωναὶ καὶ βρονταί 'lightnings and voices and thunders', some manuscripts have ἀστραπαὶ καὶ βρονταὶ καὶ φωναί 'lightnings and thunders and voices', others have βρονταὶ καὶ ἀστραπαὶ καὶ φωναί 'thunders and lightnings and voices', others have ἀστραπαὶ καὶ βρονταί 'lightnings and thunders', others have ἀστραπαὶ καὶ φωναί 'lightnings and voices', still others may possibly have φωναὶ καὶ βρονταὶ καὶ ἀστραπαί 'voices and thunders and lightnings'. GNT does not mention these alternatives. The reading 'voices and thunders and lightnings' is taken by TR and KJV.

TEXT—Instead of ἄνθρωπος ἐγένετο 'man was' some manuscripts have οἱ ἄνθρωποι ἐγένοντο 'men were'. GNT does not mention this alternative. The reading 'men were' is taken by TR and KJV.

LEXICON—a. οἷος (LN 64.1) (BAGD p. 562): 'such as' [BAGD, EC, LN, WBC; KJV, NRSV], 'such a one as' [Lns], 'such' [TEV], 'greater than' [NLT, TNT], 'worst' [CEV, NCV], 'its like' [BNTC], 'like' [LN], 'of what sort' [BAGD], not explicit [NAB, NET, NIV, REB].
  b. τηλικοῦτος (LN **78.36**) (BAGD 2. p. 814): 'so mighty' [BAGD, EC; KJV], 'so great' [BAGD, **LN**, WBC], 'so tremendous' [NET, NIV], 'so violent' [BNTC; NRSV, REB], 'such a violent' [NAB], 'such' [Lns], 'that great, so much' [LN], not explicit [CEV, NCV, NLT, TEV, TNT].
  c. οὕτω (LN 78.4) (BAGD 3. p. 598): 'so' [BAGD, EC, LN, Lns; KJV], 'so much' [LN], not explicit [BNTC, WBC; all versions except KJV].

QUESTION—What is the significance of the repetition of the intensifiers in the phrase τηλικοῦτος σεισμὸς οὕτω μέγας '*so mighty* an earthquake *so great*'?

The repetition emphasizes the strength of the earthquake [Be, EC, Sw, TNTC]. The emphasis is also seen in the adjective μέγας 'great' that first describes the earthquake [EC]. The negative modifier, *such as has not occurred since man was on the earth* plus two positives *so mighty...so great* serve to heighten the greatness of this phenomenon [TNTC].

QUESTION—Where else in Revelation do such atmospheric phenomena occur?

They also occur at the beginning of the trumpet judgments 8:5, and following the blowing of the seventh trumpet 11:19 [Alf, EC, Ld, NIC, TH, Wal, WBC]. They also occur at 4:5 [NIC, TH, WBC].

QUESTION—What is the significance of these phenomena?

They signify God's judgment [EC, NIGTC, Wal]. They signify God's glory and power [Ld]. They signify the end of the world [NIGTC].

QUESTION—What prophecy does this earthquake fulfill?

It fulfills the prophecy of Haggai 2:6 at which God promises to shake the earth one final time (see also Hebrews 12:26, 27) [EC, Hu, Sw]. It refers to the time of trouble prophesied in Daniel 12:1 [Hu, NIGTC, WBC].

DISCOURSE UNIT: 16:19–19:10 [REB]. The topic is the destruction of Babylon.

16:19 **And the great city was (split) into three parts and the cities of-the nations fell.**

QUESTION—To what does 'the great city' refer?
1. It refers to Babylon and is the same as 'Babylon the great' [Ld, Lns, NIGTC, TH]. Babylon symbolizes the evil world system [NIGTC].
2. It refers to Rome and is the same as 'Babylon the great' [Alf, Be, ICC, NIC, Sw].
3. It refers either to Rome (spiritual Babylon) or to the city of Babylon on the Euphrates River and is the same as 'Babylon the great' [Wal].
4. It refers to Babylon-Rome and is the same as 'Babylon the great' [WBC].
5. It refers to Sodom and Egypt and is the same as 'Babylon the great' (see 11:8) [Hu].
6. It refers to civilized man apart from God and is the same as 'Babylon the great' [TNTC].

7. It refers to Jerusalem and is different from 'Babylon the great' [EC]. Revelation 11:8 and the fact that this city is contrasted with 'the cities of the nations/Gentiles' supports this view. 'Babylon the great' should be identified with the city located on the Euphrates River [EC].
8. It refers to the world city and is different from 'Babylon the great' [NTC]. 'Babylon the great' refers to Rome [NTC].

QUESTION—What is the significance of becoming split into three parts?
It signifies the completeness of the destruction [Ld, NIC, TNTC]. It does not mean three literal parts but simply signifies utter destruction [Lns]. It signifies the breaking of Babylon's power [Hu].

QUESTION—What is signified by αἱ πόλεις τῶν ἐθνῶν ἔπεσαν 'the cities of the nations fell'?
It signifies that they were destroyed [Be, Ld, WBC]. The phrase shows that the destruction was worldwide [NIGTC, Sw, WBC]. It signifies that they no longer existed as a place for normal life [TH].

And Babylon the great was-remembered before God to-give her the cup of-the wine of-the fury of his wrath.

QUESTION—Who is the implied agent of the passive ἐμνήσθη 'was remembered'?
The agent is God [EC, NIC, TH, TNTC, WBC; CEV, NAB, NCV, NIV, NLT, NRSV, REB, TEV]: God remembered.

QUESTION—What is indicated by δοῦναι αὐτῇ τὸ ποτήριον 'to give her the cup'?
It means 'to cause her to drink from the cup' [Alf, Ld, TH; CEV, NLT, REB, TEV].

QUESTION—How are the nouns related in the genitive construction τὸ ποτήριον τοῦ οἴνου 'the cup of the wine'?
1. The cup contains the wine [EC, Lns, TH; NAB, NCV, NET, NIV, NLT, REB, TEV]: the cup containing wine.
2. Wine modifies cup [BNTC; CEV, NRSV]: the wine cup.

QUESTION—How are the nouns related in the genitive construction τοῦ οἴνου τοῦ θυμοῦ τῆς ὀργῆς αὐτοῦ 'the wine of the fury of his wrath'?
1. The fury of his wrath is in apposition to wine [EC, Lns, NIGTC, WBC; CEV, NET, TEV]: wine, *that is*, his fierce anger.
2. The wine either represents or brings God's wrath [TH].

QUESTION—How are the nouns related in the genitive construction τοῦ θυμοῦ τῆς ὀργῆς αὐτοῦ 'the fury of his wrath'?
1. The fury modifies his wrath [EC, Lns, NIC, NIGTC, TH, WBC; NCV, NET, NLT, TNT]: his furious wrath.
2. Wrath and fury are coordinate [NAB]: fury and wrath.

16:20 **And every island fled[a] and (the) mountains were- not -found.**
LEXICON—a. aorist act. indic. of φεύγω (LN **13.65, 24.6**) (BAGD 5. p. 856): 'to flee' [EC, Lns, WBC; NAB], 'to flee away' [KJV, NET, NIV, NRSV], 'to run away' [CEV, NCV], 'to disappear quickly' [**LN** (13.65, 4.6)], 'to

disappear' [BAGD; NLT, TEV], 'to vanish' [BAGD, BNTC; REB, TNT], 'to become invisible' [LN], 'to cease quickly' [LN (13.65)]. Θέργω may indicate 'to become invisible' or 'to rapidly cease to exist' [LN].

QUESTION—What is signified by πᾶσα νῆσος ἔφυγεν 'every island fled'?
It signifies that the islands disappeared [BAGD, BNTC, LN, TH; NLT, REB, TEV, TNT]. It signifies that they sank into the sea [Be, EC].

QUESTION—What is signified by ὄρη οὐ εὑρέθησαν 'mountains were not found'?
It signifies that the mountains disappeared [ICC, NIC, TH, Wal, WBC; NAB, NCV, TEV, TNT]. The passive use of εὑρίσκω 'to find' with the negative can mean 'to disappear' [BAGD (1.b. p. 325), WBC]. It signifies that they were leveled [NLT].

16:21 And great hailstones[a] about[b] weighing-a-talent[c] comes-down from heaven on men, and men blasphemed God because-of the plague of hail, because extremely[d] great is the plague of-it.

LEXICON—a. χάλαζα (LN 2.13): 'hailstone' [BNTC, WBC; CEV, NAB, NCV, NET, NIV, NRSV, REB, TEV], 'hail' [EC, LN, Lns], 'hailstorm' [**LN**; NLT, TNT]. See this word also at 8:7.

b. ὡς (LN 78.42) (BAGD IV.5. p. 899): 'about' [BAGD, BNTC, EC, LN; CEV, KJV, NCV, NET, NIV, NRSV], 'approximately' [BAGD, LN], 'nearly' [BAGD, WBC], 'as much as' [REB, TEV], 'as of' [Lns], 'like' [NAB], not explicit [TNT].

c. ταλαντιαῖος (LN 86.5) (BAGD p. 803): 'weighing a talent' [BAGD, EC, LN, Lns; KJV, TNT], 'weighing a hundred pounds' [WBC; CEV, NCV, NET, NIV, NRSV, TEV], 'weighing a hundredweight' [BAGD, BNTC; REB], 'weighing ninety pounds' [**LN**], 'weighing seventy-five pounds' [NLT], 'huge weights' [NAB].

d. σφόδρα (LN 78.19) (BAGD p. 796): 'extremely' [BAGD], 'exceedingly' [EC, LN, Lns], 'exceeding' [KJV], 'terrible' [**LN**, WBC; CEV, NCV, NIV, NLT, TEV], 'severe' [BNTC; NAB, REB], 'horrendous' [NET], 'fearful' [NRSV], 'great' [TNT], 'greatly' [BAGD, LN], 'violently' [LN], 'very much' [BAGD]. The phrase modifying 'plague', μεγάλη...σφόδρα 'great...extremely' is translated: 'so severe' [BNTC; NAB, REB], 'so terrible' [WBC; CEV, NCV, NIV], 'such (a) terrible' [TEV], 'very terrible' [NLT], 'so horrendous' [NET], 'exceeding(ly) great' [EC, Lns; KJV]. 'very great' [TNT]. Σφόδρα indicates a very high degree on a scale of intensity and in many contexts implies vehemence or violence [LN].

QUESTION—How much did ταλαντιαία 'weighing a talent' indicate?
It indicated between 60 and 130 pounds [Be]. It indicated between 108 and 130 pounds [EC, ICC]. It indicated between 60 and more than 100 pounds [Lns, NIC]. It indicated between 80 and 120 pounds [TH]. It indicated about 90 pounds (English weight) or 40 kilograms [LN]. It indicated a bit over 100 pounds [Ld].

QUESTION—What is symbolized by hail in Scripture?
It symbolizes the judgment of God (see Joshua 10:11; Job 38:22–23; Isaiah 28:2, 17; Ezekiel 13:11–13, 38.22) [EC, Hu, NIC].

QUESTION—In what sense is οἱ ἄνθρωποι 'the men' used in this verse and who are these men?
It refers to people in general [Alf, EC, Lns, TH, WBC; CEV, NAB, NCV, NET, NLT, REB, TEV]. It refers to those who worshiped the beast [EC, Lns].

DISCOURSE UNIT: 17:1–21:8 [Ld]. The topic is the third vision [Ld].

DISCOURSE UNIT: 17:1–20:15 [TNTC]. The topic is the triumph of Almighty God.

DISCOURSE UNIT: 17:1–20:10 [TH]. The topic is the destruction of Babylon, the defeat of the Beast, the False Prophet and the Devil.

DISCOURSE UNIT: 17:1–19:21 [NIGTC]. The topic is the final judgment of Babylon and the beast [NIGTC].

DISCOURSE UNIT: 17:1–19:10 [Alf, EC, Lns, WBC]. The topic is the judgment of Babylon [Alf, WBC; NAB], the great whore [Lns].

DISCOURSE UNIT: 17:1–19:5 [Be, Hu, NIC, NTC]. The topic is the destruction of Rome by the Antichrist [BNTC], the fall of Babylon the great [Hu, NIC], Babylon the great [NTC].

DISCOURSE UNIT: 17:1–18:8 [Hu]. The topic is the judgment of the great harlot.

DISCOURSE UNIT: 17:1–18 [BNTC, EC, GNT, Ld, NIC, NIGTC, NTC, TNTC, Wal; CEV, NCV, NET, NIV, NLT, NRSV, TEV]. The topic is the last days of Babylon [BNTC, EC, Wal], the great harlot and the beast [GNT, NIC; CEV, NCV, NET, NIV, NRSV], the mystery of Babylon [Ld], the scarlet woman [NTC; NLT, TEV], the judgment of the great whore [TNTC; KJV].

DISCOURSE UNIT: 17:1–6 [Alf, Be, BNTC, NIC, Sw, TNTC]. The topic is Babylon the harlot [Alf], the woman on the scarlet beast [Be, TNTC], the great whore [BNTC], the vision [NIC], Babylon seated on the beast [Sw].

DISCOURSE UNIT: 17:1–6a [EC; NAB]. The topic is the harlot and the beast [EC], Babylon the great [NAB].

17:1 And one of the seven angels having the seven bowls came and spoke with me saying, "Come, I-will-show you the judgment[a] of-the the great prostitute[b] sitting on[c] many waters,

TEXT—Some manuscripts include μοι 'to me' after λέγων 'saying'. GNT does not mention this alternative. 'To me' is included by TR, KJV.

TEXT—Instead of ὑδάτων πολλῶν 'many waters', some manuscripts have τῶν ὑδάτων τῶν πολλῶν 'many waters'. GNT does not mention this alternative. The reading with the articles is included by TR.

LEXICON—a. κρίμα (LN 30.110, 56.24, 56.30) (BAGD 4.b. p. 450): 'judgment' [EC, LN (30.110, 56.24), Lns, WBC; KJV, NAB, NLT, NRSV, TNT], 'condemnation and punishment' [BAGD; NET], 'punishment' [TH, TNTC; NCV, NIV], 'verdict' [LN (56.24), Lns; REB], 'condemnation' [LN (56.30), TH], 'decision, evaluation' [LN (30.110)], 'sentence' [LN (56.24)]. This noun is also translated as a verb: 'to punish' [CEV, TEV], 'to pass sentence on' [BNTC].

b. πόρνη (LN 88.275) (BAGD 2. p. 693): 'prostitute' [BAGD, LN; all versions except KJV, NRSV, REB], 'harlot' [BAGD, EC], 'whore' [BNTC, Lns, WBC; KJV, NRSV, REB]. Πόρνη is used figuratively here to indicate a government that is hostile to God and his people [BAGD].

c. ἐπί (LN 83.23, 83.46): 'on' [BNTC, LN (83.46); CEV, NET, NIV, NRSV, TNT], 'upon' [LN (83.46), Lns; KJV], 'by' [LN (83.23), NIC, TH, WBC], 'at' [LN (83.23)], 'near' [NIC, TH; NAB, TEV], 'beside' [EC], 'over' [NCV, REB]. The preposition ἐπί can mean 'on the shore of' (see John 21:1) [Be, EC].

QUESTION—How are the nouns related in the genitive construction τὸ κρίμα τῆς πόρνης 'the judgment of the prostitute'?

Someone will judge the prostitute [BNTC, EC, Lns, NIGTC, TH, WBC; CEV, NAB, NCV, NLT, REB, TEV, TNT].

QUESTION—Who is the implied actor of the event noun κρίμα 'judgment'?

The implied actor is God [TH; CEV]: God will judge the great prostitute.

QUESTION—What does 'the prostitute' symbolize?

She symbolizes: civilized man apart from God and a world empire dominating many nations [TNTC], a seductive appeal to draw people away from Christ [NIGTC], an authoritarian world system that seduces people for its own benefit [NIC], the world's people organized in opposition to God [Ld], ungodly civilization estranged from God [Hu], counterfeit religion [EC, Wal], a false religious system [EC, Wal], an economic-religious system [NIGTC], antichristian seduction [Lns].

QUESTION—What is symbolized by prostitution?

It indicates the perversion of everything for financial gain [Ld]. It indicates the perversion of everything good for power and luxury [NIC]. It indicates idolatry or a turning away from God [EC, Hu].

QUESTION—What entity may 'the prostitute' symbolize?

1. She symbolizes Babylon [EC, Hu, Ld, Lns, NIGTC, TNTC, Wal]. Babylon is situated on 'many waters' in that the Euphrates river runs through it and there is a network of canals in and around the city (see Jeremiah 51:13) [EC, Ld, NIGTC, TNTC].
2. She symbolizes Rome [Be, BNTC, ICC, NIC, NTC, WBC]. This is supported by the description in verse 17:18 [Be].
3. She symbolizes papal Rome [Alf].

QUESTION—In what sense is 'great' used to describe the prostitute?

It is used in the sense of notorious, infamous, or powerful [TH].

QUESTION—What do 'the waters' symbolize?

They symbolize peoples and multitudes and nations and languages (see 17:15) [Alf, EC, Hu, Lns, NIC, NTC, Sw, TNTC, WBC].

QUESTION—What is indicated by the 'sitting' position of the prostitute?

It indicates that she rules over that on which she is seated [Lns, NIGTC, TNTC, Wal, WBC].

17:2 **With whom the kings of-the earth committed-fornication^a and the-ones living-on the earth became-drunk^b from the wine of her fornication.**

TEXT—Some manuscripts possibly place the phrase οἱ κατοικοῦντες τὴν γῆν 'the ones inhabiting the earth' at the end of this verse instead of following ἐμεθύσθησαν 'have been made drunk', although GNT does not mention this alternative. TR places the phrase at the end of the verse.

LEXICON—a. aorist act. indic. of πορνεύω (BAGD 2. p. 693): 'to commit fornication' [BNTC, EC; KJV, NRSV, REB], 'to fornicate' [WBC], 'to commit adultery' [NIV], 'to commit whoredom' [Lns], 'to practice sexual immorality' [BAGD; TEV], 'to practice sexual vice' [TNT], 'to have immoral relations with' [NLT], 'to commit sexual immorality' [NET], 'to sin sexually' [NCV], 'to sleep with' [CEV], 'to have intercourse with' [NAB]. Πορνεύω is used figuratively here to indicate 'practice idolatry' [BAGD]. See this word also at 2:14.

b. aorist pass. indic. of μεθύσκομαι, μεθύσκω (LN 88.285) (BAGD p. 499): 'to become drunk' [WBC; NAB, NCV, NRSV, TEV, TNT], 'to get drunk' [BAGD, EC, LN; NET], 'to become intoxicated' [BAGD], 'to make drunk' [CEV], 'to make oneself drunk' [BNTC; REB], 'to be made drunk' [Lns; KJV, NLT], 'to be intoxicated' [NIV].

QUESTION—What is the point of similarity in the verb ἐμεθύσθησαν 'they got drunk'?

The point of similarity is insensitivity and loss of mental sharpness. They become insensitive to God as their true source of security and they become numb to any concern of coming judgment [NIGTC].

QUESTION—How are the nouns related in the genitive construction τοῦ οἴνου τῆς πορνείας αὐτῆς 'the wine of her fornication'?

1. Wine is her fornication [TH, WBC]: the wine, *that is*, her fornication.
2. Wine causes or results in fornication [Ld, NIGTC]: wine *resulting in* fornication with her. She uses wine to entice the nations to share her evil character [Ld].
3. Her fornication is like wine [CEV].

QUESTION—How are the nouns related in the genitive construction τῆς πορνείας αὐτῆς 'the fornication of her'?

1. Fornication is in association with her [NIGTC]: fornication *with* her.
1. She uses fornication to seduce those living on earth [Be, Ld].

QUESTION—What is indicated by fornication?
  It indicates idolatry involving worshiping the beast [EC, NIC]. It indicates alliances with the world system for economic prosperity [Ld, NIGTC, WBC]. These alliances probably involve some kind of idolatry [Ld, NIGTC].

17:3 And he-carried-away[a] me in spirit into (a) wilderness.[b] And I-saw (a) woman sitting on (a) scarlet[c] beast, being-filled[d] (with) names of-blasphemy, having seven heads and ten horns.
LEXICON—a. aorist act. indic. of ἀποφέρω (LN 15.202) (BAGD 1.a.α. p. 101): 'to carry away' [BAGD, BNTC, EC, LN; KJV, NAB, NCV, NET, NIV, NRSV, TNT], 'to carry' [WBC; REB, TEV], 'to bear away' [Lns], 'to take' [CEV, NLT], 'to take away' [BAGD, LN].
  b. ἔρημος (LN 1.86) (BAGD 2. p. 309): 'wilderness' [BAGD, EC, LN, Lns; KJV, NET, NLT, NRSV, REB, TNT], 'desert' [BAGD, BNTC, LN, WBC; CEV, NCV, NIV, TEV], 'deserted place' [NAB]. An ἔρημος is a mainly uninhabited area, usually with sparse vegetation [LN]. See this word also at 12:6.
  c. κόκκινος (LN 79.29) (BAGD p. 440): 'scarlet' [BAGD, BNTC, EC, LN, Lns, WBC; NAB, NET, NIV, NLT, NRSV, REB, TNT], 'red' [BAGD, LN; CEV, NCV, TEV], 'scarlet-colored' [KJV].
  d. pres. act. participle of γέμω (BAGD 3. p. 153): 'to be full' [BAGD, EC, LN; KJV, NET, NRSV], 'to be filled' [Lns], 'to be covered' [BNTC, WBC; CEV, NAB, NCV, NIV, REB, TNT], 'to be written all over' [NLT, TEV], 'to contain' [LN]. See this word also at 4:6.
QUESTION—Who carried away John?
  'He' refers to the angel of verse 1 [Alf, Lns].
QUESTION—What is indicated by the phrase ἐν πνεύματι 'in spirit' (see this question also at 1:10)?
  1. It indicates being in God's Spirit [Ld, NIGTC, Sw, TH, TNTC; CEV, NCV, NIV, TEV, TNT]. It was an ecstatic experience [Ld, TH, TNTC]. God's Spirit made it possible for John to see the vision [NIGTC, TH]. That John is under the influence of the Spirit stresses that the message comes from God [NIGTC]. The action happens in John's spirit but the power comes from God's Spirit [Sw]. The Spirit makes John receptive to the vision [TNTC].
  2. It indicates a special state of John's own spirit [Alf, BNTC, EC, Lns, Wal, WBC; KJV, NAB, NET, NLT, NRSV, REB]. This was a state of spiritual ecstasy or trance [Alf, NIC, Wal, WBC]. It is a prophetic trance [EC, WBC]. This made John receptive to the vision that he would experience [Alf].
  1. It indicates either of the above [Hu].

QUESTION—On which beast is the woman sitting?
It refers to the same beast that emerged from the sea (see 13:1) [Alf, BNTC, EC, Hu, Ld, Lns, NIC, NIGTC, NTC, Sw, TH, TNTC, Wal]. Revelation 19:19, 20 confirm this identification [Alf, EC]. This is the Antichrist [Ld].

QUESTION—What is the significance of the color κόκκινος 'scarlet'?
It signifies: splendor [EC, NTC, Sw, TNTC], magnificence [Sw], luxury, [EC], sin [Lns, TNTC], persecuting nature [NIGTC], blood [Alf]. It is the same color as the πυρρός 'red' dragon in 12:3 [Be, Ld]. The Greek words for the color are different, but the basic color (red) is the same [Ld]. It identifies him with the dragon of 12:3 [Ld, NIC, NIGTC]. Or, it simply intensifies the dreadful appearance of the beast [NIC].

QUESTION—What is indicated by the woman καθημένην 'sitting' on the beast?
It indicates a position of dominance over the beast [Alf, EC, Lns, Wal, WBC]. It indicates that the woman guides the beast [Alf, Wal]. It indicates dependence on the beast for transportation [Lns]. She is supported by the political strength of the beast [Wal]. It indicates a close association with the beast that supports her [TNTC]. It indicates an alliance with the beast [NIGTC].

QUESTION—What is represented by the woman and the beast?
The woman symbolizes the apostate church and the beast symbolizes the revived Roman Empire [Wal]. The woman represents the false religion that causes the empire represented by the beast to cohere together [EC]. The beast represents the antichristian power while the woman represents the antichristian seduction [Lns]. The beast represents the ungodly government while the woman represents the social, cultural, economic, and religious aspects of the government [NIGTC]. The woman represents Rome and she is maintained by the Roman Empire, the beast [NTC].

QUESTION—How are the nouns related in the genitive construction ὀνόματα βλασφημίας 'names of blasphemy'?
The second noun modifies the first [BNTC, NIGTC, WBC; CEV, NAB, NCV, NET, NIV, NLT, NRSV, REB, TEV, TNT]: blasphemous names.

QUESTION—What is indicated by βλασφημίας 'blasphemy'?
It indicates the act of ascribing to oneself the attributes of God and so insulting God [EC, Ld, NIC, Sw, TH].

17:4 And the woman was dressed-in purple[a] and scarlet[b] and adorned[c] with-gold[d] and precious[e] stones and pearls,[f] having (a) golden cup in her hand being-full of-obscenities[g] and the impurities of her fornication

TEXT—Instead of ἦν περιβεβλημένη 'was dressed', some manuscripts possibly read ἡπεριβεβλημένη 'the one dressed', although GNT does not mention this alternative. The reading 'the dressed one' is taken by TR.

TEXT—Instead of the accusative cases πορφυροῦν καὶ κόκκινον 'purple and scarlet', some manuscripts possibly read the dative cases πορφύρᾳ καὶ κοκκίνῳ, although GNT does not mention this alternative. The dative-case reading is taken by TR.

TEXT—Instead of τὰ ἀκάθαρτα 'the impurities', some manuscripts possibly read ἀκαθάρτητος 'impurities' although GNT does not mention this alternative. The reading 'impurities' is taken by TR and KJV.

TEXT—Instead of πορνείας αὐτῆς 'her fornication', some manuscripts have πορνείας τῆς γῆς 'fornication of the earth' and others have πορνείας αὐτῆς καὶ τῆς γῆς 'fornication of her and of the earth'. GNT selects the reading 'her fornication' with a B decision, indicating that the text is almost certain.

LEXICON—a. πορφυροῦν (LN **6.169**) (BAGD p. 694): 'purple' [BNTC, EC, Lns, WBC; NAB, NCV, NIV, NRSV, REB, TEV, TNT], 'purple cloth' [BAGD, **LN**], 'purple clothing' [NET, NLT], 'purple robe' [CEV], 'purple garment' [BAGD], 'purple color' [KJV]. Πορφυροῦν is a reddish-purple cloth dyed with a substance obtained from the murex shellfish [LN].

b. κόκκινον (LN **6.170**): 'scarlet' [BNTC, EC, Lns, WBC; NAB, NIV, NRSV, REB, TEV, TNT], 'scarlet cloth' [**LN**], 'scarlet clothing' [NET, NLT], 'scarlet robe' [CEV], 'scarlet color' [KJV], 'red' [NCV]. Κόκκινον is obtained from a worm called a *kermas* [EC]. See this word also at 17:3.

c. perfect pass. participle of χρυσόομαι, χρυσόω (LN **49.29**) (BAGD p. 889): 'to be adorned' [**LN**, WBC; NAB, NET, NRSV, TNT], 'to be covered' [TEV], 'to be bejeweled' [BNTC], 'to be decked' [EC; KJV], 'to be decked out' [REB], 'to be shining' [NCV], 'to be glittering' [NIV], 'to be goldened' [Lns], 'to be gilded' [BAGD], 'to be adorned with gold' [BAGD, LN], 'to be dressed with gold, to be covered with gold adornments' [LN], 'to be made golden' [BAGD]. This word is also translated actively: 'to wear' [CEV, NLT]. The phrase κεχρυσωμένη χρυσίῳ 'being adorned with gold with gold' involves semantic redundancy or what one may also speak of as semantic reinforcement [LN].

d. χρυσίον (LN **6.189**) (BAGD p. 888): 'gold' [BNTC, EC, Lns; KJV, NAB, NCV, NET, NIV, NRSV, REB], 'gold ornaments' [**LN**, WBC; TEV], 'gold jewelry' [LN; CEV, NLT], 'golden jewelry' [BAGD; TNT].

e. τίμιος (LN 65.2) (BAGD 1.a. p. 818): 'precious' [BAGD, BNTC, EC, LN, Lns, WBC; all versions except NRSV], 'valuable' [LN], 'costly' [BAGD]. The phrase λίθῳ τιμίῳ 'with precious stones' is translated: 'with jewels' [NRSV].

f. μαργαρίτης (LN 2.43) (BAGD 1. p. 491): 'pearl' [BAGD, BNTC, EC, LN, Lns, WBC; all versions].

g. βδέλυγμα (LN 25.187) (BAGD 2. p. 138): 'obscenity' [BNTC; NLT, REB], 'obscene thing' [TEV], 'abomination' [BAGD, EC, Lns, WBC; KJV, NRSV, TNT], 'abominable thing' [NIV], 'abominable deed' [NAB],

'detestable thing' [BAGD; NET], 'evil thing' [NCV], 'nasty thing' [CEV], 'what is detestable, what is abhorrent' [LN].
QUESTION—What is meant by βδελυγμάτων 'obscenities'?
It refers to idolatry [WBC]. Βδέλυγμα is used in the OT to indicate idolatry and that is its significance here [EC, Ld, NIC, Sw, TNTC].
QUESTION—What is meant by ἀκάθαρτα 'impurities'?
It is associated in the NT with idolatry (see 2 Corinthians 6:17) [EC]. In Revelation John uses this word to refer to the demonic and, since demons are behind idols, to idolatry [NIGTC]. In general it indicates immorality but also implies the demonic and false gods [BNTC].
QUESTION—What relationship is indicated by καί 'and' in the phrase 'obscenities and impurities'?
The καί 'and' is explanatory [Lns, NIC, NIGTC, TNTC]: the obscenities, *that is*, the impurities of her fornication.
QUESTION—How are the nouns related in the genitive construction βδελυγμάτων τὰ ἀκάθαρτα τῆς πορνείας αὐτῆς 'the obscenities and impurities of her fornication'?
Obscenities and impurities are the result of her fornication [TEV]: the obscenities and impurities *resulting from* her fornication.
QUESTION—What is symbolized by the colors purple and scarlet?
Purple symbolizes royalty [Alf, EC, Lns, NIC, NIGTC, TH, TNTC, WBC]. Scarlet symbolizes splendor [NIC]. Scarlet symbolizes luxury and splendor [EC, Sw, WBC]. Purple and scarlet symbolize luxury [Be, Ld, NIC, TH] and splendor [Be, Ld, NIC]. Only the wealthy could afford these dyes because they were costly to extract [NIC, TNTC]. Scarlet symbolizes the persecuting nature of the woman [NIGTC].

17:5 And (a) name was-written on her forehead "Mystery,[a] Babylon the great, the mother[b] of prostitutes and of-the abominations of-the earth."
LEXICON—a. μυστήριον (LN 28.77) (BAGD 3. p. 530): 'mystery' [BAGD, BNTC, EC, LN, Lns; KJV, NET, NIV, NRSV]. This noun is also translated as an adjective: 'mysterious (name)' [WBC; CEV, NLT], 'cryptic (name)' [TNT], 'symbolic (name)' [BNTC; NAB]; as a phrase: 'with a secret meaning' [REB]; and as a clause: 'that was secret' [NCV], 'that had a secret meaning' [TEV]. See this word at 1:20.
b. μήτηρ (LN 58.64, 10.16) (BAGD 5. p. 520): 'mother' [BAGD, BNTC, EC, LN (58.64, 10.16), Lns, WBC; all versions], 'archetype' [LN (58.64)], 'spiritual mother' [LN (58.64)]. Μήτηρ may indicate an archetype anticipating a later reality and suggesting a derivative relationship [LN (58.64)].
QUESTION—What is implied by having the name on her forehead?
It was a mark of identification [EC]. It was customary for prostitutes to have their names on their foreheads [Alf, Be, Sw, WBC]. It could have been either on her skin or on a band like those worn by Roman prostitutes [EC, Lns]. The Roman prostitutes wore a headband that had their name on it [Be, ICC,

Ld, Lns, NIC, TNTC]. Being a tattooed slave indicated that she was the worse kind of prostitute [WBC]. Names on foreheads in Revelation announce the true character of the person or announce the person to whom they are closely allied [NIGTC].

QUESTION—Should the word μυστήριον 'mystery' be taken as part of the woman's title or is it part of the introduction to the title?

1. It should not be taken as part of the title, rather it modifies the name [BNTC, EC, Hu, Ld, NIC, NTC, Sw, TNTC, Wal, WBC; CEV, NAB, NCV, NET, NLT, NRSV, REB, TEV, TNT]: a mysterious name or a name, a mystery This interpretation is supported by 18:2 [EC, Wal], 14:8 [EC], and 16:19 [Wal]. The word 'mystery' is in apposition to Babylon [Sw]: Babylon, that is, mystery. As such it indicates that the name should not be taken literally but interpreted figuratively [Ld, NIC, NTC, WBC]. It does not indicate that the name should be taken figuratively [EC]. It indicates a name with a secret meaning [NIC].
2. It should be taken as part of the title [Alf, Lns; KJV, NIV]: Mystery, Babylon the great. As such it indicates that the name should not be taken literally but interpreted figuratively [Alf].
3. It could be either 1 or 2 above and indicates that the name should be taken symbolically [Be, NIGTC].

QUESTION—What is indicated by the phrase ἡ μήτηρ τῶν πορνῶν καὶ τῶν βδελυγμάτων τῆς γῆς 'the mother of prostitutes and of the abominations of the earth'?

It indicates that she is the source or origin of these things [Alf, Be, EC, NIC, Sw, TH, TNTC, WBC]. It may indicate that she is the prototype on which all others are patterned [Alf, WBC]. It indicates that she is the symbol of all that degrades society [Hu].

17:6 And I-saw the woman drunk from the blood of-the saints and from the blood of the witnesses[a] of-Jesus.

LEXICON—a. μάρτυς (LN **20.67**) (BAGD 3. p. 494): 'witness' [BAGD, BNTC, EC, Lns, WBC; NAB, NLT, NRSV, TNT], 'martyr' [BAGD, **LN**; KJV]. This noun is also translated as a clause: 'who had given their lives' [CEV], 'those who were killed because they had been loyal' [TEV], 'who were killed because of their faith' [NCV], 'those who testified' [NET], 'who bore testimony' [NIV, REB].

QUESTION—Are τῶν ἁγίων 'the saints' and τῶν μαρτύρων 'the witnesses' two different groups or one group?

1. They are the same group [Be, EC, Ld, Lns, NIC, NIGTC, Sw, TH, TNTC; CEV, NIV, NLT]: the saints, *that is* the witnesses. The second group more precisely defines the first group [Be, NIC, TH]. The blood is mentioned twice for emphasis [EC]. The repetition of blood heightens the guilt of Babylon [Sw]. The descriptions are repeated for emphasis [Lns, TNTC]. They are called saints because they belong to God and they are called martyrs because they have shed their blood [Ld].

2. They are two different groups [BNTC, Hu, Lns, WBC; KJV, NAB, NCV, NET, NRSV, REB, TEV, TNT]: the saints *and* the witnesses. The first group represents those who will be persecuted for living and witnessing for Jesus, the second are those who suffer martyrdom for him [Hu].

QUESTION—What is indicated by her being drunk?

It indicates that she was dominated by her activity of persecuting Christians [NIGTC]. It indicates that she enjoyed this activity [NIC, NIGTC, TNTC]. She was maddened by the sight of the killing [Be, EC]. She greatly desired violence and widespread killing [EC].

QUESTION—What is symbolized by 'blood'?

It symbolizes the murder of the prostitute's enemies [WBC].

QUESTION—How are the nouns related in the genitive construction τῶν μαρτύρων Ἰησοῦ 'the witnesses of Jesus'?

1. The witnesses testified about Jesus to others [EC, NIC, NIGTC, Sw, TH, WBC; CEV, NAB, NIV, NLT, NRSV, REB, TEV, TNT].
2. The witnesses believed in Jesus [NCV].

DISCOURSE UNIT: 17:6b–18 [NAB]. The topic is the meaning of the beast and the harlot.

DISCOURSE UNIT: 17:6b–14 [EC]. The topic is the significance of the symbolism.

17:6b And seeing her I marveled (with) great amazement.[a]

LEXICON—a. θαῦμα (LN **25.212**) (BAGD 2. p. 252): 'amazement' [BAGD, EC, **LN**], 'wonder' [BAGD, LN, Lns], 'admiration' [KJV]. The clause ἐθαύμασα...θαῦμα μέγα 'I marveled (with) great amazement' is translated: '(the sight) amazed (me)' [CEV], 'I was greatly amazed' [NAB, NRSV], 'I was very amazed' [NCV], 'I was greatly astounded' [NET], 'I was greatly astonished' [NIV, REB], 'I was completely amazed' [TEV], '(I stared) completely amazed' [NLT], 'I was utterly astonished' [TNT], '(I stared) in great wonder' [BNTC], 'I was very perplexed' [WBC].

QUESTION—What is the significance of the redundancy expressed in the statement ἐθαύμασα...θαῦμα μέγα 'I marveled...a marvel great'?

The clause 'I marveled a marvel' is emphatic. The addition of 'great' gives additional emphasis to it [EC].

DISCOURSE UNIT: 17:7–18 [Alf, Be, BNTC, NIC, Sw]. The topic is the vision interpreted [Alf, Be, BNTC, NIC, Sw].

DISCOURSE UNIT: 17:7–14 [Alf, TNTC]. The topic is the significance of the woman and the beast [TNTC], the explanation of the beast [Alf].

17:7 And the angel said to-me, "Why did-you-marvel? I will-tell you the mystery[a] of-the woman and of-the beast carrying[b] her the-one having the seven heads and the ten horns.

LEXICON—a. μυστήριον (LN 28.77) (BAGD 3. p. 530): 'mystery' [BAGD, EC, LN, Lns; CEV, KJV, NAB, NET, NIV, NLT, NRSV], 'secret' [LN; NCV, REB, TNT], 'secret meaning' [WBC; TEV], 'symbolism' [BNTC]. See this word at 1:20 and 17:5.

b. pres. act. participle of βαστάζω (LN 15.188) (BAGD 2.a. p. 137): 'to carry' [BAGD, LN, Lns; KJV, NAB, NET, NRSV, TEV, TNT], 'to bear' [BAGD, EC, LN, WBC], not explicit [NLT]. This verb is also translated reciprocally: 'to sit on' [CEV], 'to ride' [BNTC; NCV, NIV, REB].

QUESTION—What is implied by the rhetorical question, Διὰ τί ἐθαύμασας; 'Why did you marvel?'

1. It implies that the angel was reprimanding John for his surprise [NIGTC, TH]. The angel meant that John should have understood what he was seeing [TH].
2. It implies that there is some reason for John's amazement: he has unanswered questions in mind [Lns].

17:8 The beast that you-saw was and is not and is-about-to come-up from the abyss[a] and go[b] to destruction,[c] and the-ones living on the earth, whose name has- not -been-written in the book-of-life[d] from (the) foundation[e] of the world, will-be-amazed seeing the beast because/that it-was and is not and will-be-present[f]

TEXT—Instead of ὑπάγει 'he goes', some manuscripts have ὑπάγειν 'to go'. GNT selects the reading 'he goes' with a B decision indicating that the text is almost certain. The reading 'to go' is taken by TR.

TEXT—Instead of τὸ ὄνομα 'the name', some manuscripts have the plural τὰ ὀνόματα 'the names'. GNT does not mention this alternative. The plural reading is taken by TR.

TEXT—Instead of καὶ παρέσται 'and will be present', some manuscripts possibly read καίπερ ἐστίν 'although he is', although GNT does not mention this alternative. The reading 'although he is' is taken by TR and KJV.

LEXICON—a. ἄβυσσος (LN 1.20) (BAGD 2. p. 2): 'abyss' [BAGD, BNTC, EC, LN, Lns, WBC; NAB, NET, REB, TEV], 'Abyss' [NIV], 'bottomless pit' [KJV, NCV, NLT, NRSV, TNT], 'deep pit' [CEV]. See this word at 9:1.

b. pres. act. indic. of ὑπάγω (LN **13.54**) (BAGD 2. p. 836): 'to go' [BNTC **LN**, Lns; KJV, NET, NIV, NLT, NRSV, REB, TNT], 'to go away' [NCV], 'to go off' [TEV], 'to depart' [EC], 'to be headed (for)' [WBC; NAB]. The phrase εἰς ἀπώλειαν ὑπάγει 'he goes to destruction' is translated 'to be destroyed' [**LN**; CEV].

c. ἀπώλεια (LN 20.31) (BAGD 2. p. 103): 'destruction' [BAGD, LN, WBC; NCV, NET, NIV, NRSV, TNT], 'eternal destruction' [NLT],

'perdition' [BNTC, EC, Lns; KJV]. This noun is also translated as a verb: 'to be destroyed' [CEV, NCV, REB, TEV].
d. βιβλίον τῆς ζωῆς. This phrase is translated: 'book of life' [BNTC, EC, WBC; all versions except NLT, TEV], 'Book of Life' [NLT], 'Book of the Life' [Lns], 'book of the living' [TEV]. See this phrase also at 3:5 and 13:8.
e. καταβολή (LN 42.37) (BAGD 1. p. 409): 'foundation' [BAGD, BNTC, EC, Lns; KJV, NAB, REB], 'creation' [LN, WBC; CEV, NET, NIV, NRSV, TEV, TNT], 'beginning' [NCV, NLT]. See this word at 13:8.
f. future middle (deponent = active) indicative of πάρειμι (LN 85.23) (BAGD): 'to be present' [EC LN, Lns, WBC], 'to be' [BNTC; CEV], 'to come (again)' [NAB, NCV, TNT], '(yet) to come' [NIV], 'to be to come' [NET, NRSV], 'to appear' [REB], 'to be at hand' [LN]. This verb is also translated as a verbal noun: 'reappearance' [NLT].

QUESTION—Which beast does this refer to?
It refers to the beast that came up from the sea (see 13:1) [Be, BNTC, Ld, Lns, NIC, NIGTC, NTC, TH, TNTC, Wal, WBC]. This beast is the same as the little horn referred to in Daniel 7:19, 21 [NIC]. Also Daniel 7:3, 11, 17–18, 23, and 26 describe this beast [NIGTC].

QUESTION—To what time does 'is not' refer and what is meant by 'and will be present'?
It refers to the defeat of the beast at Christ's exaltation [Lns]. It refers to his defeat by Christ at his death and resurrection [NIGTC]. It means that he is dead [WBC]. After the beast's appearance on earth, the time came that he was no longer in evidence, but he shall ascend from the abyss [TNTC]. People will wonder at the beast's reappearance to the scene after it has disappeared for a time [Ld]. The beast had received a death blow on one of its seven heads, but when it recovered, the whole world would be amazed that the beast could not be defeated [Lns].

QUESTION—To whom does the description 'those whose name has not been written in the Lamb's book of life' refer?
It refers to the unbelieving people of the world [NIGTC, TNTC].

QUESTION—What is meant by the phrase 'goes to destruction'?
It refers to 19:20 and 20:10 where reference is made to the beast being thrown into the Lake of fire and brimstone [Lns, NIC, WBC]. 'Destruction' indicates 'eternal doom' (see Matthew 7:13; Philippians 1:28, 3:19; Hebrews 10:39 and 2 Peter 3:7) [Ld]. It refers to eternal damnation [Wal].

QUESTION—How does the beast 'go to destruction'?
It should not be implied that he goes willingly, but that he is destined by Christ or God to go there [TH].

QUESTION—What relationship is indicated by ὅτι 'because/that'?
1. It indicates a relationship of description modifying the beast [TH; CEV, KJV, NLT, REB, TEV]: they will be amazed seeing the beast *that* was and is not and will be present.

2. It indicates a relationship of cause [Be, WBC; NAB, NCV, NIV, NRSV, TNT]: they will be amazed seeing the beast *because* he was and is not and will be present.
3. It indicates that the following clause is the complement of the verb 'seeing' [BNTC, EC, Lns; NET]: they will be amazed seeing *that* the beast was and is not and will be present.

17:9 Here (is) the mind having wisdom. The seven heads are seven mountains, on which the woman sits. Also they are seven kings;
QUESTION—What is meant by the sentence, 'Here is the mind having wisdom'?
It means that wisdom is required to interpret this mystery [EC, ICC, NIGTC, TH; NCV, NET, NIV, NRSV, REB, TEV, TNT]. It is an invitation to listen carefully and think clearly [EC, NIC]. It means that John is now going to give them a wise interpretation [Hu]. It means that only the spiritually enlightened will understand this [Ld]. It means that wise people can figure this out [TNTC]. The following are ways that different versions have rendered this: 'this calls for a mind with wisdom' [NIV, NRSV, REB], 'this calls for wisdom and understanding' [TEV], 'here there is need for the understanding mind' [TNT], 'this requires a mind that has wisdom' [NET], 'you need a wise mind to understand this' [NCV], 'anyone with wisdom can figure this out' [CEV], 'here is a clue for one who has wisdom' [NAB], 'now understand this' [NLT].
QUESTION—What is meant by the 'seven mountains'?
1. The seven mountains are the seven hills on which the city of Rome is built and so this refers to Rome itself [Alf, Be, BNTC, NIC, NIGTC, NTC, Sw, TH, TNTC, Wal, WBC]. The seven hills were a very well known feature of the topography of Rome [Be, BNTC]. This indicates that the center of religious power will be geographically in Rome [Wal]. Mountains in Scripture symbolize strength. While this is a literal reference to Rome, it is a symbolical reference to kingdoms [NIGTC]. While Rome is indicated, it symbolizes organized man in opposition to God and has its realization in every age [NIC].
2. The seven mountains have a symbolical reference [EC, Hu, Ld, Lns]. In Scripture, a mountain is figurative of power or rule. So here the seven mountains are seven empires [EC, Ld]. The harlot sits on these empires and forms a treacherous connection with each as it comes to power down through the centuries [Ld]. Since seven is symbolical of divine authority, these empires symbolize the desire to gain world domination in opposition to God [Hu]. The seven mountains refer to the proud thoughts and plans of the antichristian power [Lns].
QUESTION—Who are the 'seven kings'?
1. This is a literal reference to seven emperors or kings of Rome [NTC, Sw, TH].

2. The seven kings are used symbolically [Alf, Be, EC, Ld, Lns, NIC, NIGTC, TNTC, Wal, WBC]. Seven stands for the authority of the Roman Empire seen historically as a whole [Be, NIC, TNTC]. They refer to secular antichristian authority and are the same as the seven heads of the dragon (see 12:3) [Alf]. They refer to the personifications of the seven empires. Rome is probably the sixth of these [EC]. They probably refer to a series of empires rather than kings [Ld]. Kings and kingdoms are used interchangeably here [NIGTC]. They represent seven forms of the kingdom successively [Wal].

17:10 The five fell,[a] one is, the other came not-yet, and when he-comes he must remain for-a-little-while.[b]

TEXT—Some manuscripts possibly include καί 'and' after ἔπεσαν 'fell', although GNT does not mention this alternative. 'And' is included by TR and KJV.

LEXICON—a. aorist act. indic. of πίπτω (LN **13.97**) (BAGD 2.a.δ. p. 660): 'to fall' [BNTC, EC, LN, Lns, WBC; all versions except CEV, NCV], 'to come to an end' [**LN**], 'to die' [CEV], 'to perish, to disappear, to pass from the scene' [BAGD] 'to cease' [LN]. This active voice is also translated passively: 'to be destroyed' [NCV]. See this word also at 11:13.

b. ὀλίγος (LN 67.106) (BAGD 3.a. p. 563): 'for a little while' [NIV], '(for) only a little while' [CEV, NRSV, REB, TEV], '(for) only a short while' [WBC; NAB], 'only a brief time' [NET], '(for) a little time' [BAGD, EC], '(for) a short time' [NCV, TNT], 'a short space' [KJV], 'for a little' [Lns]. This adverb is also translated as an adjective: 'brief (reign)' [NLT], 'short (stay)' [BNTC]. See this word also at 12:12.

QUESTION—What is meant by the kings falling?
1. It simply indicates that they died [NIGTC, TH, TNTC; CEV].
2. It points to some other kind of end than simple death [Alf, Be, Ld, Sw, WBC; NCV]. It refers to someone of relatively high rank 'falling' from that position by death or other means [Be, Sw]. It represents a violent form of death or overthrow [Alf, WBC]. It points to the collapse of a kingdom [Ld].

QUESTION—If the seven kings are literal, to whom do they refer?
They refer to Egypt, Assyria, Babylon, Persia, Greece, Rome and the Christian Empire under Constantine [Alf]. They refer to Egypt, Assyria, Babylon, Persia, Greece, Rome and a future kingdom under the beast [EC]. They refer to Augustus, Tiberius, Gaius (Caligula), Claudius, Nero, Vespasian and Titus (whose reign was short) [ICC, NTC].

QUESTION—If the seven kings are figurative, what do they symbolize?
Seven symbolizes the Roman authority as a whole [Be, NIC, TNTC]. They symbolize five kingdoms that are historically past, one current one, Rome, and one that will have a short reign [Ld]. Seven symbolizes the emperors as a whole [BNTC]. Seven symbolizes kings throughout history through whom the beast has ruled [NIGTC].

QUESTION—What is meant by the phrase 'for a little while'?

It refers to the time that the dragon will be released from the Abyss (see 20:3b) [NIGTC]. It refers to the reign of the Antichrist [Ld].

17:11 And the beast that was and is not, even/and-also he-himself is an-eighth and he-is of the seven, and he-goes to destruction.

QUESTION—Which beast is this?

It refers to the beast that is described at 17:8 [Alf, EC, Hu, Ld, Lns, TH].

QUESTION—What is indicated by the presence of αὐτός 'he'?

It indicates that the pronoun is emphatic [Be, EC, Lns, NIGTC]: *he himself.*

QUESTION—What relationship is indicated by the καί 'and' before αὐτός 'he (is an eighth)'?

1. It indicates an intensive relationship [Be, EC, NIGTC; KJV]: *even* he himself is an eighth.
2. It indicates a conjoining relationship [BNTC, Lns]: *and also* he himself is an eighth.

QUESTION—How can the beast be an eighth king but be 'of the seven'?

He is a reincarnation of one of the seven [Ld, NTC]. He belongs to the seven in that he is Nero reincarnated [NTC]. The solution to the problem is that the beast is the Antichrist who appears twice, once in the person of Antiochus Epiphanes and once again at the end as the Antichrist himself [Ld]. The Greek does not say he is 'one of the seven' but that he is 'of the seven' [Alf, Lns, NIC, NIGTC]. That is to say, he comes out of the seven and so is a successor to them [Alf, Lns]. He is 'of the seven' in that he has a similar role to play [NIC]. The first seven were not kings per se, but kings that symbolized kingdoms. The eighth however is a king, a world ruler who arises from the seventh kingdom, the one that received the fatal wound but recovered from it, and rules over it [EC]. He has an intimate relation with the seven but is not one of them [Hu]. Or, it means that one of the kings will rule twice [TH].

17:12 And the ten horns that you-saw are ten kings, that not-yet received (a) kingdom,ᵃ but will-receive authority as kings (for) one hour with the beast.

LEXICON—a. βασιλεία (LN 1.82) (BAGD 1. p. 134): 'kingdom' [BAGD, EC, LN, Lns; KJV, NET, NIV, NRSV]. The phrase βασιλείαν οὔπω ἔλαβον 'did not yet receive a kingdom' is translated: 'not yet begun to rule' [NCV, REB, TEV, TNT], 'not yet come into power' [CEV], 'not yet risen to power' [NLT], 'not yet been crowned' [NAB], 'not yet come to the throne' [BNTC], 'not yet become kings' [WBC]. See this word also at 1:6.

QUESTION—Are these ten literal kings or is the number ten used symbolically?

1. Ten is symbolic of completeness or totality [Be, Hu, Ld, Lns, NIC, NIGTC, TNTC]. Here ten indicates all the kingdoms of the world [Be, Ld, Lns, NIC]. It indicates the totality of the power of the beast [Lns,

NIGTC]. See 16:12–15 where all the kings of the earth come together for the final conflict [Hu, Lns]. These are the same as 'the kings of the earth' in 17:18 [NIGTC]. Or, these are not the same as 'the kings of the earth' since they hate the prostitute (see verse 17:16) whereas 'the kings of the earth' mourn over the destruction of the city in 18:9 [TNTC].
2. Ten should be taken literally [EC, TH, WBC].

QUESTION—Will the reign of these kings be simultaneous or successive to each other?

They will all reign at one time with the beast [Be, EC, TH, Wal, WBC].

QUESTION—What is meant by the phrase μίαν ὥραν 'for one hour'?

It means: a short period of time [Be, ICC, NIC, NIGTC, Wal, WBC; CEV, NLT, REB], a very short period of time [EC, Ld, TH], a specified length of time [Alf], one hour as God thinks of time [TNTC]. The 'hour' was the shortest period of time that people of those times conceived [NIGTC]. It coincides with the length of the reign of the beast as noted in 17:10 [Alf, Be, ICC, TNTC]. During his three and a half year reign the beast will give these kings the power to reign until the war with the Lamb (see 17:14) [EC]. This time coincides with the present time between the two comings of Christ [Hu].

QUESTION—From whom do these kings receive their power?
1. They will receive their power from God (see 17:17) [Be, NIGTC, WBC].
2. They will receive their power from the beast or some other source [EC, Hu, TH].

17:13 **These have one purpose[a] and their power and authority they give to the beast.**

TEXT—Instead of διδόασιν 'they give', some manuscripts possibly read διαδιδώσουσιν 'they give out', although GNT does not mention this alternative. The reading 'they give out' is taken by TR.

LEXICON—a. γνώμη (LN **30.67**) (BAGD 1. p. 163): 'purpose' [BAGD, EC, **LN**; NCV, NIV, REB, TEV, TNT], 'mind' [BAGD, BNTC; KJV, NAB], 'intent' [NET], 'intention' [BAGD, LN], 'consent' [Lns]. The clause μίαν γνώμην ἔχουσιν 'they have one purpose' is translated: 'they think alike' [CEV], 'they agree (to give)' [NLT], 'they are united' [NRSV], 'they are of one accord' [WBC].

QUESTION—What single purpose ruled their thinking?

They were unified in their support of the beast and their opposition to Christ [Be, EC, Ld, Sw].

QUESTION—What does it mean to give one's authority to someone?

It means to become that person's subordinate [Alf, NIGTC, TH]. It means to give that person the credit for their authority [Hu]. It means to be loyal to that person [Ld, Sw]. It means to become allied with that person [Alf, Ld, TNTC].

17:14 These will-make-war with the Lamb and the Lamb will-conquer them, for he-is Lord of-lords and King of-kings and the-ones with him, called and chosen and faithful."

QUESTION—Who is the antecedent of οὗτοι 'these'?
1. It is the ten kings and their armies [Hu, WBC].
1. It is the beast *and* the ten kings (see 19:19) [Alf, Be, TH].

QUESTION—Who conquers those who make war with the Lamb?
1. The Lamb conquers them [Hu, Lns, NIC, TNTC; TNT]. The Lamb conquers them, but the called, chosen, and faithful ones share in his victory [Hu, Lns, TNTC]. The role of the faithful in battle is not stated but they share in his victory [NIC].
2. The Lamb *and* those called, chosen, and faithful conquer them [Alf, Be, BNTC, EC, Ld, NIGTC, TH, WBC; NCV, TEV]. If the faithful are not included in the conquering, they have no relevance to the subject of this clause (see also 19:14) [EC].

QUESTION—What relationship is indicated by ὅτι 'for'?
It indicates that what follows is the reason why the Lamb can conquer them [Be, BNTC, EC, Ld, Lns, NIC, TH, WBC; all versions]: the Lamb will conquer them *because* he is Lord of lords and King of kings. The Lamb conquers on two counts: (1) He is the Supreme Lord, and (2) his companions are called and chosen and faithful [BNTC].

QUESTION—Who is the implied actor of κλητοί καὶ ἐκλεκτοί 'called and chosen'?
God is the implied actor [NIC, TH]: God called and chose them.

DISCOURSE UNIT: 17:15–18 [Alf, EC, TNTC]. The topic is the judgment of the great harlot.

17:15 And he-says to me, "The waters that you-saw where the prostitute sits, are peoples and multitudes^a and nations and languages.

LEXICON—a. ὄχλος (LN 11.1) (BAGD 4. p. 601): 'multitude' [BAGD, EC, LN, Lns; KJV, NIV, NRSV], 'crowd' [BAGD, LN, WBC; TNT], 'throng' [BAGD; NET], 'people' [BAGD; TEV], 'mass' [BNTC], 'population' [REB], 'race' [NCV]. The phrase λαοὶ καὶ ὄχλοι 'peoples and crowds' is translated: 'large numbers of peoples' [NCV], 'crowds of people' [CEV], 'masses of people' [NLT]. The word ὄχλος stands as a synonym for 'peoples' and 'nations' [BAGD]. See this word also at 7:9.

QUESTION—What does the pronoun 'he' refer to?
It refers to the angel, the same one who had been speaking in 17:7–14 [TH, WBC].

QUESTION—To what specific 'waters' is the angel referring?
He is referring to the waters mentioned in 17:1 [Hu, TNTC].

QUESTION—What is the significance of the 'sitting' position of the prostitute?
It indicates that she rules over the peoples on whom she sits [Be, EC, TH, TNTC, Wal].

QUESTION—What is the significance of the fourfold statement 'peoples and multitudes and nations and languages'?

It signifies the totality of human society [Hu, NIC, NIGTC].

QUESTION—What is meant by the verb εἰσίν 'they are'?

It means that they 'represent' or 'stand for' [TH]: the waters...*represent* peoples and multitudes and nations and languages.

17:16 And the ten horns and the beast you-saw, these will-hate the prostitute and they-will-make her having-been-made-desolate[a] and naked and devour her flesh and burn-up her with fire.

TEXT—Instead of καὶ τὸ θηρίον 'and the beast', some manuscripts possibly have ἐπὶ τὸ θηρίον 'on the beast', although GNT does not mention this alternative. The reading 'on the beast' is taken by TR and KJV.

LEXICON—a. perf. pass. participle of ἐρημόομαι, ἐρημόω (LN 20.41) (BAGD p. 309): 'to be made desolate' [Lns], 'to be destroyed, to suffer destruction, to suffer desolation' [LN], 'to be laid waste' [BAGD], 'to be depopulated' [BAGD, WBC]. This verb is also translated actively: 'to make desolate' [BNTC, EC, WBC; KJV, NET, NRSV, TNT], 'to bring to ruin' [NIV], 'to take everything one has' [NCV, TNT], 'to strip' [NLT], 'to strip off finery' [NAB], 'to leave destitute' [REB]. Indicates suffer destruction, with the implication of being deserted and abandoned [LN].

QUESTION—Why do the ten kings and the beast turn against the prostitute?

They turn because evil is self-destructive [BNTC, NIC, TNTC]. They turn because evil is internally rotten [Hu]. There is a law of political history that states that every revolutionary authority contains in itself the seed of self-destruction [NIC]. They turn because God brings it about (see 17:17) [Lns].

QUESTION—Who is the person who is made desolate and who does it?

The ten horns make the prostitute desolate [BNTC, EC, WBC; KJV, NAB, NCV, NET, NIV, NRSV, REB, TEV].

QUESTION—What is meant by τὰς σάρκας αὐτῆς φάγονται 'they will eat her flesh'?

It is a figure that implies complete destruction of people by people [Be, EC, Ld].

QUESTION—What is the force of using the four verbs: make desolate, make naked, devour, and burn?

Together they indicate complete destruction [Lns, TNTC] because of their hate [Lns]. Once dressed in finery, the woman will be stripped bare; having her flesh devoured suggests wild beasts tearing her body; in Lev. 21:9, burning is the fate of a priest's daughter who becomes a harlot [NIC].

QUESTION—What is a possible interpretation of this verse?

Since Babylon refers to the apostate world church, this indicates that the beast will turn against it and destroy and substitute in its place the worship of himself [Wal].

17:17 For God put (it) into their hearts to do his purpose and to-act (with) one purpose and to-give their kingdom[a] to-the beast until the words of God will-be-fulfilled.

TEXT—Instead of τελεσθήσονται οἱ λόγοι 'will be fulfilled the words', some manuscripts possibly read τελεσθῇ 'have been completed the words', although GNT does not mention this alternative. The reading 'have been fulfilled the words' is taken by TR.

LEXICON—a. βασιλεία (LN 1.82) (BAGD 1. p. 134): 'kingdom' [EC, Lns; KJV, NAB, NRSV], 'power' [CEV], 'power to rule' [NCV, NIV, TEV], 'royal power' [WBC; NET], 'authority' [NLT], 'sovereignty' [BNTC; REB, TNT]. See this word also at 1:6.

QUESTION—What relationship is indicated by γάρ 'for'?
  1. It indicates that this clause stands as the reason why the kings and beast acted as they did in the preceding verse [Be, EC, Ld, Lns, NIC, NIGTC, TNTC]: they destroyed the prostitute *because* God put it into their hearts. This indicates that God's purposes lie behind this internal fighting in the camp of evil [EC].
  2. It indicates why the kings were united [ICC, NTC, TH]: the kings acted with one purpose *because* God put it into their hearts.

QUESTION—What is meant by the clause θεὸς ἔδωκεν εἰς τὰς καρδίας 'God put into their hearts'?

It means that: God made them decide to accomplish his will [TH], God put the thoughts into their hearts to accomplish his will [WBC], God made them have one purpose [CEV], God made them want to accomplish his purpose [NCV], God placed in their hearts the will to accomplish his purpose [TEV], God prompted them to accomplish his purpose [WBC].

QUESTION—What is indicated by the aorist tense in θεὸς ἔδωκεν 'God put'?

It is a proleptic use of the aorist that refers to a future event as though it had already occurred [Alf, Be, EC].

QUESTION—What is meant by the phrase ποιῆσαι τὴν γνώμην αὐτοῦ 'to do his purpose'?

It means that they executed his purpose [Alf, Be, EC].

QUESTION—What do οἱ λόγοι τοῦ θεοῦ 'the words of God' refer to?

They refer to the final events until the defeat of the Antichrist [Be, EC, Lns, NIC]. They refer to the destruction of Babylon [Alf]. They refer to what God has said will take place in the End [TH]. They refer to the defeat of the beast and his Parthian allies [ICC].

17:18 And the woman whom you-saw is the great city having (a) kingdom[a] over the kings of-the earth."

LEXICON—a. βασιλεία (See this word at 17:17): 'kingdom' [EC], 'kingship' [Lns], 'dominion' [WBC], 'sovereignty' [BNTC; NAB, NET]. The phrase ἔχουσα βασιλείαν 'having a kingdom' is translated: 'ruling' [CEV, NCV, NIV, NLT, NRSV, TEV], 'reigning' [KJV, TNT], 'holding sway' [BNTC].

QUESTION—What is 'the great city' (see this question also at 1:1)?
1. It refers to Rome [Alf, ICC, Sw, TH, WBC].
2. It refers to Babylon [EC, Hu, Ld, Lns, NIC, Wal]. The great city stood for Rome in the past, but in the final days it refers to Babylon [Ld, NIC]. It symbolizes a false religious system [Wal]. Here it symbolizes a false religious system associated with geographic Babylon [EC]. It symbolizes antichristian seduction [Lns].
3. It symbolizes the evil economic-religious system of earth through history. Because of her dominion over the kings of the earth it cannot refer to the apostate church [NIGTC].
4. It symbolizes mankind in organized society [TNTC].

DISCOURSE UNIT: 18:1–19:10 [NIGTC]. The topic is the saints rejoicing about God's judgment.

DISCOURSE UNIT: 18:1–19:5 [Be, Ld, TNTC; NET]. The topic is the sevenfold declaration of Rome's ruin [Be], the judgment of Babylon [Ld, TNTC; NET].

DISCOURSE UNIT: 18:1–19:4 [GNT; CEV, NAB]. The topic is the fall of Babylon.

DISCOURSE UNIT: 18:1–24 [EC, Lns, NIC, NTC, Sw, Wal, WBC; all versions except REB, TNT]. The topic is the destruction of Babylon [EC, Sw, Wal, WBC; all versions except REB, TEV, TNT], the great whore and lament over her [Lns], funeral dirge over Babylon/Rome [EC, NTC], the famous prostitute [TEV].

DISCOURSE UNIT: 18:1–8 [BNTC, NIC]. The topic is the lament of Heaven [BNTC], Babylon declared desolate [NIC].

DISCOURSE UNIT: 18:1–3 [Alf, Be, EC, Ld, Lns, NIGTC, Sw, TNTC, Wal, WBC]. The topic is the announcement of the fall of Babylon [Alf, EC, TNTC, Wal], the first part of the vision [Lns], angelic taunt song [WBC].

18:1 **After these-things I-saw another angel coming down from heaven having great authority, and the earth was-illuminated^a from his glory.^b**

TEXT—Some manuscripts include καί 'and' before the initial μετά 'after'. GNT does not mention this alternative. 'And' is included by TR and KJV.

TEXT—Some manuscripts possibly do not include ἄλλον 'another', although GNT does not mention this alternative. The word 'another' is omitted by TR.

LEXICON—a. aorist pass. indic. of φωτίζω (LN 14:39) (BAGD 2.a. p. 873): 'to be illuminated' [BAGD, EC, LN, WBC; NIV], 'to be illumined' [NAB], 'to be lit up' [BAGD; NET, TNT], 'to be lightened' [KJV], 'to be made bright' [CEV], 'to be made light' [Lns], 'to be shone on' [LN], 'to be given light' [BAGD]. This passive verb is also translated actively: 'to grow bright' [BNTC; NLT], 'to make bright' [NCV, TEV], 'to be bright' [CEV], 'to shine' [REB].

b. δόξα (LN 14.49) (BAGD 1.a. p. 203): 'glory' [EC, Lns; CEV, KJV, NCV], 'splendor' [BAGD, BNTC, WBC; NAB, NIV, NLT, NRSV, REB, TEV, TNT], 'radiance' [BAGD, LN; NET]. Here δόξα has a physical sense of 'brilliant light' [TH]. See this word also at 15:8.

QUESTION—What is the significance of the phrase μετὰ ταῦτα εἶδον 'after these things I saw'?

It marks a new unit in the text (see 4:1; 7:1, 9 and 15:5) [WBC]. It indicates the next item in the sequence of visions [EC, NIGTC]. It refers to the events that immediately preceded [TH]. It indicates a later time than the events of chapter 17 [Wal].

QUESTION—Who is this angel?

It is a different angel than the one speaking with John in chapter 17 [Alf, Be, EC, ICC, Ld, Lns, NIC, Sw, TH, Wal]. It may be Christ himself since every other mention of 'glory' in Revelation in connection with a heavenly figure has to do with either God or Christ [NIGTC].

18:2 And he shouted with (a) strong voice saying, "Fallen, Fallen (is) Babylon the great, and became (a) dwelling-place[a] of-demons and (a) haunt[b] of-every unclean spirit and (a) haunt of-every unclean bird[c] [and (a) haunt of-every unclean] and detested[d] [beast],

TEXT—Instead of ἰσχυρᾷ 'strong', some manuscripts have the near synonym ἰσχύϊ. GNT does not mention this alternative.

TEXT—Some manuscripts do not include the phrase καὶ φυλακὴ παντὸς θηρίου ἀκαθάρτου 'and haunt of every unclean beast'. Others do not include this phrase or the preceding phrase καὶ φυλακὴ παντὸς ὀρνέου ἀκαθάρτου 'and haunt of every unclean bird'. Still others do not include this phrase or the preceding phrase καὶ φυλακὴ αντὸς πνεύματος ἀκαθάρτου 'and haunt of every unclean spirit'. One Church Father omits all of this verse beginning with the first occurrence of καὶ φυλακή 'and a haunt'. GNT includes the phrase 'and haunt of every unclean beast' in brackets with a C rating indicating difficulty in deciding whether or not to include it. The reading 'and haunt of every unclean beast' is not included by BNTC, Lns, WBC; KJV, NIV, REB, TEV, TNT.

LEXICON—a. κατοικητήριον (LN **85.70**) (BAGD p. 424): 'dwelling place' [BAGD, **LN**; NRSV], 'dwelling' [REB, TNT], 'home' [CEV, NCV, NIV], 'habitation' [EC, Lns, WBC; KJV], 'haunt' [NAB], 'lair' [NET], 'hideout' [NLT], 'den' [BNTC]. This noun is also translated as a verb: 'to be haunted' [TEV].

b. φυλακή (LN **85.85**): 'haunt' [BNTC, **LN**; NET, NIV, NRSV, REB, TNT], 'den' [CEV], 'nest' [NLT], 'preserve' [WBC], 'cage' [NAB], 'prison' [EC; NCV], 'hold' [Lns; KJV], 'lair, dwelling place' [LN], not explicit [TEV]. Φυλακή indicates a place for wild animals and evil spirits to dwell [LN]. See this word also at 2:10.

c. ὄρνεον (LN 4.38) (BAGD p. 582): 'bird' [BAGD, BNTC, EC, LN, Lns, WBC; all versions except NLT], 'buzzard' [NLT].

d. perf. pass. participle of μισέω (BAGD 3. p. 523): 'detested' [NET], 'detestable' [NIV, TNT], 'disgusting' [NAB], 'loathsome' [BNTC; REB], 'hated' [EC, Lns; CEV], 'hateful' [KJV, NRSV, TEV], 'dreadful' [NLT], not explicit [WBC; NCV]. Μισέω indicates to strongly dislike, implying aversion and hostility [LN]. See this word also at 2:6.

QUESTION—What does the total scene of this verse depict?
It is a picture of utter destruction [BNTC, EC, Hu].

QUESTION—What is indicated by the aorist tense in ἔπεσεν 'fallen'?
It is a proleptic use of the aorist that refers to a future event as though it had already occurred [Be, EC, TH].

QUESTION—What is meant by the word ἀκαθάρτου 'unclean'?
Certain birds and animals were classified as 'unclean' by Jewish law and as such should not be eaten. Such birds included hawk, owl, and raven (see Deuteronomy 14:12–18) [TH]. Unclean animals included jackals and hyenas [EC].

18:3 **Because all the nations have-drunk of the wine of the passion/wrath of her fornication and the kings of the earth committed-fornication with her and the merchants^a of the earth became-rich by the power^b of her luxury.^c**

TEXT—Instead of τοῦ οἴνου τοῦ θυμοῦ τῆς πορνείας 'the wine of the wrath of the fornication', some manuscripts have τοῦ θυμοῦ τοῦ οἴνου τῆς πορνείας 'the wrath of the wine of the fornication', others have τοῦ θυμοῦ τῆς πορνείας 'the wrath of the fornication', still others have τοῦ οἴνου τῆς πορνείας 'the wine of the fornication'. GNT accepts the reading 'the wine of the wrath of the fornication' with a B rating, indicating that the text is almost certain.

TEXT—Instead of πέπωκαν 'have drunk', some manuscripts have πεπτώκασιν or πέπτωκαν 'have fallen', others have πέπτωκεν 'has fallen', one manuscript has πεπότικεν 'have given to drink', and one Church Father omits πέπωκαν 'have drunk' and the following phrase πάντα τὰ ἔθνη 'all the nations'. GNT accepts the reading 'have drunk' with a rare D rating, indicating difficulty in deciding whether or not to place it in the text. The reading 'have given to drink' is taken by ICC and NIC. The reading 'have fallen' is taken by Lns, WBC and NET.

LEXICON—a. ἔμπορος, (LN **57.203**) (BAGD p. 257): 'merchant' [BAGD, BNTC, EC, **LN**, Lns, WBC; all versions], 'trader' [LN].

b. δύναμις (LN 76.1) (BAGD 5. p. 208): 'power' [EC, LN, Lns; NET, NRSV], 'wealth' [NTC; REB], 'excessive wealth' [BAGD], 'great wealth' [NCV], 'abundance' [KJV], not explicit [CEV, NLT], 'drive' [NAB]. This noun is also translated as an adjective: 'excessive (luxury)' [WBC; NIV, TNT], 'unrestrained (lust)' [TEV], 'overwhelming (lust)' [LN], 'lavish (wealth)' [BNTC]. Δύναμις indicates the potentiality to exert force in performing some function [LN].

c. στρῆνος (LN **88.254**) (BAGD p. 771): 'luxury' [BAGD, WBC; NAB, NCV, NIV, NRSV, REB, TNT], 'wealth' [BNTC], 'sensuality' [BAGD], 'sensual living' [LN], 'sensual behavior' [NET], 'lust' [**LN**; TEV], 'wantonness' [EC, ICC, Lns, NTC], 'evil desire' [CEV], 'delicacy' [KJV]. The phrase τῆς δυνάμεως τοῦ στρήνους αὐτῆς 'the power of her luxury' is translated: 'her luxurious living' [NLT]. This noun is related to the verb στρηνιάω meaning to live sensually by gratifying the senses with sexual immorality [LN].

QUESTION—What relationship is indicated by ὅτι 'because'?

It indicates that this verse gives the reason for Babylon's downfall [EC, Ld, Lns, NIC, NIGTC, TNTC, Wal, WBC]: Fallen is Babylon the great...*because* all the nations have drunk of the wine of the passion of her immorality. There are three reasons given: (1) Babylon had a bad influence on the nations, (2) the kings of the earth committed fornication with her, and (3) the merchants became rich because of her luxury [WBC].

QUESTION—How are the nouns related in the genitive construction τοῦ οἴνου τοῦ θυμοῦ 'the wine of the passion' (also see this question at 14:8)?

1. 'Passion' modifies 'wine' [NIC, TNTC; NIV]: maddening wine.
1. 'Passion' restates 'wine' [WBC]: wine, *that is*, her immoral passion.

QUESTION—How are the nouns related in the genitive construction τοῦ θυμοῦ τῆς πορνείας αὐτῆς 'the passion of her fornication' (also see this question at 14.8)?

1. 'Fornication' modifies 'passion' [NIGTC, WBC; NAB, NET, TEV]: immoral passion.
1. 'Passion' modifies 'fornication' [NLT]: passionate immorality.
3. 'Passion (wrath)' results from 'fornication' [Alf, EC; REB]: God's anger roused by her fornication. God's anger is against Babylon [Alf, EC]. God's anger is against the nations [REB].

QUESTION—How are the nouns related in the genitive construction τῆς δυνάμεως τοῦ στρήνους αὐτῆς 'the power of her luxury'?

1. 'Luxury' is the source of 'power' [Be, NIGTC]: power *coming from* her luxury.
2. 'Power' modifies 'luxury/wealth' [BNTC, LN, WBC; NIV, TEV, TNT]: excessive luxury/lavish wealth/overwhelming lust.
3. 'Power' causes one to seek 'luxury' [NAB]: her drive for luxury.
4. 'Power/wealth' is addition to 'luxury' [REB]: wealth *and* luxury.

QUESTION—Should στρῆνος be taken to refer to 'luxury/wealth' or to 'sexual desire'?

1. It should be taken to refer to 'luxury/wealth' [BAGD, Be, BNTC, Ld, Lns, NIC, NIGTC, Sw, TNTC, WBC; NAB, NCV, NIV, NRSV, REB, TNT]. There are also the added senses of: self-indulgence [Be, Lns, TNTC], arrogance [Be, Hu, Lns, TNTC], lack of discipline [Be, EC, Lns], and extravagance [Lns].
2. It should be taken to refer to 'sexual desire' [LN, TH; CEV, NET, TEV]. This noun is related to the verb στρηνιάω meaning to live sensually by gratifying the senses with sexual immorality [LN].

DISCOURSE UNIT: 18:4–20 [Alf, EC, WBC]. The topic is a prediction of Babylon's fall [EC].

DISCOURSE UNIT: 18:4–19 [Lns, Sw]. The topic is the second part of the vision [Lns].

DISCOURSE UNIT: 18:4–8 [NIGTC]. The topic is the command to separate from Babylon.

DISCOURSE UNIT: 18:4–5 [Be, Ld, TNTC, Wal]. The topic is a warning to God's people [Be, Ld], a call to leave the city [TNTC, Wal].

18:4 **And I-heard another voice from heaven saying, "Come-out of her my people lest you-participate-in**[a] **her sins, and so-that not you-may-receive her plagues.**[b]

LEXICON—a. aorist act. subj. of συγκοινωνέω (LN 34.4) (BAGD 1. p. 774): 'to participate in/with' [BAGD, LN, WBC], 'to take part in' [CEV, NAB, NET, NLT, NRSV, TEV], 'to have part in' [REB], 'to be partners in' [BNTC], 'to share in/with' [EC; NCV, NIV], 'to have share in' [TNT], 'to be partaker of' [KJV], 'to fellowship with' [Lns], 'to associate with, to be in partnership with' [LN], 'to be connected with' [BAGD].

b. πληγή (LN **22.13**): 'plague' [BNTC, EC, Lns; KJV, NAB, NET, NIV, NRSV, REB, TNT], 'severe suffering' [**LN**], 'suffering' [WBC], 'punishment' [CEV, TEV], 'disaster' [NCV]. This noun is also translated as a verb: 'to be punished' [NLT]. See this word also at 9:18.

QUESTION—Who is the implied speaker of this voice?
1. It the voice of God [TH].
2. It is the voice of Christ [ICC, WBC]. This is likely since the third person reference to God in the next verse makes it unlikely that it is God's voice [WBC].
3. It is either the voice of God or Christ [Be].
4. It is the voice of an angel speaking in the name of God [Alf, EC, NIC, Sw, TNTC]. This is so because the third person reference to God in the next verse makes it unlikely that it is God's voice [NIC].
5. It is just another voice speaking for God [Lns].

QUESTION—To whom is this addressed?
1. It is addressed to believers [Alf, EC, Ld, Lns, NIGTC, TNTC, Wal]. The verse implies that there will still be believers in Babylon [Alf, Ld].
2. It is addressed to unbelievers who will even yet repent and trust in Christ [BNTC].

QUESTION—What relationship is indicated by the two ἵνα clauses?
They both indicate purpose [EC, NIC, NIGTC, TH, Wal]: Come out of her *in order that* you not participate in her sins and *in order that* you not receive her plagues.

18:5 Because her sins were-piled-up[a] to heaven and God remembered[b] her unrighteous-acts.[c]

TEXT—Instead of ἐκολλήθησαν 'were piled up', some manuscripts possibly have ἠκολούθησαν 'followed'. GNT does not mention this alternative. The reading 'followed' is taken by TR.

LEXICON—a. aorist pass. indic. of κολλάομαι, κολλάω (LN **59.66**) (BAGD 2.a.β. p. 441): 'to be piled up' [NAB, NIV, TEV], 'to be piled' [BNTC; CEV, NLT, REB], 'to be heaped' [NRSV], 'to increase greatly, to reach to high heaven' [LN], 'to reach to heaven/to become very very many' [**LN**], 'to touch the heaven, to reach the sky' [BAGD], 'to be glued together' [Lns]. This passive verb is also translated actively: 'to pile up' [NCV, NET, TNT], 'to reach' [WBC; KJV], 'to join' [EC]. Κολλάω indicates to increase enormously the number of something, with the implication of reaching the attention of God [LN]. Κολλάω literally means 'to be glued together' giving a picture of sins sticking to each other and accumulating until the pile reaches to heaven [Be, EC, Lns, NIC, Sw, TH, Wal].

b. aorist act. indic. of μνημονεύω (LN **29.16**) (BAGD 1.b. p. 525): 'to remember' [BAGD, EC, LN, Lns, WBC; all versions except NCV, NLT, REB], 'to not forget' [NCV, REB], 'to be ready to judge' [NLT], 'to have a record' [BNTC]. This verb implies much more than God's mental state in remembering the crimes of Babylon. The reference is clearly to God's both remembering and punishing [LN]. See this word also at 2:5 and 3:3.

c. ἀδίκημα (LN 88.23) (BAGD p. 17): 'unrighteous act' [EC, LN, Lns], 'crime' [BAGD, BNTC, LN, WBC; NAB, NET, NIV, REB, TNT], 'wrong' [BAGD; NCV], 'evil deeds' [NLT], 'evil' [CEV], 'iniquity' [KJV, NRSV], 'wicked way' [TEV], 'misdeed' [BAGD].

QUESTION—What relationship is indicated by ὅτι 'because'?

It indicates that this verse stands as the reason God calls his people to come out of Babylon [EC, Lns]: Come out of her my people...*because* her sins are piled up to heaven. It indicates the reason why God will punish Babylon [NIGTC]: so you will not receive her plagues *because* her sins are piled up to heaven.

QUESTION—How are the nouns related in the genitive construction τὰ ἀδικήματα αὐτῆς 'her unrighteous acts'?

She does the unrighteous acts [CEV, NCV].

QUESTION—What is implied in the clause ἐμνημόνευσεν ὁ θεὸς τὰ ἀδικήματα αὐτῆς 'God remembered her unrighteous acts'?

It implies that he will punish Babylon for her unrighteous acts [EC, LN, NIC, NIGTC, TH, Wal]. Babylon's sins have grown so many that God must punish her to maintain his justice [NIGTC].

QUESTION—What is indicated by the picture of something reaching to heaven?

It is an hyperbole that functions to stress the great amount of something. Here that amount threatens God's sovereignty [WBC].

DISCOURSE UNIT: 18:6–8 [Be, Ld, TNTC, Wal]. The topic is a cry of vengeance [Ld], judgment on the city [TNTC], indictment against Babylon [Wal], incitement of spirits of vengeance to action [Be].

18:6 Pay-back[a] to-her as also she paid-back and double[b] the doubles[c] according-to her works, mix[d] double for-her in the cup that she-mixed,

TEXT—Instead of τὰ διπλᾶ 'the doubles', some manuscripts, have αὐτῇ διπλᾶ 'to her doubles'. GNT does not mention this alternative. The reading 'to her doubles' is taken by TR and KJV.

LEXICON—a. aorist act. imperative of ἀποδίδωμι (LN 57.153) (BAGD 3. p. 90): 'to pay back' [BNTC; NAB, REB], 'to repay' [NET], 'to pay' [LN], 'to treat' [CEV, TEV, TNT], 'to give back' [EC; NIV], 'to give' [NCV], 'to duly give' [Lns], 'to render' [BAGD, LN, WBC; NRSV], 'to reward' [BAGD; KJV], 'to do' [NLT], 'to recompense' [BAGD]. The verb ἀποδίδωμι indicates to make a payment, with the implication of such a payment being in response to an incurred obligation [LN].

b. aorist act. imperative of διπλόω (LN **59.70**) (BAGD p. 199): 'to double' [EC, LN, Lns; KJV], 'to cause twice as much as' [LN]. The phrase διπλώσατε τὰ διπλᾶ 'double the doubles' is translated: 'pay (her) back double' [NAB, NET, NIV, TEV], 'repay (her) double' [BNTC; NRSV, TNT], 'repay (her) twice over' [WBC; REB], 'pay (her) back twice as much as' [**LN**; NCV], 'give (her) a double penalty' [NLT], 'make (her) pay double' [CEV].

c. διπλοῦς (LN **60.75**) (BAGD p. 199): 'double' [BAGD, BNTC, EC, **LN**, Lns; KJV], 'twice as much' [WBC]. Most versions translated this with the verb 'to double' in b. above.

d. aorist active imperative of κεράννυμι (LN **63.9**): 'to mix' [BNTC, EC, **LN**, Lns, WBC; NET, NIV, NRSV, TNT], 'to pour' [NAB], 'to fill' [KJV, TEV], 'to prepare' [NCV], 'to give' [NLT, REB], 'to make drink' [CEV]. See this word also at 14:10.

QUESTION—What is indicated by the free pronoun αὐτή 'she'?

It indicates that the pronoun should be stressed [NRSV]: she herself.

QUESTION—Does 'pay her back double' mean a simple blow for blow, or is a punishment worse than her crime called for?

1. It simply implies a full payment for what she has given [Be, EC, Hu, Ld, Lns, NIGTC]. The phrase διπλώσατε τὰ διπλᾶ 'to double the doubles' in the LXX is used to mean 'to produce a duplicate'. The repetitive 'double the double' emphasizes the idea of giving the equivalent [NIGTC]. So here the meaning is 'to give the exact equivalent' [Hu, Lns, NIGTC]. This phrase is an idiom that indicates 'to repay in full measure' [Ld]. This is like the expression of being called someone's double, being exactly like them [Hu].

2. It implies a more severe punishment than her actual sin called for [NIC, TH, TNTC, Wal, WBC; all versions]. Because of the greatness of Babylon's sin, the normal law of punishment is doubled [Wal].

QUESTION—To whom is this command addressed?
It was addressed to the ten kings [EC, Lns, NIGTC, TH] and the beast (see 17:16) [EC, Lns, NIGTC]. It may be simply addressed to those who were assigned to carry out the task [Alf, TNTC]. It may have been addressed to angels [BNTC, TH]. It may have been addressed to 'my people' or to God [NIGTC]. It may have been addressed to Christians [WBC].

18:7 As-much-as^a she-lived-in-luxury^b and glorified herself, give her so-much^c torment^d and grief.^e Because she-says in her heart, "I sit (as a) queen and I-am not (a) widow and never^f may-I-see grief.

TEXT—Instead of αὐτήν 'her', some manuscripts have ἑαυτήν 'herself'. GNT does not mention this alternative. The reading 'herself' is taken by TR and KJV.

LEXICON—a. ὅσος (LN **78.52**) (BAGD 3. p. 586): 'as much as' [BAGD, **LN**; NET, NIV, TEV], 'as many things as' [EC], 'how many things' [Lns], 'to the measure of' [NAB], 'to the degree that, to the same degree' [LN], 'how much' [KJV], 'as' [WBC; NRSV], not explicit [CEV, NCV]. Others translate this correspondence—as much…this much—with some form of the verb 'to match' [BNTC; NLT, REB, TNT].

b. aorist act. indic. of στρηνιάω (LN 88.254) (BAGD p. 771): 'to live in luxury' [BAGD; NLT], 'to live a life of luxury' [CEV], 'to live luxuriously' [NRSV], 'to live deliciously' [KJV], 'to live in sensual luxury' [NET], 'to become wanton' [EC], 'to make someone wanton' [Lns], 'to live sensually' [BAGD, LN, WBC], 'to live intemperately' [LN]. This verb is also translated as a noun: 'wantonness' [NAB], 'rich living' [NCV], 'luxurious living' [TNT], 'luxury' [NIV, REB, TEV]. It is also rendered as an adjective: 'lavish (pomp)' [BNTC]. Στρηνιάω indicates to live sensually by gratifying the senses with sexual immorality [LN].

c. τοσοῦτος (LN 59.18) (BAGD 1.a.α. p. 823): 'so much' [BAGD, EC, LN, Lns; KJV], 'that much' [NCV], 'so great' [BAGD, LN], 'to this extent' [NET, NLT], 'so' [WBC; NRSV], not explicit [BNTC; CEV, NAB, NIV, REB, TEV, TNT]. Τοσοῦτος pertains to a quantity considerably beyond normal expectations [LN].

d. βασανισμός (LN 24.90) (BAGD 2. p. 184): 'torment' [BAGD, BNTC, EC, LN, Lns, WBC; KJV, NAB, NET, NLT, NRSV, REB, TNT], 'suffering' [CEV, NCV, TEV], 'torture' [NIV], 'severe pain, severe suffering' [LN].

e. πένθος (LN 25.142) (BAGD p. 642): 'grief' [BAGD, BNTC, LN, WBC; NAB, NET, NIV, NRSV, REB, TEV], 'sorrow' [EC, LN; KJV, NLT, TNT], 'sadness' [BAGD; NCV], 'mourning' [BAGD, Lns], 'pain' [CEV].

f. οὐ μή. This phrase is translated 'never' [BNTC, WBC; CEV, NAB, NCV, NET, NIV, NRSV, TEV, TNT], 'in no way' [EC], 'not' [Lns; NLT]. This adverb is also translated as an adjective: 'no (sorrow)' [KJV, REB].

QUESTION—What relationship is indicated by ὅτι 'because'?
It indicates the reason for the result given in verse 8 [NIGTC, TH; KJV, NAB, NET, NRSV, TEV]: *Because* she says in her heart, 'I sit as queen...' *therefore* in one day her plagues will come, death and grief and famine.

QUESTION—What specific kind of πένθος 'grief' does she think she will not see?
The sorrow here refers to that of becoming a widow [TH; REB]. It refers to the sorrow brought about by war and loss of life [NIC].

QUESTION—What tense is indicated by the subjunctive in ἴδω 'I may see'?
It is a subjunctive that indicates future tense [Lns; all versions]: I will not see grief.

18:8 Therefore in one day the plagues will-come (on) her, death[a] and grief and famine,[b] and she-will-be-burned-up[c] with fire, because (the) Lord God, the-one having-judged[d] her (is) strong.

LEXICON—a. θάνατος (LN 23.99) (BAGD 1.a. p. 350, 1.e. p. 351): 'death' [BAGD (1.a.), EC, LN (23.99), Lns; CEV, KJV, NCV, NET, NIV, NLT], 'pestilence' [BAGD (1.e.), BNTC, ICC, LN (23.158), TH, WBC; NAB, NRSV, REB, TNT], 'disease' [TEV], 'plague' [LN (23.158)], 'fatal illness' [BAGD (1.e.)]. See this word also at 1:18, 2:23 and 6:8.

b. λιμός (LN 23.33) (BAGD 2. p. 475): 'famine' [BAGD, BNTC, EC, LN, Lns, WBC; all versions except CEV, NCV], 'hunger' [LN; CEV], 'great hunger' [NCV]. See this word also at 6:8.

c. future pass. indic. of κατακαίω (LN 14.66) (BAGD p. 411): 'to be burned up' [BAGD, EC, LN; TNT], 'to be utterly burned' [KJV], 'to be burned to ashes' [BNTC], 'to be burned down' [LN; NET], 'to be burned' [WBC; NRSV, TEV], 'to be consumed' [NAB, NIV,], 'to be utterly consumed' [NLT], 'to be destroyed' [NCV]. The passive mood of the verb is also translated actively: '(fire) will destroy' [CEV], '(she) will perish' [REB], '(they) shall burn (her) up' [Lns]. See this word also at 8.7.

d. aorist act. indic. of κρίνω (LN 56.20, 56.30) (BAGD 4.b.a. p. 452): 'to judge' [BAGD, EC, LN (56.20), Lns, WBC; all versions except CEV, REB, TNT], 'to pronounce one's doom' [REB], 'to condemn' [LN (56.30), TH; TNT]. This verb is also translated as a noun: 'Judge' [BNTC], 'judge' [CEV]. See this word also at 6:10.

QUESTION—What relationship is indicated by διὰ τοῦτο 'therefore'?
It indicates that this verse is the result of Babylon's sins as detailed in 18:7 [NIC, NIGTC, Sw, TH, TNTC]: she glorified herself and lived in luxury...*therefore* in one day the plagues will come on her. It is political and economic pride that caused her judgment [NIGTC].

QUESTION—What is meant by the phrase ἐν μιᾷ ἡμέρᾳ 'in one day'?
It indicates suddenness [Be, EC, Lns, NIC, TH]. It indicates a short period of time [NTC, TH]. The fronted position of this phrase in the sentence emphasizes it [EC, Wal].

QUESTION—What relationship is indicated by ὅτι 'because'?
It indicates that the Lord's strength stands as the reason for Babylon's judgment [EC, Lns, NIGTC, WBC]: the plagues will come on her…she will be burned up with fire *because* the Lord God is strong. This clause answers the question of how such a sudden and complete defeat is possible [WBC].
QUESTION—Which word is emphasized in this final clause?
The word ἰσχυρός 'strong' is emphasized [EC, TNTC], being placed forward in the clause [EC]: the Lord God is very strong.

DISCOURSE UNIT: 18:9–24 [Hu]. The topic is the lamentation over Babylon's fall.

DISCOURSE UNIT: 18:9–20 [NIC]. The topic is the lament of kings merchants and seamen.

DISCOURSE UNIT: 18:9–19 [Be, BNTC, Ld, NIGTC, TNTC]. The topic is the lament of the kings and the merchants [Ld, NIGTC, TNTC], the lament of the earth [BNTC], a dirge over the ruins [Be].

DISCOURSE UNIT: 18:9–10 [Wal]. The topic is the lament of the kings of the earth.

18:9 **And the kings of-the earth who committed-fornication and lived-in-luxury**[a] **with her will-weep**[b] **and mourn**[c] **over her, when they-see the smoke of her burning,**

LEXICON—a. aorist act. participle of στρηνιάω (LN **88.254**): 'to live in luxury' [NRSV, TNT], 'to live luxuriously' [WBC], 'to share (in) one's luxury' [BNTC; CEV, NIV, NLT], 'to wallow in one's luxury' [CEV], 'to share one's wealth' [NCV], 'to live deliciously' [KJV], 'to live intemperately' [**LN**], 'to live in sexual luxury' [NET], 'to take part in one's lust' [TEV], 'to become wanton' [EC], 'to wanton' [Lns]. This verb is also translated as a noun: 'wantonness' [NAB]. See this word also at 18:7.

b. future act. indic. of κλαίω (LN 25.138): 'to weep' [BNTC, LN, WBC; CEV, NAB, NET, NIV, NRSV, REB,], 'to wail' [LN], 'to lament' [LN; KJV, TNT], 'to cry' [EC; NCV, TEV], 'to sob' [Lns]. Κλαίω indicates 'to weep or wail', with emphasis on the noise accompanying the weeping [LN]. It indicates a loud expression of sorrow and could therefore be rendered 'to sob openly' [NIC]. The phrase κλαύσουσιν καὶ κόψονται 'weep and mourn' is translated: 'to mourn' [NLT]. See this word also at 5:4.

b. future middle (deponent = active) indic. of κόπτω (BAGD 2. p. 444): 'to mourn' [EC; CEV, NAB, NIV, NLT], 'to wail' [BNTC, Lns, WBC; NET, NRSV, REB], 'to weep' [TEV], 'to bewail' [KJV], 'to be sad' [NCV], 'to be filled with sorrow' [TNT].

QUESTION—Who are these kings?
They are not the ten kings who with the beast destroyed the city (see 17:16), but a wider group of the kings of the earth [EC, ICC, Ld, NIC, NIGTC, Wal].

18:10 Standing from afar[a] because-of the fear of-her torment saying, "Woe, woe, (O) great city, Babylon the strong city, because in-one hour your judgment came.

LEXICON—a. μακρόθεν (LN 83.30) (BAGD p. 488): 'afar' [Lns], 'a distance' [BAGD, LN; NAB, REB]. 'far, some distance away, far away' [LN]. The phrase ἀπὸ μακρόθεν 'from afar' is translated: 'afar off' [KJV], 'far off' [BNTC, WBC; NIV, NRSV], 'far away' [NCV], 'at a distance' [EC; CEV, NLT, TNT], 'a long way off' [NET, TEV].

QUESTION—Why are the kings afraid?
The kings are afraid because they do not want to be a part of Babylon's judgment [EC, NIGTC, TH, TNTC, Wal, WBC].

QUESTION—What emotion is expressed by the phrase οὐαὶ οὐαί 'woe, woe'?
It expresses sorrow [EC, NIC, NIGTC, TH, TNTC, Wal] or hopelessness [NIC, TH]. The doubling of the word emphasizes the intensity of the sorrow [EC, TNTC].

QUESTION—What is meant by the phrase μιᾷ ὥρᾳ 'in one hour'?
It indicates a short time [TH, WBC]. It indicates suddenness [EC, NIGTC, TH]. This phrase is emphasized by being placed first in its clause after 'because' [NIGTC].

DISCOURSE UNIT: 18:11–19 [Wal]. The topic is the lament of the merchants of the earth.

18:11 And the merchants of-the earth weep and mourn[a] for her, because no-one buys their goods[b] any-longer

LEXICON—a. pres. act. indic. of πενθέω (LN 25.142) (BAGD 1. p. 642): 'to mourn' [BAGD, BNTC, Lns, WBC; all versions except NCV], 'to be sad' [BAGD, LN; NCV], 'to grieve' [BAGD, EC, LN], 'to weep' [LN].
b. γόμος (LN 15.208) (BAGD p. 165): 'goods' [CEV, NLT, TEV, TNT], 'cargo' [BAGD, BNTC, LN, Lns; NAB, NCV, NET, NIV, NRSV, REB], 'merchandise' [EC, WBC; KJV], 'load' [BAGD, LN], 'freight' [BAGD], 'burden' [LN]. Γόμος indicates chiefly the cargo of a ship [BAGD, EC, ICC, LN, Sw, TH], or any merchandise [EC].

QUESTION—What relationship is indicated by ὅτι 'because'?
It indicates that the following clause is the reason for the merchants' sorrow [EC, Ld, NIC, NIGTC, NTC, Sw, TNTC, Wal, WBC]: the merchants weep...*because* no one buys their goods any longer.

18:12 Goods of-gold and of-silver and of-precious stone and of-pearls and of-fine-linen[a] and of-purple[b] and of-silk[c] and of-scarlet, and every (kind of)

citron[d] wood[e] and every (kind of) ivory[f] vessel and every (kind of) vessel of valuable wood and of-bronze[g] and of-iron[h] and of-marble,[i]

TEXT—Instead of ξύλου 'wood', some manuscripts have λίθου 'stone'. GNT selects the reading 'wood' with an A rating, indicating that the text is certain.

LEXICON—a. βύσσινον (LN **6.167**) (BAGD p. 148): 'fine linen' [BAGD, EC; all versions except TEV], 'linen' [BNTC; TEV], 'cloth of fine linen' [**LN**, WBC], 'made of fine linen' [BAGD, Lns], 'linen garment' [BAGD], 'byssus' [Lns]. Βύσσινον was made from Egyptian flax [EC].

b. πορφύρα (LN 6.169) (BAGD p. 694): 'purple' [BNTC, EC, Lns; KJV, NAB, NIV, NRSV, TNT], 'purple cloth' [BAGD, LN; CEV, NCV, NET, REB, TEV], 'purple material' [WBC], 'purple garment' [LN], 'purple dye' [NLT]. 'Purple dye' was associated with extreme luxury [EC]. Both 'purple' and 'scarlet' were expensive dyes [Ld]. Πορφύρα refers to cloth and clothing more than to the dye [WBC]. See this word also at 17:4.

c. σιρικόν (LN **6.168**) (BAGD p. 751): 'silk' [BAGD, BNTC, EC, **LN**, Lns, WBC; all versions], 'silk cloth' [BAGD, LN].

d. θύϊνος (LN **3.63**) (BAGD p. 365): 'citron' [NCV, NET, NIV, TNT], 'made of citron' [**LN**], 'from the citron tree' [BAGD], 'citron wood' [BAGD, LN, WBC], 'sweet smelling' [CEV], 'fragrant' [NAB, REB], 'perfumed' [NLT], 'scented' [BNTC; NRSV], 'rare' [TEV], 'thyine' [EC, Lns; KJV]. Θύϊνος grew in North Africa and is probably *Thuia articulata* [ICC, Sw]. It is a hardwood [Be, Ld, TNTC, WBC]. It is a fragrant wood [Alf, BNTC, Lns, TH, TNTC, Wal; CEV, NAB, NLT, NRSV, REB]. It was valued for its beautiful grain patterns [Sw, TNTC, WBC]. It was used to make expensive furniture [Alf, Be, EC, ICC, Ld, NIC, TH, Wal].

e. ξύλον (LN **3.60**) (BAGD 1. p. 549): 'wood' [BAGD, BNTC, EC, **LN**, Lns, WBC; all versions].

f. ἐλεφάντινος (LN **2.44**) (BAGD p. 251): 'ivory' [BNTC, EC, Lns; all versions], 'made of ivory' [BAGD, **LN**, WBC], 'consisting of ivory' [LN]. The word ἐλεφάντινος means 'consisting of the tusks of elephants' [LN].

g. χαλκός (LN **2.54**) (BAGD 1. p. 875): 'bronze' [BAGD, BNTC, **LN**; all versions except CEV, KJV], 'made of bronze' [CEV], 'brass' [BAGD, EC, LN, Lns, WBC; KJV], 'copper' [BAGD, LN]. See a cognate word at 2:7.

h. σίδηρος (LN **2.58**) (BAGD p. 750): 'iron' [BAGD, BNTC, EC LN, Lns, WBC; all versions], 'made of iron' [**LN**].

i. μάρμαρος (LN **2.45**) (BAGD): 'marble' [BAGD, BNTC, EC, **LN**, Lns, WBC; all versions]. Μάρμαρος is a colorful, relatively hard form of limestone that may be polished to a lustrous finish [LN].

QUESTION—Does the phrase 'goods of gold and of silver and of precious stone' refer to the material 'stone' or to 'jewels'?

1. It refers to jewels or precious stones [Be, BNTC, EC, ICC, Ld, NIC, NTC, TH, Wal, WBC; all versions].

1. It is singular and may refer to the material stone, such as granite [Alf, Lns, TNTC].

QUESTION—What words modify γόμον 'goods'?

The genitives 'of gold, of silver, of precious stone, of pearls, of fine linen, of purple, of silk, of scarlet' all modify 'goods' [ICC].

QUESTION—What words constitute the objects of ἀγοράζει 'buys' from the previous verse?

The words: goods, every kind of citron wood, and every kind of ivory vessel, every kind of vessel of valuable wood, of bronze, of iron and of-marble constitute the objects of 'buys' [EC].

QUESTION—What is meant by ἐκ 'of' in the phrase ἐκ ξύλου τιμιωτάτου καὶ χαλκοῦ καὶ σιδήρου καὶ μαρμάρου 'of valuable wood and of bronze and of iron and of marble'?

It means 'made from' [EC, WBC; NCV, NET, NIV, NLT, REB, TEV]: vessels *made from* valuable wood, and bronze and iron and marble.

18:13 And cinnamon[a] and spice[b] and incense and myrrh[c] and frankincense[d] and wine and olive-oil[e] and fine-flour[f] and wheat and cattle[g] and sheep, and of-horses and of-chariots[h] and of-slaves,[i] and souls[j] of-men.

TEXT—Some manuscripts do not include καὶ ἄμωμον 'and spice'. GNT does not mention this alternative. TR and KJV also do not include these words.

LEXICON—a. κιννάμωμον (LN **5.24**) (BAGD p. 432): 'cinnamon' [BAGD, BNTC, EC, **LN**, Lns, WBC; all versions]. Κιννάμωμον is a type of spice obtained from certain aromatic plants [LN]. The bark of the plant was used [EC, WBC] as well as the wood and shoots [WBC]. The oil extracted from cinnamon was sweet smelling and it was used for burning [TH].

b. ἄμωμον (LN **5.23**) (BAGD p. 47): 'spice' [BNTC, EC, **LN**, WBC; all versions except KJV], 'amomum' [BAGD, LN, Lns, WBC], not explicit [KJV]. The word ἄμωμον indicates an Indian spice plant [BAGD, LN]. It was a perfume [Be, EC, ICC, Lns, NIC, TH, Wal, WBC]. It was used on the hair [Alf, EC, ICC, NIC]. It was an ointment [Alf, Be, ICC, TH, Wal].

c. μύρον (LN 6.205) (BAGD p. 530): 'myrrh' [BNTC, WBC; all versions except CEV, KJV, NET] 'perfume' [BAGD, EC, LN, Lns; REB], 'perfumed oil' [LN], 'perfumed ointment' [NET], 'ointment' [BAGD; KJV]. Μύρον was fragrant [BAGD, Be, EC, LN, TH, Wal]. It was expensive [LN, TH]. It was an ointment [Be, LN, TH, Wal]. It referred to perfume in general, not just to the specific perfume of this name [EC].

d. λίβανος (LN 6.212) (BAGD p. 473): 'frankincense' [BAGD, BNTC, EC, LN, Lns, WBC; all versions]. Λίβανος is a resinous gum from certain trees in Arabia [BAGD]. It is aromatic [Be, LN, TH].

e. ἔλαιον (LN 6.202) (BAGD 1. p. 247): 'olive oil' [EC, LN; CEV, NAB, NCV, NET, NIV, NLT, NRSV], 'oil' [BNTC, Lns, WBC; KJV, REB, TEV, TNT]. See this word also at 6:6.

f. σεμίδαλις (LN **5.10**) (BAGD p. 746): 'fine flour' [BAGD, BNTC, EC, **LN**, Lns, WBC; CEV, KJV, NAB, NCV, NIV, NLT, TNT], 'flour'

[BNTC; REB, TEV], 'choice flour' [NRSV], 'costly flour' [NET]. Σεμίδαλις is a fine grade of wheat flour [BAGD, LN].

g. κτῆνος (LN **4.6**) (BAGD p. 455): 'cattle' [BAGD, BNTC, EC, **LN**, Lns, WBC; all versions except KJV], 'beast' [KJV], 'domesticated animal, pet, pack-animal, animal used for riding' [BAGD]. A κτῆνος is a larger type of domesticated animal, primarily used for riding or carrying loads [LN].

h. ῥέδη (LN **6.53**) (BAGD p. 734): 'chariot' [BNTC, EC, Lns; CEV KJV, NAB, NLT, NRSV, REB], 'carriage' [BAGD, **LN**, WBC; NCV, NIV, TEV, TNT], 'four-wheeled carriages' [NET], 'wagon' [**LN**]. A ῥέδη is a four-wheeled carriage [BAGD, ICC, LN, NIC, TH].

i. σῶμα (LN **87.78**) (BAGD 2. p. 799): 'slave' [BAGD, BNTC, EC, **LN**, WBC; all versions except NIV], 'body' [Lns; NIV].

j. ψυχή (BAGD 1.e. p. 894): 'soul' [EC, Lns; KJV, NIV]. The phrase ψυχὰς ἀνθρώπων 'souls of men' is translated: 'bondmen' [BAGD], 'other humans' [CEV], 'human beings' [WBC; NAB], 'human lives' [BNTC; NCV, NET, NLT, NRSV, REB, TEV, TNT]. See this word also at 6:6 and 8:9.

QUESTION—What relationship is indicated by σωμάτων καὶ ψυχὰς ἀνθρώπων 'slaves and souls of men'?

1. The last two nouns further define the first [Alf, Be, EC, Lns, NTC, WBC; NAB, NLT]: slaves, *that is* the souls of men. It is difficult to find a difference between the two terms [Alf]. The καί 'and' should be translated 'even' [Be, EC, Lns; NLT]: slaves, *even* the souls of men.
2. The nouns are in a conjoining relationship [BNTC, TH; CEV, KJV, NCV, NET, NIV, NRSV, REB, TEV, TNT]: slaves *and* the souls of men. The phrase probably indicates 'slaves and captives' [TH].

QUESTION—What do 'of horses, of carriages, of slaves' modify?

They relate to the word γόμον 'goods' in verse 12 [EC, Lns, Sw]: *goods* of horses, of carriages and of slaves.

QUESTION—Why is ψυχάς 'souls' in the accusative case?

It is in the accusative case because it is the direct object of ἀγοράζει 'he buys' of verse 11 [EC]: no one buys…slaves any longer.

18:14 **And the fruit[a] of-your soul's desire[b] departed from you, and all the luxurious[c] and splendid-things[d] perished from you and never no-longer will-they-find them.**

TEXT—Instead of ἀπώλετο 'perished', some manuscripts have ἀπῆλθεν 'departed'. GNT does not mention this alternative. The reading 'departed' is taken by TR and KJV.

TEXT—Instead of εὑρήσουσιν 'they will find', some manuscripts have εὑρήσῃς 'you will find'. GNT does not mention this alternative. The reading 'you will find' is taken by TR and KJV.

LEXICON—a. ὀπώρα (LN **3.34**) (BAGD p. 576): 'fruit' [BAGD, BNTC; KJV, NAB, NIV, NRSV, TNT], 'ripe fruit' [**LN**, WBC; NET], 'ripe autumn fruit' [EC], 'harvest' [REB], 'flush season' [Lns], 'things' [CEV], 'good things' [NCV, TEV], 'fancy things' [NLT]. The word ὀπώρα indicates 'autumn fruit' [EC, Sw], ready for harvesting [Sw].

b. ἐπιθυμία (LN 25.12) (BAGD 1. p. 293): 'desire' [BAGD, LN], 'lust' [EC, Lns]. This noun is also translated as a verb: 'to desire' [WBC; CEV], 'to greatly desire' [NET], 'to long for' [NIV, NRSV, REB, TNT], 'to long to own' [TEV], 'to lust after' [KJV], 'to crave' [NAB], 'to want' [NCV], 'to greatly love' [NLT], 'to set one's heart on' [BNTC].

c. λιπαρός (LN **79.21**) (BAGD 2. p. 475): 'luxurious' [BAGD, LN], 'splendid' [EC **LN**], 'rich' [BAGD], 'glamorous' [LN], 'costly, bright' [BAGD]. This adjective is translated as a noun: 'luxury' [CEV, NAB, NET, NLT, TNT], 'riches' [NCV, NIV], 'wealth' [TEV], 'dainties' [KJV, NRSV], 'glitter' [REB], 'glamour' [BNTC], 'fat things' [Lns], 'expensive trinkets' [WBC], 'luxurious things' [EC]. Λιπαρός refers to fatty things [EC, TH, TNTC].

d. λαμπρός (LN **27.90**) (BAGD 5. p. 466): 'splendid' [LN], 'glamorous' [**LN**], 'bright, radiant, shining, splendorous' [BAGD]. This adjective is translated as a noun: 'splendor' [NAB, NET, NIV, NLT, NRSV, TNT], 'glamour' [REB, TEV], 'glory' [CEV], 'brilliance' [BNTC], 'splendid things' [EC], 'brilliant things' [Lns], 'beautiful trinkets' [WBC], 'goodly things' [KJV], 'fancy things' [NCV].

QUESTION—Who is the implied speaker of these words?
1. The merchants of verse 11 are the implied speakers [EC, NIC, TH; NCV, TEV]: The merchants said to her
2. God himself is the speaker [Lns]: God said to her.
3. It should be left unspecified [NIV, NLT, REB]: They said to her.

QUESTION—To what specific things does the term λιπαρός 'luxurious' refer?
It probably refers to rich foods [EC, NIC, Sw, TNTC]. Taken together with the following word (splendid), they refer to the items listed in the preceding verses [Alf, EC, Hu]. These are delicacies or luxuries [TH].

QUESTION—To what specific things does the term λαμπρός 'splendid' refer?
It probably refers to clothing [EC, NIC, Sw, TNTC], decorative objects [NIC, TNTC] and expensive furniture [Sw]. These are things that sparkle like gold and silver and jewels [TH].

QUESTION—What is the significance of the negative phrase οὐκέτι οὐ μὴ 'no longer in no way'?
It is a double negative plus a double negative, literally, 'no longer, not not', and is as strong a negative as the Greek language is capable of to express that they will not be found [EC].

QUESTION—Who is the implied actor of εὑρήσουσιν 'they will find'?
The actor is an indefinite 'they' [NIGTC].

18:15 The merchants of-these-things the-ones (who) became-rich[a] from[b] her will-stand from afar weeping and grieving because-of[c] the fear of her torment.

LEXICON—a. aorist act. participle of πλουτέω (LN **57.28**) (BAGD 1. p. 674): 'to become rich' [BAGD, EC, **LN**, Lns; CEV, NCV, TEV], 'to be made rich' [KJV, TNT], 'to grow rich' [NAB, REB], 'to get rich' [NET], 'to become wealthy' [LN, WBC; NLT], 'to gain wealth' [NIV, NRSV], 'to make one's fortune' [BNTC], 'to prosper' [LN]. See this word also at 3:17.

b. ἀπό with genitive object (LN **89.25**) (BAGD V.2. p. 88): 'from' [BNTC, EC LN, Lns; NAB, NCV, NET, NIV, NRSV, TEV], 'because of' [**LN**; CEV], 'by' [KJV, NLT, TNT], 'by means of' [WBC], 'on' [REB]. This preposition here marks cause or reason with focus on the source [LN]. See this word also at 9:18.

c. διά with accusative object (LN 90.44): 'because of' [EC, LN, Lns, WBC; NET, TEV], 'for' [KJV, NAB], 'in' [BNTC; NRSV REB, TNT], not explicit [CEV, NCV, NIV, NLT].

QUESTION—What verses parallel this verse?

Verses 9–11 parallel this verse [NIGTC, TH].

QUESTION—What are τούτων 'these things'?

They are the items listed in verses 12 and 13 [Alf, EC, ICC].

QUESTION—Why are the merchants afraid?

They are afraid the same thing will happen to them [EC, Ld, WBC].

18:16 Saying, "Woe woe, the great city, the-one (that) clothed-herself-with fine-linen and purple and scarlet and having-been-adorned [with] gold and precious stone and pearl,

TEXT—Before λέγοντες 'saying', some manuscripts include καί 'and'. GNT does not mention this alternative. 'And' is included by TR and KJV.

TEXT—Some manuscripts do not include ἐν 'with.' GNT does not deal with this alternative in the apparatus, but brackets it in the text, indicating doubt about including it.

QUESTION—What verse does this parallel?

It parallels the description of the prostitute in 17:4 [BNTC, EC, WBC].

QUESTION—How does the mourning of the merchants contrast with the mourning of the kings?

The kings mourned the city's loss of power, the merchants mourn its loss of wealth [EC, NIC, TNTC].

18:17 Because in-one hour so-much[a] wealth was-destroyed."[b] And every ship-captain[c] and everyone sailing[d] to (a) place and sailors[e] and as-many-as work (by) the sea,[f] stood from afar

TEXT—Instead of ὁ ἐπὶ τόπον πλέων 'the one sailing to (a) place', some manuscripts have ὁ ἐπὶ τὸν τόπον πλέων 'the one sailing to the place', others have ὁ ἐπὶ πόντον πλέων 'the one sailing on (the) sea', others have ὁ ἐπὶ τὸν πόταμον πλέων 'the one sailing on the river', and others have ἐπὶ τῶν πλοίων πλέων 'sailing on the ships'. Still others possibly have ἐπὶ τῶν πλοίων ὁ ὅμιλος 'the company on the ships', although GNT does not mention this alternative. GNT selects the reading ὁ ἐπὶ τόπον πλέων 'the one sailing to (a) place' with a B rating, indicating that the text is almost certain. The reading 'the company on the ships' is taken by TR and KJV.

LEXICON—a. τοσοῦτος (LN **59.18**): 'so much' [BNTC, **LN**; REB], 'so great' [Lns; KJV], 'such great' [NET, NIV], 'such fabulous' [WBC], 'such' [EC], 'this great' [NAB], 'these' [NCV], 'all these' [TNT], 'all this' [NRSV, TEV], 'all' [NLT], not explicit [CEV]. See this word also at 18.7.
  b. perf. pass. indic. of ἐρημόομαι, ἐρημόω (LN **20.41**) (BAGD): 'to be destroyed' [**LN**, WBC; NCV, NET], 'to be ruined' [NAB], 'to be brought to ruin' [NIV], 'to be laid waste' [BNTC; NRSV, REB, TNT], 'to be made desolate' [Lns], 'to suffer destruction, to suffer desolation' [LN]. The passive mood is also translated actively: 'to lose' [TEV], 'to become desolate' [EC], 'to disappear' [CEV], 'to come to nought' [KJV], 'to be gone' [NLT]. See this word also at 17:16.
  c. κυβερνήτης (LN 54.28) (BAGD 1. p. 456): 'ship captain' [BNTC, LN, Lns; CEV, NAB, NCV, NET, NIV, TEV, TNT], 'captain' [BAGD], 'sea captain' [REB], 'shipmaster' [WBC; KJV, NRSV], 'helmsman' [EC], 'steersman, pilot' [BAGD], 'shipowner' [NLT].
  d. πλέω (LN **54.27**, 54.1) (BAGD p. 668): 'to sail' [BAGD, EC, LN (54.1), Lns], 'to travel by sea' [BAGD], not explicit [KJV]. The phrase ὁ ἐπὶ τόπον πλέων 'the one sailing to a place' is translated: 'sea traveler' [**LN**; NAB], 'passenger' [BAGD; CEV, NCV, TEV, TNT], 'sea merchant' [LN], 'seafarer' [NRSV], 'seafaring man' [BNTC], 'voyager' [REB], 'captain of a merchant ship' [NLT], 'one who sails along the coast' [BAGD; NET], 'one who travels by ship' [NIV].
  e. ναύτης (LN 54.30) (BAGD p. 534): 'sailor' [BAGD, BNTC, EC, LN, Lns, WBC; all versions except NET, NLT], 'seaman' [NET], 'crew' [NLT].
  f. θάλασσα (LN **1.73**) (BAGD p. 691): 'sea' [BNTC, EC, **LN**, Lns, WBC; all versions except NLT], 'open sea, ocean' [LN], 'high sea' [BAGD, LN], not explicit [NLT].

QUESTION—What relationship is indicated by ὅτι 'because'?
It indicates that this verse stands as the reason for the cry of woe in verse 16 [NIGTC]: Woe woe, the great city...*because* in one hour so much wealth was destroyed.

QUESTION—What is meant by the phrase πᾶς ὁ ἐπὶ τόπον πλέων 'everyone sailing to a place'?
  1. It means a person who travels on the sea, a seafarer or a passenger [BAGD, BNTC, ICC, NIC, TH, WBC; all versions except KJV, NLT].
  2. It means a sea merchant or one who uses the sea for commercial purposes [NLT].
  3. It could be either of the above [Sw, TNTC].

QUESTION—What is meant by the phrase ὅσοι τὴν θάλασσαν ἐργάζονται 'as many as work the sea'
It refers to those who make their living from the sea [Alf, ICC, NIC, TH, TNTC].

18:18 Seeing the smoke of-her burning[a] were-crying-out, "What (city is) like the great city?"
TEXT—Instead of βλέποντες 'seeing', some manuscripts possibly have the synonym ὁρῶντες 'seeing', although GNT does not mention this alternative. TR accepts the alternative reading.
LEXICON—a. πύρωσις (LN **14.63**): 'burning' [BNTC, EC, **LN**, Lns, WBC; all versions]. See this word also at 4:5.
QUESTION—What is implied by this rhetorical question?
It implies that there is no city like this one [Be, EC, Lns, TH, TNTC, WBC].
QUESTION—How are the nouns related in the genitive construction τῆς πυρώσεως αὐτῆς 'her burning'?
The fire burns her [LN, WBC; NET, TEV, TNT].

18:19 And they-threw dust on their heads and weeping and grieving were-crying-out, "Woe woe, the great city, by which the-ones having the ships in the sea became-rich from[a] her wealth[b] because in-one hour she-was-destroyed."
TEXT—Instead of τὰ πλοῖα 'the ships', some manuscripts have πλοῖα 'boats'. GNT does not mention this alternative. The reading 'boats' is taken by TR and KJV.
LEXICON—a. ἐκ with genitive object (LN 89.77): 'from' [LN, WBC; CEV, NAB, NET, NLT, REB], 'by' [NRSV], 'by means of' [LN], 'by reason of' [Be, Sw; KJV], 'through' [NIV, TNT], 'because of' [EC; NCV], 'due to' [Lns], 'on' [BNTC; TEV].
  b. τιμιότης (LN **57.35**) (BAGD p. 818): 'wealth' [BNTC, **LN**, WBC; NAB, NCV, NET, NIV, NRSV, TEV, TNT], 'great wealth' [NLT], 'prosperity' [REB], 'abundance of costly things' [BAGD], 'treasure' [EC; CEV], 'costliness' [BAGD; KJV], 'expensiveness' [Lns].
QUESTION—What does ἔβαλον χοῦν ἐπὶ τὰς κεφαλὰς αὐτῶν 'they threw dust on their heads' imply?
It is a sign of grief, sorrow, or mourning [EC, NIC, TH, TNTC, WBC; NLT].

DISCOURSE UNIT: 18:20–19:4 [BNTC]. The topic is the judgment of Babylon.

DISCOURSE UNIT: 18:20–24 [Lns, NIGTC, TNTC]. The topic is the third part of the vision [Lns], destruction of the city [TNTC].

DISCOURSE UNIT: 18:20 [Be, Ld, Sw, Wal]. The topic is an outburst of praise [Be, Ld], a call to rejoice [Sw, Wal]. BNTC,

18:20 Rejoice[a] over her (O) heaven and saints and apostles and prophets, because God judged your judgment against[b] her.

TEXT—Instead of οἱ ἅγιοι καὶ οἱ ἀπόστολοι 'the saints and the apostles', some manuscripts have οἱ ἅγιοι ἀπόστολοι 'the holy apostles'. GNT does not mention this alternative. The reading 'the holy apostles' is taken by TR and KJV.

LEXICON—a. pres. pass. imperative of εὐφραίνω (LN 25.1341) (BAGD 2. p. 327): 'to rejoice' [BAGD, BNTC, WBC; KJV, NAB, NET, NIV, NLT, NRSV, TNT], 'to be happy' [LN; CEV, NCV], 'to be glad' [LN; TEV], 'to make merry' [EC], 'to exult' [REB], 'to celebrate' [Lns]. See this word also at 11:10.

b. ἐκ (LN **90.16**): 'against' [NAB, NET, NRSV, TNT], 'from' [LN, Lns], 'by' [LN], 'on' [BNTC, EC; KJV, REB]. The clause ἔκρινεν ὁ θεὸς τὸ κρίμα ὑμῶν ἐξ αὐτῆς 'God judged your judgment against her' is translated: 'God condemned her for what she did to you' [**LN**]. Some versions treated this preposition as the marker of the direct object: 'God judged her' [WBC; CEV, NCV, NIV, NLT, REB].

QUESTION—Who is the speaker of this verse?
1. It is the angel of 18:4 [BNTC, EC, Lns].
1. It is the writer of Revelation [Be, TH].
1. It is the angel of verse 18:1 [NIGTC].

QUESTION—Who is addressed in the vocative οὐρανέ 'heaven'?
All heavenly beings are being addressed [TH].

QUESTION—Are all those addressed in heaven or on earth?
1. They are the ones who already in heaven [BNTC, EC, ICC, Lns, NIC, TH, WBC]. The saints and apostles and martyrs are those who have been martyred for Christ [BNTC]. It refers to martyrs because the verse compares what God is doing to Babylon with what Babylon had done to them [TH, WBC].
2. It is addressed both to those in heaven and on earth [NIGTC].

QUESTION—Do οἱ ἅγιοι καὶ οἱ ἀπόστολοι καὶ οἱ προφῆται 'the saints and the apostles and the prophets' refer to three distinct groups of people or one?
1. It refers to three distinct groups of people [Lns, WBC; all versions except KJV]: the saints *and* the apostles *and* the prophets.
2. It refers to one composite group of people, the first being generic, the last two specifics [Be, EC]: the saints, *even* the apostles and the prophets.
3. It refers to two groups of people [KJV]: you holy apostles and prophets.

QUESTION—To whom does οἱ ἀπόστολοι 'the apostles' refer?
1. It refers to the apostles in the narrow sense, to the original 12 [EC, Lns, WBC].
2. It refers to the apostles in the wider sense, to the original 12 plus those who were also called apostles [Sw].

QUESTION—To whom does οἱ προφῆται 'the prophets' refer?
1. It refers to the prophets of the NT [EC, WBC]. It must refer to NT prophets because they were persecuted for Christ's sake [EC].

150   REVELATION 18:20

   1. It refers to the prophets of the OT [Lns].
QUESTION—What relationship is indicated by ὅτι 'because'?
   It indicates that the following clause is the reason for which they should be glad [NIGTC]: Be glad...*because* God judged your judgment against her.
QUESTION—How are the nouns related in the genitive construction τὸ κρίμα ὑμῶν 'your judgment'?
   1. You judged Babylon [Be, EC, Ld, Sw; NAB, NET, NIV, NLT, NRSV, TEV, TNT]. God has vindicated your judgment in his judgment against Babylon. Κρίμα has here the sense of 'a case for trial' as it does in Exodus 18:22 and 1 Corinthians 6:7 [Sw].
   2. Someone judged you, the Roman law court judged you [BNTC, Hu, NIC, TH, WBC; REB]: God imposed on her the judgment that she made against you. See verse 18:6 for this interpretation [Hu, NIC]. Κρίμα does not have the sense of a lawsuit in its NT usage. It is used here in the sense of judgment passed by a judge and in particular the judgment of the Roman law court on the martyrs [BNTC].
   3. God judged *in relation to* you [Lns]: God has judged her in the case that involved you.
   4. Either 1 or 2 above is a correct interpretation [NIGTC].

DISCOURSE UNIT: 18:21–24 [Alf, Be, EC, Ld, NIC, Sw, Wal, WBC]. The topic is the announcement of destruction of Babylon [EC, Ld, NIC, Wal, WBC].

DISCOURSE UNIT: 18:21–23 [Alf]. The topic is the announcement of Babylon's ruin.

18:21 And one strong angel picked-up (a) stone like (a) great millstone[a] and threw (it) into the sea saying, "In-this-way Babylon the great city will-be-thrown with-violence[b] and never would-be-found any-more.
   LEXICON—a. μύλινος (LN **7.70**) (BAGD p. 529): 'millstone' [BAGD, BNTC, EC, **LN**, Lns, WBC; all versions except CEV, NCV], 'a stone used for grinding' [NCV], not explicit [CEV].
   b. ὅρμημα (LN **68.82**) (BAGD p. 581): 'violence' [BAGD; KJV], 'sudden violence' [**LN**, WBC], 'such violence' [NIV, NRSV], 'sudden violent force' [NET], 'such force' [NAB], 'headlong' [BNTC; TNT], 'rush' [EC], 'swift rush' [Lns], 'sudden force' [LN], 'violent rush' [BAGD], not explicit [CEV, NCV]. The sense of this word is implied in the verb and translated: '(sent) hurtling down' [REB]. The dative of this word is translated as an adverb: 'violently' [NLT, TEV]. This noun is also used in a cognate verb form in Mark 5:3 where the herd of pigs rushed down a steep bank into a lake and in Acts 19:29 where the crowd of people rushed into the theater in Ephesus [NIC].
QUESTION—What was the form of this 'millstone'?
   It was the doughnut-shaped upper stone of a mill that was turned by human or animal power [WBC]. It was a larger kind that needed to be turned by an

animal [EC, ICC, Lns, Sw]. It was four to five feet in diameter and a foot thick and weighed thousands of pounds [EC].

QUESTION—What does this action symbolize?

It symbolizes the destruction of the city [Ld]. It symbolizes the sudden and impressive way that God's judgment will come on the whole antichristian world [EC].

QUESTION—What is indicated by the double negative οὐ μή 'never' and ἔτι 'any more'?

The double negative is emphatic and this is further stressed by 'any longer' [EC, NIGTC, TNTC]: never any more.

QUESTION—What Scripture paints a similar figure?

Jeremiah 51:59–64 closely resembles this symbolic action [EC, Hu, ICC, Ld, NIC, NIGTC, NTC, WBC].

18:22 **And (the) sound of-harpists and musicians[a] and flutists[b] and trumpeters[c] never would-be-heard in you any-more, and every craftsman[d] of-every trade[e] never would-be-found in you any-more, and (the) sound of-a-mill[f] never would-be-heard in you any-more,**

TEXT—Instead of καὶ πᾶς τεχνίτης πάσης τέχνης 'and every craftsman of every craft', some manuscripts have καὶ πᾶς τεχνίτης καὶ πάσης τέχνης 'and every craftsman and of every craft', others have καὶ πᾶς τεχνίτης 'and every craftsman'. GNT selects the reading 'and every craftsman of every craft' with a B rating, indicating that the text is almost certain.

TEXT—One important manuscript does not include καὶ φωνὴ μύλου...ἔτι 'and (the) sound of a millstone shall by no means be heard in you any longer', and a few versions do not include from καὶ πᾶς τεχνίτης 'and every craftsman' to the end of the verse. GNT includes these two readings.

LEXICON—a. μουσικός (LN **14.84**) (BAGD p. 528): 'musician' [BAGD, EC, **LN**, Lns; KJV, NAB, NET, NIV], 'singer' [WBC; CEV, TEV, TNT], 'minstrel' [BNTC; NRSV, REB], 'music' [NCV], 'song' [NLT]. Here μουσικός probably refers to a 'singer' [LN].

b. αὐλητής (LN 6.88) (BAGD p. 121): 'flutist' [EC, LN, WBC; NAB, NRSV], 'flute player' [BAGD, BNTC, Lns; NET, NIV, REB, TEV, TNT], 'piper' [KJV], 'flute' [CEV, NCV, NLT].

c. σαλπιστής (LN **6.91**) (BAGD p. 741): 'trumpeter' [BAGD, BNTC, EC, **LN**, Lns, WBC; all versions except CEV, NLT], 'trumpet' [CEV, NLT].

d. τεχνίτης (LN **42.53**) (BAGD p. 814): 'craftsman' [BAGD, BNTC, EC, **LN**, Lns, WBC; KJV NAB, NET, REB, TNT], 'workman' [NCV, NIV, TEV], 'worker' [CEV], 'artisan' [BAGD; NRSV], 'industry' [NLT], 'designer' [BAGD]. Τεχνίτης refers to a skilled worker, not to a common laborer [TH].

e. τέχνη (LN 42.51) (BAGD p. 814): 'trade' [BAGD, BNTC; NAB, NET, NIV, NRSV, REB, TEV, TNT], 'craft' [EC, LN, Lns; KJV], 'occupation' [LN, WBC], 'job' [NCV], 'skill' [BAGD], 'kind of industry' [NLT], not explicit [CEV].

f. μύλος (LN **7.68**) (BAGD 1, p. 529): 'mill' [BAGD, BNTC, EC, **LN**, WBC; NET, REB, TNT], 'millstone' [Lns; KJV, NAB, NIV, NRSV, TEV]. This noun is also translated as a phrase: 'grinding grain' [CEV, NCV, NLT]. Here the sound a mill makes when it turns is indicated [BAGD].

QUESTION—What is symbolized by the absence of the sounds of musical instruments?

It is a poetic way of picturing desolation [WBC]. The varied activities of the city have ceased [Ld].

QUESTION—What is indicated by the numerous repetitions of οὐ μή...ἔτι 'never...anymore'?

It indicates the permanence of their disappearance [EC].

18:23 **And (the) light of-(a)-lamp**[a] **never would-shine in you any-more, and the voice of-(a)-bridegroom**[b] **and bride**[c] **never would-be-heard in you any-more,**

LEXICON—a. λύχνος (LN 6.104) (BAGD 1. p. 483): 'lamp' [BAGD, BNTC, EC, LN, Lns, WBC; CEV, NCV, NET, NIV, NLT, NRSV, REB, TEV], 'burning lamp' [NAB], 'candle' [KJV]. Λύχνος refers to a light made by burning a wick saturated with oil in a relatively small vessel [LN]. The container was either metal or clay [BAGD].

b. νυμφίος (LN 10.56) (BAGD p. 545): 'bridegroom' [BAGD, BNTC, EC, LN, Lns, WBC; KJV, NCV, NET, NIV, NRSV, REB, TNT], 'groom' [NAB, NLT, TEV], not explicit [CEV].

c. νύμφη (LN 10.57) (BAGD 1. p. 545): 'bride' [BAGD, BNTC, EC, LN, Lns, WBC; all versions except CEV], not explicit [CEV].

QUESTION—What is implied by the word λύχνος 'lamp'?

It indicates that not even the smallest of lights would shine [EC, ICC].

because your merchants were the great-people[a] **of-the earth, because all the nations were-deceived by your sorcery,**[b]

LEXICON—a. μεγιστάν (LN 87.41) (BAGD p. 498): 'great person' [LN; NCV], 'great man' [BAGD, EC; KJV, NIV], 'leading man' [TNT], 'prominent person' [WBC], 'magnate' [BAGD, BNTC; NRSV], 'tycoon' [NET], 'very important person' [BAGD, LN], '(the) greatest' [NLT], '(the) most powerful' [TEV], 'merchant prince' [REB], 'nobility' [NAB], 'grandee' [Lns], 'courtier' [BAGD]. This noun is also translated as a verb phrase: '(her merchants) ruled the earth' [CEV].

b. φαρμακεία (LN **53.100**) (BAGD p. 854): 'sorcery' [BAGD, BNTC, EC, LN, Lns; KJV, NLT, NRSV, REB, TNT], 'magic spell' [**LN**, WBC; NET, NIV], 'witchcraft' [CEV], 'magic' [BAGD, LN; NCV], 'magic potion' [NAB], 'false magic' [TEV]. See a similar word at 9:21.

QUESTION—What relationship is indicated by the first ὅτι 'because'?

It indicates that the following clause is the reason for Babylon's destruction [Be, Ld, NIC, NIGTC, TNTC, WBC]: Babylon the great city will be violently thrown down *because* her merchants were the great ones of the

earth. The word μεγιστάν 'great one' implies arrogance [Be, EC, Ld, NIC]. This pride is the cause of God's destruction of Babylon [EC]. The merchants took the credit for their greatness and did not acknowledge God [NIGTC]. Rome exploited the Mediterranean world by her economic domination. It is this for which she is being judged [WBC]. They credited their greatness to their wealth and forgot God [TNTC].
QUESTION—What relationship is indicated by the second ὅτι 'because'?
1. It indicates that the following clause gives another reason for the Babylon's destruction [Be, Ld, NIC, NIGTC, TNTC]: Babylon the great city will be violently thrown down *because* she deceived the nations with her sorcery. Her sorcery or deception lay in leading the nations to feel that ultimate security was to be had in wealth and luxury [Ld]. She deceived the nations into believing that she was the eternal city [NIC]. She led the nations astray to worship idols [Be, NIGTC]. It was her magic that caused the deception [TNTC].
2. It indicates that the following clause gives the reason for preceding one [EC, Sw, WBC]: Babylon's merchants were the great ones of the earth *because* all the nations were deceived by her sorcery. The merchants became great men because they had been drawn in by her deception [EC]. Rome's economic domination of her world could only be because of her use of magic [WBC].

18:24 **And (the) blood of prophets and saints and all the-ones having-been-slaughtered**[a] **on the earth was-found in her."**
LEXICON—a. perf. pass. participle of σφάζω (LN **20.72**) (BAGD): 'to be slaughtered' [**LN**, WBC; NRSV, TNT], 'to be slain' [EC, Lns; KJV, NAB, REB], 'to be killed' [NCV, NET, NIV, TEV], not explicit [CEV]. This verb is also translated as a noun: 'slaughter' [BNTC]. The passive mood is also translated actively: 'to slaughter' [NLT]. Σφάζω implies the use of violence [BAGD, LN] and mercilessness [LN]. See this word also at 5:6 and 6:4.
QUESTION—What is the function of this verse?
It provides the third reason for the destruction of Babylon [Be, EC, NIC, NIGTC, Sw]: Babylon is thrown down violently *because* she slaughtered the prophets and saints. This is the primary reason for its destruction [NIC].
QUESTION—Who is the speaker of this verse?
1. It continues to be the strong angel who was speaking in 18:21 [Alf, BNTC, EC; CEV, NAB, NCV, NET, NIV, NLT, NRSV].
2. It is now a comment made by the writer [TH; REB, TEV, TNT].
QUESTION—Is the phrase προφητῶν καὶ ἁγίων 'of prophets and saints' referring to two groups or one?
1. It refers to two groups, prophets and saints [BNTC, Lns, WBC; CEV, KJV, NAB, NCV, NET, NIV, NLT, NRSV, REB, TEV].
2. It is referring to one group. The first is a specific of the more general second [Be, EC, NIC]: of saints *including* prophets.

QUESTION—To whom does πάντων τῶν ἐσφαγμένων ἐπὶ τῆς γῆς 'all who have been slaughtered on the earth' refer?
1. It refers to all who have been slaughtered for the cause of Christ [Alf, EC, ICC, Ld, Lns, Sw].
1. It refers to all in general who have been murdered beginning with Abel [Hu, NIC, NIGTC].

DISCOURSE UNIT: 19:1–22:5 [EC]. The topic is the closing visions of John.

DISCOURSE UNIT: 19:1–21 [Wal; NRSV]. The topic is the Second Coming of Christ [Wal], rejoicing in heaven [NRSV].

DISCOURSE UNIT: 19:1–10 [EC, Lns, Sw; NCV, NIV, NLT]. The topic is rejoicing over Babylon's fall.

DISCOURSE UNIT: 19:1–8 [Alf, WBC; KJV]. The topic is the song of praise for Babylon's destruction [Alf; KJV], heavenly throne-room audition [WBC].

DISCOURSE UNIT: 19:1–6 [NIGTC]. The topic is the saints honor God for Babylon's fall.

DISCOURSE UNIT: 19:1–5 [Hu, Ld, NIC, NTC, TNTC]. The topic is rejoicing over Babylon's fall [Hu, NTC], a hymn of vindication [NIC], thanksgiving for Babylon's judgment [Ld, TNTC].

19:1 **After these-things I-heard something-like (a) loud voice of-(a)-great crowd in heaven saying, "Hallelujah;[a] the salvation and the glory and the power (is) of our God,**
TEXT—Instead of μετά 'after', some manuscripts have καὶ μετά 'and after'. GNT does not mention this alternative. The reading 'and after' is taken by TR and KJV.
TEXT—Instead of ὡς φωνήν 'like a voice', some manuscripts have φωνήν 'a voice'. GNT does not mention this alternative. The reading 'a voice' is taken by TR and KJV.
TEXT—Instead of the plural λεγόντων 'saying', some manuscripts possibly have the singular λέγοντος 'saying', although GNT does not mention this alternative. The singular reading is taken by TR.
TEXT—Following δόξα 'glory', some manuscripts include καὶ ἡ τιμή 'and the honor'. GNT does not mention this alternative. The reading 'and the honor' is included by TR and KJV.
TEXT—Instead of τοῦ θεοῦ ἡμῶν 'of our God', some manuscripts possibly have κυρίῳ τῷ θεῷ ἡμῶν 'to (the) Lord our God', although GNT does not mention this alternative. The reading 'to (the) Lord our God' is taken by TR and KJV.
LEXICON—a. ἁλληλουϊά (LN **33.363**) (BAGD p. 39): 'hallelujah' [BAGD, EC, **LN**, Lns, WBC; NCV, NET, NIV, NLT, NRSV, REB, TNT], 'alleluia' [BNTC; KJV, NAB], 'praise God' [**LN**; TEV], 'praise the Lord' [CEV]. The word ἁλληλουϊά is Hebrew and literally means 'praise Yah'.

Yah is a shortened form of Yahweh [TH]. Or it means 'Praise Jah' which is a shortened form of Jehovah [Alf, TNTC].

QUESTION—What is the antecedent of ταῦτα 'these things'?

The antecedent is Babylon's destruction in 18:20–24 [NIGTC]. The antecedent is what the angel was saying in chapter 18 [TH]. The antecedent is the events in chapters 17 and 18 [Lns].

QUESTION—To whom does this ὄχλου πολλοῦ 'great crowd' refer?
1. It probably refers to believers [Lns, NIC, NIGTC, Wal]. This is the same group as seen in 7:9 because they refer to God as 'our God' [Lns]. The use of the word 'salvation' and the reference to 'avenging the blood of the martyrs' in the next verse make it likely that this refers to believers [NIC]. Verse 18:20 calls on the saints to rejoice and implies that the crowd in this verse is the whole assembly of the saints. But angels may be included as well [NIGTC]. It probably is a general reference to all people in heaven, but it seems to be specifically martyrs from the great tribulation who are indicated [Wal].
2. It probably refers to angels [EC, Hu, ICC, Ld, Sw, TH, TNTC, WBC]. This probably refers to angels since elders and living creatures are mentioned in verse 4 and the movement is from the periphery in toward the throne [ICC]. It probably refers to the crowd of angels around God's throne (see 5:11) [Ld, WBC].

QUESTION—What is indicated by the term δόξα 'glory'?

It indicates all of the facets of God's character [Lns].

QUESTION—How are the nouns related in the genitive construction ἡ σωτηρία καὶ ἡ δόξα καὶ ἡ δύναμις τοῦ θεοῦ 'the salvation and the glory and the power of God'?

It indicates that the salvation and glory and power *belong to* God [Be, BNTC, Lns, NIC, NIGTC, TH, WBC; CEV, NAB, NET, NIV, REB, TEV, TNT], or *are from* God [EC; NLT]. These *should be ascribed* to God [KJV, NRSV]. God has bestowed salvation to them and this bestowal has revealed God's glory, while God's power has brought about the fall of Babylon [Lns]. Salvation includes the saving of God's people from the hatred of the beast and Babylon, but it also covers the safeguarding of the whole cause of God's kingdom [Ld]. Salvation is God's redemptive program and this has been effected by God's glorious majesty and power [NIC]. The preceding event is an example of salvation from evil and the attributes of God's glory and power [TNTC].

19:2 Because true[a] and just[b] (are) his judgments; because he-judged the great prostitute who was-corrupting[c] the earth with her fornication, and he-avenged[d] the blood of his servants from[e] her hand."

LEXICON—a. ἀληθινός (LN 73.2) (BAGD 1. p. 37): 'true' [BAGD, BNTC, EC, LN, WBC; all versions except CEV], 'honest' [CEV], 'genuine' [Lns]. The adjective ἀληθινός indicates that God's judgments are in keeping with reality [EC]. See this word also at 15:3.

b. δίκαιος (LN 88.12) (BAGD 4. p. 196): 'just' [BNTC, LN, WBC; NAB, NET, NIV, NLT, NRSV, REB, TEV, TNT], 'fair' [CEV], 'right' [NCV], 'righteous' [BAGD, EC, LN, Lns; KJV]. Δίκαιος indicates that they are impartial [EC]. See this word also at 15:3.

c. imperfect act. indic. of φθείρω (LN **88.266**) (BAGD 2.a. p. 857): 'to corrupt' [BAGD, BNTC, EC, Lns, WBC; KJV, NAB, NET, NIV, NLT, NRSV, REB, TEV], 'to pervert' [LN], 'to lead into moral ruin' [**LN**], 'to ruin' [BAGD; CEV], 'to bring ruin' [TNT], 'to make evil' [NCV], 'to deprave, to cause the moral ruin of' [LN]. Φθείρω means to ruin someone's inner life by erroneous teaching or immorality [BAGD]. It means 'to corrupt morally' but here has the sense of 'to destroy' [NIGTC].

d. aorist act. indic. of ἐκδικέω (LN 38.8, 39.33) (BAGD 2. p. 238): 'to avenge' [BNTC, EC, Lns, WBC; KJV, NAB, NET, NIV, NLT, NRSV], 'to take vengeance' [BAGD; REB], 'to punish' [BAGD, LN (38.8); TEV, TNT], 'to make someone pay a price for' [CEV], 'to pay someone back' [NCV], 'to pay back, to revenge, to seek retribution' [LN (39.33)]. See this word also at 6:10.

e. ἐκ (BAGD 6.b. p.236): 'from' [Alf, EC, Lns], 'on' [BNTC; NAB, NIV, NRSV, REB], 'against' [BAGD], 'at' [KJV], 'by' [NET], not explicit [NCV, NLT]. Some take this prepositions as a marker of the direct object of 'to avenge' translating: 'punish her' [TEV, TNT], 'make her pay' [CEV], '(deaths) caused by her' [WBC].

QUESTION—What relationship is indicated by the first ὅτι 'because'?

It indicates that the clause that follows is the reason for the praise of verse 1 [EC, ICC, Lns, NIC, NIGTC, Sw, TNTC, WBC]: Hallelujah...*because* God's judgments are true and just.

QUESTION—What relationship is indicated by the second ὅτι 'because'?

1. It also indicates the reason for the praise of verse 1, but whereas the first ὅτι clause gives the general grounds, this gives the specific grounds [Lns, NIC, NIGTC, WBC]: Hallelujah...*because* he judged the great prostitute.
2. It indicates the reason for why the first is true by giving a specific example of God's true and just judgments [EC, ICC, Sw, TNTC]: God's judgments are true and just *because* he has judged the great prostitute.

QUESTION—What is meant by τὸ αἷμα των τῶν δούλων αὐτοῦ 'the blood of his servants'?

It refers to the *death* of his servants [NIGTC; CEV, NCV, NLT, TEV, TNT].

QUESTION—Should χειρὸς αὐτῆς 'her hand' be taken literally or as a figure?

1. It should be taken figuratively, indicating the woman herself [NIC, WBC; CEV, NAB, NCV, NIV, NRSV, REB, TEV, TNT]: from her.
2. It should be taken literally [NIGTC; KJV, NET]: from her hand.

QUESTION—What is meant by the phrase ἐκ χειρὸς αὐτῆς 'from her hand'?

1. It refers back to 'blood' and indicates that the shedding of blood was caused by her [NIGTC, WBC; NET]. The blood was shed *by* her hand [NIGTC].

2. It indicates that God has taken vengeance, viewed as a penalty, *from* her hand [Alf, EC, Lns].

19:3 And a-second-time[a] they-said, "Hallelujah; and[b] her smoke ascends for-ever-and-ever."

LEXICON—a. δέρτερος (BAGD 4. p. 177): 'a second time' [BAGD, BNTC, EC, Lns, WBC; NAB, NET], 'again' [KJV, NCV, NIV, TEV, TNT], 'once more' [NRSV, REB], 'again and again' [NLT], not explicit [CEV].

b. καί (L 89.92): 'and' [EC, LN, Lns; KJV, NCV], 'for' [WBC], not explicit [BNTC; all versions except KJV, NCV].

QUESTION—What is indicated by the καί 'and' after 'hallelujah'?

1. It indicates an additional reason for praising God [Alf, EC, ICC, NIC, NIGTC, WBC]: Hallelujah *because* her smoke ascends forever and ever. It corresponds to Hebrew usage and means 'because' [EC, ICC, NIC].
2. It simply means 'and' [EC, Lns; KJV, NCV].
3. It need not be translated [BNTC; all versions except KJV, NCV].

QUESTION—What is indicated by ὁ καπνὸς αὐτῆς ἀναβαίνει εἰς τοὺς αἰῶνας τῶν αἰώνων 'her smoke ascends forever and ever'?

It indicates the complete finality of Babylon's destruction [EC, Ld, NIC, NIGTC, TH, WBC].

QUESTION—How are the nouns related in the genitive construction ὁ καπνὸς αὐτῆς 'the smoke of her'?

Smoke rises from her because she is burning [NIC, TH, WBC; CEV, NET, NIV, NLT, NRSV, REB, TEV, TNT].

19:4 And the twenty-four elders and the four living-creatures[a] fell-down and worshiped God who sits on the throne saying, "Amen Hallelujah,

TEXT—Instead of οἱ εἴκοσι τέσσαρες 'the twenty four', some manuscripts possibly have οἱ εἴκοσι καὶ τέσσαρες 'the four and twenty', although GNT does not mention this alternative. The reading 'the four and twenty' is taken by TR and KJV.

LEXICON—a. ζῷον (LN 4.2, 12.32) (BAGD 1. p. 341): 'living creature' [BNTC, LN (4.2); CEV, NAB, NCV, NET, NIV, NRSV, REB, TEV, TNT], 'living being' [EC, LN (12.32); NLT], 'living one' [Lns], 'cherubim' [WBC], 'beast' [KJV]. See this word also at 4:6.

QUESTION—What is implied by the description of God as τῷ καθημένῳ ἐπὶ τῷ θρόνῳ 'the one sitting on the throne'?

The throne is a symbol of God exercising his authority and dominion [Lns].

QUESTION—What is indicated by Ἀμήν 'Amen'?

It indicates that the elders and cherubim assent to what the crowd had said [Alf, EC, Hu, Lns, NIGTC, TNTC].

DISCOURSE UNIT: 19:5–19:10 [GNT; CEV, NAB]. The topic is the marriage supper of the Lamb [GNT], the song of victory [NAB].

19:5 And (a) voice came from the throne saying, "Praise[a] our God all his servants [and][b] the-ones-fearing him, the small and the great."

TEXT—Instead of αἰνεῖτε τῷ θεῷ ἡμῶν 'praise to our God', some manuscripts have αἰνεῖτε τὸν θεὸν ἡμῶν 'praise our God'. GNT does not mention this alternative. The reading 'praise our God' is taken by TR and KJV.

TEXT—Instead of καὶ οἱ φοβούμενοι 'and the ones fearing', some manuscripts have οἱ φοβούμενοι 'the ones fearing'. GNT has '[and] the ones fearing' bracketing καί with a C rating indicating difficulty in making the rating.

TEXT—Instead of οἱ μικροί 'the small', some manuscripts possibly have καὶ οἱ μικροί 'both the small (and)' although GNT does not mention this alternative. The reading 'both the small (and)' is taken by TR and KJV.

LEXICON—a. pres. act. imperative of αἰνέω (LN 33.354) (BAGD p. 23): 'to praise' [BAGD, BNTC, EC, LN, Lns, WBC; all versions except CEV, TNT], 'to give praise' [CEV, TNT]. The present imperative indicates a continuous aspect: 'keep on praising' [EC, Lns, Wal].

b. καί (LN 89.92): 'and' [LN; CEV, KJV, NAB, NCV, NET, NRSV, TEV], 'even' [EC, WBC], not explicit [BNTC, Lns; NIV, NLT, REB]. If καί is the correct reading, it means 'even' here [EC, ICC, NIC, NIGTC, WBC]: all his servants, *even* those who fear him.

QUESTION—Whose voice is this ?

It probably is the voice of one of the living creatures [Be, ICC, Ld, NIC, TH]. Coming from the throne, the voice appears to be God speaking, but since the voice says 'praise our God', it must be the voice of one the four living creature who were standing closest to the throne [Ld]. It probably is the voice of one of the cherubim or elders [ICC]. It is probably the voice of one of the heavenly beings around the throne [NIC]. It is probably the voice of an angel [Sw, Wal]. It may be one of the angels who is close to God's presence [Sw]. It cannot be determined who the speaker is [EC, Lns, NIGTC, WBC]. All we can say is that it is the voice of someone who can say, 'Our God.' [Lns]. It at least indicates that the voice has God's approval [WBC].

QUESTION—Are two groups of people addressed here or only one?

1. Only one group is addressed and the second clause further describes the first [BNTC, EC, Lns, NIGTC, Sw, TH, Wal, WBC; CEV, NIV, NLT, REB, TNT]: all his servants, *even* those who fear him. If καί is rejected as not being part of the text then clearly one group is intended [Sw].

2. Two groups may be indicated [Sw]. If καί 'and' is taken as the correct reading, then the second group may refer to unbaptized inquirers who are undergoing teaching (see 11:18) [Sw].

QUESTION—Who are οἱ δοῦλοι αὐτοῦ 'his servants' ?

1. This refers to all believers [Hu, Lns, NIC, NIGTC, Sw, Wal].

2. This refers specifically to the martyrs [ICC].

QUESTION—What is meant by οἱ μικροὶ καὶ οἱ μεγάλοι 'the small and the great'?

This is an idiomatic way of referring to people of low status and people of high status [WBC]. It refers to people of all intellectual, social or spiritual classes or stages of progress [Sw]. It includes people of all social and economical strata [EC].

DISCOURSE UNIT: 19:6–21:8 [Ld]. The topic is the final triumph and consummation [Ld].

DISCOURSE UNIT: 19:6–20:15 [NIC]. The topic is the final victory.

DISCOURSE UNIT: 19:6–20:6 [Be]. The topic is the sequel to the fall of Rome.

DISCOURSE UNIT: 19:6–16 [Hu]. The topic is the marriage of the Lamb.

DISCOURSE UNIT: 19:6–10 [Hu, Ld, NIC, NTC, TNTC; NET]. The topic is the marriage of the Lamb [Ld, NIC, NTC, TNTC; NET], the bride is prepared [Hu].

19:6 And I-heard something-like (a) sound of (a) great crowd and like (a) sound of-many waters and like (a) sound of-mighty thunder saying, "Hallelujah, because (the) Lord [our] God the Almighty[a] reigned.[b]

TEXT—Instead of κύριος ὁ θεὸς ἡμῶν '(the) Lord our God', some manuscripts have ὁ θεὸς ὁ κύριος ἡμῶν 'God our Lord', others have κύριος ὁ θεὸς '(the) Lord God', others have ὁ θεὸς ἡμῶν 'our God', and still others have κύριος 'Lord'. GNT selects the reading '(the) Lord our God' with a C rating, indicating difficulty in choosing the selection and brackets ἡμῶν 'our' in the text. The reading '(the) Lord God' is taken by TR and KJV.

LEXICON—a. παντοκράτωρ (LN **12.7**): 'Almighty' [EC, LN, Lns, WBC; NCV, NIV, NLT, NRSV, TEV, TNT], 'almighty' [NAB], 'all-powerful One' [**LN**], 'All-Powerful' [CEV, NET], 'omnipotent' [KJV], 'Omnipotent' [BNTC], 'sovereign over all' [REB]. See this word also at 1:8.
- b. aorist act. indic. of βασιλεύω (BAGD p. 1.b.α. p. 136): 'to reign' [Lns; KJV, NET, NIV, NLT, NRSV], 'to establish one's reign' [NAB], 'to enter on one's reign' [BNTC; REB], 'to begin to reign' [EC, WBC; TNT], 'to rule' [BAGD; CEV, NCV], 'to be king' [BAGD; TEV]. The aorist is proleptic, that is, it states a future event as though it had already happened [Ld]. See this word also at 5:10 and 11:16.

QUESTION—Who are the speakers referred to here?
1. They are the great crowd that was spoken of in 19:1 [EC, Ld, NIGTC, Wal].
2. They are distinct from those mentioned in 19:1 [WBC]. The fact that φωνὴν 'sound' is without a definite article implies that this is not the same group as that referred to in 19:1 [WBC].
3. It the voice of all of God's servants, angelic as well as human [Hu].
4. It is the voice of all of God's people as seen in 7:9 [Sw].

QUESTION—What relationship is indicated by ὅτι 'because'?
It indicates the grounds for praising God [EC, Lns, NIGTC, Sw, TNTC, WBC]: Hallelujah *because* the Lord our God reigned.
QUESTION—What is the significance of the aorist tense of ἐβασίλευσεν 'reigned'?
1. It should be taken as an inceptive aorist [Be, BNTC, EC, Ld, NIC, NIGTC, WBC; NAB, REB, TNT]: The Lord our God *has begun* to reign.
2. It should be taken as a present tense [NTC; CEV, KJV, NCV, NET, NIV, NLT, NRSV, TEV]: The Lord our God *reigns*. The aorist is the equivalent of the Hebrew perfect and means 'reigns' [NTC].
3. The aorist is historical and denotes action completed in the past [Lns, Sw]. The aorist points back to Babylon's fall [Sw].
4. Either interpretation one or two are acceptable [TNTC].
QUESTION—In what sense has the Lord our God reigned?
He has reigned in the sense that His Kingdom is now established and the powers of evil have been destroyed [Be, BNTC, NIC].
QUESTION—What is the significance of the three similes—like a sound of a great crowd, like a sound of many waters, and like a sound of mighty thunder?
They are grouped together to stress the loudness of the sound [WBC]. It has an inconceivable volume [Lns].

DISCOURSE UNIT: 19:7–10 [NIGTC]. The topic is the marriage of the Lamb.

19:7 **Let-us-rejoice and exult[a] and give him the honor, because the wedding[b] of the Lamb came and his bride[c] prepared herself."**
TEXT—Instead of the aorist verb δώσωμεν 'let us give', some manuscripts have δῶμεν 'let us give', and others have δώσομεν 'we shall give'. GNT has the aorist 'let us give' with a C rating indicating difficulty making the selection. The reading δῶμεν 'let us give' is taken by TR.
LEXICON—a. pres. act. subj. of ἀγαλλιάω (LN 25.131) (BAGD p. 4): 'to exult' [BAGD, EC, WBC; NET, NRSV], 'to shout for joy' [REB], 'to be jubilant' [BNTC], 'to jubilate' [Lns], 'to be overjoyed' [BAGD, LN], 'to greatly rejoice, to be extremely joyful' [LN], 'to rejoice' [KJV, NLT, TNT], 'to be happy' [CEV, NCV], 'to be glad' [BAGD; NAB, NIV, TEV]. The present subjunctive indicates a continuative aspect 'keep on exulting' [EC].
  b. γάμος (LN 34.67, 34.68) (BAGD 1.b. p. 151): 'wedding' [BNTC, LN (34.67), Lns; NCV, NIV, TEV], 'wedding day' [WBC; CEV, NAB, REB], 'wedding banquet' [BAGD], 'wedding feast' [NLT], 'wedding celebration' [Sw; NET], 'marriage' [EC, LN (34.67); KJV, NRSV, TNT], 'marriage feast' [Wal].
  c. γυνή (LN 10.54) (BAGD 3. p. 168): 'bride' [BAGD, BNTC; all versions except KJV], 'wife' [EC, LN, Lns, WBC; KJV].
QUESTION—What relationship is indicated by ὅτι 'because'?
It indicates that the clause that follows is the reason for rejoicing and giving the credit to God [Be, EC, Hu, Lns, TNTC, WBC]: Let us rejoice and exult

and give God the honor *because* the wedding of the Lamb has come and his bride has prepared herself.

QUESTION—To what does the word γάμος 'wedding' refer?

The Jewish marriage had three parts: (1) the betrothal in which the formal engagement was agreed on, the bride price paid, and the couple legally became husband and wife; (2) the coming of the bridegroom to the house of the bride with his friends to get the bride and take her to his home; and (3) the wedding banquet [Wal]. The wedding began with the groom going to the bride's house to get her and bringing her back to his house for the wedding banquet [NIC]. The festivities continued for a week or longer [Lns].

QUESTION—Who is the bridegroom?

The bridegroom is Christ [Alf, Be, EC, Hu, ICC, Ld, Lns, NIC, NIGTC, NTC, Sw, TH, Wal, WBC].

QUESTION—Who is the bride?

The bride is the community of believers, the Church [Alf, Be, EC, Hu, ICC, Ld, Lns, NIC, NIGTC, NTC, Sw, TH, Wal, WBC].

QUESTION—What is the point of similarity between a wedding and the Lamb's relationship to the Church?

The point of similarity is: an intimate relationship [NIGTC], a union [Alf], an intimate permanent union [EC, ICC], a perfect union [Be, Hu, Ld, TH], the intense love of the groom for the bride and the bride for the groom [Hu].

QUESTION—In what way had the bride prepared herself?

She had prepared herself by putting on her wedding dress (see verse 8) [BNTC].

QUESTION—In what sense are the aorist verbs ἦλθεν 'came' and ἡτοίμασεν 'prepared' used in this verse?

They are used proleptically in that they speak of a future event as though it had already happened [Alf, EC]. The Greek aorist describes an event that has recently happened. We should translate, 'has come' [Lns].

19:8 And it-was-given to-her that she-should-be-clothed-with fine-linen bright (and) clean; for the fine linen is the righteous-acts[a] of-the saints.

TEXT—Following λαμπρόν 'bright', some manuscripts include καί 'and'. GNT does not mention this alternative. Both TR and KJV include 'and'.

LEXICON—a. δικαίωμα (LN 88.14) (BAGD 2. p. 198): 'righteous act' [LN, Lns; NIV, TNT], 'righteous deeds' [BAGD, EC, WBC; NAB, NET, NRSV, REB], 'good things done' [CEV, NCV, NLT], 'good deeds' [TEV], 'righteousness' [KJV], 'sanctity' [BNTC]. See this word also at 15:4.

QUESTION—Is this entire verse a continuation of the quote from verse 6?
  1. The entire verse is still part of the quote from verse 6 [EC, Lns; CEV].
  2. The explanatory comment after the γάρ 'for' is the writer's comment [TH, TNTC, WBC; all versions except CEV, KJV].
  3. The entire verse is a comment by the writer [Alf].

QUESTION—Who is the implied actor of ἐδόθη 'it was given'?
  God is the implied actor [Be, EC, Ld, Lns, Sw, TH]: God gave her. 'Given' here is used in the sense of privilege, right, or permission [NIC, TH, WBC; NAB, NET, NLT, TNT]: God permitted her.
QUESTION—What relationship is indicated by γάρ 'for'?
  It indicates the explanation of the fine linen dress of the bride [EC, Lns, NIC, Sw]: she should be clothed with fine linen bright and clean, *that is*, the fine linen is the righteous acts of the saints. This clause explains how the saints have preparation to do [EC].
QUESTION—In what sense is the fine linen the righteous acts of the saints?
  The verb 'is' indicates 'signifies' or 'represents' [BNTC, NTC, Sw, TH, WBC; CEV, NAB, NCV, NIV, NLT, REB]: the fine linen *represents* the righteous acts of the saints.
QUESTION—What is meant by τὰ δικαιώματα τῶν ἁγίων 'the righteous acts of the saints'?
  1. It refers to the good works of the saints after they have been purified by their faith in Christ [Alf, EC, Hu, Ld, Lns, NIC NIGTC, NTC, Sw, Wal]. There is no conflict here between the righteousness of Christ and that of his people. These acts are the correct response to the bridegroom's call. It is for these kinds of acts that believers were created (see Ephesians 2:10). The bride was not given the fine linen, but she was given the privilege to dress herself in it [NIC]. These acts are performed in the saints by the Spirit of Christ [NTC, Sw]. This refers to the on-going sanctification of the saints who have been justified by their faith in Christ [Wal].
  2. It refers to the purity of the saints that has been gained by washing their robes in the blood of the Lamb (see 7:9, 14) [TNTC]. Δικαίωμα does not mean 'righteous act' elsewhere but has the sense of 'sentence of justification'. It is in the plural because there are many people involved [TNTC].

DISCOURSE UNIT: 19:9–10 [Alf, WBC; KJV]. The topic is the angelic revelation [WBC], the marriage supper of the Lamb [KJV].

19:9 And he-says to-me, "Write: Blessed[a] (are) the-ones invited[b] to the feast[c] of-the wedding of-the Lamb." And he-says to-me, "These are the true words of God."
LEXICON—a. μακάριος (LN 25.119) (BAGD 1.b. p. 486): 'blessed' [BAGD, BNTC, EC, Lns; KJV, NAB, NET, NIV, NLT, NRSV], 'happy' [BAGD, LN; NCV, REB, TEV, TNT], 'fortunate' [BAGD], 'how fortunate' [WBC]. This adjective is also translated as a verb: 'to bless' [CEV]. See this word at 1:3.
  b. perf. pass. indic. of καλέω (LN 33.307, 33.315) (BAGD 1.b. p. 399): 'to be invited' [BNTC, EC, LN (33.315), WBC; all versions except KJV, NAB], 'to be called' [LN (33.307), Lns; KJV, NAB], 'to be summoned' [LN (33.307)].

c. δεῖπνον (LN 23.22, 23.25) (BAGD 2. p. 173): 'feast' [BNTC LN (23.22), WBC; CEV, NAB, NLT, TEV, TNT], 'supper' [EC, LN (23.25), Lns; KJV, NIV, NRSV], 'meal' [LN (23.22); NCV], 'banquet' [BAGD, LN (23.22); REB], 'celebration' [NET], 'formal dinner' [BAGD], 'main meal' [LN (23.25)].

QUESTION—Who is the speaker of λέγει 'he says'?
1. It is the angel who began speaking in 17:1 [Alf, Be, EC, NIC, NTC, Sw, TH, WBC]. A similar statement at 22:6 confirms this identification [EC]. It is the interpreting angel of 1:1; 17:1, and 21:9 [NTC].
2. It is the angel of 14:13 who said, 'Write: Blessed are the dead who died in the Lord' [Hu, Wal].
3. It is the voice that spoke from the throne in verse 5. This is supported by John's attempt to worship the being in verse 10 [Lns].

QUESTION—Who is the implied actor of the passive verb κεκλημένοι 'invited'?

The implied actor is God [EC, Ld, TNTC]: whom God invited to the feast.

QUESTION—Are those invited to the wedding feast the same as the Bride or different?
1. They are the same [Be, Hu, ICC, Ld, NIC, NIGTC, NTC, Sw, WBC]. The picture has changed perspective. In 19:7–8 the church is pictured as the bride about ready to be married to the Lamb, but now individual Christians are pictured as guests at the marriage banquet [NIGTC]. The Bride is the body of believers viewed as a whole, the invited guests are the individual members of that body [NIGTC, NTC]. The picture now is of the church awaiting the Parousia when the heavenly groom comes for his bride and takes her to heaven for the marriage feast [NIC].
2. There are two distinct groups referred to [EC, Wal]. The Bride is the Church and the guests are others who are devoted to Jesus [EC]. The Bride is the Church and the guests are the holy ones of the OT period and also of the future millennial period [Wal].

QUESTION—What is the purpose of repeating the words καὶ λέγει μοι 'and he says to me'?

This repetition indicates the importance of the following statement [Alf, EC].

QUESTION—To what specific words do οὗτοι οἱ λόγοι 'these words' refer?
1. They refer only to the blessing just given in this verse [Hu, Ld, Lns, TNTC, Wal]: the words of this blessing are the true words of God.
2. They refer to the praise of the crowd in verses 6–8 [Be, TH].
3. They refer to all the prophecies and revelations since 17:1 [Alf, EC, NIC].

QUESTION—What is the function of the clause, 'These are the true words of God'?

They emphasize the importance of the blessing [TNTC, Wal].

19:10 And I-fell at his feet to-worship him. And he-says to-me, "See-(that)-you[a] (do it) not; I-am (a) fellow-servant[b] of-you and your brothers, those having the testimony of-Jesus; worship God.

LEXICON—a. pres. act. imperative of ὁράω (LN 13.134) (BAGD 2.b. p. 578): 'to see' [EC; KJV], 'to see to it' [BAGD, LN, Lns], 'to take care' [BAGD]. The phrase Ὅρα μή 'See you not' is translated: 'See thou do it not' [KJV], 'See that you do not do this' [EC], 'See to it, not' [Lns], 'Don't do it!' [WBC; CEV, NCV, NET, NIV, NRSV, REB, TEV, TNT], 'Don't!' [NAB], 'No, don't worship me' [NLT], 'No, not that!' [BNTC].

b. σύνδουλος (BAGD 4. p. 875): 'fellow servant' [BNTC, WBC; KJV, NAB, NET, NIV, NRSV, REB, TNT], 'fellow slave' [BAGD, EC, Lns]. This noun is also translated as a phrase: '(I am) a servant just like you' [CEV, NCV, TEV], '(I am) a servant of God just like you' [NLT]. See this word also at 6:11.

QUESTION—What is significant about the angel's reply, Ὅρα μή 'See you not'?

There is an implied 'do it' that is not spoken [Be, EC, NIC, NIGTC, Sw; all versions]: See you *do it* not. It is a figure of speech called *aposiopesis* in which part of the reply is left implied owing to a strong underlying emotion [EC]. The brevity of the command serves to emphasize it [TNTC].

QUESTION—In what sense is τῶν ἀδελφῶν 'the brothers' used here?

It is used in the sense of 'fellow believers' including both men and women [Be, Hu, TH, WBC; CEV, NCV, NET, NLT, NRSV, TEV].

QUESTION—How are the nouns related in the genitive construction τὴν μαρτυρίαν Ἰησοῦ 'the testimony of Jesus'? (See similar questions at 1:2, 1:9, and 12:17).

1. Jesus gave this testimony to others [Be, BNTC, EC, ICC, Lns, NIC; TEV, TNT]: the testimony Jesus bore. Here it means the testimony that Jesus gave, but in the next clause it means the testimony that others give about him [ICC, Ld].
2. The testimony is about Jesus [Alf, Hu, Sw, Wal, WBC; CEV, NAB, NCV, NET, NLT, REB]: the testimony about Jesus.
3. It may be either 1 or 2 above [Ld, NIGTC, TNTC].

QUESTION—What is indicated by ἐχόντων τὴν μαρτυρίαν Ἰησοῦ 'having the testimony of Jesus?

1. It indicates that they believed in Jesus' testimony [Be, BNTC, Lns; NET, NIV, TEV, TNT]. It means that they made Jesus' life and teaching their guiding principle and bore witness to it by martyrdom [BNTC].
2. It means that they testified about Jesus to others [Alf, Hu, Sw, Wal, WBC; CEV, NAB, NLT, REB].
3. It can mean either 1 or 2 [Ld, NIGTC].

REVELATION 19:10

For the testimony of-Jesus is the spirit of prophecy."
QUESTION—Who is the speaker in this final clause?
1. The speaker is still the angel, not John [Alf, EC, NIC]. This must be the angel speaking because it is an explanation of why the angel told him to worship God [EC].
2. The speaker is now John who is adding a comment to explain the angel's prohibition to worship him [Ld].

QUESTION—What relationship is indicated by γάρ 'for'?
It indicates an explanation [Be, EC, Hu, ICC, Ld, NIGTC]. It indicates that this clause gives an explanation of how angels and people are fellow servants [Be, Hu, ICC, NIGTC]. The reasoning is that a prophet simply tells the message he is given by God. Both angels and believers are merely servants entrusted with God's messages [Hu]. This clause explains the angel's command to worship God [EC, Ld].

QUESTION—How are the nouns related in the genitive construction ἡ μαρτυρία Ἰησοῦ 'the testimony of Jesus'?
1. Jesus gave this testimony to others [NIC].
2. The testimony is about Jesus [ICC, Ld].

QUESTION—How are the nouns related in the genitive construction τὸ πνεῦμα τῆς προφητείας 'the spirit of prophecy'?
1. The *Spirit* of God inspires the *prophet* to speak [BNTC, TH].
2. Prophecy modifies spirit [NIGTC, Sw, WBC]: prophetic Spirit/spirits. The prophetic Spirit is the power to give people visions and supernatural insights [WBC].

QUESTION—How is the testimony of Jesus the 'spirit of prophecy'?
1. If the testimony is about Jesus, it may mean: the true essence (spirit) of prophecy has as its primary purpose the revelation of Jesus' beauty [Wal], any testimony about Jesus is prophecy [WBC], those who testify about Jesus are prophetic people (prophetic spirits) [NIGTC], the witness about Jesus indicates that a person possesses the prophetic Spirit [Sw], prophecy is telling the message that was given by God [Hu], the one who testifies about Jesus does it through the enabling of the Spirit [CEV], the essence of prophecy is giving a witness for Jesus [NLT], or to testify for Jesus is to have the spirit of prophecy [REB].
2. If Jesus gave the testimony, it may mean: the testimony Jesus bore is prophecy's primary principle [NIC], a believer and a prophet are both agents through whom the Spirit of Jesus testifies [Be], God's Spirit takes God's word and puts it into the mouth of the prophet [BNTC], a person who has the spirit of prophecy will proclaim the testimony of Jesus [EC], by holding to the testimony Jesus gave, we actually hold the spirit of prophecy [Lns], Jesus' testimony inspires prophets [TEV, TNT], or Jesus' revelation of the truth enables people to proclaim God's message [TH].
3. If the genitive 'testimony of Jesus' is ambiguous and it may mean: either the source of all true prophecy is the acts and teaching of Jesus or the witness about Jesus is true prophecy [NIGTC], either Jesus' teaching is

the essence of all prophecy or that true prophecy always results in people's witnessing about Jesus [TNTC], either any testimony about Christ's person and work is inspired by the spirit of prophecy or the witness Jesus gave to men happened only through the spirit of prophecy [Ld].

DISCOURSE UNIT: 19:11–22:5 [Alf, EC]. The topic is the closing visions of John.

DISCOURSE UNIT: 19:11–21:8 [WBC]. The topic is the final defeat of God's remaining foes.

DISCOURSE UNIT: 19:11–20:15 [TNTC]. The topic is the final victory.

DISCOURSE UNIT: 19:11–21 [GNT, Lns, NIGTC, NTC, WBC; KJV, NCV]. The topic is the battle [Lns], the divine warrior and his conquests [WBC], the rider on the white horse [GNT; KJV, NCV, NLT].

DISCOURSE UNIT: 19:11–16 [Alf, EC, Hu, Ld, NIC, NIGTC, Sw, TNTC; NET, NIV]. The topic is the coming of the King of kings [EC, Ld], the rider on the white horse [Hu; NIV], the warrior Messiah appears [NIC, Sw], the one called the Word of God [TNTC], the Son of God goes forth to war [NET].

19:11 And I-saw heaven opened, and behold (a) white horse and the-one sitting on it [being called] faithful^a and true,^{b} and he-judges and makes-war^c in justice.^{d}

TEXT—Some manuscripts do not include καλούμενος 'being called'. GNT includes it with a C rating and brackets it in the text, indicating difficulty in making the decision.

LEXICON—a. πιστός (LN 31.87) (BAGD 1.a.α. p. 664): 'faithful' [BAGD, EC, LN, WBC], 'Faithful' [BNTC, Lns; all versions], 'reliable, dependable' [LN], 'trustworthy' [BAGD, LN]. See this word also at 1:5.
  b. ἀληθινός (LN 70.3) (BAGD 1. p 10): 'true' [BAGD, EC, LN, WBC], 'True' [BNTC; all versions], 'Genuine' [Lns], 'genuine, sincere' [LN]. See this word also at 3:7.
  c. pres. act. indic. of πολεμέω (LN 55.5) (BAGD 1.a. p. 685): 'to make war' [BNTC; KJV, NCV, NIV, NRSV], 'to go to war' [CEV, NET, NLT], 'to wage war' [EC, LN, WBC; NAB], 'to war' [BAGD], 'to fight a battle' [TEV], 'to do battle' [Lns]. This verb is also translated as a noun: 'war' [REB], 'warrior' [TNT]. See this word also at 2:16.
  d. δικαιοσύνη (LN 88.13) (BAGD 1. p. 196): 'justice' [BAGD, BNTC, WBC; NET, NIV, TEV], 'righteousness' [BAGD, EC, LN, Lns; KJV, NAB, NRSV], 'uprightness' [BAGD], 'doing what God requires, doing what is right' [LN]. This noun is also translated as a verb: 'to be fair' [CEV], 'to be right' [NCV], 'to be just' [REB, TNT]; and as an adverb: '(judges) fairly' [NLT].

QUESTION—What is the significance of the phrase καὶ εἶδον 'and I saw'?
  It indicates that this is a new vision [NIGTC, WBC].

QUESTION—What is the significance of the phrase τὸν οὐρανὸν ἠνεῳγμένον 'heaven opened'?
It signals the start of a new major literary section—one that depicts judgment as it does in 4:1, 11:19, and 15:5 [NIGTC]. Heaven is opened to make way for the rider on the white horse [Ld].

QUESTION—What is symbolized by the color white?
It symbolizes victory [Be, EC, Ld, NIC, NTC, Sw, TH, TNTC, Wal]. It symbolizes holiness [Lns]. It symbolizes vindication [NIGTC].

QUESTION—Who is the rider?
The rider is the Messiah [Be, BNTC, EC, Hu, ICC, Ld, Lns, NIC, NIGTC, NTC, Sw, TNTC, Wal, WBC].

QUESTION—What is symbolized by this figure of a rider on a white horse?
It symbolizes the Second Coming of Christ [Lns, Wal, WBC].

QUESTION—Where else in Revelation is Christ called πιστὸς καὶ ἀληθινός 'faithful and true'?
At 3:14 Christ is described as 'faithful and true' [Be, BNTC, Hu, ICC]. At 1:5 he is described as 'the faithful witness' [BNTC, Hu, ICC, Sw, Wal]. At 3:7 he is described as 'holy and true' [ICC, Sw, Wal].

19:12 **And his eyes (were) [like] (a) flame of-fire, and on his head (were) many crowns,**[a] **having (a) name written that no-one knew except himself,**

TEXT—Some manuscripts do not include ὡς 'like'. GNT includes it in brackets with a C rating indicating difficulty in deciding whether or not to include it.

LEXICON—a. διάδημα (LN **6.196**): 'crown' [CEV, KJV, NCV, NIV, NLT, TEV, TNT], 'diadem' [BNTC, EC, **LN**, Lns, WBC; NAB, NRSV, REB], 'diadem crown' [**LN**; NET]. See this word also at 12.3.

QUESTION—What relationship is indicated by δέ 'and'?
It indicates emphasis in both places where a description of the exalted Christ occurs—here and at 1:14 [WBC]: now. It should be rendered here 'moreover' [Lns].

QUESTION—Where else in Revelation is the figure of 'eyes like a flame of fire' used?
It is used to describe Christ in 1:14 and 2:18 [Be, BNTC, EC, Hu, ICC, Lns, NIC, NIGTC, NTC, Sw, Wal].

QUESTION—What is meant by having 'eyes like a flame of fire'?
It indicates that he is aware of everything [EC, Ld, TNTC]. It indicates that his sight can penetrate [Lns, NIC]. It indicates that he is a divine judge [NIGTC]. It indicates that he is a righteous judge of sin [Wal].

QUESTION—What is symbolized by a διάδημα 'crown'?
It symbolizes sovereignty [BNTC, NIC, Sw, Wal]. It symbolizes regal power and authority [Hu, Lns]. It symbolizes the loyalty he receives from his subjects [NIC].

QUESTION—What is the significance of διαδήματα πολλά 'many crowns'?
In ancient times a crown indicated sovereignty over one nation. The dragon had seven crowns (see 12.3) and the beast ten (see 13.1) [WBC]. Christ's

'many crowns' were appropriate for one who was 'King of kings' and 'Lord of lords' (see 17:14 and 19:16) [Alf, Be, ICC, Ld, NIC, WBC]. Many diadems indicate sovereignty over the world [BNTC]. They indicate absolute sovereignty [Hu, NIC]. They indicate widespread dominion [TNTC]. These crowns were not metal crowns, but were bands around the brow, and wearing many is quite possible [Lns].

QUESTION—What is meant by ἔχων ὄνομα...ὃ οὐδεὶς οἶδεν 'having a name...that no one knows'?

It may indicate that the person was divine (see Genesis 32:29) or that he was angelic (see Judges 13:17, 18) [WBC]. Some believed that to know a person's name meant to have power over that person. This may then be an indication that no one has power over Jesus [TNTC]. Having a secret name indicated wonderful power [Be]. It indicates that the human mind is unable to comprehend the depth of Christ's being [Ld, Sw]. (Other references to secret names are at 2:17 and 3:12).

QUESTION—Where was this name written?

It may have been written on his forehead [Alf, EC, NIGTC, TH]. This may be supported by the fact that the previous clause was about Christ's head [EC]. It may have been written on his crowns [NIGTC].

19:13 **And he-was-dressed (in a) robe[a] dipped[b] in-blood, and his name was-called the Word of God.**

TEXT—Instead of βεβαμμένον 'dipped', some manuscripts have ἐρραμμένον 'sprinkled', others have ἐρραντισμένον 'sprinkled', and one important manuscript has περιρεραμμένον 'sprinkled around'. GNT has 'dipped' with a B rating, indicating that the text is almost certain. The reading ἐρραντισμένον 'sprinkled' is taken by Lns.

LEXICON—a. ἱμάτιον (BAGD 2. p. 376): 'robe' [BAGD, Lns; CEV, NCV, NIV, NLT, NRSV, TEV], 'garment' [BNTC, EC, WBC; REB, TNT], 'cloak' [BAGD; NAB], 'vesture' [KJV], 'clothing' [NET]. This word refers to his outer clothing [BAGD]. It could refer to a rider's cloak or to the cloak of a Roman general [EC, Sw]. See this word also at 3:4.

b. perf. pass. participle of βάπτω (LN 47.11) (BAGD 1. p. 132, 2. p. 133): 'to be dipped in' [BAGD (1), EC, LN; all versions except CEV, REB, TEV], 'to be soaked in' [BNTC], 'to be bathed with' [Lns], 'to be stained with' [WBC], 'to be dyed in' [BAGD (2); REB], 'to be covered with' [CEV, TEV], 'to be dipped' [BAGD (1)], 'to be dipped into dye' [BAGD (2)].

QUESTION—In whose blood was his robe dipped?

1. It was dipped in his own blood [Lns, NTC, TNTC]. The Savior is also the Judge (see John 5:27) [Lns]. Christ conquered by shedding his own blood, not that of others. Also at this point the battle has not yet begun so the blood could not be that of his enemies [TNTC].

2. It was dipped in the blood of his enemies [Alf, Be, EC, Hu, ICC, Ld, NIC, NIGTC, Sw, TH, Wal, WBC]. The imagery is similar to Isaiah 63:1ff

[Alf, Be, EC, Hu, ICC, Ld, NIC, NIGTC, Sw, Wal, WBC]. This verse alludes to the description of God judging the nations in Isaiah 63 [NIGTC]. This passage is about Christ as warrior, not as Redeemer [ICC, Ld, Sw]. The argument that the battle is not yet begun and so it is not possible for the blood to be that of his enemies fails to understand the flexibility of figurative language [Ld, NIGTC]. It must have been the blood of the Parthian kings and their armies as was prophesied in Revelation 17:14 [ICC]. Blood symbolizes God's judgment on the wicked [Wal].
3. It was dipped in the blood of his martyrs [BNTC]. The persecution of the Church that seemed to be a great defeat was in reality the ingathering of the saints and the means by which Christ turned defeat into victory over his enemies [BNTC].

19:14 And the armies^a [the ones] in heaven clothed in clean white fine-linen were-following him on white horses.

TEXT—Instead of τὰ ἐν τῷ οὐρανῷ 'the ones in heaven', some manuscripts have ἐν τῷ οὐρανῷ 'in heaven'. GNT does not deal with this alternative in the apparatus but brackets τά 'the ones' in the text, indicating doubt about the selection. The reading 'in heaven' is taken by TR and KJV.

TEXT—Instead of λευκὸν καθαρόν 'white clean', some manuscripts have λευκὸν καὶ καθαρόν 'white and clean'. GNT does not mention this alternative. The reading 'white and clean' is taken by TR and KJV.

LEXICON—a. στράτευμα (LN 55.7) (BAGD p. 770): 'army' [BAGD, BNTC, EC, LN, Lns, WBC; all versions]. See this word also at 9:16.

QUESTION—Who are the armies of heaven?
1. They are the angels [Hu, Ld, Lns, Sw, TNTC]. This refers to Michael and his angels (see 12:7) [Hu]. That they are angels is supported by Mark 8:38; Luke 9:26; 1 Thessalonians 3:13, and 2 Thessalonians 1:7 [Ld]. It is also supported by Matthew 13:31; 24:31; 1 Thessalonians 4:16 [Lns].
2. They are the Christian martyrs [ICC, TH]. Verses 3:5, 7:14, and 19:8 indicate that these are victorious martyrs [TH].
3. They are angels and martyrs [NIC]. While Matthew 26:53 indicates they may be angels, 17:14 identifies the martyrs as those who are 'called, chosen, and faithful' so they should be included as well [NIC].
4. They are the saints [EC, NTC]. Two facts support this view: (1) they are dressed in white clothing as is the bride (see 19:8), and (2) 17:14 indicates that the 'called, elect, and faithful' will be with Christ in the final battle against the beast and his armies [EC].
5. They are angels and saints [Alf, NIGTC, Wal, WBC]. These are not only the angels, but also those who are with the Lamb when he is victorious over the beast in 17:14 [Alf].

QUESTION—What is symbolized by the color white?
'White' symbolizes victory [Be, BNTC, Ld, Sw]. It symbolizes holiness [Lns]. It symbolizes the rightness of God's vengeance [NIC]. It indicates that the side of truth is the right side [NIGTC].

19:15 And out-of his mouth goes (a) sharp sword, that with it he-might-strike-down[a] the nations,
LEXICON—a. aorist act. subj. of πατάσσω (LN 20.73): 'to strike down' [LN; NIV, NLT, NRSV, TNT], 'to strike' [BAGD; NAB, NET], 'to smite' [BNTC, EC, Lns, WBC; KJV, REB], 'to defeat' [NCV, TEV], 'to attack' [CEV], 'to slay' [LN], See this word also at 11:6.
QUESTION—What other verses also have reference to the figure of a sword coming from the mouth of Christ?
This same figure is seen in Revelation 1:16; 2:12, 16 [Alf, ICC, Lns, NIC, NIGTC, NTC, TH, WBC]. It also occurs in 2 Thessalonians 2:8 [NIC, WBC]. A similar figure is seen in Isaiah 11:4 [EC, Hu, Ld, WBC]. Other similar Scriptures are Isaiah 49:2, Hebrews 4:12 and Ephesians 6:17 [BNTC].
QUESTION—What does πατάσσω 'to strike down' indicate in this context?
1. It indicates that he will destroy the nations [EC, NIC, WBC]. From Isaiah 11:4 we see that the wicked are destroyed, not merely reprimanded [EC]. His condemnation of the nations means death to them [NIC].
2. It indicates that he will bring them under his control [BNTC, ICC, Sw, TH, Wal]. He will speak like a prophet and reprimand the nations [BNTC]. He will condemn them with his words [ICC]. The word πατάσσω means 'to conquer, to punish, to defeat' [TH]. The Word of God fights with the word, not a literal sword. By this he forces them to obey and believe in Him [Sw].

and he-(himself) will-rule[a] them with (an) iron rod,
LEXICON—a. fut. act. indic. of ποιμαίνω (LN 37.57, 44.3) (BAGD 2.a.γ. p. 683): 'to rule' [LN (37.57), WBC; all versions except TEV], 'to rule over' [TEV], 'to smash' [BNTC, ICC], 'to destroy' [EC, NIC, NIGTC], 'to shepherd' [BAGD, LN (44.3), Lns]. See this word also at 2:27.
QUESTION—What other verses also refer to the figure of ruling with a rod of iron?
This same figure is seen in 2:27 and 12:5 [EC, Hu, ICC, Lns, NTC, Sw, TH, TNTC]. This same figure is also seen in Psalm 2:9 [Hu, ICC, Lns, NIC, NIGTC, NTC, Sw, Wal, WBC]. A similar figure is seen in Isaiah 11:4 [EC, Ld, Sw, WBC].
QUESTION—What is meant by ποιμαίνω 'to rule' in this context?
1. It means that he will rule over them [Sw, Wal, WBC; all versions]. The wicked will be brought to obey Christ and brought under his rule [Sw]. This will be a stern absolute government that exacts obedience to righteous standards [Wal].

2. It means that he will destroy them [EC, ICC, Lns, NIC, NIGTC]. The figure indicates that he will destroy them, not just severely rule them [EC]. Ποιμαίνω has a negative connotation here and indicates punishment and destruction. Better to render it as 'break' [ICC].

QUESTION—What words are emphasized in this verse?

The word αὐτός 'he himself' is emphasized at both occurrences (he himself will rule, he himself treads) [Alf, Be, EC, ICC, Lns, TNTC]. In the second occurrence the use of αὐτός 'he himself' adds gravity to the statement [Sw]. This indicates that Christ alone will do these things [TNTC].

and he-(himself) treads[a] the winepress[b] of-the wine of-the fury of-the anger of God the Almighty.

TEXT—Instead of θυμοῦ τῆς ὀργῆς 'fury of the anger', some manuscripts have θυμοῦ καὶ τῆς ὀργῆς 'fury and of the anger'. GNT does not mention this alternative. The reading 'fury and of the anger' is taken by TR and KJV.

LEXICON—a. pres. act. indic. of πατέω (LN **19.51**) (BAGD 1.a.α. p. 634): 'to tread' [BAGD, BNTC, EC, Lns, WBC; KJV, NIV, NLT, NRSV, REB, TNT], 'to tread out' [NAB], 'to trample' [**LN**; CEV], 'to trample out' [TEV], 'to stomp' [NET], 'to crush out' [NCV].

b. ληνός (LN 7.66) (BAGD p. 473): 'winepress' [BAGD, BNTC, EC, LN, Lns, WBC; all versions except CEV]. This noun is also translated as a phrase: 'the pit where wine is made' [CEV].

QUESTION—What other verses also refer to the figure of treading a winepress?

This same figure is seen in 14:19, 20 [EC, NTC, Sw, TH, Wal]. It is also referred to in Isaiah 63:1–3 [EC, Ld, Lns, NIGTC, NTC, TNTC, Wal, WBC].

QUESTION—What other verses also refer to the figure of the fury of the wrath of God?

This same figure is also seen at 16:19 [TH].

QUESTION—How are the nouns related in the genitive construction τὴν ληνὸν τοῦ οἴνου 'the winepress of the wine'?

The two nouns either together mean 'winepress' [Lns, WBC; all versions except KJV] or a 'winepress *for* the wine' [Lns].

QUESTION—How are the nouns related in the genitive construction τοῦ οἴνου τοῦ θυμοῦ τῆς ὀργῆς 'the wine of the fury of the anger'?

1. The second noun (phrase) is in apposition to the first [Lns]: the wine/winepress, *that is* the fury of the anger.
2. The second noun symbolizes the first [NIGTC, WBC]: the winepress *representing* the furious anger.

QUESTION—How are the nouns related in the genitive construction τοῦ θυμοῦ τῆς ὀργῆς 'the fury of the anger'?

1. The first noun modifies the second [NIC, NIGTC, WBC; CEV, NCV, NET, NLT, REB, TEV, TNT]: furious anger.
2. The two nouns are in a conjoining relationship [KJV, NAB]: the fury and the anger.

QUESTION—What is symbolized by the figure of treading a winepress of God's anger?

It symbolizes that the nations will be crushed just like grapes are crushed in a winepress [Lns, NIGTC]. It symbolizes that the wine that flows from the winepress is God's anger and the nations will be made to drink it [BNTC, EC, ICC]. It symbolizes the utter defeat of God's enemies [TNTC]. The winepress is the place where God turns the evil acts of men into the instrument of their own judgment [BNTC].

19:16 And he-has (a) name written on (his) robe and on his thigh:[a] "King of-kings and Lord of-lords."

TEXT—Instead of ὄνομα '(a) name', some manuscripts possibly have τὸ ὄνομα 'the name' although GNT does not mention this alternative. The reading 'the name' is taken by TR.

LEXICON—a. μηρός (LN **8.48**) (BAGD p. 519): 'thigh' [BAGD, BNTC, EC, LN, Lns, WBC; all versions except NCV], 'upper leg' [NCV].

QUESTION—What relationship is indicated by the καί 'and' after 'robe'?

1. It indicates that the phrase following defines further the location 'on the robe' [Alf, Be, EC, Hu, Ld, NIC, Sw, TH, WBC; CEV]: on the robe, *that is*, where the robe covers his thigh. It indicates that it is on that part of his robe that covers his thigh [Be, EC, Hu, Ld, NIC]. Or, it indicates that it is partly on his robe, partly on his thigh [Alf].
2. It indicates a conjoining relationship [BNTC, Lns, TNTC, Wal; KJV, NAB, NCV, NET, NIV, NLT, NRSV, REB, TEV]: on the robe *and* on his thigh. It may have been written on a banner and hung over the place where his robe covered his thigh [Lns].
3. Either 1 or 2 is correct [NIGTC]. It was either written in two places, on his robe *and* his thigh, or in one, on his robe, *even* on his thigh [NIGTC].

QUESTION—What significance may there be to the double reference βασιλεὺς βασιλέων καὶ κύριος κυρίων 'king of kings and lord of lords'?

This figure was used by the Persians and Parthians to stress the preeminence of their leaders [EC, NIC]

DISCOURSE UNIT: 19:17–20:15 [Hu]. The topic is the enemies of the Word of God destroyed.

DISCOURSE UNIT: 19:17–21 [Alf, EC, Hu, Ld, NIC, Sw, TNTC; NIV]. The topic is the great supper of God [EC], the doom of the beast and the false prophet [Hu, NIC, Sw, TNTC], the battle of Christ and Antichrist [Ld], King of kings and Lord of lords [NIV].

DISCOURSE UNIT: 19:17–18 [NIGTC]. The topic is the angelic declaration of the Last Enemy's destruction.

19:17 And I-saw one angel standing in the sun and he-shouted [with] (a) loud voice saying to-all the birds[a] flying in midheaven,[b] "Come gather to the great feast of God

TEXT—Instead of ἐν φωνῇ μεγάλῃ 'with a loud voice', some manuscripts do not include ἐν 'with', which does not alter the translation. GNT does not deal with this alternative in the apparatus but brackets ἐν in the text, indicating doubt about the selection. TR does not include 'with'.

TEXT—Instead of δεῦτε 'come', some manuscripts possibly have δεῦτε καί 'come and', although GNT does not mention this alternative. The reading 'come and' is taken by TR and KJV.

TEXT—Instead of τὸ δεῖπνον τὸ μέγα τοῦ θεοῦ 'the great feast of God', some manuscripts have τὸ δεῖπνον τοῦ μεγάλου θεοῦ 'the feast of the great God'. GNT does not mention this alternative. The reading 'the feast of the great God' is taken by TR and KJV.

LEXICON—a. ὄρνεον (LN **4.38**): 'bird' [BAGD, BNTC, EC, **LN**, Lns, WBC; all versions except KJV, NLT], 'fowl' [KJV], 'vulture' [NLT]. See this word also at 18:2.

b. μεσουράνημα (LN 1.10) (BAGD p. 508): 'midheaven' [BAGD, BNTC, EC, Lns, WBC; NRSV, REB, TNT]. The phrase ἐν μεσουρανήματι 'in midheaven' is translated: 'in the sky' [CEV, NCV], 'high in the sky' [LN; NET, NLT], 'in the midst of heaven' [KJV], 'high overhead' [NAB], 'in midair' [NIV, TEV]. See this word at 8:13.

QUESTION—What is the significance of the phrase καὶ εἶδον 'and I saw'?
It signifies that a new vision begins here [WBC].

QUESTION—What is signified by the angel shouting with a loud voice?
It signifies the importance of what he is about to say [Wal].

QUESTION—What is signified by the invitation to this feast?
It emphasizes the sureness of the defeat that will follow [NIGTC].

QUESTION—Is ἑστῶτα ἐν τῷ ἡλίῳ 'standing *in* the sun' a good translation?
It may be better to translate: 'standing *on* the sun' [TH].

QUESTION—How are the nouns related in the genitive construction τὸ δεῖπνον τὸ μέγα τοῦ θεοῦ 'the great feast of God'?
The feast is provided, prepared, or given by God [Be, EC, Ld, NIC, Sw, TH, TNTC; NLT]: the feast that God *provides*.

QUESTION—What OT Scripture also prophesies a similar feast?
Ezekiel 39:17–20 prophesies a similar feast [Alf, Be, BNTC, EC, Hu, ICC, Ld, Lns, NIC, NIGTC, NTC, Sw, TH, TNTC, Wal, WBC].

19:18 That you-may-eat (the) flesh[a] of-kings and (the) flesh of-generals[b] and (the) flesh of-strong-men and (the) flesh of-horses and of-the-ones sitting on them and (the) flesh of-all both freemen and slaves both small and great.

TEXT—Instead of ἐλευθέρων τε 'both freemen', some manuscripts possibly do not include τε 'both' although GNT does not mention this alternative.

LEXICON—a. σάρξ (LN **8.63**) (BAGD 1. p. 743): 'flesh' [BAGD, EC, **LN**; all versions except NCV], 'flesh part' [Lns], 'body' [NCV], 'carrion' [WBC], 'carcass' [BNTC]. Σάρξ here refers to dead bodies [TH].
  b. χιλίαρχος (LN 55.15) (BAGD p. 882): 'general' [WBC; NCV, NET, NIV, TEV], 'captain' [KJV, NLT, NRSV], 'commander' [REB, TNT], 'officer' [BNTC], 'commanding officer' [LN], 'military officer' [NAB], 'military leader' [BAGD], 'ruler' [CEV], 'chiliarch' [EC, LN, Lns]. The χιλίαρχος was a commander of 1,000 soldiers and was equivalent to a 'tribune' [WBC]. See this word also at 6:15.
QUESTION—What relationship is indicated by ἵνα 'that'?
  It indicates that the following is the purpose for which the birds are summoned [EC]: Come, gather to the great feast of God *so that* you may eat the flesh of kings.
QUESTION—What is indicated by the use of these eight conjunctions καί 'and'?
  They emphasize the absolute total of all these things [WBC].
QUESTION—What is indicated by the naming of these many groups 'kings, generals, mighty men, cavalry, slaves, and freemen both small and great'?
  It signifies the totality of mankind of every status of life [EC].
QUESTION—Who are these people?
  They are those who have taken the mark of the beast and allied themselves with it [EC, Ld, Wal].
QUESTION—What is indicated by their bodies being left on the battlefield for birds to eat?
  In those days such a fate indicated total dishonor [NIC].

DISCOURSE UNIT: 19:19–21 [NIGTC]. The topic is the defeat of the beast and the false prophet.

19:19 And I-saw the beast and the kings of-the earth and their armies[a] having-been-gathered to make war with the-one sitting on the horse and with his army.
TEXT—Instead of τὸν πόλεμον 'the war', some manuscripts have πόλεμον 'war'. GNT does not mention this alternative. The reading 'war' is taken by TR.
LEXICON—a. στράτευμα (LN **55.7**): 'army' [BNTC, EC, **LN**, Lns, WBC; all versions].
QUESTION—What is the significance of the phrase καὶ εἶδον 'and I saw'?
  It signifies a new phase of the vision [WBC].
QUESTION—Which 'beast' is referred to here?
  It is the first beast, the one mentioned in 13:1 that came out of the sea [Hu, Lns, TH, Wal]. The beast is the Antichrist [Hu, Ld, NIC]. The beast is the Nero-antichrist [ICC].
QUESTION—Who are these kings?
  They are the ten kings who give their authority to the beast (see 17:12–14) [BNTC, EC, Sw, WBC]. They are the kings referred to in 16:14 [Alf, Hu,

ICC, Ld, Lns, NIC, NIGTC, TH, WBC]. They are also referred to in 17:2, 18 [Hu, ICC, Ld]. They are also referred to in 18:3 [ICC, Ld].

QUESTION—Who is the implied actor of the passive verb συνηγμένα 'having been gathered'?

The actors are the evil spirits (see 16:14), and Satan himself (see 20:8) [NIGTC]: the evil spirits and Satan gathered the kings and their armies.

QUESTION—What is signified by the article in the phrase ποιῆσαι τὸν πόλεμον 'to make *the* war'?

The references 16:14; 19:19 and 20:8 all have the article with πύλεμον 'war' and all refer to *the* final battle [NIGTC].

QUESTION—To which battle does this refer?

It refers to the battle of Armageddon (see 16:16) [Alf, Be, Ld, Lns, NIC, Sw]. This is the final battle between Christ and Antichrist [Sw].

QUESTION—Who is 'the one sitting on the horse'?

The one sitting on the horse is Christ [EC, NIGTC, TH].

19:20 **And the beast was-captured[a] and with it the false-prophet who performed the miraculous-signs before it, by which he-deceived the-ones (who) received the mark of-the beast and who worship its image; the two were-thrown alive into the lake[b] of-fire burning with sulfur[c]**

TEXT—Instead of μετ' αὐτοῦ 'with it', some manuscripts have μετὰ τούτου 'with this one'. GNT does not mention this alternative. The reading 'with this one' is taken by TR.

TEXT—Instead of ἐν τῷ θείῳ 'with the sulfur', some manuscripts have ἐν θείῳ 'with sulfur'. GNT does not mention this alternative. The reading 'with sulfur' is taken by TR.

LEXICON—a. aorist pass. indic. of πιάζω (LN **18.3**) (BAGD 2.b. p. 657): 'to be captured' [EC, Lns, WBC; CEV, NCV, NIV, NLT, NRSV], 'to be taken prisoner' [REB, TEV, TNT], 'to be taken' [KJV], 'to be caught' [BAGD, LN; NAB], 'to be seized' [**LN**; NET, TNT], 'to be taken hold of, to be grasped firmly' [LN].

b. λίμνη (LN 1.72) (BAGD 1. p. 475): 'lake' [BNTC, EC, LN, Lns, WBC; all versions except NAB], 'pool' [LN; NAB].

c. θεῖον (LN 2.26) (BAGD p. 353): 'sulfur' [BAGD, LN, WBC; all versions except KJV, REB], 'brimstone' [EC, LN, Lns; KJV]. This noun is also translated as an adjective: 'sulphurous (flames)' [BNTC; REB]. See this word also at 14:10.

QUESTION—Who is the implied actor of ἐπιάσθη 'was captured'?

The implied actor is probably Christ [EC, TH]: Christ captured the beast and with it the false prophet.

QUESTION—Who is the beast?

This refers to the first beast that came up out of the sea (see 13:1) [Hu].

QUESTION—Who is the false prophet?
   This refers to the second beast, the one that came up out of the land (see 13:11ff.) [Alf, Be, Hu, ICC, Lns, Wal, WBC]. See also 16:13 [Lns, TH, TNTC].
QUESTION—Are 'those who received the mark of the beast and who worship its image' one group or two?
   They are the same group defined by two activities [TH].
QUESTION—Who is the implied actor of ἐβλήθησαν 'were thrown'?
   The implied actor is probably Christ [EC, TH]: Christ threw the beast and the false prophet into the lake of fire.
QUESTION—How are the nouns related in the genitive construction ἣν λίμνην τοῦ πυρός 'the lake of fire'?
   The second noun modifies the first [EC, NIC; NAB]: the fiery lake.
QUESTION—What is another name for 'the lake of fire'?
   This is the same as Gehenna [Alf, EC, Ld, NIC, TH]. Gehenna is the same as hell [Alf]. Gehenna was the place where the evil dead existed and it was a place of fire (see Matthew 5:22 and Mark 9:43) [NIC]. (In these two places, and in Matthew 10:28 Gehenna is translated 'hell' by CEV, KJV, NCV, NET, NIV, NLT, NRSV, REB, and TEV).

19:21 And the rest were-killed with the sword of-the-one sitting on the horse the-one going-out from his mouth, and all the birds were-gorged[a] with their flesh.

LEXICON—a. aorist pass. indic. of χορτάζω (LN 23.16) (BAGD p. 1. p. 884): 'to be gorged' [NRSV], 'to be filled' [EC; KJV], 'to be caused to eat ones fill, to be satisfied with food' [LN]. It is also translated reflexively: 'to gorge oneself' [BAGD, BNTC, Lns; NAB, NET, NIV, NLT, REB, TNT], 'to stuff oneself' [CEV], 'to eat until full' [NCV], 'to eat all one can' [TEV], 'to feast' [WBC].

QUESTION—What other Scriptures have a similar content to this verse?
   Isaiah 11:42 has a similar content to this verse [Alf, Be, TNTC]. 2 Thessalonians 2:8 does as well [Alf, Be, Lns]. See also Hebrews 4:12 [Be].
QUESTION—Who are οἱ λοιποί 'the rest'?
   It refers to the kings of the earth and their armies (see verse 19) [ICC, Lns, NIGTC, Sw, WBC]. It refers to the kings of the earth and those who had the mark of the beast [EC, Ld]. It refers to the soldiers [TH, Wal].
QUESTION—Should the 'killing' be taken literally or spiritually?
   1. It should be taken literally to mean physical death [Alf, EC, ICC, Ld, Lns, NIC, NIGTC, TNTC, Wal]. Although the means of death is not a literal sword, the enemies of the Lord are destroyed by the Word that goes out of Lord's mouth [Alf, Be, EC, ICC, NIC]. The Word of God was a decree of death to the armies [NIGTC].
   2. It should be taken spiritually to symbolize conversion [NIC, NTC, Sw]. The Lord conquered his enemies by the power of the Gospel as he had

always conquered [NTC]. The Lord causes his enemies to believe by destroying their hostility to himself [Sw].

DISCOURSE UNIT: 20:1–10 [BNTC, Hu, WBC; KJV, NAB, NCV]. The topic is the millennium [BNTC; KJV, NAB, NCV], an intervening vision [Hu], the final defeat of Satan [WBC].

DISCOURSE UNIT: 20:1–6 [GNT, Hu, Ld, NIGTC, NTC, Sw; CEV, NET, NIV, NLT, NRSV, TEV]. The topic is Satan bound [Hu], the binding of Satan, the Resurrection and the Millenial Kingdom [NIC, NIGTC], Satan's captivity and the martyrs' reign [NTC, Sw], the thousand years [GNT; CEV, NET, NIV, NLT, NRSV, TEV].

DISCOURSE UNIT: 20:1–3 [Alf, EC, ICC, Lns, NIC, NIGTC, TNTC, Wal, WBC]. The topic is Satan bound [Alf, EC, NIC, TNTC, Wal, WBC], introduction [ICC].

20:1 **And I-saw an-angel coming-down from heaven having the key of-the abyss^a and (a) big^b chain^c in his hand.**

LEXICON—a. ἄβυσσος (LN 1.20) (BAGD 2. p. 2): 'abyss' [BAGD, BNTC, EC, LN, Lns, WBC; NAB, NET, REB, TEV], 'Abyss' [NIV], 'bottomless pit' [KJV, NCV, NLT, NRSV, TNT], 'deep pit' [CEV]. The word ἄβυσσος originally meant 'bottomless' or 'unfathomed' [NIC]. It is a huge hole [Lns, NIC, TNTC] with an entrance that can be locked [Lns, TNTC]. It is the place where the demons in the pigs thought they would be sent (see Luke 8:31). Paul used it as the place of the dead (see Romans 10:7) [TNTC]. It is a living place of the devil (see 9:1) [Alf], evil spirits (see 9:1) [Alf, TNTC], demonic locusts (see 9:1) [Ld], or the beast (see 11:7) [Ld]. Its purpose is to confine [Sw, TNTC, Wal]. See this word also at 9:1 and 11:7.

b. μέγας (LN **79.123**): 'big' [**LN**; CEV], 'large' [LN, WBC; NCV], 'huge' [NET], 'great' [BNTC, EC, LN, Lns; KJV, NIV, NRSV, REB, TNT], 'heavy' [NAB, NLT, TEV]. See this word also at 6:4.

c. ἅλυσις (LN 6:16) (BAGD 1. p. 41): 'chain' [BAGD, BNTC, EC, LN, Lns, WBC; all versions]. This is linked, metal instrument for binding [LN].

QUESTION—What is indicated by the phrase καὶ εἶδον 'and I saw'?
  1. It indicates that this event chronologically follows the events of chapter 19, the destruction of the Beast, the False Prophet and their army [NIC, TH]. The sequence of events extends from the Rider on the white horse of 19:11 to the new Heaven in 21:1 [NIC].
  2. It indicates simply that this is a new event that John saw with no necessary reference to sequence in time [Sw, WBC].

QUESTION—If τὴν κλεῖν 'the key' is symbolic, what does it symbolize?
  It symbolizes: the ability to open something [Lns], authority over the abyss [TNTC], authority over the devil [NIGTC].

QUESTION—If ἅλυσιν 'chain' is symbolic, what does it symbolize?
It symbolizes: the ability to make someone helpless [EC, Lns, TNTC, Wal], limitation of someone's strength and activity [Ld].

20:2 And he-seized[a] the dragon, the ancient serpent who is (the) Devil[b] and Satan, and bound[c] him (a) thousand years

TEXT—Instead of the (grammatically incorrect) nominative ὁ ὄφις ὁ ἀρχαῖος 'the ancient serpent', some manuscripts have the accusative τὸν ὄφιν τὸν ἀρχαῖον with the same translation. GNT does not mention this alternative. The accusative reading is also taken by TR.

LEXICON—a. aorist act. indic. of κρατέω (LN 37.110) (BAGD 1.a. p. 448): 'to seize' [BNTC, EC, LN, Lns; NAB, NET, NIV, NLT, NRSV, REB, TEV, TNT], 'to grab' [NCV], 'to apprehend' [BAGD, WBC], 'to arrest' [BAGD, LN], 'to lay hold on' [KJV], 'to take into custody' [BAGD], not explicit [CEV].
    b. διάβολος (LN **12.34**): 'Devil' [BNTC, **LN**; KJV, NAB, NLT, NRSV, REB, TEV, TNT], 'devil' [EC, Lns, WBC; CEV, NCV, NET, NIV], 'Satan' [LN]. See this word also at 2:10 and 12:9.
    c. aorist act. ind. of δέω (LN 18.13) (BAGD 2. p. 178): 'to bind' [EC, Lns, WBC; KJV, NIV, NLT, NRSV], 'to tie up' [LN; NAB, NCV, NET], 'to tie' [BAGD, LN], 'to chain' [CEV], 'to chain up' [REB, TEV, TNT], 'to put in chains' [BNTC]. This does not mean that the angel tied up Satan for 1,000 years and then threw him into the abyss but that he tied him and threw him into the abyss where he stayed for 1,000 years [TH]. See this word also at 9:14.

QUESTION—Where else in Revelation does such a four-fold description of Satan occur?
A similar description of Satan also occurs in Revelation 12:3 and 9 [Alf, EC, TNTC].

QUESTION—What is the significance of the nominative case of the phrase ὁ ὄφις ὁ ἀρχαῖος 'the ancient serpent', in apposition to the accusative τὸν δράκοντα 'the dragon', where the accusative would be grammatically correct?
The use of the nominative case here serves to emphasize the phrase [EC].

QUESTION—When does the binding of Satan begin?
    1. It began at the first coming of Jesus Christ [Hu, Lns, NIGTC]. It began at the cry of Jesus from the cross, 'It is finished!' The 1,000 years is the present time in which we are now living [Lns]. The binding of Satan is the result of Christ's resurrection [NIGTC]. It begins with the ascension of Christ to glory and ends when Satan is loosed for 'a short time' [Hu].
    2. It begins at a time associated more with the last days [Ld, NIC, NTC, Wal]. Since Satan is loosed at the end of this 1,000 years, it seems unlikely that this particular binding of Satan is that accomplished at Jesus death and resurrection. From that victory Satan is never loosed [Ld].
    3. It is not certain when it begins [TNTC].

QUESTION—Does the binding merely limit the activity of Satan or does it make him completely inactive?
1. It limits his ability to use all of his powers [Hu, Ld, NIGTC, TNTC]. This limiting is major and includes both his activity and strength [Ld]. Satan is restrained chiefly in his power to deceive the nations [Ld, NIGTC].
2. It makes him completely inactive [Be, EC, NIC, Wal]. The rather involved means of making his incarceration secure, points toward the full cessation of his activities [NIC].

QUESTION—Should the 1,000 years be taken literally or figuratively?
1. It should be taken as referring to a literal 1,000-year period [EC, NTC, Wal]. The fact that the phrase '1,000 years' is repeated six times between 20:2–7 stresses the importance of this phrase. Also, if an indefinite period of time is referred to, the author uses a phase like μικρὸν χρόνον 'a little time' (see 20:3) [EC]. When a period of time such as a month or year occurs in the Bible, it always is used literally [Wal]. This cannot refer to the present age since verses like 1 Peter 5:8 indicate that Satan is active now [Wal].
2. It should be taken figuratively to refer to a period of time [Hu, Ld, Lns, NIC, NIGTC, Sw, TNTC]. It indicates a relatively long period of time [Hu, NIC, Sw]. The number 1,000 is composed of 10 x 10 x 10 to indicate completeness [LN, TNTC], or an ideal time period [Ld]. It refers to the authority of Christ limiting Satan's activities during the church age, the time between Christ's first and second comings [NIGTC].

20:3 And threw him into the abyss[a] and shut and sealed[b] (it) over him, so-that he-might-deceive the nations not anymore until the thousand years were-ended.[c] After these-things he must be-released (a) short time.

TEXT—Instead of μετὰ ταῦτα 'after these things', some manuscripts have καὶ μετὰ ταῦτα 'and after these things'. GNT does not mention this alternative. The reading 'and after these things' is taken by TR and KJV.

LEXICON—a. ἄβυσσος (LN **1.20**): 'abyss' [BNTC, EC, **LN**, Lns, WBC; NAB, NET, REB, TEV], 'Abyss' [NIV], 'bottomless pit' [KJV, NCV, NLT, NRSV, TNT], 'deep pit' [CEV]. See this word also at 9:1 and 11:7.

b. aorist act. indic. of σφραγίζω (LN **6.33**) (BAGD 1. p. 796): 'to seal' [BAGD, BNTC, EC, **LN**, Lns, WBC; CEV, NAB, NET, NIV, NRSV, REB, TEV], 'to set a seal' [KJV, TNT], 'to lock' [NCV, NLT], 'to put a seal on, to make secure' [LN], 'to provide with a seal' [BAGD]. This 'shutting' and 'sealing' assumes that there is a device like a door to shut. It may be necessary to make this explicit [TH]. See this word also at 10:4.

c. aorist pass. subj. of τελέω (LN **67.67**): 'to be ended' [LN; NCV, NIV, NRSV, REB], 'to come to an end' [**LN**], 'to be completed' [EC, WBC; NAB, TNT], 'to be finished' [Lns; NET, NLT], 'to be over' [BNTC; TEV], 'to be fulfilled' [KJV], 'to go by' [CEV]. See this word also at 11:7.

QUESTION—What relationship is indicated by ἵνα 'so that'?
 It indicates purpose [Be, EC, NIGTC, TNTC]: he threw him into the abyss...*so that* he might not deceive the nations anymore.
QUESTION—What is meant by δεῖ 'must'?
 It indicates that this is God's plan that has to be carried out [Alf, EC, TH, TNTC].
QUESTION—Who is the implied actor of the passive verb λυθῆναι 'to be released'?
 It is probably the same angel who bound Satan in the beginning [TH]: it is necessary that the angel release him for a short time.

DISCOURSE UNIT: 20:4–10 [EC]. The topic is the Millenial Reign [EC].

DISCOURSE UNIT: 20:4–6 [Alf, ICC, Lns, NIC, NIGTC, TNTC, WBC]. The topic is the Millenial Reign [Alf, Lns, NIC, NIGTC, WBC], the first resurrection [TNTC], the glorified martyrs [ICC].

20:4 And I-saw thrones and they-(who)-sat on them and judgment[a] was-given to-them, and (I saw) the souls of-the-ones who-were-beheaded[b] because-of the testimony of-Jesus and because-of the word of-God

LEXICON—a. κρίμα (LN **56.22**) (BAGD 3. p. 450): 'judgment' [BNTC, EC, Lns; KJV, NAB, REB], 'the authority to judge' [BAGD, **LN**, WBC; NET, NIV, NLT, NRSV, TNT], 'the right to judge' [LN; CEV], 'the power to judge' [NCV, TEV]. See this word also at 17:1.
 b. perf. pass. participle of πελεκίζω (LN **20.80**) (BAGD p. 641): 'to be beheaded' [BAGD, EC, **LN**, Lns, WBC; all versions except CEV, NCV, TEV], 'to have one's head cut off' [LN; CEV], 'to be killed' [NCV], 'to be executed' [BNTC; TEV]. This verb is derived from the noun πέλεκυς 'axe' [EC, LN, NIC] and the instrument of beheading was an axe [Alf, BAGD, Be, ICC, TH, WBC]. This use of 'to behead', is representative of all forms of execution [Be, Lns, NIC, NIGTC, TNTC]. The axe was the instrument of beheading used by Republican Rome [EC, ICC, Sw, TNTC]. At that time, the time of Imperial Rome, the sword had replaced the axe [Be, Sw, TNTC].

QUESTION—Does this action take place on earth or in heaven?
 1. It takes place on earth [Alf, Be, EC, ICC, NIC, NIGTC, Wal, WBC].
 2. It takes place in heaven [Lns, TH, TNTC]. The martyrs lived and reigned in heaven with Christ for a thousand years. John uses 'throne' 47 times in Revelation and all occur in heaven except two, those of Satan and the Beast (see 2:13 and 13:2) [TNTC].

QUESTION—Who are those who sat on the thrones?
 1. The martyrs of the following clause are the ones who sat on the thrones [Alf, Be, BNTC, Hu, Lns, TH, TNTC, WBC]: I saw thrones and those that sat on them, *that is*, the souls of those who were beheaded. The καί 'and' is explanatory and further defines who were seated on the thrones [WBC]. Luke 22:30 and Matthew 19:28 states that the disciples would sit

on twelve thrones judging the twelve tribes of Israel thus showing that 'ruling' and 'judging' are synonymous and therefore that the identity of those seated is the martyrs [Be].
2. The saints or the Lamb's Bride are those who sat on the thrones [EC, Ld, NIGTC, Wal]. In 3:21 Christ promised that all overcomers would sit with him on his throne, so this privilege is not limited to martyrs only [Ld]. The primary focus is on saints although angels are also included (see 4:4 and 11:16) [NIGTC].
3. The Apostles and saints are those who sat on the thrones [Alf, Sw]. This is supported in 1 Corinthians 6:2, 3 where it is said that the saints will judge the world and angels [Alf, Sw] and Matthew 19:28 where the apostles are to judge the twelve tribes of Israel [Sw].

QUESTION—Who are the actors of the verb implied in the noun κρίμα 'judgment'?
1. Those who sat on the thrones are the judges [Sw, WBC; CEV, NCV, NET, NIV, NLT, NRSV, TEV, TNT].
2. Judgment is passed by God against Satan on behalf of those who sat on the thrones [NIGTC].

QUESTION—Does this verse refer to one group or two?
1. It refers to one group [Alf, Be, BNTC, Hu, TH, TNTC, WBC]. There is one group of 'souls' divided into two categories: those who are martyred and those who do not worship the Beast. All will reign with Christ 1,000 years [Hu]. There is one group who had been executed for two reasons: for their witness and for their refusal to worship the Beast [WBC]. The saints are those who sat in judgment. This linked with the fact that the martyred souls were those who reigned with Christ, show that they are the same persons [Alf]. The first general statement about thrones and those who sat on them, is further amplified by the rest of the verse [Be].
2. It refers to two groups [EC, Ld, Lns, NIC, Sw]. The first group is composed of those who sit on the thrones, that is, to the armies of heaven who accompanied Christ at his return (see 19:14). The second group refers to the 'souls' John saw, that is, those who were beheaded. Both groups will reign with Christ 1,000 years, even though the latter is singled out to do so here [EC]. The first group refers to all the saints, the second group refers specifically to the martyrs [Ld]. The first group refers to those who were beheaded, the second group refers to those who did not worship the Beast [Lns]. The first group, the ones who sat on the thrones, may be an unspecified group who assist in judgment. The second group is those who were beheaded, who are further defined as those who did not worship the Beast [NIC].

QUESTION—Who is the implied actor of the passive verb ἐδόθη 'was given'?
The implied actor is God [EC, TH] or Christ [EC, Lns]. The verb ἐβασίλευσαν 'they reigned' ('with Christ') tells who the giver of 'judgment' is [Lns].

QUESTION—Who is the implied actor of the passive verb πεπελεκισμένων 'having been beheaded'?
   The implied actor is a general word such as 'others' [TH]: souls...whom *others* had beheaded.
QUESTION—How are the nouns related in the genitive construction τὸν λόγον τοῦ θεοῦ 'the Word of God'?
   1. Others proclaimed the Word of God [Wal; CEV, NLT, TEV, TNT].
   1. God spoke the Word or sent the message [TH; NCV].

and the-ones-who worshiped not the beast nor its image and received not the mark[a] on the forehead and the hand of-them. And they-lived[b] and reigned[c] with Christ (a) thousand years.
TEXT—Instead of τὸ μέτωπον 'the forehead', some manuscripts have τὸ μέτωπον αὐτῶν 'their forehead'. GNT does not mention this alternative. The reading 'their forehead' is taken by TR.
LEXICON—a. χάραγμα (LN **33.482**) (BAGD 1. p. 876): 'mark' [BNTC, EC, LN, Lns; all versions except TNT], 'brand-mark' [TNT], 'brand' [LN, WBC]. See this word also at 14.9.
   b. aorist act. indic. of ζάω (LN 23.88) (BAGD 1.a.b. p. 336): 'to live' [EC, Lns; KJV], 'to come to life' [BNTC, WBC; CEV, NAB, NET, NIV, NRSV, TEV, TNT], 'to come back to life' [NCV], 'to come to life again' [NLT, REB]. The aorist means: 'to come to life' [EC, NIGTC, NTC] or 'to live again' [Alf, Be, EC, Wal]. The aorist is constative (action completed in the past and viewed as a whole) and indicates 'they did live' [Lns]. Whether or not this refers to a resurrection of their bodies or an entrance into spiritual life is key in the exegesis of this passage and the meaning of 'resurrection' in the next verse [Ld]. See this word also at 2:8.
   c. aorist act. indic. of βασιλεύω (LN 37.64) (BAGD 1.b.δ. p. 136): 'to reign' [BNTC, EC, Lns, WBC; all versions except CEV, NCV, TEV], 'to rule' [BAGD, LN; CEV, NCV], 'to rule as king' [TEV]. See this word also at 5:10 and 11:15.
QUESTION—Does καὶ οἵτινες 'and those' (who did not worship...) indicate a new group or further define the preceding one?
   1. It further defines those who had been beheaded [EC, NIC, NTC, TNTC; CEV, KJV, NAB, NCV, NET, NIV NRSV, REB, TEV, TNT]. The καὶ is explanatory and should be translated 'even' [EC]: those who had been beheaded...*even* those who did not worship the Beast.
   2. It introduces a new group separate from the martyrs who did not worship the Beast [Lns, Sw].
QUESTION—How are the nouns related in the implied genitive construction 'its mark'?
   The mark is one that shows one's relationship to the beast, one that was a mark of loyalty to the beast or a mark of the party of the beast [LN].

QUESTION—How are the nouns related in the genitive construction τὴν μαρτυρίαν Ἰησοῦ 'the testimony of Jesus'?
1. Others gave this testimony about Jesus [Ld, TH, Wal, WBC; CEV, NAB, NET, NIV, NLT, NRSV, REB, TEV, TNT].
2. Jesus gave this testimony about the truth to others [Be, EC, Lns, NIC].

QUESTION—What other Scriptures are similar to the contents of this verse?
Daniel 7:9, 13, 22 are similar to the contents of this verse [Ld].

20:5 The rest of-the dead lived^a not until the thousand years were-ended. This (is) the first resurrection.^b

TEXT—Instead of οἱ λοιποί 'the rest', some manuscripts possibly have οἱ δὲ λοιποί 'but the rest', although GNT does not mention this alternative. The reading 'but the rest' is taken by TR and KJV.

TEXT—Instead of ἔζησαν 'lived', some manuscripts possibly have ἀνέζησαν 'lived again', although GNT does not mention this alternative. The reading 'lived again' is taken by TR and KJV.

LEXICON—a. aorist act. indic. of ζάω (LN 23.88) (BAGD 1.a.b. p. 336): 'to live' [EC, Lns], 'to come to life' [BNTC; NAB, NET, NIV, NRSV, REB, TEV, TNT], 'to come back to life' [NLT], 'to come to life again' [WBC], 'to be raised to life' [CEV], 'to live again' [KJV, NCV]. The word must mean 'to live again' here [EC]. See this verb in the preceding verse.
b. ἀνάστασις (LN 23.93) (BAGD 2.b. p. 60): 'resurrection' [BAGD, BNTC, EC, LN, Lns, WBC; all versions except CEV, NCV, TEV], 'raising of the dead' [NCV, TEV]. This noun is also translated as a verb: 'to be raised to life' [CEV].

QUESTION—Who are οἱ λοιποὶ 'the rest'?
1. They are unbelievers who are physically dead [EC, Hu, Ld, Lns, Wal]. To say that this group included the righteous would by implication indicate that the second death had power over them and this is not reasonable (see verse 6) [EC]. The rest are those who died in unbelief and they did not live with everlasting life [Lns].
2. They are all those who are not martyrs, both the righteous and the unrighteous [Be, ICC, NIC, TH]. This first resurrection is limited to the martyrs (see 20:12, 15). The second resurrection implies the presence of both the righteous and the unrighteous. [Be].

QUESTION—Is this resurrection physical or spiritual?
1. It is physical [Alf, Be, EC, ICC, NIC, NIGTC, Wal]. This refers to a bodily resurrection since its counterpart (an implied second resurrection) at the end of the 1,000 years is bodily [Alf, NIC, NIGTC]. Justin Martyr, Tertullian, Irenaeus, Hippolytus and Victorinus, early commentators on Revelation, all take the words in their literal rather than spiritual sense [ICC].
2. It is spiritual [Hu, Lns, TNTC]. John speaks of 'souls' not bodies and so the souls of the martyrs reign with Christ for 1,000 years [TNTC]. It is the 'souls' who live and reign with Christ [Hu, Lns].

QUESTION—Is this first resurrection limited to the martyrs?
1. No, this resurrection includes all believers [EC, Hu, Ld, Lns, Sw, Wal]. Although this resurrection is limited to martyrs, there were earlier phases of this resurrection that include the resurrection of the just (Luke 14:4; Acts 24:15), the resurrection from the dead (Luke 20:34–36), the resurrection of life (John 5:29), and the resurrection to everlasting life (Daniel 12:2) [EC]. The church is raptured first and then at the end of the great tribulation, the martyrs for Christ will be raised. So the first resurrection is a series of resurrections that includes all believers [Wal].
2. Yes, this resurrection is limited to martyrs only [Be, ICC, NIC]. Not even those believers who have died have a part in this resurrection [ICC]. The judgment of the people from the opened books in 20:12, 15 imply the presence of the righteous along with the unrighteous [Be].

20:6 Blessed[a] and holy[b] (is) the-one having-part-in[c] the first resurrection; the second death has not power on these, but they-will-be priests of-God and of Christ and will-reign with him [the] thousand years

TEXT—Instead of τὰ χίλια ἔτη 'the thousand years', some manuscripts have χίλια ἔτη '(a) thousand years'. GNT reads [τὰ] χίλια ἔτη '[the] thousand years' with a C decision, indicating that the Committee had difficulty making the decision. The reading '(a) thousand years' is taken by TR.

LEXICON—a. μακάριος (LN 23.119) (BAGD 1.b. p. 486): 'blessed' [BAGD, BNTC, EC, Lns; all versions except CEV, NCV, TEV], 'especially blessed' [CEV], 'happy' [BAGD, LN; NCV, TEV], 'fortunate' [BAGD], 'how fortunate' [WBC]. The word μακάριος is more accurately translated 'happy' [TH]. See this word also at 1:3 and 16:15.

b. ἅγιος (LN 88.24) (BAGD 1.b.d. p. 10): 'holy' [BAGD, BNTC, EC, LN, Lns, WBC; all versions except TEV], 'greatly blessed' [TEV], 'dedicated to God' [BAGD]. The word ἅγιος has the sense of 'set apart [Be] and belonging to God' [Be, TH]. It indicates complete dedication to God [TH]. The word ἅγιος 'holy', joined with μακάριος 'blessed', indicates that to be holy is to be blessed [EC]. See this word at 3:7 and 4:8.

c. ἔχων μέρος ἐν (LN 90.83). This phrase is translated: 'to have part in' [EC, Lns; KJV, NIV], 'to share in' [NAB, NCV, NLT, NRSV, REB, TNT], 'to have a share in' [BNTC, WBC], 'to experience along with others' [LN], 'to take part in' [NET], 'to be included in' [TEV], 'to experience together with, to share in experiencing' [LN], not explicit [CEV].

QUESTION—To what does τῇ ἀναστάσει τῇ πρώτῃ 'the first resurrection' refer?
1. It refers to the resurrection of the martyrs in verse 4 [NTC, Sw, TH].
2. It refers to the 'first' resurrection of Jesus in which all believers have a part by identification with him [Hu].

QUESTION—What is ὁ δεύτερος θάνατος 'the second death'?
It is being thrown into the lake of fire (see 20:10, 14, 15) [NIC]. It is the lake of fire (see 20:10, 14, 15) [Hu]. It is eternal death in the lake of fire [TH].

DISCOURSE UNIT: 20:7–22:5 [Be]. The topic is the end.

DISCOURSE UNIT: 20:7–15 [Ld]. The topic is the final destruction of Satan and Death.

DISCOURSE UNIT: 20:7–10 [Alf, GNT, Hu, Lns, NIC, NIGTC, NTC, Sw, TNTC, WBC; CEV, NET, NIV, NLT, NRSV, TEV]. The topic is Satan defeated [GNT, NIC, TNTC; CEV, NET, NIV, NLT, NRSV, TEV], the battle [Lns], Satan loosed, his final assault [Hu, NIGTC, Sw], Gog and Magog [NTC], Satan's release, defeat, and punishment [WBC].

20:7 **And when the thousand years would-be-ended, Satan will-be-released from his prison**
QUESTION—Who is the implied actor of λυθήσεται 'will be released'?
The actor is God [WBC]. The actor is either God or an angel who will release Satan [TH].

20:8 **And he-will-go-out to-deceive the nations in the four corners of-the earth, Gog[a] and Magog[b], to-gather them to the war, of-whom the number of-them (is) as the sand of-the sea.**
TEXT—Instead of τὸν πόλεμον 'the war', some manuscripts have πόλεμον 'war'. GNT does not mention this alternative. The reading 'war' is taken by TR and KJV.
TEXT—Instead of ὧν ὁ ἀριθμὸς αὐτῶν 'of whom the number of them', some manuscripts have ὧν ὁ ἀριθμος 'of whom the number'. GNT does not mention this alternative. The reading 'of whom the number' is taken by TR.
LEXICON—a. Γώγ (LN **98.87**) (BAGD): 'Gog' [BAGD, BNTC, EC, **LN**, Lns, WBC; all versions except CEV, REB, TNT], 'country of Gog' [CEV], 'host of Gog' [REB], 'Gog, the nation' [TNT]. Γώγ is an obscure name to indicate an enemy to be conquered by the Messiah [LN].
  b. Μαγώγ (LN **93.243**) (BAGD): 'Magog' [BAGD, BNTC, EC, **LN**, Lns, WBC; all versions except CEV, REB, TNT], 'country of Magog' [CEV], 'host of Magog' [REB], 'Magog, the nation' [TNT]. Μαγώγ is an obscure name to indicate an enemy to be conquered by the Messiah [LN].
QUESTION—What is meant by the phrase ἐν ταῖς τέσσαρσιν γωνίαις τῆς γῆς 'in the four corners of the earth'?
It refers to the whole earth [EC, Lns, NIC, NIGTC, Sw; TEV]: to deceive the nations in the whole earth. It means that all the nations will be included, however far away they may be [Sw, TH].
QUESTION—What other Scripture has a similar account of Gog and Magog?
Chapters 38 and 39 of Ezekiel have a similar account of Gog and Magog opposing the forces of God [Alf, EC, Hu, NIC, NIGTC, Sw, TH, TNTC]. The features of a temporary Messianic kingdom, followed by the eternal

kingdom, are the same in both Ezekiel and Revelation [Ld]. In both Ezekiel and Revelation, the Messianic Kingdom is followed by the attack of evil forces [NIC].

QUESTION—What is meant by the terms Gog and Magog?

The phrase, 'Gog and Magog', is in apposition to the nations [WBC]: the nations, *that is*, Gog and Magog. Gog and Magog symbolize the enemies of God and his people [EC, Ld, NIC, NTC, WBC]. They refer to the nations that were deceived [WBC; CEV, NAB, NCV, NET, NIV, NLT, NRSV, REB, TEV, TNT]. They symbolize all the unbelievers on earth [ICC]. John uses the names to refer to the armies of evil [TNTC]. Magog may refer to the nations, while Gog is their leader [Alf]. Gog (Satan) refers to the commander while Magog refers to the army itself [Lns].

QUESTION—What is meant by the figure ὡς ἡ ἄμμος τῆς θαλάσσης 'as the sand of the sea'?

It means that the people making up this group are innumerable [BNTC, NIGTC, TH, Wal; NLT, REB]: whose number is innumerable. It refers to all the people living on earth [Lns]. It refers to the greatest possible number [TNTC]. It indicates that the army will be enormous [WBC]. It is the people who are innumerable, like the sand, not the nations themselves [TH]. It stresses the overwhelming odds against the forces of good [NIGTC].

20:9 **And they-went-up over the breadth^a of-the earth and surrounded^b the camp^c of-the saints and the beloved city, and fire^d came-down out-of heaven and consumed them.**

TEXT—Instead of ἐκ τοῦ οὐρανοῦ 'out of heaven', some manuscripts have ἀπὸ τοῦ θεοῦ 'from God', others have ἀπὸ τοῦ θεοῦ ἐκ τοῦ οὐρανοῦ 'from God out of heaven', still others have ἐκ τοῦ οὐρανοῦ ἀπὸ τοῦ θεοῦ 'out of heaven from God'. GNT selects the reading 'out of heaven' with an A rating, indicating that the text is certain. The reading 'from God out of heaven' is taken by TR and KJV.

LEXICON—a. πλάτος (LN 81.15) (BAGD 1. p. 666): 'breadth' [BAGD, BNTC, EC, LN, Lns, WBC; KJV, NAB, NIV, NRSV, REB], 'width' [BAGD, LN]. The phrase ἐπὶ τὸ πλάτος τῆς γῆς 'over the breadth of the earth' is translated: 'across the earth' [NCV], 'all the way across the earth' [CEV], 'over the earth' [TEV], 'over the earth's expanse' [TNT], 'on the broad plain of the earth' [NET, NLT]. Here πλάτος indicates 'the broad plain of the earth' [BAGD].

b. aorist act. indic of κυκλεύω (LN **15.147**) (BAGD p. 456): 'to surround' [EC, **LN**, Lns, WBC; CEV, NAB, NIV, NLT, NRSV, TEV, TNT], 'to encircle' [BNTC; NET], 'to lay siege to' [REB], 'to encompass' [KJV], 'to gather around' [NCV], 'to be around' [LN].

c. παρεμβολή (LN 1.94) (BAGD 1. p. 625): 'camp' [BAGD, BNTC, EC, LN, Lns; all versions], 'encampment' [WBC]. A παρεμβολή is a temporary population center consisting of an encampment [LN]. It is a fortified camp [BAGD].

d. πῦρ (LN **2.5**) (BAGD 1.b. p. 730): 'fire' [BAGD, BNTC, EC, **LN**, Lns, WBC; all versions]. Here fire is being used as a destructive agent [LN].

QUESTION—What is meant by the phrase τὸ πλάτος τῆς γῆς 'the breadth of the earth'?
1. It indicates they went up over the surface of the whole earth [Alf, Be, Hu, Lns, NIGTC, TH, WBC]. It indicates that the army covers the whole earth. It is an hyperbole or overstatement [Be]. It stresses the huge distance that must be traveled to the scene [WBC].
2. It probably has a more localized meaning here [EC, NIC, TNTC]. It refers to the whole land of Palestine [EC, NIC]. It refers to a plain large enough to contain the vast army of attackers [NIC]. It indicates that they had very large armies [TNTC].

QUESTION—What relationship is indicated by καί in the phrase τὴν παρεμβολὴν τῶν ἁγίων καὶ τὴν πόλιν τὴν ἠγαπημένην 'the camp of the saints and the beloved city'?
1. An appositional relationship is indicated [Alf, EC, Hu, Lns, NIC, NIGTC, Sw, TH, Wal, WBC; NIV]: the camp of the saints, *that is*, the beloved city. The word καί is used in an explanatory manner here [Alf, EC].
1. A locative relationship is indicated [Ld]: the camp of the saints *in* the beloved city.
3. A conjoining relationship is indicated [CEV, KJV, NAB, NCV, NET, NLT, NRSV, REB, TEV]: the camp of the saints *and* the beloved city.

QUESTION—Who is the implied actor of 'beloved'?
1. God is the actor [Be, BNTC, EC, Lns, NIC, NTC, TH, Wal; NCV, NIV, REB, TEV, TNT]: the city God loves.
2. The people of God are the actors [CEV]: the city that the people of God love.

QUESTION—Is the 'beloved city' literal Jerusalem or a heavenly Jerusalem?
1. It refers to a literal Jerusalem [Alf, Be, EC, Ld, Lns, TH, Wal, WBC]. The saints' center during the millennium is the beloved city [Ld]. The saints live in the city [Lns, TH]. The adjective 'beloved' tends to indicate that earthly Jerusalem is intended (see Psalms 78:68 and 87:2) [EC].
2. It refers to a heavenly or spiritual Jerusalem [BNTC, Hu, ICC, NIGTC, NTC, Sw, TNTC]. The beloved city is the people of God under his dominion [TNTC]. This is the city that comes down from heaven and is comprised of the people of God wherever they gather together [BNTC]. God's people make up the city and no geographical location is intended [Hu]. The two entities, the camp of the saints and the beloved city, are the church around the world [NIGTC]. Jerusalem does not refer to a walled city, but to the company of true Israel [NTC].

20:10 And the devil that deceived them was-thrown into the lake-of-fire-and-sulfur[a] where both the beast and the false-prophet (are), and they-will-be-tormented[b] day and night forever-and-ever.[c]

TEXT—Instead of ὅπου καί 'where also', some manuscripts have ὅπου 'where'. GNT does not mention this alternative. The reading 'where' is taken by TR and KJV.

LEXICON—a. θεῖον (LN 2.26) (BAGD p. 353): 'sulfur'. The phrase λίμνην τοῦ πυρὸς καὶ θείου (LN **1.22, 1.72**) 'lake of fire and sulfur' [**LN** (1.22); NET, NRSV, REB, TEV, TNT] is also translated 'lake of fire and burning sulfur' [CEV], 'lake of fire that burns with sulfur' [NLT], 'lake of burning sulfur' [NCV, NIV], 'pool of fire and sulfur' [NAB] 'lake of fire and brimstone' [EC, Lns, WBC; KJV], 'lake of fire' [BNTC], 'hell' [LN]. This idiom indicates a place of eternal punishment and destruction [LN]. See a similar phrase at 19:20.

b. fut. pass. indic. of βασανίζω (LN 38.13) (BAGD 2.a. p. 134): 'to be tormented' [BAGD, BNTC, EC, LN, Lns, WBC; all versions except CEV, NCV, TNT], 'to suffer torment' [TNT], 'to be punished' [NCV], 'to be in pain' [CEV]. See this word also at 14:10.

c. εἰς τοὺς αἰῶνας τῶν αἰώνων (See this phrase at 11:15): 'forever and ever' [BNTC, EC; all versions except REB], 'for ever' [WBC; REB], 'for the eons of the eons' [Lns].

QUESTION—What verb should be supplied after the phrase 'the beast and the false prophet'?

1. Some form of the verb 'to be' should be supplied [EC, Lns, WBC; KJV, NAB, NET, NRSV]: where the beast and false prophet *are*.
2. Some form of the verb 'to throw' should be supplied [NCV, NIV, REB, TEV]: where the beast and false prophet *had been thrown*.

QUESTION—What is the meaning of the phrase ἡμέρας καὶ νυκτός 'day and night'?

It is a figure that indicates a complete 24-hour day implying 'without ceasing' or 'without interruption' [WBC]. It means 'unceasing' [EC, NIGTC]. See a similar question at 7:15.

QUESTION—What are the implications of this action?

It indicates the final and eternal crushing of the evil that had afflicted mankind from the very beginning [Ld, NIC].

QUESTION—What words of Jesus are similar to this verse?

Matthew 25:41 is similar to this verse where Jesus spoke of 'the eternal fire prepared for the devil and his angels' [Ld, NTC].

DISCOURSE UNIT: 20:11–22:5 [TH]. The topic is the final judgment, the new Heaven, the new earth and the new Jerusalem.

DISCOURSE UNIT: 20:11–15 [Alf, BNTC, EC, GNT, Hu, Lns, NIC, NIGTC, NTC, Sw, TNTC, WBC; CEV, KJV, NAB, NCV, NET, NIV, NLT, NRSV, TEV]. The topic is final judgment.

20:11 And I-saw (a) great[a] white throne and the-one sitting on it, from whose presence the earth and heaven fled and (a) place was-found not for-them.

LEXICON—a. μέγας (LN 79.123) (BAGD 1.a. p. 497): 'great' [BAGD, BNTC, EC, LN, Lns, WBC; all versions except NAB, NET], 'large' [LN; NAB, NET]. The adjective μέγας has the sense of 'large' here [NIC, TH, WBC]. See this word also at 6:4 and 6:17.

QUESTION—What is indicated by the phrase καὶ εἶδον 'and I saw'?
> It introduces a new vision [WBC]. It introduces the next phase of the revelation [Wal].

QUESTION—What other Scripture is similar to this scene of judgment?
> Chapter 7 of Daniel has a similar scene of God as judge [NIC, NIGTC].

QUESTION—Who is 'the one sitting' on the throne?
> 1. The one sitting on the throne is God [Alf, Be, EC, ICC, NIC, Sw, TH, TNTC, WBC]. John 5:22 seems to indicate that Christ will be the judge, but Revelation 4:2, 9; 5:1, 7, 13; 6:16; 7:10, 15; 19:4; 21:5 suggest that God is the one sitting on the throne. The two positions can be reconciled by the unity of the Father and Son in all they do [Sw]. Though it is the Father who judges, he does so through the Son (see John 5:22) [TNTC].
> 2. The one sitting on the throne is Christ [Lns, NTC, Wal]. It is Christ because God has given all authority to judge to the Son (see John 5:22) [Wal]. Matthew 25:31 and John 5:27 support this interpretation [Lns, NTC].

QUESTION—In what sense was this throne 'great'?
> It was 'great' in contrast to previously mentioned thrones in 20:4 [Alf, EC, ICC].

QUESTION—What is meant by the phrase τόπος οὐχ εὑρέθη αὐτοῖς 'a place was not found for them'?
> It means that they disappeared [ICC, TH], they ceased to exist [EC, ICC], or that they were destroyed [TNTC, Wal].

QUESTION—What is meant by the phrase ἡ γῆ καὶ ὁ οὐρανὸς 'the earth and the heaven'?
> It means the whole universe [Ld, TH].

QUESTION—What is the reason that the earth and heaven fled away?
> They fled because they feared the judgment of God [WBC]. They fled from the awesome majesty of God [Wal].

20:12 And I-saw the dead, the great and the small, standing before the throne. And books were-opened and another book was-opened, which is the (book) of-life, and the dead were-judged from the-things written in the books according-to[a] their works.

TEXT—Instead of τοὺς μεγάλους καὶ τοὺς μικρούς 'the great and the small', some manuscripts possibly read μικροὺς καὶ μεγάλους 'small and great', although GNT does not mention this alternative. The reading 'small and great' is taken by TR and KJV.

TEXT—Instead of θρόνου 'throne', some manuscripts possibly have θεοῦ 'God', although GNT does not mention this alternative. The reading 'God' is taken by TR and KJV.

LEXICON—a. κατά with accusative object (LN 89.8) (BAGD II.5.a.β. p. 407): 'according to' [BAGD, EC, Lns, WBC; KJV, NAB, NIV, NLT, NRSV, TEV, TNT], 'in accordance with' [LN], 'by' [BNTC; CEV, NCV, NET, REB]. The phrases ἐκ τῶν γεγραμμένων ἐν τοῖς βιβλίοις κατὰ τὰ ἔργα αὐτῶν 'from the things written in the books according to their works' are translated: 'by what those books said they had done' [CEV]. See this word also at 2:23.

QUESTION—Who are 'the dead' that the writer saw?

1. They are the unbelieving dead [Alf, EC, Ld, NTC, TH, Wal]. They are 'the rest of the dead' referred to in verse 5 [Alf, Ld, NTC, TH].
2. They are all of the dead who have ever died, including believers and unbelievers [Lns, NIC, NIGTC]. 1 Corinthians 5:10 and Romans 14:10 state that all must appear before Christ's judgment seat. Matthew 25:32 states that all will be gathered before the Son of Man and he will separate them, the sheep from the goats. John 5:28 states that all the dead who hear the voice of the Son of Man will rise, some to life and others to punishment [Lns]. The martyrs of verse 4 are the only ones who would be missing from this group [NIC].

QUESTION—What is meant by the phrase τοὺς μεγάλους καὶ τοὺς μικρούς 'the great and the small'?

It means the common as well as the important people [Sw, TH]. It means that all classes of mankind are included [EC]. It indicates that there will be no exceptions to this category of dead people [Hu, TNTC]. See a similar question at 13:16.

QUESTION—What books are these?

They are the record books in which the works of all people have been written down [Be, BNTC, EC, Ld, Lns, NIC, NTC, Sw, TH, TNTC, WBC]. They are the basis of the judgment [Be, BNTC, EC, WBC]. These probably include good and evil works [Be, Ld, Lns, WBC].

QUESTION—How are the nouns related in the genitive construction τῆς ζωῆς 'the (book) of life'?

This book contains the names of those to whom have God has given eternal life [BNTC, EC, Hu, ICC, Ld, Lns, Sw, TH, TNTC, Wal]. The names in this book have been written down since the creation of the world (see 17:8) [BNTC]. See this question also at 13:8.

QUESTION—Who is the implied actor of ἠνοίχθη 'were opened'?

The actors are probably the angels who were present [TH, WBC]: the angels opened the books. God may have been the one who opened the books [WBC].

QUESTION—Who is the implied actor of ἐκρίθησαν 'were judged'?

The implied actor is God [TH]: God judged them.

20:13 And the sea gave (up) the dead in it and death and Hades[a] gave (up) the dead in them, and they-were-judged each according-to their works.

LEXICON—a. ᾅδης (LN 1.19) (BAGD 1. p. 17): 'Hades' [BAGD, BNTC, EC, LN, WBC; NAB, NCV, NET, NIV, NRSV, REB, TNT], 'hades' [Lns], 'the kingdom of death' [CEV], 'hell' [KJV], 'the grave' [NLT], 'the world of the dead' [LN; TEV]. See this word also at 1:18 and 6:8.

QUESTION—If the sea, death, and Hades cannot be personified, how can this verse be translated?

It could be translated as: And those dead people who were in the sea and in Hades went to be judged, each according to their works [TH].

QUESTION—Why does John describe this resurrection after already speaking of the dead appearing before the throne in verses 11 and 12?

These words chronologically belong before the opening of the books. He simply returns to fill in the details of the more general statement in verses 11 and 12. [Be, EC]. This verse gives a description of the resurrection that was implied in verse 12 [Sw].

QUESTION—Why is the sea mentioned in this list?

It is mentioned because there was an implied abhorrence of the dead being unburied [Be, EC]. The Greeks and Romans felt it important that a person be buried and were horrified at the thought of drowning or being buried at sea [Sw]. It is mentioned to show that everyone would face resurrection and judgment, even those lost at sea [NIC]. It was thought that resurrection was possible only for those buried on land [NTC]. It was thought that those who died at sea without burial could not enter Hades and so were in a tragic situation [BNTC]. The sea is therefore mentioned to make the resurrection inclusive of all [BNTC, Ld].

QUESTION—What is the significance of the mention of the three entities—the sea, Death, and Hades as giving up their dead?

It signifies that *all* the dead are included [Hu, NIC, TNTC]. The mention of both Death and Hades indicates all the dead—both buried and unburied [Alf].

QUESTION—Is Hades the place of the dead for both the righteous and unrighteous?

1. Hades is the place of the dead for both the righteous and the unrighteous [EC, NIC, TNTC]. The word ᾅδης refers to the realm of the dead, both righteous and unrighteous (see Acts 2:27, 31) [NIC]. It includes both Paradise (Luke 23:43) and Gehenna (Luke 12:5), as seen in the story Jesus told about the rich man and Lazarus (Luke 16:22–28) [EC].
2. Hades is the place of the dead for the unrighteous only [ICC]. This is clear by the fact that it is thrown into the Lake of Fire in verse 14 [ICC].

20:14 And death and Hades were-thrown into the lake of fire. This is the second death, the lake of fire.

TEXT—Some manuscripts do not include οὗτος ὁ θάνατος ὁ δεύτερός ἐστιν, ἡ λίμνη τοῦ πυρός 'this is the second death, the lake of fire'. Some manuscripts possibly do not include only ἡ λίμνη τοῦ πυρός 'the lake of fire', although GNT does not mention this alternative. The phrase 'the lake of fire' is not included by TR and KJV.

QUESTION—What is symbolized by the figure of death and Hades being thrown into the lake of fire?

1. It symbolizes the final destruction of death and Hades [Be, BNTC, EC, Ld, NIC, NTC, Sw, TNTC]. 1 Corinthians 15:26 describes death as being the final enemy to be destroyed. This is what is referred to here [Be, BNTC, EC, NIC, NTC, Sw]. It indicates that death and Hades are rendered powerless, as are the other evil entities [TNTC].
2. It symbolizes the punishment of the unrighteous dead, those described in verse 15 [WBC].

QUESTION—What is meant by the statement, 'This is the second death, the lake of fire'?

It indicates that *being consigned to* the lake of fire is the second death [Be, TNTC].

QUESTION—What other Scriptures describe the second death?

Revelation 2:11; 20:6, 14; and 21:8 all describe the second death [EC].

20:15 **And if anyone was-found not written in the book of life, he-was-thrown into the lake of fire.**

QUESTION—Who is the antecedent of the pronoun 'he' in the verb ἐβλήθη '*he* was thrown'?

It refers to any person and so should be translated in a neutral way lest it be taken to refer only to men [TH, WBC; all versions except NIV, TNT]: and if anyone was not found written…that person was thrown into the lake of fire.

QUESTION—Does Jesus refer to this lake of fire?

Jesus speaks of eternal fire as the punishment of those on his left in Matthew 25:41 [Sw].

QUESTION—Where is the 'book of life' alluded to in Daniel?

Daniel 12:1 refers to God's people being delivered if their names were in the book [NIGTC].

DISCOURSE UNIT: 21:1–22:5 [Alf, EC, Hu, NIC, NIGTC, TNTC; NAB]. The topic is the new heaven and the new earth [Alf, Hu, NIC, TNTC; NAB], the new creation [EC, NIGTC].

DISCOURSE UNIT: 21:1–27 [NIV]. The topic is the new Jerusalem.

DISCOURSE UNIT: 21:1–8 [BNTC, EC, GNT, Hu, Ld, Lns, NIC, NIGTC, NTC, Sw, WBC; CEV, NET, NRSV, TEV]. The topic is the new heaven and earth [BNTC, EC, Lns, Sw, WBC; CEV, KJV, NET, NRSV], the new creation [Hu, Ld, NIC, NIGTC, NTC].

DISCOURSE UNIT: 21:1–4 [TNTC]. The topic is God with them.

21:1 And I-saw (a) new heaven and (a) new earth. For the first heaven and the first earth passed-away[a] and the sea is no longer.[b]

TEXT—Instead of ἀπῆλθαν 'passed away', some manuscripts have the nearly synonymous παρῆλθεν 'passed by'. GNT does not mention this alternative. The reading 'passed by' is taken by TR.

LEXICON—a. aorist act. indic. of ἀπέρχομαι (LN 13.93) (BAGD 1.b. p. 84): 'to pass away' [BAGD, EC, LN, WBC; KJV, NAB, NIV, NRSV], 'to go away' [BNTC, Lns; TNT], 'to disappear' [CEV, NCV, NLT, TEV], 'to vanish' [REB], 'to cease to exist' [LN; NET]. See this word also at 9:12.

b. ἔτι (LN 67.128): 'longer' [EC, Lns, WBC; NIV, REB, TNT], 'more' [BNTC; KJV, NAB, NRSV], 'anymore' [NCV], 'yet' [LN], not explicit [CEV, NET, NLT, TEV].

QUESTION—What is indicated by the phrase καὶ εἶδον 'and I saw'?
It indicates a new vision [TH].

QUESTION—What relationship is indicated by γάρ 'for'?
It introduces a reason for the preceding clause [EC, Lns, NIGTC]: I saw a new heaven and a new earth *because* the first heaven and the first earth passed away.

QUESTION—Does this mean that the earth and heaven are renewed or completely replaced?
1. It means that they are renewed [Alf, Hu, Lns, NIGTC]. The renewal of the earth is supported by such Scriptures as Romans 8:19–22 and 2 Corinthians 5:17 [Hu].
2. It means that they are completely replaced [EC, TH, Wal, WBC]. The complete dissolution of the first heaven and first earth is indicated (see 20:11) [EC, WBC].

21:2 And I-saw the holy city new Jerusalem coming-down out-of heaven from God prepared as (a) bride adorned[a] for her husband.

TEXT—Instead of καὶ τὴν πόλιν τὴν ἁγίαν Ἰερουσαλὴμ καινὴν εἶδον 'and I saw the holy city new Jerusalem', some manuscripts possibly have, καὶ ἐγὼ Ἰωάννης εἶδον τὴν πόλιν τὴν ἁγίαν Ἰερουσαλὴμ καινὴν 'and I John saw the holy city new Jerusalem', although GNT does not mention this alternative. The reading 'and I John saw the holy city new Jerusalem' is taken by TR and KJV.

TEXT—Instead of ἐκ τοῦ οὐρανοῦ ἀπὸ τοῦ θεοῦ 'out of heaven from God', some manuscripts have ἀπὸ τοῦ θεοῦ ἐκ τοῦ οὐρανοῦ 'from God out of heaven'. GNT does not mention this alternative. The reading, 'from God out of heaven' is taken by TR and KJV.

LEXICON—a. perf. pass. participle of κοσμέω (LN 79.12) (BAGD 2.a.α. p. 445): 'to be adorned' [BAGD, BNTC, EC, LN, Lns, WBC; KJV, NAB, NET, NRSV, REB, TNT], 'to be beautifully dressed' [NIV], 'to be dressed' [NCV, TEV], 'to be dressed in one's wedding gown' [CEV], 'to be beautified' [LN], 'to be decorated' [BAGD, LN]. This verb is also translated as an adjective: '(a) beautiful (bride)' [NLT].

QUESTION—What other verse in Revelation refers to 'new Jerusalem the city'?

'New Jerusalem the city' is referred to in 3:12 where Jesus promises to write the name of new Jerusalem, the city of his God, on the one who overcomes [Hu, Sw, TH, Wal, WBC].

QUESTION—Does new Jerusalem symbolize the saints or the place in which they live?

1. It symbolizes the place where the saints will live [Be, NIC, Wal, WBC]. Jerusalem is the place where God lives in the same way that the people of God are His temple (see 1 Corinthians 3:16, 17) [NIC]. The city is compared to a bride so it cannot be the bride. If the believers will inherit the city (21:7), they cannot be the city. The city is the place where the believers will live (21:24–26) [WBC].
2. It symbolizes the saints [Alf, NTC]. The city is named for its inhabitants [Alf]. New Jerusalem is the body of believers (see Galatians 4:26; Hebrews 12:22). The church is 'the city…whose builder and maker is God' (see Hebrews 11:10) [NTC].
3. It may symbolize both [EC, Ld]. Although new Jerusalem symbolizes the place the believers will live, it may also be identified with God's people (see 1 Corinthians 3:16 and Ephesians 2:21) [Ld].

QUESTION—What relationship is indicated by ἐκ in the phrase ἐκ τοῦ οὐρανοῦ 'out of heaven'?

It indicates that heaven is the place *from which* new Jerusalem descends [Be, EC, NIC, Sw, TH].

QUESTION—What relationship is indicated by ἀπό in the phrase ἀπὸ τοῦ θεοῦ 'from God'?

It indicates that God is the person who *sends* new Jerusalem down [Be, EC, NIC, Sw, TH].

QUESTION—What is the point of similarity between Jerusalem and a bride adorned for her husband?

The point of similarity is *beauty* [Lns, TNTC, Wal]: New Jerusalem is beautiful like a bride adorned for her husband.

QUESTION—Who is the implied actor of the passive participle ἡτοιμασμένην 'prepared'?

The actor is God [NIGTC]: coming down from God and prepared by him like a bride adorned for her husband.

21:3 And I-heard (a) loud voice from the throne saying, "Behold[a] the dwelling[b] of God (is) with men,[c] and he-will-live[d] with them, and they will-be his peoples, and God himself with them will-be [their God],"

TEXT—Instead of θρόνου 'throne', some manuscripts have οὐρανοῦ 'heaven'. GNT does not mention this alternative. The reading, 'heaven' is taken by TR and KJV.

TEXT—Instead of the plural λαοί 'peoples', some manuscripts have the singular λαός 'people'. GNT selects the reading 'peoples' with a B decision, indicating that the text is almost certain. Either reading is translated 'people' by [BNTC, EC, Lns, WBC; all versions except CEV, NRSV]; or 'peoples' by [NRSV].

TEXT—Instead of μετ' αὐτῶν ἔσται αὐτῶν θεός 'with them will be, their God', some manuscripts have ἔσται μετ' αὐτῶν θεός αὐτῶν 'will be with them, their God', others have μετ' αὐτῶν ἔσται θεός 'with them will be God', still others have μετ' αὐτῶν ἔσται 'with them will be'. GNT has μετ' αὐτῶν ἔσται [αὐτῶν θεός] 'with them will be, [their God]' with a C rating, indicating difficulty in deciding which alternative to place in the text. The reading, 'will be with them, their God' is taken by TR. The reading, 'with them will be' is taken by BNTC, Lns; NLT, NRSV, and REB.

LEXICON—a. ἰδού (LN 91.13) (BAGD 1.a. p. 370): 'behold' [BAGD, EC, WBC; KJV, NAB], 'look' [BAGD, LN; NET, NLT], 'see' [BAGD; NRSV], 'lo' [Lns], 'now' [BNTC; NCV, NIV, REB, TEV], 'pay attention' [LN], not explicit [CEV, TNT]. See this word also at 1:7.

b. σκηνή (LN 7.17) (BAGD p. 754): 'dwelling' [BAGD, BNTC, WBC; NAB, NIV, REB], 'home' [CEV, NLT, NRSV, TEV], 'residence' [NET], 'presence' [NCV], 'tent' [BAGD, LN], 'tabernacle' [EC; KJV], 'Tabernacle' [Lns], 'tabernacle tent' [LN]. This noun is also translated as a verb phrase: 'to come to live' [TNT]. See this word also at 13:6.

c. ἄνθρωπος (LN 9.1): 'man' [BNTC, EC, LN; KJV, NIV, TNT]. The plural of ἄνθρωπος (as here) is translated: 'people' [WBC; CEV, NCV, NLT, TEV], 'men and women' [NET], 'mankind' [REB], 'human beings' [Lns], '(the) human race' [NAB], 'mortals' [NRSV].

d. fut. act. indic. of σκηνόω (LN **85.75**): 'to live' [CEV, NCV, NET, NIV, NLT, TEV], 'to dwell' [BNTC, EC, WBC; KJV, NAB, NIV, REB, TNT], 'to come to dwell' [**LN**], 'to tabernacle' [Lns], 'to come to reside, to take up residence' [LN]. See this word also at 7:15.

QUESTION—What is the significance of the word ἰδού 'behold'?

It calls attention to what follows [EC, TH].

QUESTION—What is the significance of the *loud* voice?

The loudness of the voice indicates the importance of the words it announces [EC, TNTC, Wal]. It indicates the authority of the announcement [Wal]. It indicates the amazing significance of the announcement [EC].

QUESTION—Whose voice was heard from the throne?

1. The speaker is not God [EC, Lns, Sw, TNTC, WBC]. This voice speaks about God and therefore it is someone else used by God [Lns]. God only begins to speak at verse 5 [EC]. The speaker is one of the angels [Sw].
2. Although it might be the cherubim around the throne speaking, verse 5 seems to confirm that it is God himself who is speaking [NIGTC].

QUESTION—How should the clause αὐτὸς ὁ θεὸς μετ' αὐτῶ ἔσται αὐτῶν θεός 'God himself with them will be their God' be translated?

1. It should be translated: 'God himself will be with them and be their God' [KJV, NCV, NIV, TEV, TNT].

2. It should be translated: 'God himself will be with them as their God' [EC, WBC; NAB, NET].

QUESTION—What is the significance of the five-fold repetition in this verse of God's presence with people?

It indicates the prominence of the theme that God is now present with his people [EC].

QUESTION—What is the significance of the addition of the pronoun αὐτός 'he', with 'God'?

It intensifies the word 'God' [EC]: God *himself*.

QUESTION—How are the nouns related in the genitive construction λαοὶ αὐτοῦ 'his peoples'?

Either the peoples *belong to* God or the peoples *worship* God [TH].

QUESTION—What is indicated by the plural noun λαοί 'peoples'?

It is a specific reference to the many kinds of people or nations who together make up the people of God [Alf, EC, Hu, NIC, NIGTC, Sw, TNTC]. It refers to peoples of every tribe, tongue, people, and nation (see 5:9 and 7:9) [NIGTC]. God promised Abraham to make him a blessing to all the peoples/nations of the earth (see Genesis 12:3 and Galatians 3:8) [EC, Hu].

21:4 **And he-will-wipe-away every tear from their eyes, and death will-be no longer nor grief[a] nor crying[b] nor pain[c] will-be any longer, [because] the first-things passed-away.**

TEXT—Instead of ἐξαλείψει 'he will wipe away', some manuscripts have ἐξαλείψει ὁ θεός 'God will wipe away'. GNT does not mention this alternative. The reading, 'God will wipe away' is taken by TR and KJV.

TEXT—Instead of ὅτι τὰ πρῶτα 'because the first things', one manuscript reads ὅτι ταῦτα 'because these things', others read τὰ πρῶτα 'the first things', and one important manuscript reads τὰ πρόβατα 'the sheep'. GNT reads [ὅτι] τὰ πρῶτα '[because] the first things' with a C decision, indicating difficulty in deciding which alternative to place in the text.

LEXICON—a. πένθος (LN 25.142) (BAGD p. 642): 'grief' [BAGD, BNTC, LN, WBC; TEV], 'mourning' [BAGD, Lns; NAB, NET, NIV, NRSV, REB, TNT], 'sorrow' [EC, LN; KJV, NLT], 'sadness' [BAGD; NCV], 'suffering' [CEV]. See this word also at 18:7.

b. κραυγή (LN **25.138**) (BAGD 1.a. p. 449): 'crying' [BAGD, BNTC, EC, **LN**, WBC; all versions except NAB], 'outcry' [Lns], 'wailing' [NAB], 'weeping' [LN].

c. πόνος (LN **24.77**): 'pain' [BNTC, EC, **LN**, Lns, WBC; all versions], 'suffering' [LN]. See this word also at 16:10. In this verse physical pain is indicated [Be, EC].

QUESTION—Where else in Scripture is the action of this verse described?

The action of this verse is also described in Isaiah 25:8 and Revelation 7:17 [BNTC, WBC].

QUESTION—Are these tears caused by grief, or suffering, or remorse?
They are tears caused by grief and suffering [EC, Ld]. They are caused by suffering for Christ, not by any remorse for the past [NIC, Wal].
QUESTION—What relationship is indicated by ὅτι 'because'?
It indicates the reason for the absence of death, grief, crying, and pain [EC, Hu, NIGTC, TNTC]: death will be no longer nor will there be any more grief, or crying or pain *because* the first things passed away.
QUESTION—To what does the phrase τὰ πρῶτα 'the first things' refer?
It refers to the conditions existing under the first heaven and the first earth [EC, Lns, Sw, TH, TNTC, WBC]. It refers to death, grief, crying, and pain [Be, EC, TH].

DISCOURSE UNIT: 21:5–8 [TNTC]. The topic is the separation between good and evil.

21:5 **And the-one sitting on the throne said, "Behold I-make all-things new," and he-says, "Write (this), because these words are trustworthy[a] and true."**

TEXT—Following λέγει 'he says', some manuscripts include μοι 'to me'. GNT does not mention this alternative. The reading, 'to me' is included by TR and KJV.
LEXICON—a. πιστός (LN 31.87) (BAGD 1.a.α. p. 664): 'trustworthy' [BAGD, LN, WBC; NAB, NIV, NLT, NRSV, REB, TNT], 'faithful' [BAGD, BNTC, EC, LN, Lns; KJV], 'reliable' [LN; NET]. This adjective is also translated as a verb phrase: 'to be able to be trusted' [CEV, NCV, TEV]. See this word also at 1:5.
QUESTION—Who is ὁ καθήμενος ἐπὶ τῷ θρόνῳ 'the one sitting on the throne'?
  1. It is God the Father [Alf, Be, BNTC, EC, Hu, Ld, NIGTC, Sw, TH, TNTC, WBC].
  2. It is Christ [Wal]. The speaker of verse 6 is Christ because he introduces himself as the Alpha and Omega as he did in 1:8 [Wal].
QUESTION—Who is the speaker of the verb λέγει 'he says'?
  1. The speaker is God himself [Be, NIC, NIGTC, TH, WBC]. Although the verb is 'says' (present tense) here while the previous and following clauses which are spoken by God use the past tense 'said', there is no reason to postulate a change of speaker for what may be an alteration of tense for stylistic reasons [NIC].
  2. The speaker is an angel [Alf, EC, Sw, TNTC]. It is a voice from heaven, perhaps an angel [Alf]. This is an interjection by someone else, perhaps an angel, who seeing that John was so astounded that he forgot to write, had to remind John to continue writing [TNTC].
  3. The speaker is Christ [Wal].
QUESTION—What is the implied object of Γράψον 'Write!'?
  1. The implied object is what has been said in verses 1–4 or 1–5 [Be, EC, NIC, TH].

2. The implied object is the whole book of Revelation [WBC]. At some places (4:13 and 19:9), only a small portion was to be written. Here it includes the whole as it does in 1:11, 19 (see also 10:4) [WBC].
3. The implied object is the statement, "Behold, I make all things new" [NIGTC].

QUESTION—What relationship is indicated by ὅτι 'because'?
It indicates the reason for writing [Be, EC, NIC, NIGTC, Sw, TH, WBC; all versions except CEV]: Write, *because* these words are trustworthy and true.

QUESTION—To what does οὗτοι οἱ λόγοι 'these words' refer?
1. These words refer to what has been said in verses 1–5 [EC, NIC].
1. They refer to the statement, 'Behold, I make all things new' [NIGTC].
3. They refer to the words that are about to be spoken [TNTC]. It is probably the words about to be spoken but it may refer to the words about making all things new [TNTC].

21:6 And he said to-me, "They-have-come-to-pass. I [am] the Alpha and the Omega, the beginning and the end.

TEXT—Instead of the plural γέγοναν 'they have come to pass', some manuscripts possibly read the singular γέγονεν 'it has come to pass', although GNT does not mention this alternative. The reading 'it has come to pass' is taken by TR.

TEXT—Instead of ἐγώ εἰμι τὸ Ἄλφα 'I am the Alpha', some manuscripts do not include εἰμι 'am'. GNT does not deal with this alternative in the apparatus but brackets εἰμι in the text, indicating doubt about including it.

QUESTION—Who is the speaker of εἶπέν 'he said'?
1. The speaker is God [Alf, Be, BNTC, EC, Hu, ICC, Ld, NIC, NIGTC, Sw, TNTC, WBC]: And God said to me.
2. The speaker is Christ [Lns, Wal]: And Christ said to me.

QUESTION—How is the verb γέγοναν 'they have come to pass' translated?
It is translated: 'it is finished' [WBC; NCV, NLT], 'it is done' [KJV, NET, NIV, NRSV, REB, TEV], 'everything is finished' [CEV], 'they have occurred' [Lns], 'they are accomplished' [NAB], 'they are done' [EC], 'they are fulfilled' [TNT], 'all is over' [BNTC].

QUESTION—What does 'they' refer to in the verb γέγοναν 'they have come to pass'?
'They' refers to the words 'these words' of the previous verse [Alf, Be, Sw, TH]. 'They' refers to the 'all things' in the phrase 'I make *all things* new' [BNTC, EC, NIGTC]. It is possible that 'they' refers to 'all things' (of 21:5), but 'these words' is the preferred reference [Alf]. 'They' may refer to 'all these things' of Matthew 24:33–34, namely all the things that have to happen before the end [WBC]. 'They' probably refers to all the events that were supposed to happen [TNTC]. 'They' refers to the descent of the new Jerusalem and its benefits [NIC]. 'They' refers to all the work done throughout history [Wal].

REVELATION 21:6

QUESTION—What is the significance of the explicit use of the pronoun ἐγώ 'I'?

It makes the pronoun emphatic [Lns]: I myself.

QUESTION—What is meant by the metaphors τὸ Ἄλφα καὶ τὸ Ὦ, ἡ ἀρχὴ καὶ τὸ τέλος 'the Alpha and the Omega, the beginning and the end'?

They emphasize everything that lies between the extremes. Here they signify God's sovereignty over history [NIGTC]. They signify that God starts and completes all things [BNTC, EC, TH, TNTC]. They signify that Christ starts and completes all of God's saving work [Lns]. They signify absolute control over all things [EC]. They signify that God is the origin of all things and is their goal [NIC].

To-the-one being-thirsty[a] I-will-give freely[b] from the spring[c] of-the water of life.

LEXICON—a. pres. act. participle of διψάω (BAGD 2. p. 200): 'to be thirsty' [WBC; CEV, NCV, NET, NIV, NLT, TEV, TNT], 'to thirst' [BAGD, EC, Lns], 'to be athirst' [KJV]. This verb is also translated as a noun: '(the) thirsty' [BNTC; NAB, NRSV, REB]. See this word also at 7:16.

b. δωρεάν (LN 57.85) (BAGD 1. p. 210): 'freely' [EC, WBC; CEV, KJV], 'without cost' [LN; NIV, TNT], 'as a (free) gift' [BAGD, LN; NRSV, REB], 'without paying' [BAGD, LN; TEV], 'free of charge' [BNTC; NET, NLT], 'gratis' [BAGD, Lns]. This verb is also translated as a noun: 'gift' [NAB]; and as an adjective: 'free (water)' [NCV].

c. πηγή (LN 1.78) (BAGD 2. p. 656): 'spring' [BAGD, BNTC, LN, Lns; all versions except CEV, KJV], 'fountain' [EC; CEV, KJV], 'well' [WBC]. See this word also at 7:17.

QUESTION—What is signified by the verb 'to be thirsty'?

It signifies: the sense of need [BNTC], the sense of spiritual need [Be, EC, Ld, TNTC], the desire of the soul for God [NIC], soul thirst [Hu], a longing for fellowship with God [Be].

QUESTION—What is the significance of the explicit use of the pronoun ἐγώ 'I'?

It emphasizes the pronoun [TNTC]: I myself. It makes the pronoun exclusive [EC]: I, and no other.

QUESTION—How are the nouns related in the genitive construction τῆς πηγῆς τοῦ ὕδατος 'the spring of the water'?

The water *comes from* the spring [TH].

QUESTION—How are the nouns related in the genitive construction τοῦ ὕδατος τῆς ζωῆς 'the water of life'?

1. Life modifies water [WBC]: living water.
2. The water gives life [TH; CEV, NAB]: life-giving water.
3. Life is either in apposition to water (water, that is, life) or life modifies water (living water) [NIGTC].

QUESTION—To what does the 'water of life' refer?

It refers to never ending fellowship with God and Christ [NIGTC].

21:7 The-one overcoming will-inherit[a] these-things and I-will-be God to-him and he will-be (a) son to me.

TEXT—Instead of ταῦτα 'these things', some manuscripts possibly read πάντα 'all things', although GNT does not mention this alternative. The reading 'all things' is taken by TR and KJV.

TEXT—Instead of υἱός '(a) son', some manuscripts possibly read ὁ υἱός 'the son', although GNT does not mention this alternative. The reading 'the son' is taken by TR.

LEXICON—a. fut. act. indic. of κληρονομέω (LN 57.138) (BAGD 2. p. 434): 'to inherit' [EC, LN, Lns, WBC; KJV, NAB, NET, NIV, NLT, NRSV], 'to receive' [NCV, TEV], 'to possess' [TNT], 'to acquire, to obtain, to come into possession of' [BAGD]. This verb is also translated by its reciprocal: 'to be given' [CEV]. It is also translated as a noun: '(his) heritage' [BNTC; REB]. Κληρονομέω here indicates simply 'to receive as a gift' as there is no reference to the death of a donor [TH].

QUESTION—What is meant by 'overcoming'?

It means continuing to believe in spite of persecution [NIGTC].

QUESTION—To what does ταῦτα 'these things' refer?

It refers to all the promises made to those who overcome (see 2:7, 11, 17, 26; 3:5, 12, 21) [NIC, NTC, Sw]. It refers to all the blessings of the new heaven and earth [Alf, Hu, ICC, Lns]. It refers to the benefits named in verses 21:1–6 [NIGTC, TH]. It refers to the 'all things' of verse 5 [EC]. It refers to the benefits named in verse 4 [WBC]. It refers to the water from the fountain of life [Ld].

QUESTION—Does αὐτῷ 'to him' only refer to men?

No, it refers to men and women and perhaps should be translated with a generic plural [TH, WBC; CEV, NCV, NLT, NRSV, REB, TEV]: I will give these things to *those* who overcome, and I will be *their* God and *they* will be my *children*.

21:8 But for-the cowards[a] and unbelieving[b] and abominable[c] and murderers[d] and sexually-immoral[e] and sorcerers[f] and idolaters[g] and all liars[h]

TEXT—Instead of τοῖς δὲ δειλοῖς 'but to the cowardly', some manuscripts possibly have δειλοῖς δέ 'but to cowardly', although GNT does not mention this alternative. The reading 'but to cowardly' is taken by TR.

LEXICON—a. δειλός (LN **25.286**) (BAGD p. 173): 'coward' [BNTC, **LN**, Lns, WBC; CEV, NAB, NCV, NET, TEV, TNT], 'the cowardly' [BAGD, EC, LN; NIV, NRSV, REB], 'cowards who turn away from me' [NLT], 'the fearful' [KJV], 'timid' [BAGD].

b. ἄπιστος (LN 31.98, 31.106) (BAGD 2. p. 85): 'the unbelieving' [BAGD, LN (31.98); KJV, NIV], 'unbeliever' [LN (31.106), Lns, WBC; NET, NLT, TNT], 'traitor' [TEV], 'the unfaithful' [EC; CEV, NAB], 'the faithless' [BAGD, BNTC; NRSV, REB], 'one who refuses to believe' [NCV], 'lacking in trust' [LN (31.98)]. The word ἄπιστος implies a refusal to believe [LN (31.98); NCV].

c. perf. pass./mid. (deponent = act.) participle of βδελύσσομαι (LN **25.186**) (BAGD p. 138): 'to abominate' [LN], 'to abhor, to detest' [BAGD, LN]. This verb is translated as an noun: 'the abominable' [BAGD, EC, **LN**, WBC; KJV], 'the dirty-minded' [CEV], 'the depraved' [NAB], 'the loathsome' [TNT] 'a detestable person' [NET], 'the vile' [NIV], 'the corrupt' [NLT], 'the polluted' [BNTC; NRSV], 'the obscene' [REB], 'a pervert' [TEV], 'one who does evil things' [NCV], 'such as have become an abomination' [Lns].

d. φονεύς (LN 20.85) (BAGD p. 864): 'murderer' [BNTC, EC, LN, Lns, WBC; all versions except NCV], 'one who kills' [NCV].

e. πόρνος (LN 88.274) (BAGD p. 693): 'the sexually immoral' [BAGD, LN; CEV, NET, NIV], 'the immoral' [WBC; NLT, TEV, TNT], 'fornicator' [BAGD, BNTC, EC; NRSV, REB], 'one who sins sexually' [NCV], 'whore-monger' [KJV], 'the unchaste' [NAB], 'whorer' [Lns].

f. φάρμακος (LN 53.101) (BAGD p. 854): 'sorcerer' [BNTC, EC, LN, Lns, WBC; KJV, NAB, NRSV, REB, TNT], 'one who uses witchcraft' [CEV], 'one who does evil magic' [NCV], 'one who practices magic (spells)' [NET, TEV], 'one who practices magic arts' [NIV], 'one who practices witchcraft' [NLT], 'magician, poisoner' [BAGD].

g. εἰδωλολάτρης (LN 53.64) (BAGD p. 221): 'idolaters' [BAGD, BNTC, EC, LN, Lns, WBC; KJV, NIV, NRSV, REB, TNT], 'idol-worshipers' [LN; CEV, NAB, NCV, NLT, TEV], 'the idolatrous' [NET].

h. ψευδής (LN 33.255) (BAGD 1. p. 891): 'liar' [BNTC, EC, LN, Lns, WBC; KJV, NIV, NLT, NRSV, REB, TEV, TNT], 'deceivers' [NAB], 'one who tells lies' [CEV, NCV], 'one who lies' [NET], 'false' [BAGD]. See this word also at 2:2.

QUESTION—What relationship is indicated by δέ 'but'?

It indicates an adversative relationship [EC, NIGTC; all versions]: *But* for the cowardly.... Those persons listed in this verse contrast with 'the one overcoming' of verse 7 [EC, NIGTC].

QUESTION—What is meant by δειλός 'coward'?

It indicates those who deny their faith in Christ when faced with persecution [EC, ICC, Ld, NIGTC]. It indicates those who because of fear avoid conflict [Alf, Be]. It indicates those who fear men rather than God [Hu]. It indicates those who prefer personal safety to remaining loyal to Christ [NIC, TNTC]. It indicates those who are not brave in witnessing for Christ [TH].

QUESTION—What is meant by ἄπιστος '(the) unbelieving'?

It indicates: those who do not believe in Jesus or to those whom God cannot trust to be witnesses for Jesus [Ld], those who reject the Good News [Hu], those who refuse to believe in Christ [Hu, ICC], Christians who deny their faith in Christ [EC, ICC, NIC, TH], those whose faith does not prove genuine when tested [Be, TNTC].

QUESTION—What is meant by ἐβδελυγμένοις 'the abominable'?

It indicates: those who worship the emperor [NIC], those who worship the emperor or those who participate in the immorality of unbelievers [Be, TH], those who worship the Beast and participate in the detestable practices of unbelievers [EC], those who worship the Beast or to those who are morally impure [Ld, TH], idolaters [NIGTC], those who accept concepts and practices from the religion of unbelievers [TNTC]. It may indicate: sodomites or homosexuals [WBC], or sexual perverts [LN (25.168); TEV].

their part[a] (will be) in the lake burning with-fire and sulfur, that is the second death.

LEXICON—a. μέρος (BAGD 2. p. 506): 'part' [EC, Lns; KJV], 'lot' [BNTC; NAB], 'place' [BAGD; NCV, NET, NIV, NRSV, TEV, TNT], 'portion' [REB], 'doom' [NLT], 'share' [BAGD]. The clause τὸ μέρος αὐτῶν ἐν τῇ λίμνῃ 'their part (will be) in the lake' is translated: 'they will experience the lake' [WBC], 'they will be thrown into the lake' [CEV]. See this word also at 20:6.

DISCOURSE UNIT: 21:9–22:9 [WBC]. The topic is the vision of the new Jerusalem.

DISCOURSE UNIT: 21:9–22:5 [BNTC, EC, Ld, Lns, NTC, Sw; CEV, NET, REB, TEV]. The topic is the holy city.

DISCOURSE UNIT: 21:9–27 [Hu, NIC; NRSV]. The topic is the new Jerusalem [GNT, NIC; NRSV], the Lamb's bride [Hu].

DISCOURSE UNIT: 21:9–21 [TNTC]. The topic is the holy city.

DISCOURSE UNIT: 21:9–14 [NIGTC]. The topic is the holy city.

21:9 **And one of-the seven angels who-had the seven bowls filled with the seven last plagues came and spoke with me saying, "Come,[a] I-will-show you the bride[b] the wife[c] of-the Lamb.**

TEXT—Following ἦλθεν 'came', some manuscripts possibly include πρός με 'to me', although GNT does not mention this alternative. The reading 'to me' is included by TR and KJV.

TEXT—Instead of ἐκ τῶ ἑπτά 'of the seven', some manuscripts have τῶ ἑπτά with the same translation. GNT does not mention this alternative.

TEXT—Instead of the (grammatically incorrect) genitive τῶ γεμόντων 'the ones being filled', some manuscripts have the (grammatically correct) accusative τὰς γεμούσας. GNT does not mention this alternative. The accusative reading is taken by TR.

LEXICON—a. aorist act. impera. of δεῦρο (LN 84.24) (BAGD 1. p. 176): 'come' [BAGD, BNTC, EC, WBC; NET, NIV, NRSV, REB, TEV, TNT], 'come here' [BAGD, LN; NAB], 'come hither' [KJV], 'come on' [CEV], 'come with me' [NCV, NLT], 'hither' [LN, Lns], 'here' [LN].

b. νύμφη (LN 10.57) (BAGD 1. p. 545): 'bride' [BNTC, EC, Lns, WBC; all versions]. See this word also at 18:23.

c. γυνή (LN 10.54) (BAGD 3. p. 168): 'wife' [BNTC, EC, LN, Lns, WBC; all versions], 'bride' [BAGD]. See this word also at 19:7.

QUESTION—What does the verb γεμόντων 'filled' modify?
1. It modifies bowls [Be, BNTC, EC, ICC, NIC, WBC; all versions]: seven bowls filled with the seven last plagues.
2. It modifies angels [Alf, Lns]: seven angels filled with the seven last plagues. Here it is best to translate τὴν γεμὺντων as 'laden with' [Lns]: seven angels *laden with* the seven last plagues.
3. It may be taken to modify either bowls or angels [Sw]. If it modifies angels, since being masculine grammatically modifies them, it may mean that the angels were fresh from their work of pouring out the bowls of plagues [Sw].

QUESTION—In what sense is the word γυνή 'wife' used here?
It is used in the sense of 'wife to be' [Be, EC, TH]. In Biblical culture the concepts of engagement and marriage were more closely associated [NIGTC]. It could be rendered, 'bride who would become the Lamb's wife' [TH].

21:10 And he-carried-away[a] me in Spirit/spirit to (a) big high mountain, and showed me the holy city Jerusalem coming-down out-of heaven from God

TEXT—Instead of τὴν ἁγίαν Ἰερουσαλήμ 'the holy Jerusalem', some manuscripts have τὴν μεγάλην καὶ ἁγίαν Ἰερουσαλήμ 'the great and holy Jerusalem'. Others possibly have τὴν μεγάλην τὴν ἁγίαν Ἰερουσαλήμ 'the great the holy Jerusalem', although GNT does not mention this alternative. The reading 'the great the holy Jerusalem' is taken by TR and KJV.

LEXICON—a. aorist act. indic. of ἀποφέρω (LN 15.202) (BAGD 1.a.α. p. 101): 'to carry away' [BAGD, BNTC, EC, LN; KJV, NCV, NIV, NRSV, REB], 'to carry' [TEV], 'to take away' [BAGD, LN; NET], 'to take' [CEV, NAB, NLT, TNT], 'to bear away' [Lns] 'to transport' [WBC]. See this word also at 17:3.

QUESTION—What is meant by the phrase ἐν πνεύματι 'in spirit' (see this question also at 1:10 and 17:3)?
1. It indicates being in God's Spirit [Be, Ld, NIC, NIGTC, Sw, TH, TNTC; CEV, NCV, NET, NIV, TEV, TNT]. The action happens in John's spirit but the power comes from God's Spirit [Sw]. It was an ecstatic experience [Be, Ld, TH, TNTC]. It indicates that the Spirit possessed or controlled John [TH]. The Spirit makes John receptive to the vision [TNTC].
2. It indicates a special state of John's own spirit [Alf, BNTC, EC, Lns, WBC; KJV, NAB, NLT, NRSV, REB]. This was a state of spiritual ecstasy or trance [Alf, BNTC, EC, WBC]. It indicates a prophetic trance [WBC]. This made John receptive to the vision that he would experience [Alf].

21:11 Having the glory^a of God, the radiance^b of-it (was) like (a) precious^c stone as (a) jasper^d stone shining-like-crystal.^e

TEXT—Before ὁ φωστὴρ αὐτῆς 'its radiance', some manuscripts include καί 'and'. GNT does not mention this alternative. The word 'and' is included by TR and KJV.

LEXICON—a. δόξα (LN 14.49) (BAGD 1.a. p. 203): 'glory' [BNTC, EC, Lns, WBC; all versions except NAB], 'splendor' [BAGD; NAB]. Δόξα here indicates 'brightness, radiance' [BAGD, LN], 'shining' [LN], 'splendor' [BAGD]. See this word also at 15:8.

  b. φωστήρ (LN **14.49**) (BAGD 2. p. 872): 'radiance' [BAGD, BNTC, **LN**, WBC; NAB, NRSV, REB, TNT], 'brilliance' [EC; NET, NIV], 'light' [KJV], 'luminary' [Lns], 'splendor' [BAGD]. This noun is also translated as an adjective: 'bright (city)' [CEV, NCV]. It is also translated as a verb: 'to sparkle' [NLT], 'to shine' [TEV].

  c. τίμιος (LN 65.2) (BAGD 1.a. p. 818): 'precious' [BAGD, LN, WBC; CEV, NAB, NET, NLT, TEV], 'very precious' [BNTC, EC; NIV, TNT], 'most precious' [Lns; KJV], 'very expensive' [NAB], 'very rare' [NRSV], 'priceless' [REB], 'valuable' [LN], 'costly' [BAGD]. See this word also at 17:4.

  d. ἴασπις (LN 2.30) (BAGD p. 368): 'jasper' [BAGD, BNTC, EC, LN, WBC; all versions], 'diamond' [Lns]. The comparison of jasper to crystal stresses its value and pureness since jasper is opaque [WBC]. The jasper we know is opaque, so it may be that a diamond is meant [TNTC]. This could have the meaning of 'diamond' [EC, Lns]. See this word also at 4:3.

  e. pres. act. participle of κρυσταλλίζω (LN 2.47) (BAGD p. 454): 'to shine like crystal' [BAGD, LN], 'to shine clear as crystal' [**LN**], 'to shine brightly' [LN], 'to scintillate' [Lns], 'to be as transparent as crystal' [BAGD]. This verb is also translated as an adjective: 'crystal clear' [BAGD (p. 368), EC; CEV, NET, NLT, TNT], 'clear as crystal' [BNTC; KJV, NAB, NCV, NIV, NRSV, REB, TEV], 'transparent as crystal' [WBC].

QUESTION—What is meant by ἔχουσαν τὴν δόξαν τοῦ θεοῦ 'having the glory of God'?

  It means that it shone with the light of God's presence [TH]. It means that the glory of God made the city bright [BNTC; CEV]. It means that it shone with the glory of God [NAB, NCV, NIV, REB, TEV].

QUESTION—What is the point of similarity intended with the verb κρυσταλλίζω 'to shine like crystal'?

  1. The point of similarity is 'clearness' or 'transparency' [EC, Sw, Wal, WBC; all versions]. A jasper stone *clear* like crystal.

  2. The point of similarity is 'shining, sparkling, scintillating' [LN, Lns, NIC]. A jasper stone *shining* like crystal.

QUESTION—What else is compared to a jasper stone in Revelation?

  The person sitting on the throne in heaven is compared to jasper (see 4:3) [BNTC, EC, Hu, ICC, Ld, Lns, TNTC].

21:12 Having (a) great^a and high wall, having twelve gates^b and at the gates twelve angels and names written-on^c (them) that are [the names] of-the twelve tribes of-the-sons of-Israel;

TEXT—Instead of ἔχουσα τεῖχος 'having a wall' (nominative), some manuscripts have ἔχουσάν τε τεῖχος (accusative) 'and having a wall', although GNT does not mention this alternative. The reading 'and having a wall' is taken by TR and KJV.

TEXT—Instead of τὰ ὀνόματα 'the names', some manuscripts have ὀνόματα 'names'. Others do not include τὰ ὀνόματα 'the names'. GNT includes 'the names' in brackets with a C decision, indicating difficulty in deciding whether or not to include them in the text. The reading 'the names' is not included by TR.

LEXICON—a. μέγας (LN 78.2): 'great' [EC, LN, Lns; KJV, NCV, NIV, NRSV, REB, TEV, TNT], 'massive' [NAB, NET], 'huge' [BNTC], 'broad' [NLT], 'thick' [CEV], 'wide' [WBC]. See this word also at 6:4.
  b. πυλών (LN 7.38, 7.48) (BAGD 1. p. 729): 'gate' [BAGD, LN (7.48)], 'portal' [Lns], 'door' [LN (7.48)], 'gateway, entrance, vestibule' [LN (7.38)].
  c. perf. pass. participle of ἐπιγράφω (LN 33.65) (BAGD 1. p. 291): 'to write on' [BAGD, LN; CEV, KJV, NCV, NET, NIV, NLT, TEV, TNT], 'to inscribe on' [EC, Lns, WBC; NAB, NRSV, REB], 'to carve on' [BNTC].

QUESTION—How should the phrase φυλῶν υἱῶν Ἰσραήλ 'tribes of the sons of Israel' be translated?

It is translated: 'tribes of Israel' [BNTC, TH; CEV, NCV, NIV, NLT, REB], 'tribes of the Israelites' [NAB, NRSV], 'tribes of the nation of Israel' [NET], 'tribes of the people of Israel' [TEV], 'tribes of the sons of Israel' [EC, Lns, WBC], 'tribes of the children of Israel' [KJV, TNT].

QUESTION—Where else in Scripture is a similar description of a city?

A similar description of a city is found in Ezekiel 48:30ff. [EC, Hu, TNTC].

21:13 On (the) east three gates and on (the) north three gates and on (the) south three gates and on (the) west^a three gates.

TEXT—Instead of καὶ ἀπὸ δυσμῶν 'and on (the) west', some manuscripts have ἀπὸ δυσμῶν 'on (the) west'. GNT does not mention this alternative. The reading 'on (the) west' is taken by TR.

LEXICON—a. δυσμή (LN 82.2): 'west' [BNTC, EC, **LN**, Lns, WBC; all versions].

21:14 And the wall of-the city having twelve foundation-stones^a and on them twelve names of-the twelve apostles of the lamb.

TEXT—Instead of ἐπ' αὐτῶν 'on them', some manuscripts possibly have ἐν αὐτοῖς 'in them', although GNT does not mention this alternative. The reading 'in them' is taken by TR and KJV.

TEXT—Instead of δώδεκα ὀνόματα 'twelve names', some manuscripts possibly read ὀνόματα 'names', although GNT does not mention this alternative. The reading 'names' is taken by TR and KJV.
LEXICON—a. θεμέλιος (LN **7.43**) (BAGD 1.a. p. 355): 'foundation stone' [BAGD, BNTC, **LN**, WBC; CEV, NCV, NLT, REB, TEV, TNT], 'foundation' [EC, Lns; KJV, NET, NIV, NRSV], 'stone as a foundation' [NAB].
QUESTION—How are the twelve foundation stones laid?
The wall had 12 sections each resting on one foundation stone [ICC]. There was either one stone between the gates [Alf, EC, TH], or a stone under each gate [TH].
QUESTION—To whom does the phrase 'the twelve apostles' refer?
It probably refers to the twelve disciples of Jesus [NIC, Sw, TH].
QUESTION—How are the names written?
There is one name written on each stone [TH; CEV]

DISCOURSE UNIT: 21:15–17 [NIGTC]. The topic is the measurements of the city.

21:15 And the-one speaking with me had (a) golden measure[a] measuring-rod,[b] so-that he-might-measure[c] the city and its gates and its wall.
TEXT—Instead of μέτρον κάλαμον 'measuring rod', some manuscripts have κάλαμον 'rod'. GNT does not mention this alternative. The reading 'rod' is taken by TR and KJV.
LEXICON—a. μέτρον (LN 81.1) (BAGD 1.b. p. 515): 'measure' [BAGD, LN]. The phrase μέτρον κάλαμον 'measure measuring rod' is translated: 'rod as a measure' [EC], 'measure (a golden) reed' [Lns], 'measuring rod' [BNTC, WBC; NAB, NCV, NET, NIV, NRSV, REB, TNT], 'measuring stick' [CEV, NLT, TEV].
b. κάλαμος (LN **6.213**) (BAGD 3. p. 398): 'measuring rod' [BAGD, LN], 'measuring stick' [**LN**], 'reed' [Lns; KJV], 'rod' [BNTC, EC, WBC; NAB, NCV, NET, NIV, NRSV, REB, TNT], 'stick' [CEV, NLT, TEV].
c. aorist act. subj. of μετρέω (LN 81.2) (BAGD 1.a. p. 514): 'to measure' [BAGD, BNTC, EC, LN, Lns, WBC; all versions].
QUESTION—What relationship is indicated by ἵνα 'so that'?
It indicates the purpose of his having the measuring rod [BNTC, EC, TNTC]: *the purpose* he had a golden measuring rod *was so that* he might measure the city and its gates and its wall.
QUESTION—What is indicated by the καί 'and' occurring before 'its gates'?
1. The καί is explanatory and means 'that is, even' [Be, EC]: so that he might measure the city, *that is*, its gates *and* its wall.
2. It is conjoining and means 'and, also' [Lns, WBC; CEV, KJV, NET, NRSV]. so that he might measure the city and its gates and its wall.

21:16 And the city lies[a] square[b] and its length[c] (is) as-much-as the width[d] [also]. And he measured the city with-the rod to-the-extent-of[e] twelve thousand stadia,[f] the length and the width and the height[g] of-it are equal.[h]

TEXT—Following τὸ μῆκος αὐτῆς 'the length of it', some manuscripts possibly include τοσοῦτόν ἐστιν 'is as much as', although GNT does not mention this alternative. The reading 'is as much as' is included by TR.

TEXT—Instead of καὶ τὸ πλάτος 'the breadth also', some manuscripts have τὸ πλάτος 'the breadth'. GNT does not deal with this alternative in the apparatus but brackets καί 'also' in the text, indicating doubt about including it.

LEXICON—a. pres. mid./pass. (deponent = act.) of κεῖμαι (LN 85.2) (BAGD 1.b. p. 426): 'to lie' [EC, LN, Lns; KJV, NRSV], 'to be' [NAB, NLT, TEV, TNT], 'to be laid (out)' [BAGD; NET, NIV], 'to be built in' [NCV], 'to stand' [BNTC]. Κεῖμαι indicates to be in a place, frequently in the sense of 'being contained in' or 'resting on' [LN].

b. τετράγωνος (LN **79.91**) (BAGD p. 813): 'square' [**LN**; NAB, NCV, NLT, TNT], 'perfectly square' [TEV], 'foursquare' [BNTC, EC, Lns; KJV, NRSV], 'as a square' [BAGD; NET, NIV], 'four-sided' [REB]. Τετρύγωνος indicates 'as a square' or possibly 'like a cube' [BAGD]. It refers to stones that are used in a building that were 'shaped like a cube' [BAGD, EC, NIC]. The verb phrase τετράγωνος κεῖται 'lies square' is translated: 'is shaped like a cube' [CEV], 'is arranged with four equal sides' [WBC].

c. μῆκος (LN **81.12**) (BAGD p. 518): 'length' [BAGD, BNTC, EC, **LN**, Lns, WBC; KJV, NAB, NCV, NET, NRSV, TNT], not explicit [CEV]. This noun is also translated as an adjective: 'long' [NIV, NLT, REB, TEV].

d. πλάτος (LN **81.15**) (BAGD 1. p. 666): 'width' [BAGD, EC, LN, WBC; NAB, NCV, NET, NRSV], 'breadth' [BAGD, BNTC, **LN**, Lns; KJV, TNT]. This noun is also rendered as an adjective: 'wide' [**LN**; CEV, NIV, NLT, REB, TEV].

e. ἐπί with genitive object (LN **78.51**) (BAGD III.1.a.α. p. 288): 'to the extent of' [EC, **LN**], 'at' [Lns, WBC; NET], 'to the point of, to the degree that, up to.' [LN], 'across, over' [BAGD], not explicit [BNTC; all versions except NET]. The preposition ἐπί indicates a degree extending to a particular point according to the context [LN].

f. στάδιος (LN 81.27) (BAGD 1. p. 764): 'stade' [BAGD, EC, LN, Lns, WBC; NCV, NIV, TNT], 'furlong' [BNTC; KJV, REB]. The phrase σταδίων δώδεκα χιλιάδων 'twelve thousand stadia' is translated: 'fifteen hundred miles' [CEV, NAB, NRSV TEV], 'fourteen hundred miles' [NET, NLT]. See this word at 14:20.

g. ὕψος (LN **81.3**) (BAGD 1.a. p. 850): 'height' [BAGD, BNTC, EC, **LN**, Lns, WBC; KJV, NAB, NET, NLT, NRSV, REB, TNT]. This noun is also translated as an adjective: 'high' [CEV, NCV, NIV TEV].

h. ἴσος (LN **58.33**) (BAGD p. 381): 'equal' [BAGD, BNTC, EC, Lns; KJV, NET, NRSV, REB, TNT], 'the same' [**LN**, WBC], 'equivalent' [LN], not explicit [CEV, NAB, NCV, NIV, NLT, TEV].

QUESTION—How big is the city?
1. It is a cube having each dimension equal to 12,000 stadia (1,500 miles) [Be, EC, ICC, Ld, NIC, NIGTC, Sw, TH, TNTC, WBC]. If it is not 1,500 miles on each dimension, then the verse does not tell us how high the city was [EC].
2. It is either a cube or a pyramid having each of its dimensions equal to 12,000 stadia (1,500 miles) [Wal].
3. It is a cube having each dimension being equal to 3,000 stadia (375 miles) [Alf].

QUESTION—Are these numbers literal or symbolic?
1. They are literal [EC, Wal, WBC].
2. They are symbolic [Be, Hu, ICC, Ld, Lns, NIC, NIGTC, NTC, Sw]. The number symbolizes: its huge size [Be, Ld, NIC, Sw], its symmetry [Be, Hu, Ld, NIC], its magnificence [Be, NIC, Sw], its perfection and completeness [Ld], the eternal union of God with mankind [Lns], the completeness of God's people both Jews and Gentiles [NIGTC].

21:17 And he-measured its wall one-hundred forty four cubits[a] (the) measure[b] of-man, which is of-an-angel.

LEXICON—a. πῆχυς (LN **81.25**) (BAGD): 'cubit' [EC, LN, WBC; KJV, NAB, NCV, NET, NIV, NRSV, REB, TNT], 'cubit (measured by a man's forearm)' [BNTC], 'half-arm length' [Lns], 'eighteen inches, half meter' [LN]. The phrase ἑκατὸν τεσσεράκοντα τεσσάρων πηχῶν 'a hundred forty four cubits' is translated: 'two hundred sixteen feet' [CEV, NLT, TEV]. A πῆχυς is traditionally the distance from the elbow to the end of the fingers [LN].

b. μέτρον (LN **81.1**): 'measure' [EC, LN, Lns; KJV, NLT], 'measurement' [CEV, NCV, NET, NIV, NRSV, REB, TNT], 'unit of measurement' [**LN**, WBC; NAB, TEV]. This noun is also translated as a verb: 'to measure (by)' [BNTC]. See this word also at 21:15.

QUESTION—Does this refer to the width or the height of the wall?
1. It refers to the height of the wall [Alf, Hu, NIGTC, Sw, TH, TNTC, Wal; CEV, NCV, REB, TEV]: two hundred sixteen feet high.
2. It refers to the thickness of the wall [Be, EC, Ld, NTC, WBC; NIV, NLT]: two hundred sixteen feet wide. It is possible that this refers to the thickness of the wall rather than its height as a wall only 216 feet high would be out of proportion to a city 1,500 miles high [Ld].

QUESTION—What is indicated by the phrase μέτρον ἀνθρώπου, ὅ ἐστιν ἀγγέλου 'measure of man which is of an angel'?
1. It indicates that the measure the angel used was the measure that was in common use by man [Alf, Be, EC, ICC, Ld, NIC, Sw, TH, TNTC, Wal; CEV, NCV, NIV, NLT, NRSV, REB, TEV, TNT].

2. It indicates that the numbers should be taken symbolically [Hu, NIGTC]. It indicates that the angel's measure is different than man's and thereby gives a hint that the figures should be taken symbolically [NIGTC]. It indicates that this is merely a human calculation and that the numbers therefore should be taken symbolically [Hu].
3. It indicates that the man, whose measurements are used as reference here, is an angel [NTC]. John intended to indicate that the cubit he meant here was the measure of man's forearm and not a standard cubit of any particular country. He also adds that by man he means angel [BNTC].

DISCOURSE UNIT: 21:18–21 [TNTC]. The topic is the material of the city.

21:18 And the material[a] of its wall (was) jasper and the city (was) pure[b] gold like pure[c] glass.[d]

TEXT—Instead of καὶ ἡ ἐνδώμησις 'and the construction material', some manuscripts have καὶ ἦν ἡ ἐνδώμησις 'and the construction material was'. GNT does not mention this alternative. The reading 'and the construction material was' is taken by TR.

LEXICON—a. ἐνδώμησις (LN **7.77**) (BAGD p. 264): 'material' [BAGD, EC, **LN**; TNT], 'material used in the construction of' [WBC], 'fabric' [BNTC], 'building material' [LN], 'building' [KJV], 'interior structure, construction' [BAGD], 'inlaying' [Lns]. This noun is also translated as a verb: 'to be built of' [CEV, NRSV, REB], 'to be constructed of' [NAB], 'to be made of' [NCV, NET, NIV, NLT, TEV]. This word may also indicate 'foundation' [BAGD, LN (7.41)].

b. καθαρός (LN 79.48) (BAGD 1. p. 388): 'pure' [BNTC, EC, Lns, WBC; all versions], 'bright' [BNTC].

c. καθαρός (See this word just above): 'pure' [BAGD; NCV, NIV], 'clear' [LN (6.222); CEV, KJV, NAB, NET, NLT, REB, TEV, TNT], 'clean' [BAGD, LN (79.48)].

d. ὕαλος (LN **6.222**) (BAGD p. 831): 'glass' [BAGD, BNTC, EC, **LN**, Lns, WBC; all versions except CEV], 'crystal' [BAGD, LN; CEV]. See the related adjective of this related word at 4:6.

QUESTION—Was the wall made of jasper, or was it inlaid with jasper?
1. It was *made of* jasper [Alf, Be, BNTC, ICC, Ld, TH, TNTC, WBC; CEV, NAB, NCV, NET, NIV, NLT, NRSV, REB, TEV].
2. It was *inlaid with* jasper [EC, Lns, NIC, Sw]. Since verse 19 indicates that the first foundation stone was jasper, it must have the meaning of 'inlaid with' here [NIC]. The verb from which ἐνδώμησις is derived actually means 'to build into' indicating that the wall had jasper built into it [Sw].

QUESTION—What quality did jasper give to the wall?
It gave splendor and value to the city [NIC]. It made the wall shine or sparkle brilliantly [EC, Ld, Sw].

QUESTION—What feature of χρυσίον καθαρὸν ὅμοιον ὑάλῳ καθαρῷ 'pure gold like pure/clear glass' is in focus?
1. The feature of its *brightness* is in focus [Alf, Be, BNTC, Lns, NIC; REB]. The gold of the city shone like highly polished glass [Lns]. Purity and brilliance are indicated [Be]. The absence of impurity in gold is like the absence of opaqueness in glass (see verse 21). Such gold shone with fiery brilliance [NIC]. The inlaid diamond made the city glitter and shine [Lns].
2. The feature of its *purity* is in focus [EC, Sw]: The gold was so pure that it was transparent [EC].
3. The feature of its *extreme value* is in focus [TNTC].
4. The feature of its *high quality* is in focus [TH].

21:19 The foundations of-the wall of-the city were-adorned[a] with-every precious stone; the first foundation (was) jasper, the second sapphire,[b] the third chalcedony,[c] the fourth emerald,[d]

TEXT—Instead of οἱ θεμέλιοι 'the foundations', some manuscripts have καὶ οἱ θεμέλιοι 'and the foundations'. GNT does not mention this alternative. The reading 'and the foundations' is taken by TR and KJV.

LEXICON—a. perf. pass. participle of κοσμέω (BAGD 2.a.β. p. 445): 'to be adorned' [BAGD, EC, Lns, WBC; NRSV, REB, TEV, TNT], 'to be decorated' [BAGD; NAB, NCV, NET, NIV], 'to be garnished' [KJV], 'to be bejewelled' [BNTC], 'to be inlaid' [NLT]. Others take this as indicating that the foundation was the same as the stone (see Question below) [CEV]. See this word also at 21:2.

b. σάπφιρος (LN 2.31) (BAGD p. 742): 'sapphire' [BAGD, EC, LN, Lns, WBC; all versions except REB], 'lapis lazuli' [BNTC, ICC, NIC, Sw; REB].

c. χαλκηδών (LN 2.32) (BAGD p. 874): 'chalcedony' [BAGD, BNTC, EC, LN, Lns, WBC; KJV, NAB, NCV, NIV, REB, TNT], 'agate' [LN; CEV, NET, NLT, NRSV, TEV].

d. σμάραγδος (LN **2.29**, 2.33) (BAGD p. 758): 'emerald' [BAGD, BNTC, EC, **LN**, Lns, WBC; all versions]. This stone was green in color [Alf, BAGD, LN]. It was transparent green [BAGD]. See the related adjective of this word at 4:3.

QUESTION—Were the foundations *adorned with* precious stones or were the foundations *made of* the precious stones?
1. They were *adorned with* precious stones [BNTC, Lns, NIC, WBC; NAB, NCV, NET, NIV, NLT, NRSV, REB, TEV, TNT].
2. The foundations *consisted of* or *were made of* precious stones [Alf, Be, EC, ICC, NIGTC; CEV].

QUESTION—How should one translate these precious stones if unknown?
It may be best to translate the stone by its color and transliterate the name [TH]: a precious blue stone called 'sapphire'. One could borrow the name from the national language and explain its color in a glossary [LN (2.29)].

QUESTION—What is the color of ἴασπις 'jasper'?
Its color is: green [BAGD, EC, ICC, LN, TNTC, WBC], crystal green [NIC, TNTC], transparent and crystal-like [EC, Ld, Lns, Sw, TNTC, Wal], white [Alf], red [BAGD, WBC], yellow or grayish blue [WBC]. See this question also at 4:3.

QUESTION—What is the color of σάπφιρος 'sapphire'?
Its color is: blue [Alf, BAGD, BNTC, EC, ICC, LN, NIC, Sw, TH, TNTC, Wal; REB], blue with flecks of iron pyrite [NIC], or blue with flecks of gold [Sw].

QUESTION—What color is χαλκηδών 'chalcedony'?
It is: green [EC, ICC, NIC, Sw, TH], blue with stripes of other colors [Alf, Wal], milky or gray [LN]. It is a silicate of copper [EC, NIC, Sw]. It is a kind of quartz [TNTC].

QUESTION—What color is σμάραγδος 'emerald'?
It is: green [EC, Lns, NIC, Sw, TH, Wal]. See this question also at 4:3.

QUESTION—How were the foundations laid?
They were layered one on the other, each layer extending around all four sides [Wal]. They were either layered on each other and extending around the city, or there were twelve sections between the twelve gates [NIC].

21:20 **The fifth sardonyx,[a] the sixth carnelian,[b] the seventh chrysolite,[c] the eighth beryl,[d] the ninth topaz,[e] the tenth chrysoprase,[f] the eleventh jacinth[g] the twelfth amethyst,[h]**

LEXICON—a. σαρδόνυξ (LN 2.35) (BAGD p. 742): 'sardonyx' [BAGD, BNTC, EC, LN, Lns; KJV, NAB, NIV, REB, TNT], 'onyx' [WBC; CEV, NCV, NET, NLT, NRSV, TEV].

b. σάρδιον (LN 2.36) (BAGD p. 742): 'carnelian' [BAGD, LN, WBC; all versions except KJV, REB, TNT], 'cornelian' [BNTC; REB], 'sardius' [BAGD, EC; KJV, TNT], 'sard' [Lns]. See this word also at 4:3.

c. χρυσόλιθος (LN 2.37) (BAGD p. 888): 'chrysolite' [BAGD, BNTC, EC, LN, Lns; all versions except TEV], 'yellow quartz' [TEV], 'yellow topaz' [WBC].

d. βήρυλλος (LN 2.38) (BAGD p. 140): 'beryl' [BAGD, BNTC, EC, LN, Lns, WBC; all versions].

e. τοπάζιον (LN 2.39) (BAGD p. 822): 'topaz' [BAGD, BNTC, EC, LN, Lns, WBC; all versions].

f. χρυσόπρασος (LN 2.40) (BAGD p. 888): 'chrysoprase' [BAGD, BNTC, EC, LN, Lns, WBC; all versions].

g. ὑάκινθος (LN 2.41) (BAGD p. 831): 'jacinth' [BAGD, BNTC, EC, LN, Lns, WBC; all versions except NAB, REB, TEV], 'hyacinth' [BAGD, LN; NAB], 'turquoise' [REB, TEV].

h. ἀμέθυστος (LN 2.42) (BAGD p. 44): 'amethyst' [BAGD, BNTC, EC, LN, Lns, WBC; all versions].

QUESTION—What color is σαρδόνυξ 'sardonyx'?
It is: white with layers of red (or brown) [EC, ICC, NIC, Sw, Wal], or red [TH]. It comes in various colors [LN, TH].

QUESTION—What color is σάρδιον 'carnelian'?
It is red [BAGD, EC, ICC, LN, NIC, Wal]. It is a kind of chalcedony [TH].

QUESTION—What color is χρυσόλιθος 'chrysolite'?
It is: yellow [EC, ICC, LN, NIC, Sw, TNTC, Wal, WBC; TEV], yellowish green [TH], or pale green [Alf].

QUESTION—What color is βήρυλλος 'beryl'?
It is: green [BAGD, ICC, LN, NIC], bluish green [LN, TH], sea-green [BAGD, EC, Sw, TNTC, Wal], or blue [EC, Sw].

QUESTION—What color is τοπάζιον 'topaz'?
It is: yellow [BAGD, LN, TH, TNTC, WBC], or golden green [NIC, Sw, Wal]. It is a bit transparent [BAGD, Wal].

QUESTION—What color is χρυσόπρασος 'chrysoprase'?
It is: green [BAGD, LN, Sw, Wal], apple-green [BAGD, TH, TNTC], golden-green [EC, ICC]. It is a kind of quartz [BAGD, LN, TNTC].

QUESTION—What color is ὑάκινθος 'jacinth'?
It is: blue [BAGD, LN], blue smoke color [Sw], turquoise [REB, TEV], bluish purple [NIC], violet [EC, ICC, Wal], or reddish orange [TH]. It is a variety of zircon [TH].

QUESTION—What color is ἀμέθυστος 'amethyst'?
It is: purple [Alf, EC, ICC, LN, NIC, TH, TNTC, Wal], or violet [EC, LN, TH]. It is a kind of quartz [ICC, NIC, TNTC].

21:21 And the twelve gates (were) twelve pearls[a] each[b] one each of-the gates was of one pearl. And the street of-the city (was) pure gold as transparent[c] glass.[d]

TEXT—Instead of διαυγής 'transparent', some manuscripts possibly have the synonym διαφανής, although GNT does not mention this alternative. The reading διαφανής is taken by TR.

LEXICON—a. μαργαρίτης (LN **2.43**): 'pearl' [BAGD, BNTC, EC, **LN**, Lns, WBC; all versions]. A μαργαρίτης is a smooth glossy hardened concretion formed in the shells of certain mollusks [LN]. The pearl was ranked highest among precious stones [EC]. See this word also at 17:4.

  b. ἀνά (LN 89.91) (BAGD 3. p. 50): 'each' [BAGD, LN], 'apiece' [BAGD, LN]. The phrase ἀνὰ εἷς ἕκαστος τῶν πυλώνων 'each one each of the gates' is translated: 'each gate' [BNTC; NCV, NIV, NLT, REB, TEV], 'each of the gates' [CEV, NAB, NRSV, TNT], 'each one of the gates' [EC; NET], 'each individual gate' [WBC], 'each and every one of the portals' [Lns], 'every several gate' [KJV], 'each one of the gates separately' [Alf].

  c. διαυγής (LN **79.24**) (BAGD p. 190): 'transparent' [BAGD, EC, **LN**, Lns, WBC; KJV, NAB, NET, NIV, NRSV, TEV, TNT], 'clear' [CEV, NCV, NLT], 'translucent' [BNTC; REB], 'pure' [BAGD].

d. ὕαλος (LN **2.46, 6.222**): 'glass' [BNTC, EC, **LN** (6.222), Lns; KJV, NAB, NCV, NET, NIV, NLT, NRSV, REB, TEV, TNT], 'crystal' [**LN** (2.46), WBC; CEV]. It is a very hard, translucent, and usually transparent type of quartz [LN]. See this word also at 21:18.

QUESTION—What is meant by the τῶν πυλώνων 'the gates'?
This means the actual door of a gateway [Lns]. They were gate towers [Be, EC]. They were either gateways or the watch towers above them [TH]. They were the gates and their towers [Ld].

QUESTION—What is meant by ἡ πλατεῖα τῆς πόλεως χρυσίον 'the street of the city (was) gold'?
It indicates that the street *was made of* gold [Alf, BNTC; CEV, NAB, NCV NIV, REB, TEV].

QUESTION—What is meant by ἡ πλατεῖα 'the street'?
1. It refers to the main street of the city [Be, TH; NET, NIV, NLT, REB].
2. It refers to the streets of the city [BNTC, ICC, Lns; CEV].
3. It refers to the main square of the city [WBC].
4. It refers to either the main street, the city square or the streets of the city [EC].

QUESTION—What is the point of similarity between 'pure gold' and 'transparent glass'?
If glass is transparent, every flaw shows up. Similarly, if gold is pure like transparent glass, it would indicate that it is completely flawless [TNTC].

DISCOURSE UNIT: 21:22–22:5 [TNTC]. The topic is 'no night there'.

21:22 **And I saw not (a) temple in it, for the Lord God, the Almighty is its temple and the Lamb.**
QUESTION—What is implied by the statement οὐκ εἶδον 'I did not see'?
It implies that John expected to see a temple but that he did not [WBC].

QUESTION—What relationship is indicated by γάρ 'for'?
It indicates the reason that there was no temple there [Be, EC, NIGTC, WBC]: I saw no temple in it *because* the Lord God Almighty is its temple and the Lamb. There was no temple because the whole city was now a temple [EC, Hu, Lns, Sw]. The temple was the place where people could meet with God. Now, because of the presence of God and the Lamb, there is no longer a need for a temple [EC, Ld, Wal].

QUESTION—What is indicated by καὶ τὸ ἀρνίον 'and the Lamb'?
It indicates that the Lamb is also its temple [EC, Lns, NIGTC, WBC; CEV, KJV, NAB, NCV, NIV, REB, TNT]: the Lord God Almighty and the Lamb *are* its temple.

21:23 **And the city has no need of-the sun or the moon to shine in-it, for the glory of God gave-light-to[a] it and the Lamb (is) its lamp.**
TEXT—Instead of φαίνωσιν αὐτῇ 'might illuminate it', some manuscripts have φαίνωσιν ἐν αὐτῇ 'might shine in it'. GNT does not mention this alternative. The reading 'might shine in it' is taken by TR.

LEXICON—a. pres. act. subj. of φωτίζω (LN 14:39) (BAGD 2.a. p. 873): 'to give light to' [BAGD, BNTC; NAB, NIV, REB], 'to be (its) light' [NCV, NRSV], 'to light up' [BAGD; NET], 'to lighten' [KJV], 'to shine on' [LN; CEV, TEV, TNT], 'to illuminate' [Lns; NLT], 'to illumine' [BAGD, EC, LN, WBC]. See this word also at 18:1.

QUESTION—What relationship is indicated by γάρ 'for'?

It indicates the reason that there is no need of sun or moon [EC, NIGTC]: the city does not need the sun or the moon *because* the glory of God illumines it and the Lamb is its lamp.

QUESTION—Does the fact that 'the Lamb is its lamp' diminish his part in the provision of light to the city?

Both actions—that of God and the Lamp—are of equal value in providing light for the city [Be, EC, TH, TNTC, WBC]. The difference in the two expressions for illumination is simply rhetorical [Be]. In 22:5, God replaces the lamp [Be, EC].

21:24 **And the-nations^a will-walk^b by its light, and the kings of-the earth bring their glory^c into it.**

TEXT—Instead of περιπατήσουσιν τὰ ἔθνη διὰ τοῦ φωτὸς αὐτῆς 'the nations will walk through its light', some manuscripts possibly have τὰ ἔθνη τῶν σωζομένων ἐν τῷ φωτὶ αὐτῆς περιπατήσουσιν 'the nations of the ones being saved will walk in its light', although GNT does not mention this alternative. The reading 'the nations of the ones being saved will walk in its light' is taken by TR, Wal and KJV.

TEXT—Following δόξαν 'glory', some manuscripts include καὶ τὴν τιμήν 'and the honor'. GNT does not mention this alternative. The reading 'and the honor' is included by TR and KJV.

LEXICON—a. τὰ ἔθνη (LN 11.37). This phrase is translated 'the nations' [BNTC, EC, Lns, WBC; all versions except NCV, TEV], 'the nations of the earth' [NLT], 'the people(s) of the world' [TH; NCV, TEV]. See this phrase also at 11:2

b. fut. act. indic. of περιπατέω (LN 41.11) (BAGD 1.c. p. 649): 'to walk' [BAGD, BNTC, EC, Lns, WBC; all versions], 'to live, to behave' [LN]. Περιπατέω here means 'to live' [TH, WBC], 'to conduct one's life' [WBC]. See this word also at 2:1 and 16:15.

c. δόξα (BAGD 2. p. 204): 'glory' [EC, Lns, WBC; KJV, NCV, NLT, NRSV, TNT], 'splendor' [BAGD; NIV, REB], 'grandeur' [NET], 'magnificence' [BAGD], 'riches' [CEV], 'wealth' [TEV], 'treasure(s)' [BNTC; NAB]. See this word also at 1:6.

QUESTION—What relationship is indicated by διά in the phrase διὰ τοῦ φωτὸς αὐτῆς 'by its light'?

1. It indicates means [EC, Lns, WBC; CEV, NAB, NCV, NET, NIV, NRSV, REB, TEV]: the nations will walk *by means of* its light.
2. It indicates location [KJV, NLT]: the nations will walk *in* its light.
3. It can either indicate 'by' or 'in the midst of' [ICC].

QUESTION—Who are τὰ ἔθνη 'the nations' here?
1. They are people from all nations who are believers [Be, EC, Hu, Ld, Lns, NIGTC, TR, Wal; KJV]. These people are the result of the worldwide harvest of the Good News as predicted in Isaiah 60:3 [Hu]. These are the people 'from every nation' referred to in 7:9 who have become believers [Ld, NIGTC]. They are saints 'from every tribe' (see 5:9) [Lns, NIGTC]. John is using prophetic language that foresees the Gentiles as being included in the city but refers to them by the title they had before they were redeemed [Be, NIC]. They must be believers since verse 27 says that only those whose names are written in the Book of Life may enter the city [NIGTC]. These are people who have not died but neither have they been resurrected. They are in some way transformed and will live eternally on the new earth in a kind of restored Garden of Eden [EC].
2. They are people who are unbelievers [BNTC, Sw]. These are the people who once trampled on Jerusalem but now have been brought into subjection by the forces of Christ (see 11:2; 17:3, 23; 19:15) [BNTC]. They are not yet Christian or are Christian in name only [Sw].
3. They are merely people who are not hostile to God [WBC].

QUESTION—Who are the βασιλεῖς τῆς γῆς 'kings of the earth'?
1. They are kings who have become believers [Alf, EC, NIGTC, Wal]. They must be believers since verse 27 says that only those whose names are written in the Book of Life may enter the city [Alf, NIGTC].
2. They are rulers who once brought their trade for the benefit of the whore but who now do so for the benefit of the new Jerusalem [BNTC, Sw]. They are secular princes [Sw].
3. The terms 'the nations' and 'the kings of the earth' are used synonymously here. They are not hostile to God and his people [WBC].

QUESTION—What does it mean that they bring their glory into the city?
1. It means that they bring their wealth into the city [Be, BNTC, TH; CEV, NAB, TEV].
2. It means that they bring their honor into the city [Hu, Lns, Wal; NET, NIV, REB]. The glory and honor ascribed to the kings will now be ascribed to God himself [Hu, Wal]

21:25 And its gates will- never[a] -be-closed by-day, for night will- not -be there.

LEXICON—a. οὐ μή (LN 69.6) (BAGD D.1.a. p. 517): 'never' [BNTC, WBC; all versions NAB, NCV, NET, NIV, NLT, NRSV, REB, TEV], 'not at all' [KJV], 'not' [TNT], 'in no wise' [Lns], 'in no way' [EC]. This concept is also translated by its reciprocal: 'always (open)' [CEV]. See this phrase also at 2:11.

QUESTION—Does οὐ μὴ κλεισθῶσιν ἡμέρας 'never be closed by day' mean that the gates will *never* be closed?

In view of the fact that there will be no night there, it indicates that the gates will stay open all the time [Alf, EC, Hu, Ld, NIC, NIGTC, Sw, TH, TNTC,

Wal; CEV, TEV]. Since there is no night there, if the gates were to be shut, they would have to be shut during the day [Alf].

QUESTION—What relationship is indicated by γάρ 'for'?
1. It supplies the reason why only day, and not day and night, is mentioned in the preceding clause [Be, NIC, NTC, Wal]: its gates will never be closed by day *because* there will be no night there.
2. It emphasizes that the gates will always remain open [NIGTC]: its gates will never be closed by day, *indeed* there will be no night there.

QUESTION—What is indicated by the word ἐκεῖ 'there'?

It may indicate that regular day and night continue outside of the city [WBC].

21:26 **And they-will-bring the glory and the honor of-the nations into it.**

QUESTION—Who is the implied actor of οἴσουσιν 'they will bring'?
1. It is indefinite and refers to people in general [Alf, Lns, TH; CEV, KJV, NAB, NCV, NET, NIV, NRSV, REB, TEV, TNT].
2. It refers to the kings of verse 24 [EC, Ld, NIC, Sw, Wal, WBC].
3. It refers to all the nations [NLT].

QUESTION—What is meant by τὴν δόξαν καὶ τὴν τιμὴν τῶν ἐθνῶν 'the glory and the honor of the nations'?
1. It means treasure and wealth [Be, BNTC, EC, ICC, NIC, NTC, Sw, TH; CEV, NAB]: they will bring *treasure and wealth* into it.
2. It means homage and reverence [TNTC]: they will bring *homage and reverence* into it.
3. It means glory and honor [Lns, Wal; KJV, NCV, NIV, NLT, NRSV, TNT]: they will bring *glory and honor* into it.
4. It means wealth as well as homage and reverence [WBC; NET, REB, TEV]: they will bring *wealth and reverence* into it.

21:27 **And every unclean-thing[a] and [the-one] doing what-is-abhorrent[b] and falsehood[c] never may-enter into it but-only[d] the-ones written in the book of life of-the Lamb.**

TEXT—Instead of πᾶν κοινὸν καὶ ὁ ποιῶν 'every unclean thing and the one doing', some manuscripts possibly have πᾶν κοινοῦν καὶ ποιοῦν 'everything defiling and doing'. GNT does not mention this alternative, but brackets ὁ 'the one' in the text, indicating doubt about including it. The reading 'everything defiling and doing' is taken by TR and KJV.

LEXICON—a. κοινός (LN 53.39) (BAGD 2. p. 438): 'unclean thing' [BNTC, EC, WBC; NAB, NCV, NRSV, REB], 'ritually unclean thing' [LN; NET], 'impure thing' [NIV, TEV], 'defiled thing' [LN; TNT], 'unworthy thing' [CEV], 'common thing' [BAGD, Lns], 'ordinary thing' [BAGD], 'profane thing' [BAGD], 'evil thing' [NLT]. This word is also taken as a verb: 'that which defiles' [KJV]. Κοινός here means 'ceremonially impure' [BAGD, TH].

b. βδέλυγμα (LN **25.187**): 'what is abhorrent' [EC, **LN**, WBC], 'abomination' [Lns; KJV, NRSV], 'abominable thing' [NAB], 'what is

abominable' [TNT], 'what is shameful' [NIV], 'shameful thing' [NCV, TEV], 'shameful idolatry' [NLT], 'what is detestable' [NET]. The clause, [ὁ] ποιῶν βδέλυγμα '[the one] doing abomination', is translated: 'whose ways are foul' [REB], 'whose life is obscene' [BNTC], 'who is dirty-minded' [CEV]. See this word also at 17:4.
  c. ψεῦδος (LN 33.254) (BAGD p. 892): 'falsehood' [BAGD, LN; NET, NRSV], 'lie' [BAGD, EC, LN, Lns; KJV], 'what is deceitful' [NIV], 'dishonesty' [NLT], 'what is false' [WBC; TNT]. This noun is also translated as a verb: 'one who tells a lie' [CEV, NAB, NCV, TEV], 'to be false in one's ways' [BNTC; REB].
  d. εἰ μή (LN 89.131): 'but only' [BNTC, LN; NET, NIV, NLT, NRSV, TNT], 'only' [Lns; CEV, NAB, NCV, REB, TEV], 'but' [EC, LN; KJV], 'except' [WBC], 'except that, however, instead' [LN].

QUESTION—What relationship is indicated by καί in the phrase καὶ ὁ ποιῶν βδέλυγμα 'and the one doing what is abhorrent'?
  1. It indicates a conjunctive relationship [BNTC, EC, Lns; KJV, NAB, NCV, NET, NIV, NRSV, REB, TEV, TNT]: And every unclean thing *and* the one doing what is abhorrent.
  2. It indicates an explanatory relationship [WBC; NLT]: And every unclean thing, *that is*, the one doing what is abhorrent.

QUESTION—What does the word κοινός 'unclean thing' refer to here?
  It refers to what is ritually impure [BAGD, LN, TH, WBC; NET]. It refers to what is morally impure [EC, Sw, WBC].

QUESTION—What does the word βδέλυγμα 'what is abhorrent' refer to here?
  It may refer specifically to idolatry [EC, NIGTC, Sw, TH, TNTC, WBC; NLT]. Here it refers to being sexually immoral as well as idolatrous [WBC].

QUESTION—How are the nouns related in the genitive construction τῷ βιβλίῳ τῆς ζωῆς 'the book of life'?
  If a person's name was written in this book it meant that he/she would benefit from Christ's death and receive eternal life [NIGTC]. The noun 'life' provides the purpose of the noun 'book' [NIGTC]: a book *whose purpose is* life. See this question also at 13:8.

QUESTION—How are the nouns related in the genitive construction τῷ βιβλίῳ τῆς ζωῆς τοῦ ἀρνίου 'the book of life of the Lamb'?
  The book of life belongs to the Lamb [Sw]. See this question also at 13:8.

QUESTION—Where else in Revelation is the book of life mentioned?
  It is mentioned in 3:5; 13:8; 17: 8; 20:12, 15 [NIGTC].

DISCOURSE UNIT: 22:1–5 [Alf, Hu, NIC, NIGTC, WBC; NIV, NRSV]. The topic is the water of life and the tree of life [Hu], the river of life [NIV], Eden restored [NIC], the new Jerusalem as Paradise [WBC].

22:1 And he-showed me (a) river of-water of-life sparkling[a] like crystal[b], going-out from the throne of God and of-the Lamb.

TEXT—Following ποταμόν 'river', some manuscripts include καθαρόν 'pure'. GNT does not mention this alternative. The word 'pure' is included by TR and KJV.

LEXICON—a. λαμπρός (LN **79.25**) (BAGD 2. p. 465): 'sparkling' [**LN**, WBC; NAB, REB, TEV], 'shining' [NCV, TNT], 'bright' [BNTC, EC, LN, Lns; NRSV], 'clear' [BAGD; CEV, KJV, NET, NIV, NLT], 'transparent' [BAGD]. Λαμπρός indicates the qualities of being bright and clear [LN]. See this word also at 15:6.

b. κρύσταλλος (LN **2.11**): 'crystal' [BNTC, EC, Lns, WBC; all versions except CEV], 'ice' [**LN**], 'rock-crystal' [BAGD]. This noun is also translated as an adverb: 'crystal (clear)' [CEV]. See this word also at 4:6.

QUESTION—Who is the implied actor of ἔδειξεν 'he showed'?

The actor is an angel [EC, Sw, TH, TNTC; all versions except KJV]. The angel is the one mentioned in 21:9 [EC, Sw, TH; NET].

QUESTION—How are the nouns related in the genitive construction ὕδατος ζωῆς 'water of life'? See this question also at 21:6.

1. The water gives life [EC, NIC, TH; CEV, NAB]: life-giving water.
2. Life modifies water [NIGTC, WBC]: living water. Water primarily symbolizes a life of never-ending fellowship with God and Christ [NIGTC].
3. Life is in apposition to water [Lns]: water, *that is*, life. It is the same as saying, 'a river of life' [Lns].

QUESTION—Does the word λαμπρός mean 'clear' or 'sparkling' here?

1. It means bright or sparkling [BNTC, EC, Hu, LN, Lns, NIGTC, TH, TNTC, WBC; NAB, NRSV, REB, TEV]: sparkling like crystal.
2. It means clear [CEV, KJV, NET, NIV, NLT]: clear as crystal.

QUESTION—Where else in Scripture is a similar river described?

A similar river is described in Genesis 2:9ff [Alf, Be, BNTC, EC, Hu, ICC, NIGTC, Sw, TNTC], Ezekiel 47:1ff. [Alf, Be, BNTC, EC, Hu, ICC, Ld, NIC, NIGTC, NTC, Sw, TNTC, Wal, WBC], and Zechariah 14:8 [Be, EC, ICC, Ld, NIGTC, NTC, TNTC, Wal, WBC].

QUESTION—How many thrones were there?

There was a single throne for both the Father and the Son (see 3:21) [EC, Ld, NIC, NIGTC, TH].

QUESTION—What is the central point of this verse?

The central point of this verse is that God's people will eternally live at the source of the life-giving river that flows from the very presence of God [EC, NIC].

22:2 In the-middle of its street, and from-here[a] and from-there[b] of-the river (was a/the) tree of-life producing[c] twelve fruits, yielding its fruit according-to[d] each month, and the leaves of-the tree (are) for (the) healing[e] of-the nations.

TEXT—Instead of ἐντεῦθεν καὶ ἐκεῖθεν 'from here and from there', some manuscripts have ἐντεῦθεν καὶ ἐντεῦθεν 'from here and from here'. GNT does not mention this alternative. The reading 'from here and from here' is taken by TR.

TEXT—Instead of κατὰ μῆνα ἕκαστον 'according to each month', some manuscripts have κατὰ μῆνα ἕνα ἕκαστον 'according to each one month'. GNT does not mention this alternative. The reading 'according to each one month' is taken by TR.

LEXICON—a. ἐντεῦθεν (LN 84.9) (BAGD 1. p. 268): 'from here' [BAGD, LN], 'on this side' [EC, Lns]. The phrase ἐντεῦθεν καὶ ἐκεῖθεν 'from here and from there' is translated: 'on each side' [BAGD, BNTC; CEV, NCV, NET, NIV, NLT, TEV, TNT], 'on either side' [WBC; KJV, NAB, NRSV, REB].

b. ἐκεῖθεν (LN 84.10) (BAGD p. 239): 'from there' [BAGD, LN], 'from that place' [LN], 'on that side' [EC, Lns].

c. pres. act. participle of ποιέω (LN **23.199**) (BAGD 1. p. 90): 'to produce' [EC, LN WBC; NAB, NCV, NET, NRSV], 'to yield' [BAGD, BNTC, **LN**; KJV, REB], 'to bear' [LN, Lns; NIV, NLT, TEV, TNT], 'to grow' [CEV].

d. κατά with accusative object (LN 89.8) (BAGD II.5.a.β. p. 407): 'according to' [Lns]. The phrase κατὰ μῆνα ἕκαστον 'according to each month' is translated: 'once each month' [NAB, NCV, TEV], 'one for each month' [BNTC; REB], 'each month' [EC, WBC; CEV, NLT, NRSV, TNT], 'every month' [KJV, NET, NIV].

e. θεραπεία (LN 23.139) (BAGD 1.b. p. 358): 'healing' [BAGD, EC, LN, WBC; KJV, NCV, NET, NIV, NRSV, REB, TEV, TNT], 'health' [Lns], 'cure' [BNTC], 'treatment' [BAGD], 'medicine' [NAB]. This noun is also translated as a verb: 'to heal' [CEV, NLT]. Θεραπεία indicates 'health-giving', that is, the leaves enhance the enjoyment of life in the city [Wal]. It indicates the promotion of physical health rather than spiritual health [Be]. Healing is the absence of all physical and spiritual want [NIC].

QUESTION—Does the phrase ἐν μέσῳ τῆς πλατείας αὐτῆς 'in the middle of its street' go with the preceding verse or with this verse?

1. It goes with the preceding verse [Be, BNTC, ICC, NIGTC, TH, WBC; all versions except KJV]: the river of life going out from the throne of God and of the Lamb through the middle of the street of the city. The river flows down the middle of the street with the tree of life on both of its banks [EC, ICC, NIGTC, Sw, Wal].

2. It goes with this verse [Alf, EC, Lns, Sw]. The river flows parallel to the street with a space in between. The tree(s) of life either grows in the space

along the bank of the river and the edge of the street or is a woods in a park-like space between the street and the river [Alf, Lns].

QUESTION—Should 'tree of life' be interpreted as a single tree or as several?
1. It is probably best to take it as a collective noun [Be, EC, ICC, Lns, NIGTC, Sw, TH, WBC; CEV]. One tree cannot be on each side of the river [Be, EC, ICC, NIGTC, Sw, TH, WBC].
 1.1 On each side of the river there are trees of life [CEV, NAB].
 1.2 On the strip between the street and the river there are trees of life, or better, a woods of life [Lns].
2. It is best to keep it a singular noun [BNTC, Hu; KJV, NCV, NET, NIV, NLT, NRSV, REB, TEV, TNT]. Most keep the singular 'tree of life' and do not indicate how the tree can be on both sides of the river.

QUESTION—Should ξύλον ζωῆς 'tree of life' be translated 'a tree of life' or 'the tree of life'?
1. It should be translated 'the tree of life' [BNTC; KJV, NAB, NCV, NET, NIV, NRSV, TEV, TNT]: on each side was the tree of life.
2. It should be translated 'a tree of life' [EC, Lns, WBC; NLT, REB]: on each side was a tree of life.

QUESTION—How are the nouns related in the genitive construction ξύλον ζωῆς 'tree of life'? See this question also at 2:7.
1. The tree gives life [TH; CEV, TEV]: life-giving tree.
2. Life is in apposition to tree [Lns]: the tree, *that is*, life. Life in eternal union with God is symbolized by both the river and by these trees [Lns].

QUESTION—What is meant by the clause, 'the tree of life producing twelve fruits, yielding its fruit according to each month'?
1. It probably means that the trees bear fruit twelve times a year, once each month [Be, BNTC, ICC, NIC, TH; NAB, NCV, NIV, NLT, REB, TEV, TNT].
2. It probably means that the trees bear twelve kinds of fruit, once each month [Alf, EC, Ld, Sw, WBC; CEV, KJV, NET, NRSV]. Either interpretation is possible but this one is in keeping with the symbolism because one fruit of the Spirit has many varieties [Sw].

22:3 And there-will-be no longer any accursed-thing.[a] And the throne of God and of-the Lamb will be in it, and his servants will-serve[b] him.

LEXICON—a. κατάθεμα (LN **33.474**) (BAGD): 'accursed thing' [BAGD, **LN**, Lns; NAB, NRSV, REB, TNT], 'thing under God's curse' [BNTC; TEV], 'thing judged guilty by God' [NCV], 'cursed thing' [LN], 'curse' [EC; CEV, KJV, NET, NIV], 'curse of war' [WBC]. This noun is also translated as a verb: 'to be cursed' [NLT].
 b. fut. act. indic. of λατρεύω (LN 53.14) (BAGD p. 467): 'to serve' [BAGD, EC, Lns; KJV, NIV], 'to worship' [BNTC, LN, WBC; all versions except KJV, NIV]. See this word at 7:15.

QUESTION—What is meant by λατρεύω 'to serve'?
It means: that they worship God [Be, BNTC, Ld, NIC, NTC, WBC; all versions except KJV, NIV], or that they serve as priests to God [EC, NIGTC, TH]. See this question also at 7:15.

QUESTION—To whom does αὐτῷ 'him' refer in the phrase λατρεύσουσιν αὐτῷ 'they will serve *him*'?
1. It refers to God [Be, TH; CEV, NCV]: they will serve God.
2. It refers to both God and the Lamb [EC, NIGTC, TNTC]: they will serve God and the Lamb. The singular 'him' indicates the unity of the Father and the Son [EC, NIGTC].

QUESTION—What is meant by κατάθεμα 'accursed thing'?
It probably refers to the curse that God put on the earth because of Adam's sin (Genesis 3:17) [BNTC, EC, Hu, NIC, NIGTC, NTC]. It refers specifically to the curse of war [WBC].

QUESTION—Who is the implied actor of 'accursed thing'?
God is the actor [Be, BNTC, EC, Hu, Ld, Lns, NIC, NIGTC, TH, Wal; NCV, TEV, TNT]: accursed by God.

QUESTION—Does the first clause of this verse go with the previous verse or this one?.
1. It goes with previous verse [Be, BNTC, EC, Lns, TH; CEV, NAB, NCV, NIV, REB, TEV]: the leaves of the tree are for the healing of the nations and there will be no longer any accursed thing.
2. It goes with this verse [KJV, NET]: And there will be no longer any accursed thing. And the throne of God and of the Lamb will be in it.

QUESTION—What relationship is indicated between the two clauses, 'there will be no longer any accursed thing' and 'the throne of God and of the Lamb will be in it'?
1. A reason relationship is indicated [Ld, NIGTC, NTC, Wal; NLT]: there will be no longer any accursed thing *because* the throne of God and of the Lamb will be in it.
2. A contrastive relationship is indicated [KJV, NRSV]: there will be no longer any accursed thing *but* the throne of God and of the Lamb will be in it.
3. A conjoining relationship is indicated [NET]: there will be no longer any accursed thing *and* the throne of God and of the Lamb will be in it.

22:4 And they-will-see his face, and his name (will be) on their foreheads.
QUESTION—Whose face will they see?
1. They will see the face of God [Ld, NIC, TH, WBC; CEV].
2. They will see the face of God and of the Lamb [EC, NIGTC, TNTC].

QUESTION—What is the significance of seeing God's face?
Up until this time, no one had ever seen God's face (see Exodus 33:20) [EC, Ld, NIC, TH]. For Christians, seeing God's face was the fulfillment of their highest hopes for happiness [TNTC]. This was the major goal of salvation

[Ld]. Of all of God's gifts, this was the greatest [NIC]. To see God is to be like him (1 John 3:2) [NIGTC, NTC].

QUESTION—Whose name will be on their foreheads?
1. The name of God will be on their foreheads [NIC, TH; CEV].
2. The name of God and of the Lamb will be on their foreheads [EC, NIGTC].

QUESTION—What is symbolized by 'his name on their foreheads'?
It symbolized: that they belonged to God [Hu, Ld, NIC, Wal], that they were under his protection [Ld, NIGTC], that they were their firmly devoted to him [Be, NIC, Sw], that they were like God [NIC], that they had intimate fellowship with God [NIGTC], that they were close to God and knew him [Alf]. See this question also at 13:16.

22:5 And night will-be no-longer and they-have no need of-(the)-light of-a-lamp and (the)-light of-(the)-sun, because (the) Lord God will-shine on them, and they-will-reign[a] for-ever-and-ever.[b]

TEXT—Instead of ἔσται ἔτι 'will be (no) longer', some manuscripts have ἔσται ἐκεῖ 'will be (no night) there'. GNT does not mention this alternative. The reading 'will be (no night) there' is taken by TR and KJV.

TEXT—Instead of φωτὸς λύχνου 'light of a lamp', some manuscripts have λύχνου 'of a lamp'. GNT does not mention this alternative. The reading 'of a lamp' is taken by TR and KJV.

TEXT—Instead of φωτίσει ἐπ' αὐτούς 'will shine on them', some manuscripts have φωτίζει αὐτούς 'illuminates them'. GNT does not mention this alternative.

LEXICON—a. fut. act. indic. of βασιλεύω (LN 37.64) (BAGD 1.b.δ. p. 136): 'to reign' [BNTC, EC, LN, WBC; KJV, NAB, NET, NIV, NLT, NRSV, REB, TNT], 'to reign as kings' [Lns], 'to rule' [BAGD, LN; CEV], 'to rule as kings' [NCV, TEV]. They reign in that the sense that they are worshiping servants in God's eternal reign [WBC]. See this word at 5:10.

b. εἰς τοὺς αἰῶνας τῶν αἰώνων: 'forever and ever' [EC, WBC; KJV, NAB, NCV, NLT, NRSV, TEV, TNT], 'forever' [BNTC; CEV, NET, NIV, REB], 'for the eons of the eons' [Lns]. See this phrase at 1:6.

QUESTION—Where else does it speak of no night or no need of the sun?
It speaks of no night or no need of the sun in 21:23 and 25 [Alf, Be, EC, Hu, Lns, NIGTC, Sw, TH, TNTC].

DISCOURSE UNIT: 22:6–21 [Alf, Be, BNTC, EC, GNT, Hu, Ld, NIC, NIGTC, NTC, TH, TNTC; CEV, KJV, NAB, NET, NIV, NLT, REB]. The topic is the epilogue [Be, BNTC, EC, Ld, NIC, NIGTC, NTC, TH, TNTC; NAB], the coming of Christ [GNT; CEV, KJV, NIV, NLT], assurances and exhortations [Alf], the conclusion [EC, Hu; REB], a final reminder [NET].

DISCOURSE UNIT: 22:6–20 [Sw]. The topic is the final words.

DISCOURSE UNIT: 22:6–19 [Lns]. The topic is the visions.

REVELATION 22:6 223

DISCOURSE UNIT: 22:6–17 [TEV]. The topic is the coming of Jesus.

DISCOURSE UNIT: 22:6–9 [WBC]. The topic is a transitional conclusion.

DISCOURSE UNIT: 22:6–7 [EC]. The topic the testimony of the angel.

22:6 And he-said to-me, "These words (are) trustworthy[a] and true, and the Lord God of-the spirits of-the prophets sent his angel to-show his servants things-that must happen soon.[b]

TEXT—Instead of τῶν πνευμάτων τῶν προφητῶν 'of the spirits of the prophets', some manuscripts have τῶν ἁγίων προφητῶν 'of the holy prophets'. GNT does not mention this alternative. The reading 'of the holy prophets' is taken by TR and KJV.

LEXICON—a. πιστός (LN 31.87) (BAGD 1.a.α. p. 664): 'trustworthy' [BAGD, LN; NAB, NIV, NLT, NRSV, REB, TNT], 'faithful' [BAGD, BNTC, EC, Lns, WBC; KJV], 'reliable' [NET]. This adjective is also translated as a verb phrase: 'to be able to be trusted' [CEV, NCV, TEV].

b. ἐν τάχει (LN **67.56**) (BAGD): 'soon' [BAGD, BNTC, EC, **LN**, WBC; NAB, NCV, NET, NIV, NLT, NRSV, REB, TNT], 'very soon' [LN; TEV], 'right away' [CEV], 'shortly' [Lns; KJV], 'in a short time' [BAGD]. See this phrase also at 1:1.

QUESTION—To whom does the pronoun refer in the verb εἶπέν 'he said'?
    1. It refers to an angel [Be, BNTC, EC, Hu, Ld, Lns, NIC, NIGTC, Sw, TH; NCV, NET, NLT, TEV, TNT]. It refers to the angel mentioned in 21:9, 21:15 and 22:1 [Be, EC, Hu, Ld, NIC, NIGTC, Sw, TH; NET]. It refers to the angel sent by Christ that is first mentioned in 1:1 [BNTC, Lns, WBC].
    2. It refers to Christ himself [ICC].

QUESTION—How far does the quote of this verse continue?
    1. The quote continues only through the first clause, And he said to me, 'These words are trustworthy and true' [Be, BNTC, Ld, TH, WBC; NCV]. The first clause has the words of the angel and the rest of the verse has the words of John [Be, BNTC, Ld, TH].
    2. The quote continues through the whole verse [ICC, Lns, NIC, Wal; NAB, NET, NIV, NLT, NRSV, TEV].
    3. This quote continues through both this verse and the next [REB].
    4. This quote continues through this verse and the first clause of the next [TNT].

QUESTION—To what does the phrase οὗτοι οἱ λόγοι 'these words' refer?
    1. It refers to the whole book of Revelation [Alf, Be, EC, Hu, ICC, Ld, Lns, NIC, Sw, TH, TNTC].
    2. It refers to the preceding description of the New Jerusalem beginning with chapter 21. Note the similar expression, 'these things are trustworthy and true', in 21:5 [NIGTC].
    3. It refers to the following statement [NLT]: 'These words are trustworthy and true: The Lord God, who tells his prophets....'

QUESTION—What is indicated by the καί in the phrase καὶ ὁ κύριος 'and the Lord'?
1. It indicates reason [EC, Sw; NRSV]: These word are trustworthy and true *because* the Lord God…sent his angel…. This indicates that the clause supplies the reason why these words are trustworthy [EC].
2. It indicates a conjoining relationship [WBC; KJV, NAB, TEV, TNT]: These words are trustworthy and true and the Lord God…sent his angel….

QUESTION—How are the nouns related in the genitive construction ὁ κύριος ὁ θεὸς τῶν πνευμάτων τῶν προφητῶν 'the Lord, the God of the spirits of the prophets'?
1. The Lord God *inspires* the spirits of the prophets [Be, BNTC, NIGTC, Sw, TH, TNTC; NLT, REB, TNT]. This probably refers to the God who inspired the New Testament prophets [NIC, NIGTC, TNTC]. It refers to the God who inspired the Old Testament prophets [BNTC, NIC, NIGTC].
2. The Lord God *gives his Spirit* to the prophets [TEV].
3. The Lord God *controls* the prophets [Hu, NIGTC, WBC; CEV]. God controls what the prophets say so that it is reliable and true [WBC].

QUESTION—How are the nouns related in the genitive construction τῶν πνευμάτων τῶν προφητῶν 'the spirits of the prophets'?
1. The two nouns refer to the same thing: the prophets [BNTC, EC, Hu, ICC, Lns, NIC, Sw, TNTC, WBC; NLT, REB, TEV, TNT]: The Lord, the God of the prophets. 'Spirits' probably refers to the hearts of the prophets [BNTC]. Spirits refers to their own spirits or cognitive faculties [EC, Hu, NIC, Sw]. The term 'spirit' indicates the highest faculty of a human being. As such it is the vehicle the Spirit of God uses to convey prophetic utterances [WBC]. When a prophet prophesied it was his spirit that was involved [ICC].
2. *Prophets* modifies 'spirits' [NAB]: prophetic spirits.

QUESTION—Who is τὸν ἄγγελον αὐτοῦ 'his angel'?
It refers to any angel from a group of angels that God would choose to use at any given time [Lns]. It refers to a different angel from the speaker [Lns, WBC]. It refers to the angel of Jesus Christ first mentioned in 1:1 [WBC]. It refers to some angelic intermediary [NIC].

QUESTION—Who are τοῖς δούλοις αὐτοῦ 'his servants'?
They are all believers [Lns, NIGTC, TH]. They are the members of the churches [Be]. They are the prophets of that time who were to be martyred [BNTC].

QUESTION—To what does the ἃ δεῖ γενέσθαι ἐν τάχει 'things that must happen soon' refer?
It refers to the whole book of Revelation [Be, EC, Hu, TH].

22:7 And behold[a] I-come soon.[b] Blessed[c] (is) the-one keeping[d] the words of-the prophecy of this book."

TEXT—Instead of καὶ ἰδού 'and behold', some manuscripts have ἰδού 'behold'. GNT does not mention this alternative.

LEXICON—a. ἰδού (LN 91.13) (BAGD 1.a. p. 370): 'behold' [BAGD, EC; KJV, NAB, NIV], 'lo' [Lns], 'listen' [NCV, TEV, TNT], 'remember' [CEV, REB], 'look' [BAGD, LN; NET, NLT], 'see' [BAGD; NRSV], 'indeed' [WBC], 'be sure' [BNTC]. This imperative should be translated in the plural form as it is addressed to all believers [TH].

    b. ταχύ (LN 67.56, 67.110) (BAGD 2.b. p. 807): 'soon' [BNTC, EC, LN (67.56), WBC; all versions except KJV], 'quickly' [BAGD, LN (67.110), Lns; KJV]. See this word at 2:16.

    c. μακάριος (LN 25.119) (BAGD 1.b. p. 486): 'blessed' [BAGD, BNTC, EC, Lns, WBC; KJV, NAB, NET, NIV, NLT NRSV], 'happy' [BAGD, LN; NCV, REB, TEV, TNT]. This adjective is also translated as a verb: '(God will) bless' [CEV]. See this word at 1:3.

    d. pres. act. participle of τηρέω (LN36.19, 13.32) (BAGD 5. p. 815): 'to keep' [BAGD, EC, LN (13.32), Lns; KJV, NAB, NET, NIV, NRSV, TNT], 'to obey' [Be, LN (36.19), TH, WBC; NCV, NLT, TEV], 'to heed' [BNTC], 'to pay attention to' [CEV], 'to take to heart' [REB]. See this word at 1:3.

QUESTION—Who is the speaker in this verse?
1. Jesus is the speaker of the whole verse [EC, ICC, Ld, NIGTC, Sw; TEV]: 'Behold,' says Jesus, 'I come soon....' These words may be reported by the angel [EC, Ld, NIGTC, Sw].
2. Jesus is the speaker of the first clause while John is the speaker of the second [Alf, Be, Hu, NIC, TH]. In both cases, Jesus and John's words are reported by the angel [Alf].
3. The angel of verse 6 is the speaker of the whole verse [Lns, WBC]. Although it is the angel, he is quoting Jesus' words [Lns].
4. The angel of verse 6 is the speaker of the first clause of this verse [REB, TNT].
5. Someone other than the angel of verse 6 is the speaker of this verse [NCV, NET, NLT, NRSV].
6. Someone other than the angel of verse 6 is the speaker of the first clause while someone else is the speaker of the second [NAB].

DISCOURSE UNIT: 22:8–21 [NRSV]. The topic is the epilogue and benediction.

DISCOURSE UNIT: 22:8–11 [EC]. The topic is the testimony of John.

22:8 And-I John (am) the-one hearing and seeing these-things. And when I-heard and saw, I-fell-down[a] to-worship at the feet of-the angel who was-showing me these-things.

TEXT—Instead of ὁ ἀκούων καὶ βλέπων ταῦτα 'the one hearing and seeing these things', some manuscripts have ὁ βλέπων ταῦτα καὶ ἀκούων 'the one seeing these things and hearing'. GNT does not mention this alternative. The reading 'the one seeing these things and hearing' is taken by TR and KJV.

LEXICON—a. aorist act. indic. of πίπτω (LN 17.22) (BAGD1.b.α. p. 659): 'to fall down' [LN, Lns; KJV, NAB, NIV, NLT, NRSV, TEV, TNT], 'to fall' [BAGD, BNTC, EC, WBC], 'to kneel down' [CEV], 'to bow down' [NCV] 'to throw oneself down' [NET], 'to prostrate oneself' [LN; REB]. See this word at 1:17.

QUESTION—What is the significance of the words Κἀγὼ Ἰωάννης 'And I John'?

This expression functions to emphasize who was speaking [Lns, TNTC, WBC]: It was I, John [WBC]; And I, I John [Lns].

QUESTION—To what does ταῦτα 'these things' refer?

1. It refers to the whole book of Revelation [Be, Ld, Lns, NIC, NTC, WBC]. Although the New Jerusalem is the primary reference, it refers back to all of the revelations he had received [NIC]. Specifically, it refers to all the events between 1:9 and 22:9 [WBC].
2. It refers to the description of the New Jerusalem [EC, Hu, Sw].

QUESTION—What is the significance of the two verbs 'hearing and seeing'?

These two actions formed the basis of a legal witness (see 1 John 1:1, 2) [NIGTC]. The people of those times felt that the two senses of seeing hearing were the only dependable access to a reported event [WBC] The actions of hearing and seeing an event guaranteed its veracity [WBC].

22:9 And he-says to-me, "See-(that)-you[a] (do it) not; I-am your fellow-servant[a] and (the servant) of your brothers the prophets and of-the-ones keeping the words of this book; worship God.

LEXICON—a. pres. act. imperative of ὁράω (LN 13.134) (BAGD 2.b. p. 578): 'to see' [EC; KJV], 'to see to' [BAGD, LN, Lns]. The phrase Ὅρα μή 'See you not' is translated: 'See thou do it not' [KJV], 'See to it not' [Lns], 'See that you do not do this' [EC], 'Don't do it!' [WBC; NIV, TEV], 'Don't do that' [WBC; CEV, TNT], 'Do not do this' [NET], 'Don't!' [NAB], 'No, don't worship me' [NLT], 'Do not worship me' [NCV], 'No, not that!' [BNTC], 'You must not do that' [NRSV, REB]. See this word at 19:10.

b. σύνδουλος (LN 87.81) (BAGD 3. p. 785): 'fellow servant' [BNTC, WBC; KJV, NAB, NET, NIV, NRSV, REB, TNT], 'fellow slave' [BAGD, EC, LN, Lns]. This noun is also translated as a clause: 'I am a servant just like you' [CEV, NCV], 'a servant together with you' [TEV], 'a servant of God just like you' [NLT]. See this word at 6:11 and 19:10.

QUESTION—What is significant about the angel's reply, Ὅρα μή 'See that you not'?

See this question at 19:10.

DISCOURSE UNIT: 22:10–20 [WBC]. The topic is the concluding parenthesis.

22:10 And he-says to-me, "(Do) not seal-up^a the words of-the prophecy of this book, for the time is near.

TEXT—Instead of ὁ καιρὸς γάρ 'for the time', some manuscripts have ὅτι ὁ καιρός 'because the time'. GNT does not mention this alternative. The reading 'because the time' is taken by TR.

LEXICON—a. aorist act. subj. of σφραγίζω (LN 6.55) (BAGD 2.a. p. 501): 'to seal up' [BAGD, BNTC, EC; NAB, NET, NIV, NLT, REB], 'to seal' [LN, Lns, WBC; KJV, NET], 'to put a seal on, to make secure' [LN], 'to keep something a secret' [CEV, NCV, TEV, TNT]. To seal up is to make inaccessible [Lns]. To seal up is to keep secret [Sw]. To seal up is to hide from view [TH, TNTC]. See this word at 10:4.

QUESTION—Who is referred to by the pronoun 'he' in λέγει 'he says'?
  1. An angel is the speaker [Be, Ld, Lns, NIC, NIGTC, Sw, WBC; NCV, TNT].
  2. Christ is the speaker [ICC].

QUESTION—What is indicated by the figure μὴ σφραγίσῃς 'do not seal up'?

It is a figure of *litotes* and stresses that the words of this book should be published [ICC, Lns]. It indicates that the words of this book should be kept open for all to read [EC, Hu, Ld, Sw]. It indicates that the contents of the book should be proclaimed [NIC]. John should write them down and send them to the churches [NIGTC]. The study of the book should be encouraged [Sw]. The contents of the book should not be kept secret [TH; CEV, NCV, TEV, TNT].

QUESTION—What relationship is indicated by γάρ 'for'?

It indicates that the clause, 'the time is near' stands as the reason for not sealing up the prophecy of the book [Hu, NIGTC]: do not seal up…*because the time is near.*

QUESTION—What is meant by ὁ καιρός 'the time'?

It refers to the time for fulfilling the prophecies of this book [BNTC, Hu, Lns, TH]. It refers to the time for the fulfilling of God's purposes [Sw]. It refers to the time for Christ's coming again [NTC]. It refers to the time of the conclusion of the ages [Wal]

22:11 The-one doing-wrong^a let-that-one-do-wrong still and the filthy^b let-that-one-be-filthy^c still, and the righteous^d let-that-one-do righteousness^e still and the holy-one^f let-that-one-be-holy^g still.

TEXT—Instead of ὁ ῥυπαρὸς ῥυπανθήτω 'the filthy let him be filthy', some manuscripts possibly have ὁ ῥυπῶν ῥυπωσάτω 'the one being filthy let him be filthy', although GNT does not mention this alternative. The reading 'the one being filthy let him be filthy' is taken by TR.

TEXT—Instead of δικαιοσύνην ποιησάτω 'let him do righteousness', some manuscripts have δικαιωθήτω 'let him do righteousness'. GNT does not mention this alternative. The reading δικαιωθήτω 'let him do righteousness' is taken by TR.

LEXICON—a. pres. act. participle of ἀδικέω (LN 88.22) (BAGD 1.a. p. 17): 'to do wrong' [LN], 'to act unjustly' [ICC, LN]. This verb is translated as phrase: 'one who does wrong' [EC; NIV, NLT], 'wrong-doer' [BNTC; TNT], 'evildoer' [BAGD; NET, NRSV, REB], 'evil person' [CEV], 'whoever is evil' [TEV], 'whoever does evil' [NCV], 'one who is unjust' [WBC; KJV], 'the wicked' [NAB], 'the one doing unrighteousness' [Lns].

b. ῥυπαρός (LN **88.257**) (BAGD 2. p. 738): 'filthy' [BNTC, EC Lns; KJV, NAB, NRSV, TEV], 'filthy minded' [REB, TNT], 'morally filthy' [**LN**; NET], 'morally depraved' [WBC], 'unclean' [BAGD; NCV], 'vile' [NIV, NLT], 'morally impure, morally perverted' [LN], 'morally defiled' [NIC], 'defiled' [BAGD]. This adjective is also translated as a phrase: 'one who is dirty-minded' [CEV]. The word ῥυπαρός indicates internal defilement [ICC]. It is used here in its moral or spiritual sense rather than a literal sense [TH].

c. aorist. pass. impera. of ῥυπαίνομαι (LN **88.258**) (BAGD p. 738): 'to be filthy' [EC, **LN**; KJV, NAB, NRSV, TEV, TNT], 'to be depraved' [WBC], 'to be dirty minded' [CEV], 'to be unclean' [NCV], 'to be morally filthy' [NET], 'to be vile' [NIV, NLT], 'to continue in one's filth' [REB], 'to remain in one's filth' [BNTC], 'to be made filthy' [Lns], 'to live in moral filth, to live a completely bad life' [LN], 'to be defiled' [BAGD].

d. δίκαιος (BAGD 1.a. p. 195): 'righteous' [EC, Lns, WBC; KJV, NAB, NET, NRSV], 'just' [BNTC], 'right' [NCV, NIV], 'good' [CEV, NLT, REB, TEV]. This adjective is also translated as a noun: 'good man' [TNT], 'upright man' [BNTC]; and as a clause: 'one who does what is right' [BAGD]. See this word also at 15:3.

e. δικαιοσύνη (LN 88.13) (BAGD 2.b. p. 196): 'righteousness' [BAGD, EC, LN, Lns], 'right' [BNTC; CEV, NAB, NCV, NIV, NRSV], 'righteous' [KJV], 'goodness' [REB], 'good' [NLT, TEV, TNT], 'uprightness' [BAGD]. The phrase δικαιοσύνην ποιησάτω 'let him do righteousness' is translated: 'to act righteously' [WBC; NET], 'doing what God requires, doing what is right' [LN].

f. ἅγιος (LN 88.24) (BAGD 2.c.β. p. 10): '(the) holy one' [EC, Lns], 'one who is holy' [WBC; KJV, NCV, NET, NIV, NLT, TEV, TNT], 'the holy' [BAGD, BNTC, LN; NAB, NRSV, REB], 'God's person' [CEV]. Moral purity is indicated here [TH]. See this word at 3:7.

g. aorist pass. impera. of ἁγιάζω (LN **88.26**) (BAGD 3. p. 9): 'to be holy' [EC, **LN**, WBC; all versions except NLT, REB], 'to be made holy' [Lns], 'to continue in holiness' [BNTC; NLT, REB], 'to keep oneself holy' [BAGD].

DISCOURSE UNIT: 22:12–20 [EC]. The topic is the testimony of Jesus and John's response.

22:12 Behold I-come soon,[a] and my reward[b] (is) with me to-give to-each as his work is.

TEXT—Before ἰδού 'behold', some manuscripts include καί 'and'. GNT does not mention this alternative. 'And' is included by TR and KJV.

TEXT—Instead of the present tense ἐστίν 'is', some manuscripts have the future tense ἔσται 'will be'. GNT does not mention this alternative. The reading 'will be' is taken by TR and KJV.

LEXICON—a. ταχύς (LN 67.56, 67.110) (BAGD 2.b. p. 807): 'soon' [BNTC, EC, LN (67.56), WBC; all versions except KJV], 'quickly' [LN (67.110), Lns; KJV]. See this word at 2:16 and 22:7.

  b. μισθός (LN **38.14**) (BAGD 2.c. p. 523): 'reward' [BAGD, BNTC, EC, **LN**, Lns, WBC; KJV, NCV, NET, NIV, NLT, NRSV, TEV, TNT], 'recompense' [LN; NAB, REB]. This noun is also translated as a verb: 'to reward' [CEV]. Μισθός here can indicate reward or punishment [BAGD, Be, EC, LN, NIC, TH]. It indicates 'what is due' [TNTC]. See this word also at 11:18.

QUESTION—How does this verse relate to verse 11?

Jesus words are addressed to the two classes of people in verse 11 and will reward each according to his work [Hu].

QUESTION—Who is the speaker of this verse?

  1. Jesus is the speaker [Be, BNTC, EC, Hu, Ld, NIC, NIGTC, NTC, Sw, TH, WBC; TEV, TNT].
  2. The angel is the speaker but he is quoting Jesus [Lns].

QUESTION—What relationship is indicated by the infinitive ἀποδοῦναι 'to give'?

  1. A relationship of purpose is indicated [Sw]: my reward is with me *so that I may give* to each as his work is.
  2. A explanatory relationship is indicated [EC]: my reward is with me *that is, I will give* to each as his work is.

QUESTION—What is indicated by the singular ἔργον 'work'?

It is singular to indicate the total of a man's life's works [EC, Lns].

22:13 I (am) the Alpha[a] and the Omega, the first and the last, the beginning and the end.

TEXT—Instead of ὁ πρῶτος καὶ ὁ ἔσχατος, ἡ ἀρχὴ καὶ τὸ τέλος 'the first and the last, the beginning and the end', some manuscripts have ἀρχὴ καὶ τέλος, ὁ πρῶτος καὶ ὁ ἔσχατος 'beginning and end, the first and the last'. GNT does not mention this alternative. The reading 'beginning and end, the first and the last' is taken by TR and KJV.

LEXICON—a. ἄλφα (LN **61.7**) (BAGD p. 1): 'Alpha' [BNTC, EC, Lns, WBC; all versions except TEV], 'alpha' [LN], 'the first, the beginning' [LN], not explicit [TEV]. The combination of alpha and omega in secular literature came to designate the entire universe and all kinds of divine and demonic powers [BAGD, LN], so that in Revelation this title could refer to Christ's dominion over the universe [LN]. See this word also at 1:8 and 21:6.

QUESTION—What word is emphasized in this verse?

The pronoun ἐγώ 'I' is emphasized [Lns]: *I myself* am the Alpha and the Omega.

QUESTION—What is the relationship between the first pair, 'Alpha and Omega', and the last two pairs, 'the First and the Last' and 'the Beginning and the End'?

The last two pairs function to explain the meaning of the first two [BAGD, LN, Wal]: I am the Alpha and the Omega, that is, the first and the last or the beginning and the end. All three pairs say the same basic idea in three different forms [NIC, TH, TNTC].

QUESTION—What claim is Christ making in this verse?

It is a claim to deity since God made these same claims in 1:8 and 21:6 [NIGTC, Sw, TNTC, Wal]. Since Christ is the sovereign over the beginning and end of creation he is also sovereign over all the events in between [NIGTC]. He is claiming that with him the past and the future are always present [BNTC]. These claims separate Christ from all creation [NIC, TNTC].

QUESTION—What claims did God the Father make for himself and what ones did Christ make for himself.

God the Father claimed to be the Alpha and the Omega and the beginning and the end (see 1:8 and 21:6). Christ claimed to be the Alpha and Omega, the first and the last and the beginning and the end (see 1:17; 2:8; and this verse) [EC, ICC, NIGTC, WBC].

22:14 Blessed (are) the-ones washing their robes, that their authority[a] will-be over[b] the tree of life and they-may-enter the city by-the gates.

TEXT—Instead of οἱ πλύνοντες τὰς στολὰς αὐτῶν 'the ones washing their robes', some manuscripts have οἱ πλατύνοντες τὰς στολὰς αὐτῶν 'the ones broadening their robes', others have οἱ ποιοῦντες τὰς ἐντολὰς αὐτοῦ 'the ones doing his commandments'. GNT selects the reading 'the ones washing their robes' with an A decision indicating that the text is certain. The reading 'the ones doing his commandments' is taken by TR and KJV.

LEXICON—a. ἐξουσία (BAGD 1. p. 278): 'authority' [EC], 'right' [BAGD, BNTC, Lns; CEV, KJV, NAB, NCV, NIV, NRSV, TEV, TNT], 'access' [WBC; NET]. This noun is also translated as a verb: 'to be able (to)' [NLT], 'to be free (to)' [REB]. See this word at 2:26 and 9:3.

b. ἐπί with accusative object (LN 37.9): 'over' [EC], 'to' [BNTC, LN, Lns, WBC; KJV, NAB, NET, NIV, NRSV, TNT]. This preposition is also

REVELATION 22:14　　　　　　　　　　　231

translated by a phrase: 'to eat (the fruit) from' [CEV, NCV, NLT, REB, TEV].

QUESTION—Who is the speaker of this verse?
1. John is now the speaker [Be, NIC, TNTC].
2. The speaker is still Christ [EC].

QUESTION—Where else is the action of washing one's robes mentioned in Revelation?
In Revelation 7:14 it is stated, 'they washed their robes and made them white in the blood of the Lamb' [TH].

QUESTION—What is the significance of the present tense of πλύνοντες 'washing'?
This indicates the need for continuous washing from daily defilement (see 1 John 1:7). In 7:14 the aorist tense is used of 'washing' but there it indicates the entering into salvation which is done just once [TNTC].

QUESTION—What relationship is indicated by ἵνα 'that'?
1. It indicates result [TH, TNTC]: Blessed are the ones washing their robes, *as a result* their authority will be over the tree of life.
2. It indicates either purpose or result [Be]. Blessed are the ones washing their robes, *as a result* their authority will be over the tree of life. Or, Blessed are the ones washing their robes *in order that* their authority will be over the tree of life.

QUESTION—What is meant by ἔσται ἡ ἐξουσία αὐτῶν ἐπὶ τὸ ξύλον τῆς ζωῆς 'their authority/right will be over the tree of life'?
1. It means that they will have the right to eat from the tree of life [Alf, Be, EC, NIGTC, TH; CEV, NCV, NLT, REB, TEV].
2. It means that they will have access to the tree of life [BNTC, ICC, Sw, Wal, WBC; NET].

QUESTION—How are the nouns related in the genitive construction τὸ ξύλον τῆς ζωῆς 'the tree of life'?
The tree gives life [TH; CEV]: life-giving tree. See this question also at 2:7 and 22:2.

QUESTION—What is meant by the phrase τοῖς πυλῶσιν 'by the gates' in the clause τοῖς πυλῶσιν εἰσέλθωσιν εἰς τὴν πόλιν 'they may enter by the gates into the city'?
It means that there is full and free access to the city [TH].

22:15 Outside (are) the dogs[a] and the sorcerers[b] and the fornicators and the murderers and the idolaters and everyone loving and practicing falsehood.[c]

TEXT—Instead of ἔξω 'outside', some manuscripts possibly have ἔξω δέ 'but outside', although GNT does not mention this alternative. The reading 'but outside' is taken by TR.

LEXICON—a. κύων (LN **88.282**) (BAGD 2. p. 461): 'dog' [BAGD, BNTC, EC, LN, Lns, WBC; all versions except NCV, REB, TEV], 'pervert' [**LN**; REB, TEV], 'evil person' [NCV].

b. φάρμακος (LN **53.101**): 'sorcerer' [BNTC, EC, **LN**, Lns; KJV, NAB, NET, NLT, NRSV, REB, TNT], 'magician' [WBC], 'one who practices magic (arts)' [NIV, TEV], 'one who does evil magic' [NCV], 'witch' [CEV]. See this word also at 21:8.

c. ψεῦδος (LN 33.254) (BAGD p. 892): 'falsehood' [BAGD, BNTC, LN; NET, NIV, NRSV], 'lie' [BAGD, EC, LN, Lns; KJV], 'wrong' [CEV], 'deceit' [NAB, REB], 'what is false' [TNT]. This noun is also translated as a verb: '(one who) tells a lie' [NCV], 'to live a lie' [NLT], 'to be a liar' [TEV]. The clause πᾶς φιλῶν καὶ ποιῶν ψεῦδος 'everyone loving and doing falsehood' is translated: 'everyone who is fond of lying' [WBC]. See this word at 21:27.

QUESTION—What is symbolized by κύων 'dog'?

In the east, a dog is a disgusting and contemptible animal [Sw]. A dog here may indicate someone who is: evil [Ld, TNTC, WBC], malicious [Be, Ld, NIC], impure [Alf, NIC], of low character [Wal]. It may symbolize: someone who is a sexual pervert or possibly someone who is sexually promiscuous, or it may symbolize an evil person who despises what is holy [LN], male homosexuals, pederasts or sodomites [WBC], the same thing as the word 'abominable' in 21:8 [ICC, Sw, TH].

QUESTION—What relationship exists between οἱ κύνες 'the dogs' and the other kind of people named?

'Dogs' are further defined by the other kind of people named [BNTC; NLT]: dogs, *that is*, sorcerers, fornicators, murderers, idolaters and everyone loving and practicing falsehood.

QUESTION—Where else are 'sorcerers, fornicators, murderers, and idolaters' referred to?

These kind of persons are referred to in 21:8 [Alf, BNTC, EC, ICC, Lns, NIC, NIGTC, NTC, TH, TNTC].

QUESTION—What is indicated by ἔξω 'outside (are)'?

It indicates that such kind of people are *not allowed* inside the city [NIC, NTC, Sw, TH, Wal, WBC]. 'Outside' has reference to the city [Be, EC, Hu, ICC, Ld, Lns, NIC, NIGTC, NTC, TH, Wal, WBC]: outside the city. 'Outside' is the same as the 'lake of fire' because in 21:8, all this kind of people are relegated to the lake of fire [NIGTC].

QUESTION—What is meant by πᾶς φιλῶν καὶ ποιῶνψεῦδος 'everyone loving and practicing falsehood'?

It means to be completely lacking any association with the truth [NIC].

22:16 I Jesus sent my angel to-testify these-things to-you for[a] the churches. I am the root[b] and the offspring[c] of-David, the bright[d] morning star.

TEXT—Instead of ὁ πρωϊνός 'the morning', some manuscripts possibly have καὶ ὀρθρινός 'and morning', although GNT does not mention this alternative. The reading 'and morning' is taken by TR.

LEXICON—a. ἐπί with dative object (BAGD II.1.b.δ. p. 287): 'for' [Be, BNTC, EC; all versions except KJV, TEV, TNT], 'for the benefit of'

REVELATION 22:16

[WBC; TNT], 'in' [Alf, NIGTC; KJV, TEV], 'in regard to' [Lns], 'about' [BAGD]. See this word also at 10:11.
   b. ῥίζα (LN 10.33) (BAGD 2. p. 736): 'root' [EC; KJV, NAB, NET, NRSV], 'Root' [BNTC; NIV], 'source' [NLT], 'Shoot' [Lns], 'shoot growing from (his) stock' [REB], 'descendant' [BAGD, LN; TNT]. The phrase ἡ ῥίζα καὶ τὸ γένος 'the root and the offspring' is translated: 'descendant' [TH, WBC], 'Great Descendant' [CEV], 'descendant from the family' [NCV, TEV]. See this word also at 5:5.
   c. γένος (LN **10.32**) (BAGD 1. p. 156): 'offspring' [EC, LN, Sw; KJV, NAB, REB, TNT], 'Offspring' [Lns; NIV], 'descendant' [**LN**; NET, NRSV], 'scion' [BAGD, BNTC], 'heir to (his) throne' [NLT], not explicit (see phrase under 'root' above) [WBC; CEV, NCV, TEV].
   d. λαμπρός (LN **14.50**) (BAGD 1. p. 465): 'bright' [BAGD, BNTC, EC, **LN**, WBC; all versions], 'Brilliant' [Lns], 'shining, radiant' [BAGD, LN]. See this word also at 15:6 and 22:1.
QUESTION—What word is emphatic in this verse?
   1. The first occurrence of ἐγώ is emphasized [TNTC]: *I myself,* Jesus, sent my angel.
   2. The second occurrence of ἐγώ is emphasized [Lns]: *I myself* am the root of and offspring of David.
   3. Both occurrences are emphatic [EC].
QUESTION—What does ταῦτα 'these things' refer to?
   It refers to all the things written in this book [EC, Hu, ICC, Sw]. It refers to the 'things that must happen soon' of verse 22:6 [Lns].
QUESTION—To whom does the plural ὑμῖν 'to you' refer?
   1. It refers to the members of the Asian churches [EC, ICC, NIGTC, Sw].
   2. It refers to the prophets of whom John is one [Be, WBC].
   3. It refers to all believers [Lns, NIC, TH, TNTC]. It refers to believers or the readers of this book [TH].
QUESTION—To what does the phrase ταῖς ἐκκλησίαις 'the churches' refer?
   1. It refers to the seven churches of Asia of chapters 2 and 3 [Be, EC, ICC, TH, WBC]. This phrase occurs thirteen times in Revelation and in each place it refers to the seven churches of Asia [WBC]. Although it refers to the seven churches of Asia, the message is intended for the whole church [Be, EC].
   2. It refers to the whole Church of believers in general [Hu, Sw]. The seven churches represent all churches everywhere [Hu].
QUESTION—Does ἡ ῥίζα 'the root' refer to the 'ancestor of' or to the 'descendant of David'?
   1. It refers to David's 'descendant' [Be, Lns, NIC, NIGTC, TH, TNTC, WBC; CEV, NCV, REB, TEV, TNT]: I am the shoot and descendant of David. Here 'root' is defined by the following word 'descendant' [Be, Lns]. The figure of the 'root of David' is taken from Isaiah 11:1, 10 in which a 'root of Jesse' is a Messianic title of Jesus but refers not to the

ancestor of Jesse, but to his descendant. Here 'root' is used to mean that which springs from the root [NIC].
2. It refers to David's ancestor [BNTC, EC, Hu, ICC; NLT]: I am the ancestor and descendant of David. Jesus is the root from which David sprang [BNTC, Hu]. As the source from which David sprang as well as the descendant of David, he is both truly God and truly man [Hu]. The word 'root' in Isaiah is used in the sense of 'descendant'. Here it is used in the sense of 'ancestor' [EC].

QUESTION—How is Jesus like the 'morning star'?

As the morning star signals the end of night and the dawn of a new day, so Jesus signals the end of the darkness of night and the dawn of God's new day [Hu, NIC, TH]. The star was a common Hebrew figure of the expected Davidic King (see Numbers 24:17) [Be, NIC]. The morning star seems to indicate that Jesus is the one who brings in God's perfect day [Be]. Jesus is the star that brings in eternal day [Alf]. The star is a symbol of Jesus' royalty (see Numbers 24:17) [Lns].

22:17 And the Spirit and the Bride say, "Come." And the-one hearing let-him-say, "Come." And the-one thirsting let-him-come, the-one desiring let-him-take[a] (the) water of-life freely.

TEXT—Instead of the present tense ἔρχου 'come', some manuscripts possibly have the aorist tense ἐλθέ 'come', although GNT does not mention this alternative. The aorist reading 'come' is taken by TR.

TEXT—Instead of the present tense ἐρχέσθω 'let him come', some manuscripts possibly have the aorist tense ἐλθέτω 'let him come', although GNT does not mention this alternative. The aorist reading 'let him come' is taken by TR.

TEXT—Before ὁ θέλων 'the one desiring', some manuscripts possibly include καί 'and', although GNT does not mention this alternative. The reading 'and' is included by TR and KJV.

LEXICON—a. aorist act. impera. of λαμβάνω (LN **57.125**) (BAGD 2. p. 465): 'to take' [EC, Lns; CEV, KJV, NET, NIV, NRSV, TNT], 'to accept' [BNTC, **LN**; REB, TEV], 'to receive' [BAGD, LN, WBC; NAB], 'to drink' [NLT], 'to have' [NCV].

QUESTION—Who is τὸ πνεῦμα 'the Spirit'?
1. It is the Holy Spirit of God [EC, Hu, Ld, Lns, NIC, NIGTC, TH, Wal].
2. It is the Spirit of Christ [ICC, WBC].
3. It is the Spirit of Prophecy and so it indicates the Prophets [Sw].

QUESTION—Who is the ἡ νύμφη 'the Bride'?

It is the Church of believers [Alf, Be, EC, Hu, ICC, Ld, Lns, NIC, Sw, Wal, WBC]. It is the wife of the Lamb, the people of God (see 19:7) [Ld, TH]. It is prophetic leaders of the church [NIGTC].

QUESTION—Who are addressed by the first two invitations, 'Come!'?
1. They are addressed to Jesus [Be, EC, Lns, NTC, Sw, TH, WBC]: The Spirit and the Bride say to Jesus, 'Come!' It is an appeal for Jesus to

return to earth [Be, EC, WBC]. This is the response of the church to Jesus' words in verse 22:12 [Sw, WBC].
2. They are addressed to anyone who will [BNTC, Hu, ICC, Ld, NIC, Wal]. It is an appeal to anyone who will to come and join God's family [Hu, ICC, Wal]. Since the second half of the verse is addressed to the world, it is better to take this part to be addressed to the world as well [Ld, NIC].
3. They are addressed either to Christ or to anyone who will [NIGTC].

QUESTION—Are the first two commands to come singular or plural?
They are singular [TH]: you (singular) come.
QUESTION—What is meant by the figure of διψῶν 'thirsting'?
It indicates moral and spiritual need [NIGTC].
QUESTION—Is the invitation ἐρχέσθω 'let him come' addressed only to men?
No, this invitation is addressed to whoever will [TH]. It may be better translated with a plural 'let them come' [TH; NLT], or in some other gender-neutral manner [CEV, NAB, NCV, NET, NRSV, REB, TEV, TNT].
QUESTION—How are the nouns related in the genitive construction ὕδωρ ζωῆς 'water of life'?
Water gives life [NIC; CEV, NAB]: life-giving water. See this question also at 21.6.

DISCOURSE UNIT: 22:18–21 [TEV]. The topic is the conclusion.

22:18 I testify[a] to-everyone hearing the words of the prophecy of-this book: if anyone adds[b] to them, God will-add[c] to-him the plagues written in this book,

TEXT—Instead of μαρτυρῶ ἐγὼ παντὶ τῷ ἀκούοντι 'I testify to every one hearing', some manuscripts possibly have συμμαρτυροῦμαι γὰρ παντὶ ἀκούοντι 'for I testify together with everyone hearing', although GNT does not mention this alternative. The reading 'for I testify together with everyone hearing' is taken by TR.

TEXT—Instead of ἐπ' αὐτά 'to them', some manuscripts possibly have πρὸς ταῦτα 'to these things', although GNT does not mention this alternative. The reading 'to these things' is taken by TR and KJV.

LEXICON—a. pres. act. indic. of μαρτυρέω (BAGD 1.a. p. 492): 'to testify' [EC, Lns WBC; KJV, NET], 'to warn' [NAB, NCV, NIV, NRSV], 'to give warning' [REB], 'to solemnly warn' [TNTC; TEV], 'to solemnly declare' [BNTC; NLT], 'to declare' [TNT], 'to bear witness to' [BAGD]. This verb is also translated as a noun: '(my) warning' [CEV]. See this word also at 1:2
b. aorist act. subj. of ἐπιτίθημι (LN **59.72**) (BAGD 1.b. p. 303): 'to add' [BAGD, BNTC, EC, **LN**, Lns, WBC; all versions],
c. fut. act. indic. of ἐπιτίθημι (LN **90.87**) (BAGD 1.b.β. p. 303): 'to add' [BNTC, EC, Lns, WBC; all versions except CEV, TEV], 'to add to one's punishment' [TH; TEV], 'to subject to' [**LN**], 'to make suffer' [CEV], 'to bring upon' [BAGD]. The word ἐπιτίθημι usually involves the use of force [LN].

QUESTION—Where else in Scripture is a similar warning given?

A similar warning is given in Deuteronomy 4:2 and 12:32 [Alf, Be, BNTC, EC, Ld, NIC, NIGTC, NTC, Sw, TH, TNTC].

QUESTION—Who is the speaker of this verse?
1. The speaker is Jesus [EC, ICC, Lns, NIC, Sw, Wal, WBC]: I, Jesus, testify. That this is Jesus is supported by the fact that verse 20 identifies Jesus as the speaker and there also he uses the words 'testify'. Only he would have the authority to make such a claim [EC]. The warning is so solemn it suggest that Jesus is the speaker [NIC].
2. The speaker is John [Alf, Be, Ld, NIGTC, TH, TNTC; REB, TEV]: I John testify.

QUESTION—What word is emphasized in this verse?

The word ἐγώ 'I' is emphatic [Alf, EC, Lns, WBC; TEV]: *I myself* testify.

QUESTION—What is intended by the phrase 'adding to the words of the prophecy of this book'?

It indicates the deliberate perversion of the teachings of Revelation [Be, Ld, NIC, Sw]. It indicates altering the substance of the teaching of Revelation [EC, TH]. It specifically indicates teaching that people can believe in Christ and still worship idols [NIGTC].

QUESTION—To whom is this warning addressed:
1. It is primarily a warning to copyists that they make sure that their copies are exact with nothing added or left out [BNTC].
2. It is a warning to whoever hears and is not given only to warn copyists against altering the contents of the book [Alf, Be, EC, Ld, NIC, NTC, Sw, TNTC, WBC].

QUESTION—What are the 'plagues' mentioned here?

They are the plagues listed in chapters 15 and 16 [TH, WBC]. With these we should also include the three plagues set in motion by the blowing of the sixth trumpet (see 9:18) [WBC]. They are the plagues connected with the seals, trumpets and bowls [EC].

QUESTION—What is the significance of the use of the word προφητείας 'prophecy'?

It indicates that the words of this book are the words of God [TNTC].

22:19 And if anyone takes-away[a] from the words of-the book of-this prophecy God will-take-away[b] his share[c] from the tree of-life and from the holy city of-the-things written in this book.

TEXT—Instead of τοῦ ξύλου 'the tree', some manuscripts possibly have βιβλίου 'book', although GNT does not mention this alternative. The reading 'book' is taken by TR and KJV.

TEXT—Before τῶν γεγραμμένων 'of the things written', some manuscripts possibly include καί 'and', although GNT does not mention this alternative. The reading 'and' is included by TR and KJV.

LEXICON—a. aorist. act. subj. of ἀφαιρέω (LN **68.47**) (BAGD 1. p. 124): 'to take away' [BAGD, BNTC, EC, **LN**, Lns, WBC; all versions except

NLT], 'to remove' [NLT]. The word ἀφαιρέω means to cause to cease, implying that someone is no longer permitted to enjoy or participate in some state or activity [LN].
  b. fut. act. indic. of ἀφαιρέω (BAGD 1. p. 124): 'to take away' [BNTC, EC, Lns, WBC; all versions except CEV, NLT], 'to remove' [NLT], 'to cut off' [BAGD]. The clause ἀφελεῖ ὁ θεὸς τὸ μέρος αὐτοῦ 'God will take away his share' is translated: 'God will not let you have part in' [CEV].
  c. μέρος (LN 63.14): 'share' [BNTC, WBC; all versions except CEV, KJV], 'part' [EC, LN, Lns; CEV, KJV], 'place'. See this word at 20:6 and 21:8.
QUESTION—Does the phrase τὸ μέρος αὐτοῦ 'his share' refer only to men?
  No, it is an indefinite reference to anyone [TH, WBC; CEV, NCV, NLT, NRSV, TEV]: God will take away that one's share.
QUESTION—What does it mean that God will take away that one's share in the tree of life and in the holy city?
  It means that God will take away that one's right to eat fruit from the tree and to enter the city [TH].
QUESTION—What do the words τῶν γεγραμμένων ἐν τῷ βιβλίῳ τούτῳ 'of the things written in this book' modify?
  1. They modify the tree of life and the holy city [BNTC, EC, WBC; all versions except KJV]: from the tree of life and the holy city that are described in this book. The tree of life and the holy city are described in 21:10–22:5 [Be, EC].
  2. They modify 'his share' [Lns]: God will take away his share of the things written in this book.
  3. They stand alone adding a third blessing to be taken away [KJV]: God will take away his share out of the book of life and out of the holy city and from the things written in this book.

DISCOURSE UNIT: 22:20 [Lns]. The topic is Jesus dismisses John.

22:20 The-one testifying[a] these-things says, "Yes,[b] I come soon."[c] Amen,[d] come Lord Jesus

TEXT—Before ἔρχου 'come', some manuscripts include ναί 'yes'. GNT does not mention this alternative. The reading 'yes' is included by TR and KJV.
LEXICON—a. pres. act. indic. of μαρτυρέω (BAGD 1.b. p. 492): 'to testify' [EC, Lns WBC; KJV, NET, NIV, NRSV], 'to give a testimony' [BNTC; NAB, REB, TEV, TNT], 'to be a faithful witness to' [NLT], 'to speak' [CEV], 'say' [NCV]. Μαρτυρέω is used here in the sense of to announce or proclaim [TH]. See this word also at 22:18.
  b. ναί (LN **69.1**) (BAGD 2. p. 533): 'yes' [BNTC, EC; NAB, NCV, NET, NIV, NLT, REB, TNT], 'yes, indeed' [**LN**; TEV], 'yea' [Lns], 'surely' [WBC; KJV, NRSV], 'certainly, quite so' [BAGD], 'indeed' [BAGD], not explicit [CEV]. Ναί is a particle of affirmation confirming the truth of the statement that follows it [WBC]. See this word also at 1:7.

c. ταχύς (LN 67.56, 67.110) (BAGD 2.b. p. 807): 'soon' [BNTC, EC, LN (67.56), WBC; all versions except KJV], 'quickly' [LN (67.110), Lns; KJV]. See this word at 2:16, 22:7 and 22:12.
d. ἀμήν (LN 72.6) (BAGD 1. p. 45): 'amen' [BAGD, BNTC, EC, Lns, WBC; all versions except CEV, TEV], 'so' [CEV], 'so be it' [TEV], 'truly, indeed' [LN]. The word ἀμήν confirms as true what the previous speaker has said [ICC, TNTC]. See this word at 1:6.

QUESTION—Who is the speaker of the quote 'Yes, I come soon'?

The speaker is Jesus [Alf, Be, BNTC, EC, ICC, Ld, Lns, NIC, NIGTC, NTC, Sw, TH, TNTC, WBC]. The speaker is Jesus but he is quoted by John [Be, EC].

QUESTION—To what does ταῦτα 'these things' refer?

It refers to the whole book of Revelation [Be, EC, ICC, TH]. It refers immediately to 22:12–19, but ultimately to the whole book [EC].

QUESTION—Does the particle ναί 'yes' affirm what has gone before or what follows? (Note: the version support for the following interpretations is mainly interpretive).
1. It affirms what follows [WBC; KJV, NRSV]: Surely I am coming soon.
2. It affirms what precedes it [EC, NTC, Sw; all versions except CEV, KJV, NRSV]: (Come soon!). Yes, I am coming soon. Jesus is responding to the invitation to come given by the Spirit and the Bride and those hearing in 22:17 [EC, NTC, Sw].

QUESTION—Who is the speaker of 'Amen, come Lord Jesus'?

The speaker is John [Alf, Be, EC, Ld, Lns, NIC, NIGTC]. The speakers are the Spirit and the Bride and the ones hearing of 22:17 [NTC].

DISCOURSE UNIT: 22:21 [EC, Lns, Sw, WBC]. The topic is John dismisses his readers [Lns], the benediction [EC, Sw], the epistolary postscript [WBC].

22:21 The grace of-the Lord Jesus (be) with all.

TEXT—Instead of κυρίου Ἰησοῦ 'Lord Jesus', some manuscripts have κυρίου Ἰησοῦ Χριστοῦ 'Lord Jesus Christ', others have κυρίου ἡμῶν Ἰησοῦ Χριστοῦ 'our Lord Jesus Christ', and one manuscript omits this verse. GNT selects the reading 'Lord Jesus' with an A decision, indicating that the text is certain. The reading 'our Lord Jesus Christ' is taken by TR and KJV.

TEXT—Instead of μετὰ πάντων 'with all', some manuscripts have μετὰ πάντων ἡμῶν. αμήν 'with all of us. Amen', others have μετὰ πάντων ὑμῶν. αμήν 'with all of you. Amen', others have μετὰ πάντων τῶν ἁγίων. ἀμήν 'with all the saints. Amen', and still others have μετὰ πάντων τῶν ἁγίων αὐτοῦ. ἀμήν 'with all his saints. Amen'. One important manuscript has μετὰ τῶν ἁγίων. ἀμήν 'with the saints. Amen', another has μετὰ τῶν ἁγίων σου. ἀμήν 'with your saints. Amen'. GNT selects the reading 'with all' with a B rating, indicating that the text is almost certain. The reading 'with all of you. Amen' is taken by TR and KJV.

www.ingramcontent.com/pod-product-compliance
Lightning Source LLC
Chambersburg PA
CBHW072108010526
44111CB00037B/2033